Network Sales and Services Handbook

Matthew J. Castelli

Cisco Press

Cisco Press
201 West 103rd Street
Indianapolis, IN 46290 USA

Network Sales and Services Handbook

Matthew J. Castelli

Copyright © 2003 Cisco Systems, Inc.

Published by:
Cisco Press
201 West 103rd Street
Indianapolis, IN 46290 USA

Printed in the United States of America 1 2 3 4 5 6 7 8 9 0

Library of Congress Cataloging-in-Publication Number: 619472050903

ISBN: 1-58705-090-0

Warning and Disclaimer

This book is designed to provide information about network sales and services. Every effort has been made to make this book as complete and as accurate as possible, but no warranty or fitness is implied.

The information is provided on an "as is" basis. The authors, Cisco Press, and Cisco Systems, Inc. shall have neither liability nor responsibility to any person or entity with respect to any loss or damages arising from the information contained in this book or from the use of the discs or programs that may accompany it.

The opinions expressed in this book belong to the authors and are not necessarily those of Cisco Systems, Inc.

Trademark Acknowledgments

All terms mentioned in this book that are known to be trademarks or service marks have been appropriately capitalized. Cisco Press or Cisco Systems, Inc. cannot attest to the accuracy of this information. Use of a term in this book should not be regarded as affecting the validity of any trademark or service mark.

Feedback Information

At Cisco Press, our goal is to create in-depth technical books of the highest quality and value. Each book is crafted with care and precision, undergoing rigorous development that involves the unique expertise of members of the professional technical community.

Reader feedback is a natural continuation of this process. If you have any comments regarding how we could improve the quality of this book, or otherwise alter it to better suit your needs, you can contact us through e-mail at feedback@ciscopress.com. Please be sure to include the book title and ISBN in your message.

We greatly appreciate your assistance.

Publisher	John Wait
Editor-In-Chief	John Kane
Cisco Representative	Anthony Wolfenden
Cisco Press Program Manager	Sonia Torres Chavez
Cisco Marketing Communications Manager	Tom Geitner
Cisco Marketing Program Manager	Edie Quiroz
Acquisitions Editor	Amy Moss
Managing Editor	Patrick Kanouse
Development Editor	Ginny Bess
Project Editors	Kristy Knoop, Suzanne Pettypiece
Copy Editor	Kathy Murray
Technical Editors	Deborah Dworanczyk, Lindsay Hiebert, Amir Kazemzadeh
Team Coordinator	Tammi Ross
Book Designer	Gina Rexrode
Cover Designer	Louisa Klucznik
Composition	Octal Publishing, Inc.
Indexer	Tim Wright

CISCO SYSTEMS

Corporate Headquarters
Cisco Systems, Inc.
170 West Tasman Drive
San Jose, CA 95134-1706
USA
http://www.cisco.com
Tel: 408 526-4000
      800 553-NETS (6387)
Fax: 408 526-4100

European Headquarters
Cisco Systems Europe
11 Rue Camille Desmoulins
92782 Issy-les-Moulineaux
Cedex 9
France
http://www-europe.cisco.com
Tel: 33 1 58 04 60 00
Fax: 33 1 58 04 61 00

Americas Headquarters
Cisco Systems, Inc.
170 West Tasman Drive
San Jose, CA 95134-1706
USA
http://www.cisco.com
Tel: 408 526-7660
Fax: 408 527-0883

Asia Pacific Headquarters
Cisco Systems Australia,
Pty., Ltd
Level 17, 99 Walker Street
North Sydney
NSW 2059 Australia
http://www.cisco.com
Tel: +61 2 8448 7100
Fax: +61 2 9957 4350

Cisco Systems has more than 200 offices in the following countries. Addresses, phone numbers, and fax numbers are listed on the Cisco Web site at www.cisco.com/go/offices

Argentina • Australia • Austria • Belgium • Brazil • Bulgaria • Canada • Chile • China • Colombia • Costa Rica • Croatia • Czech Republic • Denmark • Dubai, UAE • Finland • France • Germany • Greece • Hong Kong Hungary • India • Indonesia • Ireland • Israel • Italy • Japan • Korea • Luxembourg • Malaysia • Mexico The Netherlands • New Zealand • Norway • Peru • Philippines • Poland • Portugal • Puerto Rico • Romania Russia • Saudi Arabia • Scotland • Singapore • Slovakia • Slovenia • South Africa • Spain • Sweden Switzerland • Taiwan • Thailand • Turkey • Ukraine • United Kingdom • United States • Venezuela • Vietnam Zimbabwe

About the Authors

Matthew J. "Cat" Castelli has more than 14 years of experience in the telecommunications networking industry, starting as a Cryptologic Technician (Communications) in the United States Navy. Cat has since been working as a principal consultant for a Cisco® Professional Services partner, as the senior technical consultant/enterprise network design engineer, a global telecommunications integrator, and most recently as the Information Assurance (IA) Liaison for a 360,000+ user network. Cat has broad exposure to LAN/WAN, Internet, and Alternative technologies (VoX) for service provider and enterprise networks of all sizes including implementation, application, configuration, integration, network management, and security solutions.

About the Technical Reviewers

Deborah Dworanczyk has been working in telecommunications since completing graduate school in 1997. She has a background in managing staff, customers, accounts, and proposals, as well as a background in voice and data and wired and wireless technologies. She is taking these skills with her as she embarks on a new position with AT&T Technical Services Corp. as a Project/Capture Manager. Prior to making the move to AT&T TSC, Deborah was a Project Manager for Global Crossing Telecommunications. In this capacity she was responsible for the implementation of customers' global networks, as well as the ongoing maintenance and customer relations associated with these accounts. Prior to joining the Global Crossing team, Deborah had the opportunity to manage the technicians and their daily operations at the Telecommunications Service Office (TSO) of the White House and the Executive Office of the President (EOP). Deborah's primary responsibility included being the point of contact and primary point of escalation for the White House and EOP for all Lucent telecommunication services, networks, equipment, and associated systems.

Deborah has a master's degree in public administration from the American University in Washington, DC. She graduated from Albright College in Reading, PA with a dual degree in Economics and Political Science. Currently she is completing course work in telecommunications engineering at George Washington University in Washington, DC. Deborah currently resides in Washington, DC and is part owner in the independent record label Keep Safe Records.

Lindsay Hiebert is Cisco Systems, Inc. Marketing Manager and Consulting Product Manager for the Integrated Communications Business Unit. His recent responsibilities include marketing and technical marketing for the AVVID CallManager products, including the Branch Office Solutions products within the Integrated Communications Business Unit. Mr. Hiebert has three years of experience in deploying Cisco's advanced communications technologies and applications for IP Telephony, Unified Messaging, and IP Contact Centers for Cisco's 280 locations worldwide. His experience has been used in over 100 Cisco Executive Briefings to Enterprise Customers and in consulting roles to assist sales and support teams in the field.

Amir Kazemzadeh was born in 1968 in Iran and received his bachelor of science in electrical engineering from the University of Maryland in 1991. He has been taking graduate courses in Electrical Engineering at George Mason University, with a concentration of studies in Telecommunications. Since 1994, Amir has been working with the major telecommunications companies and focusing on the design of Internet backbone for small to mid-sized ISPs. In the past few years, he has gained experience and knowledge in the design of high-speed data transfer via SONET and WDM technologies.

Amir's continued training has been in the following areas: fiber Optics; wave division multiplexing; SONET technologies; network management analysis; ATM & Frame Relay services; TCP/IP protocol; introduction to Cisco Routers (CCNA); BGP-4, Internet routing, and MPLS; advanced IP design skills and understanding of Routing Protocols such as BGP, MPLS; Layer 2: Frame Relay, ATM, SONET, ISDN, PPP; Ethernet (10M/Fast/Gigabit); FDDI and Token Ring; understanding of third-generation (3G); broadband, packet-based transmission of text; digitized voice, video, and multimedia at data rates up to and possibly higher than 2 megabits per second.

Dedications

Thanks to everyone who has supported me in this and all of my endeavors. Thanks to those who have been there for me when things were going well, and most notably, when they weren't.

Special thanks go to the following people:

Kim Graves, Mike, and Matthew Forrest

LJ Bur

Deborah Dworanczyk and Hillary Dick

Bob O'Connor, Leo, and Jaime Alexander

Michelle Cornell, Andre Buckner, Kenny Rodgers, Belinda Goldsmith, Jeff Stevenson, Harrison McCoy, Michelle Romano, Erin Barker, Matt "Looch" Luetjen, John Steel, Brent Doherty, Paul DeSena, and Scott Carnley

Lisa Bickerton, Cathy Enos, John Cronley, Jon Hage, Joe Shannon, Jeff Wolfe, Jim Steinbauer, Tania Ferguson, Laura Mendenhall, Amir Kazemzadehmoran, Laura Gargiulo, Nader Bakhtiary, Bryan Thompson, the ISF TQA and IA teams, Lou Tosado and the NAE Team—you all are some of the best.

Pepe, Paul, and the rest of the gang of eCiti

Eric, Tony, John, Robin, Stephanie, Dot, Gina, and the rest of the crew at Chutzpah

Thanks to Michael T., Allie, Marvin, Mark and Dick, Reinhardt and Jim, Gloria, Mike F., Joseph, and all the rest of the Le Canard regulars.

The Boys: Spike, Zeke, Buzz, Keyser, and Sam

And last, but certainly not least, a special thanks goes to my mom Jayne, and my brother, Dan.

Acknowledgments

Thanks goes to the tech editors for keeping me honest; Deborah, Lindsay, and Amir.

Thanks to John Kane and Amy Moss, again for their motivation and encouragement.

Ginny Bess, for her extraordinary efforts and for making sure I always spelled things out.

"Knowledge is the food of the soul."

—Plato

Contents at a Glance

Table of Contents

Throughout this book, you will see the following icons used for common network devices

Router

Layer 3
Switch

Switch

PIX Firewall

Voice-Enabled
Router

Content
Switch

Route/Switch
Processor
(Layer 3 Switch)

Cisco 7500
Series Router

CSS11000
Content
Switch

Hub

Content
Engine

NetRanger
Intrusion Detection
System

Local Director

Access
Server

CiscoSecure
Scanner

IP/TV
Broadcast
Server

Cisco
CallManager

Cisco
Directory Server

PC

Laptop

CiscoWorks
Workstation

Web
Browser

Web
Server

Supercomputer

Relational
Database

Phone

IP Phone

Fax

File Server

Printer

Camera
PC/Video

Introduction

One of the most significant challenges in any technical organization is knowledge transfer; getting the knowledge from those "in the know" (network engineers or consultants) to those on the "front lines," the individuals who are selling and supporting (servicing) network services to a client (current or prospect). Individuals on a sales/service team do not have a lot of time because they are quota driven and time away from the field is potentially lost revenue. Frequently conducted formal or lengthy training sessions are not always attended. Understanding knowledge transfer is necessary for people working as customer service representatives and managers, engineering technicians, and pre-sales account managers.

Goals and Methods

This book covers the general topic of broad data and networking, including the following topics:

- Internetworking Fundamentals
- Local Area and Wide Area Networks
- Network Access Methods
- Network Design Concepts
- High Availability Concepts
- Traditional and Alternative Voice Networks
- Local and Remote Network Security Concepts
- Routing Protocol Briefs

Several chapters also provide case studies that are meant to show you how these technologies are currently being implemented in company environments. In addition, some chapters include frequently asked questions (FAQs) to enhance your understanding of the topics covered in this book. The approach and methodologies used in this book are intended to aid in the knowledge transfer process that doesn't always happen with a one-time training session or without reference material to aid in the learning process.

Who Should Read This Book?

This book provides introductory and intermediate coverage of broad data and voice networking concepts, including fundamental architecture, design, management, and security.

The primary audience is any "non-technical" individual in a networking sales or service position. By nature, individuals in these positions are not as technical as engineers or consultants, necessitating the sales engineering role. One of the challenges sales engineers face is the task of pushing knowledge to their respective sales and service teams so that these teams are better prepared when in front of a customer, either in person or via telephone, in turn providing better/more clear and complete information to the engineers and consultants.

This book addresses the following primary audiences:

- Pre-Sales and Service Representatives
- New Hires Sales and Customer Service Representatives

Secondary Audience:

- Senior Sales and Customer Service Representatives
- Sales Engineers

Anyone in a pre-sales engineering (products or services) environment

How This Book Is Organized

Although this book could be read cover-to-cover, it is designed to be flexible so that you can move easily among chapters and sections to cover only the material you want to learn. The 22 chapters cover the following topics:

- **Chapter 1, "Internetworking Basics,"** introduces foundational concepts and discussions of how networks interconnect.
- **Chapter 2, "OSI Reference Model,"** discusses how the OSI Model is fundamental for moving information between computers on an internetwork.
- **Chapter 3, "TCP/IP Introduction,"** introduces the TCP/IP Protocol Suite's functionality, addressing, and protocol operation.
- **Chapter 4, "Customer Premise Equipment (CPE),"** provides a discussion of the hardware found at a customer site.
- **Chapter 5, "Local Area Networks (LANs),"** discusses local area networking (LAN) implementations, such as Token Ring and EtherNet, and LAN equipment, such as bridges, hubs, routers, and switches.
- **Chapter 6, "Local Access,"** illustrates the different methods by which a customer site can access a network service provider's services.
- **Chapter 7, "DSL and Cable Modem Networks,"** introduces two alternative ways to connect to an IP service provider.
- **Chapter 8, "WAN Basics,"** introduces wide area networking (WAN) concepts and architecture.
- **Chapter 9, "Asynchronous Transfer Mode (ATM) Introduction,"** introduces ATM wide area networking (WAN) concepts.
- **Chapter 10, "Frame Relay Introduction,"** introduces Frame Relay wide area networking (WAN) concepts.
- **Chapter 11, "Understanding Routers and Routing,"** introduces router and routing functionality in an internetwork.
- **Chapter 12, "Virtual LAN (VLAN) Introduction,"** discusses Virtual LANs and how they can be used within an organization's network.

- **Chapter 13, "Quality of Service Introduction,"** discusses a network's capability to provide better service to select network traffic over various internetworking technologies.

- **Chapter 14, "Network Architecture Introduction,"** introduces the concepts of geographic-based networks and the three-tiered network hierarchy.

- **Chapter 15, "Network Security Basics,"** discusses threats to a network and methods of protecting a network against such threats.

- **Chapter 16, "Remote Access Virtual Private Networks (VPNs),"** discusses available methods to remote users to securely access organizational resources.

- **Chapter 17, "Voice Networks,"** discussion of the Public Switched Telephone Network (PSTN) services and customer access to those services.

- **Chapter 18, "Network Management Basics,"** discussion regarding the fundamentals of a network management system and protocols, including Telecommunications Management Network (TMN) and the Fault, Configuration, Accounting, Performance, and Security (FCAPS) Management Model.

- **Chapter 19, "High Availability Networking,"** includes discussion of how to measure the availability of a network and methods for minimizing the impact of a network outage on its users.

- **Chapter 20, "The Internet,"** explores what the Internet is and how the Internet functions from a user's perspective.

- **Chapter 21, "MPLS Introduction,"** discusses Multiprotocol Label Switching (MPLS) and how it is used in a network backbone.

- **Chapter 22, "Introduction to Fiber Optics,"** provides a discussion of the fundamentals of fiber optic networks, including Synchronous Optical Network (SONET) and Dense Wave Division Multiplexing (DWDM).

The first appendix lists the Primary Interexchange Codes (PICs) used by Local and Interexchange Carriers (LECs and IXCs). The remaining six appendices briefly discuss the common routing protocols used in an internetwork.

- Appendix A: PIC Codes
- Appendix B: RIP (Routing Information Protocol)
- Appendix C: RIP Version 2 (RIPv2)
- Appendix D: Border Gateway Protocol, Version 4 (BGP4)
- Appendix E: Interior Gateway Routing Protocol (IGRP)
- Appendix F: OSPF (Open Shortest Path First)
- Appendix G: EIGRP (Enhanced Interior Gateway Routing Protocol)

The Twelve Networking Truths

One last introductory note: I invite you to read the following, RFC 1925 (by Ross Callon), perhaps ironically published April 1, 1996. This RFC could be considered a core fundamental for anyone involved in the sale, design, service, or maintenance of a network. Following is Ross Callon's *Twelve Networking Truths*.

The Twelve Networking Truths

Status of this Memo

This memo provides information for the Internet community. This memo does not specify an Internet standard of any kind. Distribution of this memo is unlimited.

Abstract

This memo documents the fundamental truths of networking for the Internet community. This memo does not specify a standard, except in the sense that all standards must implicitly follow the fundamental truths.

Acknowledgements

The truths described in this memo result from extensive study over an extended period of time by many people, some of whom did not intend to contribute to this work. The editor merely has collected these truths, and would like to thank the networking community for originally illuminating these truths.

Introduction

This Request for Comments (RFC) provides information about the fundamental truths underlying all networking. These truths apply to networking in general, and are not limited to TCP/IP, the Internet, or any other subset of the networking community.

The Fundamental Truths

1   It Has To Work.

2   No matter how hard you push and no matter what the priority, you can't increase the speed of light.

2a   (corollary). No matter how hard you try, you can't make a baby in much less than 9 months. Trying to speed this up *might* make it slower, but it won't make it happen any quicker.

3   With sufficient thrust, pigs fly just fine. However, this is not necessarily a good idea. It is hard to be sure where they are going to land, and it could be dangerous sitting under them as they fly overhead.

4   Some things in life can never be fully appreciated nor understood unless experienced firsthand. Some things in networking can never be fully understood by someone who neither builds commercial networking equipment nor runs an operational network.

5   It is always possible to aglutenate multiple separate problems into a single complex interdependent solution. In most cases this is a bad idea.

6   It is easier to move a problem around (for example, by moving the problem to a different part of the overall network architecture) than it is to solve it.

6a (corollary). It is always possible to add another level of indirection.

7   It is always something.

7a (corollary). Good, Fast, Cheap: Pick any two (you can't have all three).

8   It is more complicated than you think.

9   For all resources, whatever it is, you need more.

9a (corollary). Every networking problem always takes longer to solve than it seems like it should.

10 One size never fits all.

11 Every old idea will be proposed again with a different name and different presentation, regardless of whether it works.

11a (corollary). See rule 6a.

12 In protocol design, perfection has been reached not when there is nothing left to add, but when there is nothing left to take away.

Command Syntax Conventions

The conventions used to present command syntax in this book are the same conventions used in the IOS Command Reference. The Command Reference describes these conventions as follows:

- Vertical bars (|) separate alternative, mutually exclusive elements.
- Square brackets ([ ]) indicate optional elements.
- Braces ({ }) indicate a required choice.
- Braces within brackets ([{ }]) indicate a required choice within an optional element.
- **Bold** indicates commands and keywords that are entered literally as shown. In configuration examples and output (not general command syntax), bold indicates commands that are manually input by the user (such as a **show** command).
- *Italic* indicates arguments for which you supply actual values.

The following topics are covered in this chapter:

- Open System Interconnection Reference Model
- Information Formats
- Network Hierarchy
- Connection-Oriented and Connectionless Network Services
- Network Addressing
- Flow Control
- Error-Checking
- Standards Organization

CHAPTER 1

Internetworking Basics

Internetworks are groups of individual networks functioning as a single large network. *Internetworking* refers to the technology and devices—such as bridges, routers, and switches—creating and administering these internetworks.

Two primary types of networks are used by customers:

- **Local-area networks (LANs)** enable multiple users in a small geographical area, such as within a building or campus, to share files and exchange messages. LANs also enable the sharing of resources, such as file servers and printers. Some examples of LAN technology are Ethernet, Token Ring, or FDDI implementations.

NOTE High-speed LANs and switched internetworks often are deployed throughout enterprise organizations because these internetworks enable high-bandwidth applications, such as videoconferencing, voice-over alternate technologies (such as VoIP and VoATM), and other multimedia applications.

- **Wide-area networks (WANs)** interconnect geographically dispersed LANs enabling these LAN users to communicate and share resources with each other. Some examples of WAN technology are Frame Relay, Asynchronous Transfer Mode (ATM), or IP Virtual Private Network (VPN).

In comparison, the roads and highways used are an internetwork. Consider the neighborhood roads and streets as part of a LAN. People living in houses attached (by driveways) to these neighborhood roads are the LAN users. When people leave their houses and drive to work, they use an internetwork of larger thoroughfares and perhaps interstates. This larger internetwork is a WAN, carrying several users from one LAN (home neighborhood) to another (workplace neighborhood).

Just as these highways and interstates create one type of WAN, the railroad creates another and the routes taken by airplanes yet another. Figure 1-1 illustrates this highway/Frame Relay and railway/ATM comparison.

Figure 1-1   *Internetwork Comparison*

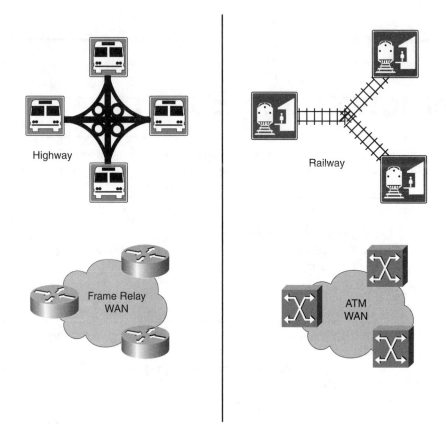

In order to use the railroad WAN, a user must be in the proper vehicle; in this case, a railroad car. An automobile, or bus, would not be able to use railroad tracks because the automobile is designed to be used on a different WAN: the highway. These differing vehicles are similar to different WAN technologies in use, such as Frame Relay, ATM, or Internet Protocol Virtual Private Networking (IP VPN). A Frame Relay user (automobile) could not use the railroad tracks (ATM) for transportation because the two are incompatible. Some form of conversion must be available to carry the data; in this case a person, from one network to another.

The key fundamental concept to an internetworked system is the Open System Interconnection (OSI) Reference Model, which is discussed in the following section.

OSI Reference Model

At the heart of any internetworked system is the OSI Reference Model. The OSI Reference Model is a conceptual model made up of seven layers, each specifying particular network functions. The OSI Reference Model was developed by the International Organization for Standardization (ISO) in 1984, and it is considered the architectural model for network-based communications. The OSI Reference Model describes how information from one computer application is transported across a network to the same (or similar) application on another computer.

The OSI Reference Model divides the processes involved with internetwork communication into smaller, more manageable pieces, or layers. Each layer is self-contained, although dependant upon the layer below for services, so that the processes assigned to each layer can be independently implemented. This layering provides for the solutions offered by one layer to be updated without affecting the other layers.

The following list details the seven layers of the OSI Reference Model:

- Layer-7: Application
- Layer-6: Presentation
- Layer-5: Session
- Layer-4: Transport
- Layer-3: Network
- Layer-2: Data-Link
- Layer-1: Physical

In order for network devices to communicate with each other, they must be able to speak the same "language," or protocol. Vendors, vendor consortiums, and technology working groups develop these protocols with the OSI Reference Model as a common reference point.

Chapter 2, "OSI Reference Model," discusses the model in further detail.

Information Formats

Data and control information transmitted across internetworks takes a variety of formats, depending on which layer of the OSI Model is being discussed. The terms describing these information formats are not used consistently in the internetworking industry and sometimes are used interchangeably.

Common information formats are listed in Table 1-1.

Table 1-1   *Information Formats*

Information Format	OSI Layer (if applicable)
Data Units / Datagrams	N/A
Frames	Layer-2
Packets	Layer-3
Segments	Layer-4
Cells	N/A

The following sections discuss these formats of information transmission.

Data Units/Datagrams

Data unit, sometimes known as *a datagram,* is a generic term referring to a variety of information units found in network environments. Some common data units are as follows:

- **Service data units (SDUs)** — Information units from upper-layer protocols that define a service request to a lower-layer protocol.

- **Protocol data units (PDUs)** — OSI terminology for a packet.

- **Bridge protocol data units (BPDUs)** — Used by the spanning-tree algorithm as "hello" messages.

Frames

Frames are data-link layer (OSI Layer-2) datagrams and are made up of the following:

- Data-link layer header
- Payload (upper-layer data)
- Trailer

The frame header and trailer contain control information, such as addressing, link management, and error-checking mechanisms, to be used by Layer-2 devices, such as LAN bridges or Frame Relay WAN switches.

The length of a frame, measured in bytes, is determined by the maximum transmission unit (MTU) setting, which can be adjusted manually or by the protocol default. Figure 1-2 illustrates a data-link layer frame.

Figure 1-2 *Layer-2 Datagram (Frame)*

Packets

Packets are network layer (OSI Layer-3) datagrams and are made up of a network layer header, payload (upper-layer data), and a trailer. The packet header and trailer contain control information, such as addressing, to be used by Layer-3 devices, such as WAN routers and Layer-3 switches.

The length of a packet, measured in bytes, is determined by the MTU setting, which can be adjusted manually or by the protocol default. Figure 1-3 illustrates the basic components of a network layer packet.

Figure 1-3 *Layer-3 Datagram (Packet)*

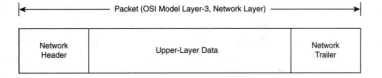

Segments

Segments are transport layer (OSI Layer-4) datagrams and are made up of a transport layer header, payload (upper-layer data), and a trailer. The segment header and trailer contain control information, such as sequencing and error checking, to be used by Layer-3 devices, such as routers. Routers use the sequencing information found in the header to ensure that all packets in a data stream have been received.

The length of a segment, measured in bytes, is determined by the MTU setting, which can be adjusted manually or by the protocol default. Figure 1-4 illustrates the basic components of a transport layer segment.

Figure 1-4 *Layer-4 Datagram (Segment)*

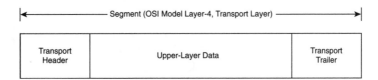

Cells

Cells are a fixed size and used in switched environments, such as ATM networks. Cells are made up of a header and payload; cells do not use trailers. The header contains control information, such as addressing, used by cell switching devices, such as ATM switches.

The length of a cell, measured in bytes, is a fixed length. For example, ATM cells are 53 bytes in length; 5 bytes for the header and 48 bytes for the payload. Figure 1-5 illustrates an ATM cell.

Figure 1-5   *ATM Cell*

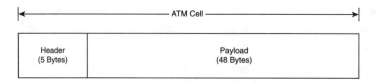

Technical Note: Transmitting Large Datagrams

If the payload of a datagram is larger than the MTU will allow, the datagram must be broken down into fragments for transmission. For example, if the MTU of a frame (Layer-2) is 1500 bytes and the data-link layer is presented with a packet of 4500 bytes in length, the packet is fragmented into three frames for transmission. These fragments are then reassembled by the receiving device for handing off to the next upper-layer.

Network Hierarchy

Large internetworks often are organized as hierarchies, providing advantages such as ease of management, flexibility, and a reduction in unnecessary traffic. It is for these reasons the ISO developed a hierarchical network model. Although this model is not as strictly adhered to in the internetworking community as the OSI Reference Model, the ISO Hierarchical model serves to define internetwork boundaries between users and user communities. Figure 1-6 illustrates this ISO Hierarchical Network model.

Figure 1-6   *ISO Hierarchical Network*

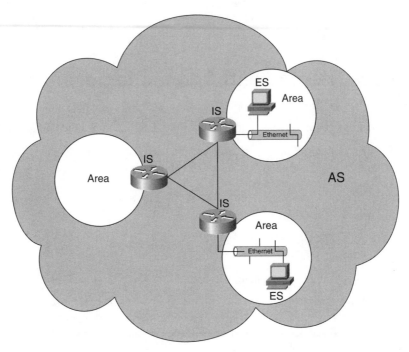

The ISO Hierarchical Network model defines some terminology conventions for addressing network entities. These terms are as follows:

- **End System (ES)**—Network device that does not perform any routing or traffic forwarding functions. Some examples of end system hardware are terminals, personal computers, and printers.

- **Intermediate System (IS)**—Network device that performs routing or other traffic-forwarding functions. Some examples of intermediate system hardware are routers, switches, and bridges. Two types of IS networks exist: intradomain IS and inter-domain IS.

  — Intradomain ISs communicate within a single autonomous system (AS)

  — Interdomain ISs communicate within and between autonomous systems

- **Autonomous System (AS)**—Collection of networks under a common administration sharing a routing strategy. Autonomous systems are subdivided into areas, and an AS is sometimes called a *domain*.

NOTE	An *area* is a logical group of network segments and their attached devices; areas are subdivisions of autonomous systems.

Connection-Oriented and Connectionless Network Services

Transport protocols are characterized as either connection-oriented or connectionless:

- Connection-oriented services must first establish a connection between the two end-points (sending/receiving) before passing any data traffic between them. An example of a connection-oriented service is Frame Relay, where a VC (virtual connection) is required between both end-points before data traffic can be exchanged. Connection-oriented service involves three phases:

  — Connection establishment

  — Data transfer

  — Connection termination

  During connection establishment, the end-points can reserve resources and negotiate traffic parameters for the connection; for example, to ensure Quality of Service (QoS), further discussed in Chapter 13, "Quality of Service Introduction."

- Connectionless services can send data without requiring an established connection. Connection-oriented services provide some level of delivery guarantee, whereas connectionless services do not. An example of a connectionless service is any IP service, such as the Internet. No established connection is made between a web browsing user and the home page being viewed.

During data transfer, most connection-oriented services will monitor for lost packets and handle resending them. The protocol also is responsible for putting the packets in the right sequence before passing the data up the protocol stack.

Connection-oriented network services have more overhead than connectionless ones. Connection-oriented services negotiate a connection, transfer data, and tear down the connection, whereas a connectionless transfer can send the data without the additional overhead required to create and tear down connections.

Network Addressing

Network addresses identify devices that are attached to an internetwork, either as individual devices or as members of a group. Three types of addressing are used in internetworks:

- Data-link layer addresses
- Media Access Control (MAC) addresses
- Network layer addresses

Each of these is discussed in the following sections.

Data-Link Layer Addresses

Data-link layer addresses identify each network device's physical network connection. Data-link addresses are referred to as *physical* or *hardware addresses* and exist within a flat address space, having a pre-established and fixed relationship to a specific device.

End systems often have one physical network connection and thus have only one data-link address, whereas routers and other internetworking devices can have multiple physical network connections, and therefore have multiple data-link addresses. This physical address is known as the *MAC*, address.

MAC Addresses

MAC addresses consist of a subset of data-link layer addresses. MAC addresses identify network entities in LANs that implement the IEEE MAC addresses of the data-link layer. As with most data-link addresses, MAC addresses are unique for each LAN interface. Figure 1-7 illustrates the relationship between MAC addresses, data-link addresses, and the IEEE sub-layers of the data-link layer.

Figure 1-7   *MAC Addresses, Data-Link Addresses, and the IEEE Sub-Layers*

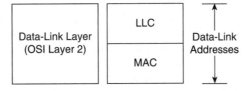

MAC addresses are 48 bits in length and are expressed as 12 hexadecimal digits (0-9, A-F). The MAC address is broken down as follows:

- **First six hexadecimal digits**—Administered by the IEEE. Identifies the manufacturer or vendor and comprises the Organizationally Unique Identifier (OUI).

- **Last six hexadecimal digits**—Administered by the specific vendor and made up of the interface serial number.

MAC addresses are also known as *burned-in addresses* (BIAs) because the address is burned into read-only memory (ROM) and copied into random-access memory (RAM) when the interface card is initialized (powered up). Figure 1-8 illustrates the MAC address format.

Figure 1-8   *MAC Address (48 Bits)*

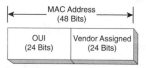

The following is an example of a MAC address:

```
00-02-3b-00-b1-5f
```

In this case, the OUI is `00-02-3b` and the vendor assigned code is `00-b1-5f`.

Network Layer Addresses

A *network layer address* identifies an internetwork device at the network layer of the OSI Model. Network addresses exist within a hierarchical address space and are often called *virtual* or *logical addresses.*

End systems require one network layer address for each network layer protocol they support. The network layer protocol in turn is defined by the internetwork to which the network device is attached. For example, suppose that on a router with three interfaces, one interface is attached to an AppleTalk network, another interface is attached to a Novell network, and the third interface is attached to an IP network. The router must have network layer addresses for each network; in this case, an AppleTalk, IPX (Novell), and an IP network address.

Because internetworks use network addresses to route traffic through the network, there is a need to map network addresses to MAC addresses. When the network layer has determined the destination host's network address, the sending device must forward the information over a physical network using a MAC address. Different protocol suites use different methods to perform this mapping of MAC-to-IP addressing, with the most popular being the Address Resolution Protocol (ARP).

Hierarchical Versus Flat Address Space

Internetwork address space takes one of two forms:

- Hierarchical address space is organized into subgroups, or subnetworks (subnets), each successively narrowing an address until it points to a single device (in a manner similar to street addresses). Telephone numbers are an example of hierarchical address space. For example, the North American Numbering Plan (NANP) users the following hierarchy: NPA-NXX-xxxx; where NPA is the area code and NXX is the central office (CO) exchange responsible for the "xxxx" extensions.

- Flat address space is organized into a single group. An example of flat address space would be the U.S. Social Security Number; no two Social Security numbers can be logically grouped together.

Hierarchical addressing offers advantages over flat-addressing schemes in that addresses can be grouped together to form a single, larger address designation. For example, if a telephone number has the area code of 202, it signifies that the number is part of the Washington, DC telephone exchange group.

Technical Note: ARP

ARP is the method used in the TCP/IP suite. When a network device needs to send data to another device on the same network, the sending device knows the source and destination network addresses for the data transfer, but must map the destination network address to a MAC address before forwarding the data.

Before sending data across the network, the sending host will check its ARP table to see whether it has already discovered the destination host's MAC address. If the sending host has not, it will send a broadcast on the network with the destination host's IP address contained in the broadcast. Every station on the network receives the broadcast and compares the received IP address to its own. Only the receiving host with the matching IP address replies to the sending host with a packet containing the MAC address for the station. The sending host then adds the learned MAC address to its ARP table for future reference and then begins to send the data.

Network Address Assignments

Network addresses are assigned to device interfaces in one of two ways:

- **Static**—Addresses are assigned by a network administrator according to an internetwork addressing plan and do not change without a network administrator manually changing the address.

- **Dynamic**—Addresses are obtained by network devices when the devices are attached to a network, by means of some protocol-specific process, such as DHCP (Dynamic Host Configuration Protocol). A device using a dynamic address is often given a different address each time the device connects to the network, usually assigned by a dynamic address pool (maintained by a dynamic address server). Server-assigned network addresses are recycled for reuse by other network devices when the device holding the address disconnects from the network.

Network Addresses Versus Names

Internetwork devices often have both a name and a network address associated with them. Internetwork names tend to be location-independent and remain associated with a device wherever that device might be located. For example, if a network device is relocated from one building or floor to another the device name does not change. Internetwork addresses often are location-dependent and change when a device is moved. MAC addresses are an exception to this rule because of their nature (MAC addresses are BIAs, embedded in the device's network card). As network addresses are mapped to MAC addresses, names are mapped to network addresses.

The Internet uses the Domain Name System (DNS) to map the name of a device to its IP address. For example, it is easier for users to remember www.cisco.com than the IP address 198.133.219.25. Therefore, when a user types **www.cisco.com** in a web browser, the user's computer (host) performs a DNS lookup of the IP address for Cisco's web server and then communicates with the web server using the learned network address.

Technical Note: DNS

The group of computers listed in a single DNS naming scheme is called a *zone*. This list is a single definitive list of DNS names and associated IP addresses. A zone might be a top-level national domain, such as .com (commercial) or .gov (government). DNS service for subsidiary zones can be delegated within that zone, along with any subsidiary domains.

The DNS system is its own network. If one DNS server doesn't know how to translate a particular domain name, it asks another DNS server, and so on, until the correct IP address is returned.

Flow Control

Flow control prevents network congestion by ensuring that sending network devices do not overwhelm the receiving devices with data. A high-speed computer, for example, could generate traffic faster than the network can transfer it or faster than the destination network device can receive and process it.

The three methods used for handling network congestion are as follows:

- **Buffering**—Used by network devices, such as routers, to temporarily store bursts of excess data in memory until the data can be processed.
  - Occasional data bursts are often handled by buffering.
  - Excess data bursts can exhaust memory forcing the network device to discard any additional datagrams that arrive for transmission. In this case, it is up to the upper-layer protocols to detect the loss of data and request retransmission of the missing data.
- **Source-quench messages**—Used by receiving network devices (routers) to prevent their buffers from overflowing. The receiving device sends source-quench messages to request that the sender reduce its current rate of data transmission.
  - The receiver begins discarding received data due to overflowing buffers.
  - The receiver then begins sending source-quench messages to the sending device at the rate of one message for each packet dropped. The source device receives these source-quench messages and slows down the sending data rate until source-quench messages are no longer received by the sender.
  - The sender gradually increases the sending data rate for as long as no further source-quench requests are received (by the distant-end).
- **Windowing**—A flow-control scheme in which the source requires an acknowledgment from the destination after a certain number of packets have been transmitted. For example, with a window size of three, the source requires an acknowledgment after sending three packets, as the following details:
  - The source device sends three packets to the destination device.
  - After receiving these three packets, the destination device sends an acknowledgment to the source.
  - The source receives the acknowledgment and sends three more packets.
  - If the destination does not receive one or more of these packets for some reason, such as overflowing buffers, the receiver does not receive enough packets to send an acknowledgment. The source then retransmits the packets at a slower transmission rate.

Error-Checking

Error-checking schemes determine whether sent data became corrupted or damaged while traveling from source to destination and is implemented at several layers of the OSI Model, such as cyclic redundancy checks (CRCs) at Layer-2 (Data-Link) or parity checking at Layer-1 (Physical).

CRC

This is the most common error-checking scheme used to detect and discard corrupted data. Error-correction functions, such as data retransmission requests and handling, are left to the upper-layer protocols, such as TCP in the TCP/IP Suite. CRC values are generated by a calculation that is performed at the sending network device. The sending device calculates the CRC value of the datagram, and the source places the calculated value in the datagram trailer and then sends the datagram to the destination. The destination device receives the datagram, calculates the CRC value, compares this value to the value included in the datagram, and then determines whether errors occurred during transmission.

If the CRC values match, no errors occurred and the datagram is processed. If errors did occur, the datagram is dropped and no further action is taken by the receiving device.

Parity Checking

Parity checking refers to the use of parity bits to check that data has been accurately transmitted across the network. A parity bit is added to every (seven or eight bit) data unit transmitted. The parity bit for each unit is set so that all bytes have either an odd number or an even number of set bits.

The following list details the parity checking process between two devices using even parity (the most common form of parity checking):

1 The sending device sends data and counts the number of set bits in each group of seven bits.

2 If the number of set bits is even, the sending device sets the parity bit to 0; if the number of set bits is odd, it sets the parity bit to 1. In this way, every byte has an even number of set bits.

3 The receiving device checks each byte to make sure that it has an even number of set bits.

4 If the receiver finds an odd number of set bits, the receiver knows there was an error during transmission and ignores the errored data.

The sender and receiver must both agree to use parity checking and whether even or odd parity is to be used. If the two sides are not configured with the same parity sense, communication will be impossible.

Parity checking is the most basic form of error detection in communications networks. Although parity checking can detect many errors, it is not foolproof, because parity checking cannot detect situations in which an even number of bits in the same data unit is changed due to some noise on the line, such as noise caused by electrical interference.

Standards Organizations

A wide variety of organizations contribute to internetworking standards by providing forums for discussion, turning informal discussion into formal specifications, and proliferating specifications after they are standardized.

Most standards organizations create a formal standard by using specific processes: organizing ideas, discussing the approach, developing draft standards, voting on all or certain aspects of the standards, and then formally releasing the completed standard to the public.

Some of the best-known standards organizations contributing to internetworking standards are these:

- **International Organization for Standardization (ISO)**—An international standards organization responsible for a wide range of standards, including many that are relevant to networking. Its best-known contribution is the development of the OSI Reference Model and the OSI Protocol Suite.

- **American National Standards Institute (ANSI)**—Also a member of the ISO, ANSI is the coordinating body for voluntary standards groups within the U.S. ANSI developed the Fiber Distributed Data Interface (FDDI) and other communications standards.

- **Electronic Industries Association (EIA)**—Specifies electrical transmission standards, including those used in networking. The EIA developed the EIA/TIA-232 standard (formerly known as RS-232).

- **Institute of Electrical and Electronic Engineers (IEEE)**—A professional organization that defines networking and other standards. The IEEE developed the LAN standards IEEE 802.3 and IEEE 802.5.

- **International Telecommunication Union Telecommunication Standardization Sector (ITU-T)**—Once called the Consultative Committee for International Telegraph and Telephone (CCITT), ITU-T is now an international organization that develops communication standards. The ITU-T developed X.25 and other communications standards.

- **Internet Architecture Board (IAB)**—IAB is a group of internetwork researchers who discuss issues pertinent to the Internet and set Internet policies through decisions and task forces. The IAB designates some Request For Comments (RFC) documents as Internet standards, including Transmission Control Protocol/Internet Protocol (TCP/IP) and the Simple Network Management Protocol (SNMP).

Summary

This chapter discussed basic internetworking concepts. Internetworks are groups of individual networks, such as LANs and WANs that function as a single large network.

As discussed, OSI Reference Model is the heart of any internetworked system. The OSI Reference Model is made up of seven layers: Physical (1), Data-Link (2), Network (3), Transport (4), Session (5), Presentation (6), and Application (7).

The ISO developed the hierarchical network model, which defines network terminology conventions such as ES, IS, and AS.

This chapter also covered network protocols, which are characterized as either connection-oriented or connectionless, and discussed the three types of addressing used in internetworks:

- Data-link layer addresses identify each network device's physical network connection.
- MAC addresses are a subset of data-link layer addresses, made up of the OUI and an interface serial number (assigned by the vendor).
- Network layer addresses identify an internetwork device at the network layer of the OSI Model.

As noted, the three methods of flow control for preventing network congestion in an internetwork are buffering, source-quench, and windowing.

As you learned in this chapter, don't forget that error-checking is not to be confused with error-correction; error-checking verifies the integrity of the data but does nothing if errors are detected.

Finally, this chapter discussed the organizations that contribute to the internetworking standards—ISO, ANSI, EIA, IEEE, ITU-T, and the IAB.

The following topics are covered in this chapter:

- OSI Layer Characteristics
- Host Communication
- Data Encapsulation

OSI Reference Model

Chapter 1, "Internetworking Basics," outlined the basic concepts of internetworking. This chapter introduces you to the fundamental concepts of the Open System Interconnection (OSI) Reference Model. If you are familiar with OSI, this chapter should serve as a refresher; if you are not familiar with it, this information should provide a good introduction.

OSI Layer Characteristics

The OSI Reference Model describes how information from a user or client application in one host, or computer, moves through an internetwork to an application on another host. The OSI Reference Model, illustrated in Figure 2-1, is a conceptual model composed of seven layers, each specifying particular network functions.

Figure 2-1   *OSI Reference Model*

Layer-7	Application
Layer-6	Presentation
Layer-5	Session
Layer-4	Transport
Layer-3	Network
Layer-2	Data-Link
Layer-1	Physical

The model was developed by the International Organization for Standardization (ISO) in 1984 and is considered the primary architectural model for internetwork communications. Each layer of the model is reasonably self-contained, so that tasks assigned to each layer can be implemented independently. This self-containment enables the solutions offered by one layer to be updated without adversely affecting the other layers. This is critical among internetwork vendors who want to focus their Research and Development (R&D) on one particular function rather than the entire OSI Model.

Figure 2-2 illustrates the OSI Model, identifying common internetworking components and the layer at which these components operate.

Figure 2-2   *Components of the OSI Model*

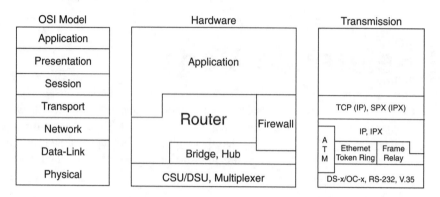

The seven layers of the OSI model are divided into two categories:

- **Upper layers (5–7)**—These layers deal with user data and application issues and are implemented only in the client software. The highest layer, Layer-7 (Application), is the layer closest to the end user and functions as the user-data interface.

- **Lower layers (1–4)**—These layers handle data transport across the internetwork. The Physical and Data-Link layers are implemented in hardware and software. The other lower layers, Network and Transport, are implemented in the communications software. The lowest layer, the Physical layer, is closest to the physical network medium, such as network cabling. The Physical layer is responsible for placing information on the medium (in the form of bits).

Each of the layers is discussed in more detail in the following sections.

NOTE   Communications software is designed for the transmission of data across a connection. Some examples of communications software are ProComm Plus or WinFax.

Layer-1: Physical Layer

The Physical layer specifications address the physical characteristics of the physical medium. Connectors, pins, use of pins, electrical currents, encoding, and light modulation are all part of different Physical layer specifications.

Examples of Layer-1 (Physical) implementation are as follows: EIA/TIA-232, EIA/TIA-449, V.35, V.24, RJ45, Ethernet, IEEE 802.3, IEEE 802.5, Fiber Data Distributed Interface (FDDI), Non-Return-to-Zero-Inverted (NRZI), Non-Return-to-Zero (NRZ), and Binary 8-Zero Substitution (B8ZS).

Layer-2: Data-Link Layer

The Data-Link layer specifications are concerned with getting data across one particular link or medium, such as a LAN (local area network) or WAN (wide area network). Data-link protocols are concerned with the type of media in question; for example, these data-link specifications define how Ethernet or point-to-point WAN links work.

The Data-Link layer is made up of two sub-layers:

- **Media Access Control (MAC)**—Protocol controlling access to the LAN's physical transmission medium

- **Logical Link Control (LLC)**—Provides a common interface point to the MAC layers specifying the access method to be used

Examples of the Layer-2 (Data-Link) implementation are Frame Relay, High-level Data-Link Control (HDLC), Point-to-Point Protocol (PPP), IEEE 802.3/802.2, FDDI, Asynchronous Transfer Mode (ATM), and IEEE 802.5/802.2

Layer-3: Network Layer

The Network layer defines end-to-end delivery of packets by defining logical (network) addressing so that any endpoint can be identified. Logical addressing is not hard-coded into the network device and can be changed, unlike physical addressing which is hard-coded into the network device and cannot be changed. The Network layer defines how routing works and how routes are learned so that packets can be delivered. The Network layer also defines fragmenting a packet into smaller packets to accommodate media with smaller maximum transmission unit (MTU) sizes.

NOTE	*MTU* is an acronym for maximum transmission unit, it is the largest frame size that can be transmitted over the network. Messages longer than the MTU must be divided into smaller frames by the network layer protocol. For example, the Layer-3 protocol, such as IP, learns the MTU from the Layer-2 protocol, such as Ethernet, fragments the datagrams into that frame size and makes these datagrams available to the lower layer for transmission.

Examples of Layer-3 (Network) implementation are Internet Protocol (IP), Novell's Internetwork Packet Exchange (IPX), and AppleTalk Datagram Delivery Protocol (DDP).

Layer-4: Transport Layer

The Transport layer includes the choice of protocols that either do or do not provide error recovery, reordering of the incoming data stream, and reassembly of the data if the packet is fragmented during transmission. For example, Transmission Control Protocol (TCP) may give a 4200 byte segment of data to IP (Internet Protocol) for delivery. IP will fragment the data into smaller sizes if a 4200 byte packet cannot be delivered across the media. The receiving TCP will get three different segments of 1400 bytes apiece, and may receive them in a different order than originally sent. TCP reorders the received segments, compiles them into the original 4200 byte segment, and then acknowledges the data to the sender.

Examples of Layer-4 (Transport) implementation are TCP, User Datagram Protocol (UDP), and Novell's Sequenced Packet Exchange (SPX).

Layer-5: Session Layer

The Session layer defines how to start, control, and end conversations (called *sessions*), including the control and management of multiple bi-directional acknowledgement messages. Acknowledgement messages serve to notify the application if a series of messages are missing. For example, an Automated Teller Machine transaction in which you withdraw cash from your checking account should not debit your account and fail before handing you the cash, and then record the transaction even though you did not receive money.

Examples of Layer-5 (Session) implementation are Remote Procedure Call (RPC), Structured Query Language (SQL), UNIX Network File system (NFS), NetBIOS names, AppleTalk ASP, and DECnet SCP.

Layer-6: Presentation Layer

The Presentation layer defines data formats, such as ASCII text, EBCDIC text, binary, Binary Code Decimal (BCD), and Joint Photographic Experts Group (JPEG). Encryption also is a Presentation layer service. The Presentation layer is the only layer that can manipulate or change user data. This change is brought about when data encryption is implemented.

Examples of Layer-6 (Presentation) implementation are Tagged Image File Format (TIFF), Graphics Interchange Format (GIF), JPEG, Apple Macintosh Picture (PICT), American Standard Code for Information Interchange (ASCII), Extended Binary Coded Decimal Interchange Code (EBCDIC), encryption, Moving Pictures Experts Group (MPEG), Musical Instrument Digital Interface (MIDI), and HyperText Markup Language (HTML).

Layer-7: Application Layer

The Application layer is the user's interface to generate data for transmission using the application's communications services. For example, a standard word processing software package does not have communications capabilities, and therefore will not be concerned with communications requirements. However, e-mail applications, such as Microsoft's Outlook or Qualcomm's Eudora, are applications requiring communications and therefore will be enabled with communications capabilities.

Examples of Layer-7 (Application) implementation include File Transfer Protocol (FTP), World Wide Web (WWW) browsers, Telnet, UNIX Network File System (NFS), Simple Mail Transfer Protocl (SMTP) gateways (Eudora, cc:mail), Simple Network Management Protocol (SNMP), X.400 mail, and File Transfer Access and Management (FTAM).

Host Communication

Layer-*N* must interact with Layer-*N* on another host to successfully implement its functions. For example, Layer-4 (Transport) can send data, but if another host does not acknowledge that the data was received, the sender does not know the data was received and will then perform error-recovery procedures. Likewise, the sending computer encodes a destination network layer (Layer-3) address in the network layer header and if the intervening network devices, such as routers, do not perform their network layer tasks, the packet will not be delivered to the intended destination.

Figure 2-3 provides a conceptual perspective of same-layer interactions. The Application layer on the sending host communicates with the Application layer on the receiving host. The Presentation, Session, and Transport layers on both the sending (Host A) and receiving host (Host B) also communicate in a similar direct fashion. The bottom three layers of the OSI Model—Network, Data-Link and Physical—have to do with delivery of the data. A network device, such as a router (shown in the figure as Router 1), will interconnect the two host devices—Host A and Host B. Router 1 is involved in this process of data delivery because it is interconnected to both Host A and B's Network, Data-Link, and Physical layers.

Figure 2-3   *OSI Model Internetworking*

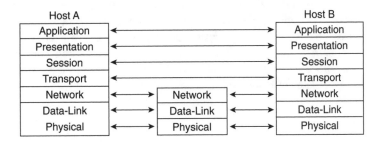

Data Encapsulation

The process by which data is handled layer-to-layer through the OSI model is referred to as *data encapsulation*. The following list shows the five steps of encapsulating data:

1 End-user information creates the data (from an OSI Model standpoint). This occurs at OSI Layers 5–7.

2 Data is converted to segments. This occurs at OSI Layer-4.

3 The segments are converted to packets or datagrams. This conversion occurs at OSI Layer-3.

4 Packets (or datagrams) are converted to frames (OSI Layer-2).

5 Frames are converted to bits, which occurs at OSI Layer-1.

NOTE   *Headers* are placed in "front" of the datagram and *trailers* are placed at the "end" of the datagram. The addition of headers and trailers wraps, or encapsulates, the data with protocol-specific information (pertinent to the protocol's respective OSI layer). OSI Layer-1 (Physical) does not encapsulate data because it does not use headers or trailers.

Common terminology is necessary to discuss the data that a particular layer is processing. Layer-*N protocol data unit* (*PDU*) is a term used to describe a set of bytes that includes the Layer-*N* header and trailer, all headers encapsulated, and the user data. For example, the Layer 2 PDU (including the data-link header and trailer) is called a *frame*; the Layer-3 PDU is called a *packet*, or sometimes a *datagram*; the Layer-4 PDU is called a *segment*.

Summary

This chapter provided a simple tutorial of the OSI Reference Model. The OSI Model was developed by the ISO in 1984 and is considered the primary architectural model for inter-network communications.

The seven layers of the OSI Model are divided into two categories: the upper layers and the lower layers. The upper layers (Layers 5–7) deal with user-data and application issues, which are implemented in client software only. The lower layers (Layers 1–4) are implemented in both hardware and software, and they handle data transport across the internetwork. The process by which data is handled layer-to-layer through the OSI Model is referred to as data encapsulation.

Frequently Asked Questions (FAQ)

1 How are the OSI Model and Transmission Control Protocol/Internet Protocol (TCP/IP) related?

TCP/IP is not an OSI protocol and does not fit into the OSI Reference Model. TCP/IP is a suite of protocols that has been developed by the U.S. Department of Defense and is used on the Internet. Software supporting TCP/IP is part of nearly every UNIX distribution today. The service provided by TCP/IP is very similar to OSI Layer-3 (Network) and Layer-4 (Transport). IP is considered a Layer-3 protocol and TCP is considered a Layer-4 protocol.

2 Which is better—the OSI Model or the TCP/IP Suite?

The answer to this question is that neither is better. The OSI Model is just that: it's a model, not to be confused with the OSI Protocol Suite, which was developed by the International Organization for Standardization (ISO). In theory, the OSI Protocol Suite has the more advanced feature set than the TCP/IP protocol suite, but the OSI Protocol Suite was loosely defined and its vendor proprietary standards were too entrenched in existing networks, making it difficult to transition to a standard protocol. The TCP/IP protocol is more tightly defined than the OSI suite, but has gained wide acceptance from vendors, making TCP/IP a *de facto* protocol standard for internetwork communications.

The following topics are covered in this chapter:

- TCP/IP Model
- TCP/IP Operation
- TCP/IP Addressing
- TCP/IP Ports and Sockets
- UDP and ICMP
- Routing

CHAPTER 3

TCP/IP Introduction

TCP/IP is a protocol suite developed to enable cooperating computers to share resources across a network. Some of the more common protocols in the suite are Internet Protocol (IP), Transmission Control Protocol (TCP), and User Datagram Protocol (UDP). There are other protocols in the TCP/IP suite used for specific tasks, such as transferring files between computers, sending mail, or determining who is logged in on another computer.

A common TCP/IP application is the sending and receiving of electronic mail (e-mail). The TCP/IP suite provisions for the handling of e-mail between hosts (users); however, the presumption is made that there is a reliable method of communication between the two hosts.

The TCP piece of the TCP/IP protocol suite is responsible for several aspects of this communication:

- Ensuring that application-related commands are exchanged between the sending and receiving hosts

- Keeping track of what is sent, and retransmitting anything that did not get through

- Splitting into several packets any message that is too large for one packet (for example, the text of the mail) and ensuring that they all arrive at the intended destination

Because these functions are needed for many applications, they are put together into a separate protocol, rather than being part of the application specifications, such as e-mail.

NOTE The key difference between TCP and UDP is the way in which network connections are established; TCP connections are connection-based, and UDP connections are connectionless. *Connection-based* means that the receiver sends acknowledgements to the packet's sender, acknowledging the sequence numbers in each sent packet. *Connectionless* means that packets are sent with no acknowledgement from the receiver. For example, if you send a package using an overnight shipping service or by certified mail, you receive an acknowledgement that the intended recipient received the package; however, if you send a postcard, there is no system in place for you to know if the recipient received the postcard.

You can think of TCP as a library of routines that applications can use when reliable network communications with another computer are required. As specific applications call on the services of TCP, TCP calls on the services of IP. As with TCP, can be thought of as a library of routines that TCP calls on. The difference is that the library of routines found with IP is available to other applications as well, not only TCP.

TCP/IP Model

The TCP/IP model does not match the seven layers of the Open System Interconnection (OSI) model. There is no universal agreement regarding how to describe TCP/IP with a layered model, but it is agreed that there are fewer layers than the OSI model. TCP/IP is often described as having four layers, as illustrated in the following figure (see Figure 3-1).

Figure 3-1 *OSI Model and TCP/IP Model Layers*

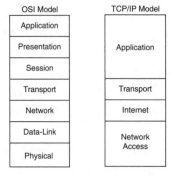

The following list describes each TCP/IP layer in relation to the OSI Network Model layers:

- **Application Layer**—In TCP/IP, the Application layer also includes the OSI Presentation layer and Session layer. Any process occurring above the Transport layer is considered to be part of the Application layer.

  In TCP/IP, the terms *socket* and *port* describe the path over which applications communicate. There are numerous application level protocols in TCP/IP, including Simple Mail Transfer Protocol (SMTP) and Post Office Protocol (POP) used for e-mail, Hyper Text Transfer Protocol (HTTP) used for the World Wide Web, and File Transfer Protocol (FTP). Most application level protocols are associated with one or more port numbers.

- **Transport Layer**—There are two Transport layer protocols:
  - Transmission Control Protocol (TCP) guarantees that information is received as it was sent.
  - User Datagram Protocol (UDP) performs no end-to-end reliability checks.

- **Internet Layer**—The OSI Network Model layer isolates the upper-layer protocols from the details of the underlying network (lower layers) and manages the connections across the network. All upper- and lower-layer communication passes through IP as it is passed through the TCP/IP protocol stack.

- **Network Access Layer**—The OSI Model Data-Link layer and Physical layer are grouped together. TCP/IP makes use of existing Data-Link and Physical layer standards instead of defining its own.

The four-layer structure of TCP/IP is built as information is passed down from applications to the Physical network layer. When data is sent from a source, each layer treats all of the information it receives from the upper layer as data. Control information is added to the front of this data (header), and error checksum information is added to the rear (trailer). This process is known as *encapsulation* and is illustrated in Figure 3-2.

Figure 3-2   *TCP/IP Encapsulation*

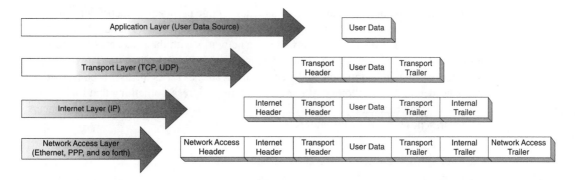

When data is received, the opposite procedure takes place as each layer removes its header before passing the data to the layer above.

TCP/IP Operation

TCP/IP is a connectionless protocol, transferring information in datagrams called *packets*. Each of these packets is individually forwarded through the network. There are limitations to the size of the packet, and if a packet exceeding this maximum size is presented to the network, it is a function of TCP to break the data down into a more manageable stream for the network.

For example, suppose a 15,000-octet file is to be sent; most networks can't handle a 15,000-octet packet. So TCP will break this single large packet into several smaller pieces; maybe 30 500-octet packets. Each of these packets is sent to the destination where these smaller packets are put back together into the 15,000-octet file.

While these packets are in transit, however, the network does not know, or care, that there is any relation between them. It is possible that packet 24 will arrive before packet 11. It is also possible that somewhere in the network an error will occur, and a packet will not be forwarded at all. In this case, the missing packet must be resent by the source.

Two separate protocols are involved:

- TCP is responsible for breaking up the message into packets, reassembling them at the other end, resending anything that gets lost, and putting these packets back in the right order.

- IP is responsible for routing individual packets from source to destination across the internetwork.

The interface between TCP and IP is simple: TCP hands IP a packet with a destination network address. IP does not know, nor care, how this packet relates to any packet before it or after it.

TCP/IP is based on the presumption that there are a large number of independent networks connected together by routers, switches, and gateways. The end-user should be able to access hosts or other resources on any of these networks with their packets often passing through a dozen different networks before reaching their final destination. The routing of these packets should be invisible to the end-user because as far as the user is concerned, all that is needed to access another system is an Internet address, something that looks like 128.6.4.194. Internet addresses are a 32-bit number, often written as four decimal numbers, each representing 8 bits of the address.

NOTE   The term *octet* is used by Internet documentation for 8-bit parts. The term *byte* is not used because TCP/IP is supported by some computers that have byte sizes other than 8 bits.

The structure of the Internet (network) address provides some information about how to get to the host. For example, 128.6.4.194 is broken down as follows:

- 128.6 is the network number assigned by a central authority (IANA) to Rutgers University.

- Rutgers uses the next octet to indicate which of the campus Ethernets is involved. 128.6.4 is the address of an Ethernet network used by the Computer Science Department.

- The last octet allows for up to 254 systems on each Ethernet network.

Internet users often refer to network systems by name rather than by Internet address. When a name is specified, the network software on the host, such as web browser, looks up the name in a database and is given the corresponding Internet address; this database is part of the Domain Name System (DNS).

TCP/IP Addressing

An IP address is a 32-bit unique identifier for a node or host connection on an IP network. This 32-bit binary number is represented as four decimal values, each representing 8 bits, in the range 0 to 255 (known as octets) separated by decimal points; this is known as *dotted decimal* notation. For example, 140.179.220.200 and 10001100.10110011.11011100.11001000 are the same address; one is represented as a decimal number, the other as a binary number, as demonstrated in the following table.

Table 3-1   *IP Address in Decimal and Binary Form*

Decimal	140	179	220	200
Binary	10001100	10110011	11011100	11001000

IP addresses have two parts—the network and the node. The Class of the Internet network address and the subnet mask determine which part belongs to the network address and which part belongs to the node address. It was during the early days of the Internet that the size of the network (active hosts) determined what Class of address space to use. With the advent of classless interdomain routing (CIDR) and variable length subnet masks (VLSM), these Classes were further broken down into more manageable sizes.

Technical Note: CIDR and VLSM

CIDR, also called *supernetting*, is an IP addressing scheme replacing the older system based on classes A, B, and C. CIDR addresses reduce the size of routing tables and make more IP addresses available within network organizations. With CIDR, a single IP address can be used to designate many unique IP addresses. A CIDR IP address looks like a normal IP address except that it ends with a slash followed by a number, called the *IP prefix*. For example:

172.200.0.0/16

The IP prefix specifies how many addresses are covered by the CIDR address, with lower numbers covering more addresses. An IP prefix of /12, for example, can be used to address 4096 former Class C addresses.

CIDR uses VLSM. VLSM was created to enable greater flexibility in routed IP networks, allowing for the accelerating expansion of the Internet.

Variable length subnet masking is a means of allocating IP addressing resources to subnets according to their individual need rather than some general network-wide rule. Therefore the network/host division can occur at any bit boundary in the address. Because the normal class distinctions are ignored, the new system is called *classless routing*, with the original system being called *classful routing*. Classless routing came into use in the mid-1990s due to the inefficiencies of the classful system.

CIDR and VLSM network addresses are used throughout the public Internet, although they also are used elsewhere, particularly in large private networks.

There are five different address classes. You can determine the class of an IP address by examining the first four bits of the IP address. The classes are as follows:

- Class A addresses begin with 0xxx, or 1 to 126 decimal.
- Class B addresses begin with 10xx, or 128 to 191 decimal.
- Class C addresses begin with 110x, or 192 to 223 decimal.
- Class D addresses begin with 1110, or 224 to 239 decimal.
- Class E addresses begin with 1111, or 240 to 254 decimal.

Addresses beginning with 01111111, or 127 decimal, are reserved for loopback and for internal testing on a local machine. Class D addresses are reserved for multicasting. Class E addresses are reserved for future use. They should not be used for host addresses.

NOTE   *Multicasting* refers to sending a message to a select group of users, *broadcasting* refers to sending a message to every user connected to the network (carrying the broadcast), and *unicasting* refers to sending a message to a single user on a network.

Technical Note: Loopback Address

The IP address 127.0.0.1 is a loopback address and will point back to the sending machine. For example, a user can ping 127.0.0.1 and should see a 100 percent success rate (0 percent failure).

For an interactive example, Microsoft Windows users can open an MS-DOS prompt and enter the following command: `ping 127.0.0.1` at the `C:>` prompt; so that the display looks like this: `C:\>ping 127.0.0.1`

You should then see the following on your screen:

```
Pinging 127.0.0.1 with 32 bytes of data:

Reply from 127.0.0.1: bytes=32 time<10ms TTL=128
Reply from 127.0.0.1: bytes=32 time<10ms TTL=128
Reply from 127.0.0.1: bytes=32 time<10ms TTL=128
Reply from 127.0.0.1: bytes=32 time<10ms TTL=128

Ping statistics for 127.0.0.1:
    Packets: Sent = 4, Received = 4, Lost = 0 (0% loss),
Approximate round trip times in milli-seconds:
    Minimum = 0ms, Maximum =  0ms, Average =  0ms

C:\>
```

This output shows that a ping of 32 bytes took less than 10 milliseconds to return from the interface; in this case, the interface is identified by the loopback address (127.0.0.1).

It can be determined by Class which part of the IP address belongs to the network (N) and which part belongs to the node (n).

- Class A—NNNNNNNN.nnnnnnnn.nnnnnnn.nnnnnnn

- Class B—NNNNNNNN.NNNNNNNN.nnnnnnnn.nnnnnnnn

- Class C—NNNNNNNN.NNNNNNNN.NNNNNNNN.nnnnnnnn

In the example, 140.179.220.200 is a Class B address, so by default the Network part of the address (also known as the *network address*) is defined by the first two octets (140.179.x.x) and the node part is defined by the last two octets (x.x.220.200).

In order to specify the network address for a given IP address, the node section is set to all 0s. In the example, 140.179.0.0 specifies the network address for 140.179.220.200. When the node section is set to all 1s, it specifies a broadcast that is sent to all hosts on the network. 140.179.255.255 specifies the example broadcast address.

There are three IP network addresses reserved for private networks, defined in RFC 1918. The addresses are as follows:

- 10.0.0.0/8

- 172.16.0.0/12

- 192.168.0.0/16

These address ranges can be used by anyone setting up internal IP networks, such as a lab, a home LAN, or an enterprise LAN behind a Network Address Translation (NAT) server, proxy server, or a router. It is always safe to use these because routers on the Internet will never forward packets coming from these addresses.

Class A Addresses (/8 Prefix)

Each Class A network address has an 8-bit network-prefix with the highest order bit set to 0 and a seven-bit network number, followed by a 24-bit host-number. Today, it is no longer considered "modern" to refer to a Class A network. Class A networks are now referred to as "/8s" (pronounced "slash eight" or just "eights") because they have an 8-bit network-prefix.

A maximum of 126 (2^7 -2) /8 networks can be defined. The calculation requires that the 2 is subtracted because the /8 network 0.0.0.0 is reserved for use as the default route and the /8 network 127.0.0.0 (also written 127/8 or 127.0.0.0/8) has been reserved for the "loopback" function. Each /8 supports a maximum of 16,777,214 (2^{24} -2) hosts per network. The host calculation requires that 2 is subtracted because the all-0s ("this network") and all-1s ("broadcast") host-numbers may not be assigned to individual hosts.

Because the /8 address block contains 2^{31} (2,147,483,648) individual addresses and the IPv4 address space contains a maximum of 2^{32} (4,294,967,296) addresses, the /8 address space is 50 percent of the total IPv4 unicast address space.

Class B Addresses (/16 Prefix)

Each Class B network address has a 16-bit network-prefix with the two highest order bits set to 1-0 and a 14-bit network number, followed by a 16-bit host-number. Class B networks are now referred to as "/16s" because they have a 16-bit network-prefix.

A maximum of 16,384 (2^{14}) /16 networks can be defined with up to 65,534 (2^{16} -2) hosts per network. Because the entire /16 address block contains 2^{30} (1,073,741,824) addresses, it represents 25 percent of the total IPv4 unicast address space.

Class C Addresses (/24 Prefix)

Each Class C network address has a 24-bit network-prefix with the three highest order bits set to 1-1-0 and a 21-bit network number, followed by an 8-bit host-number. Class C networks are now referred to as "/24s" because they have a 24-bit network-prefix.

A maximum of 2,097,152 (2^{21}) /24 networks can be defined with up to 254 (2^8 -2) hosts per network. Because the entire /24 address block contains 2^{29} (536,870,912) addresses, it represents 12.5 percent (or 1/8th) of the total IPv4 unicast address space.

Class D and Class E Addresses

Class D and Class E network address space are unique and not managed like Class A, B, and C address space.

Class D networks have addresses from 224.0.0.0 to 239.255.255.255. Class D network addresses are used for multicast protocols.

Class E networks have addresses from 240.0.0.0 to 255.255.255.255. Class E networks are reserved for future use.

TCP Ports and Sockets

Because several application programs can be running on one machine using a single network interface, TCP needs to keep track of which data goes to which program. This tracking is done by assigning a port number to every TCP connection. The TCP port number does not need to be the same on the local and remote processes. When a TCP segment is received, TCP knows which process to pass it to by looking at the port number in the TCP header. For example, a user web browsing and polling the e-mail server at the same time is not aware that TCP is playing traffic director to the received data; all data from TCP port 80 is pointed to the web browser, and all data from TCP port 25 is pointed to the e-mail client.

A TCP socket is defined as the combination of the local IP address and the TCP port number. An application wanting to use the facilities of TCP must request a unique socket from the TCP. This is known as *opening a socket*. The local socket and the remote socket define a connection. An application must know these two things in order to successfully communicate to a remote application through TCP.

Routers and firewalls use the TCP port number to block or allow traffic to pass through a network. A complete list of TCP port numbers can be found in RFC 1700 (`www.ietf.org/ rfc/rfc1700.txt?number=1700`). The following table lists some of the more common TCP port numbers.

Table 3-2   *Common TCP Port Numbers*

Port Number	Process Name (Abbreviation)	Description
20	FTP-Data	FTP (File Transfer Protocol)—Data
21	FTP	FTP—Control
23	TelNet	Telnet
25	SMTP	Simple Mail Transfer Protocol
53	DNS	Domain Name System
69	TFTP	Trivial File Transfer Protocol
80	HTTP	HTTP (HyperText Transfer Protocol) (WWW)
110	POP3	Post Office Protocol version 3
115	SFTP	Simple File Transfer Protocol
161	SNMP	SNMP (Simple Network Management Protocol)
179	BGP	Border Gateway Protocol
443	HTTPS	Secure HTTP

UDP and ICMP

User Datagram Protocol (UDP) is for applications where packet sequencing is not a concern of the application. UDP fits into the IP system much like TCP; however UDP does not split data into multiple packets as TCP does. UDP is connectionless, meaning that UDP does not keep track of what it has sent. UDP is used most often for name lookup services.

Internet Control Message Protocol (ICMP) is used for network health (measurement of availability and reliability) and error messages. For example, if a connection attempt to a host is made, the requesting system might receive an ICMP message saying the intended host is unreachable. The most popular ICMP message is ping, which is used to test reachability of a network host. ICMP is simpler than TCP or UDP; ICMP does not use port numbers. Because all ICMP messages are interpreted by the TCP/IP networking software itself, no port numbers are needed to direct ICMP messages at the receiving host.

NOTE   It is a little known fact that *ping* is an abreviation for Packet Internet Groper.

Routing

The task of finding how to get a packet to its destination is referred to as *routing*. IP presumes that a system is attached to some local network, and it is further presumed that the network system can send packets to any other system on the same network. IP faces a challenge when a system is asked to send a packet to a system on a different network. This problem of forwarding packets to different networks is handled by gateways (systems that connect a network with one or more other networks).

Gateways often are routers with more than one network interface, as illustrated Figure 3-3.

Figure 3-3   *IP Gateway*

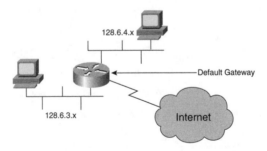

For example, a router has two different Ethernet interfaces; one connected to the 128.6.4.x network, the other connected to the 128.6.3.x network. The router can act as a gateway between these two networks. Routing in IP is based entirely upon the network number of the destination address. The router/gateway determines where to forward the packet based on its routing tables, listing the networks to which the router/gateway is connected. If there is no entry, the packet is then forwarded to the default gateway network, often the Internet.

You can find more detail regarding IP routing in Chapter 11, "Understanding Routers and Routing."

Summary

The TCP/IP protocol suite was developed so that cooperating computers can share resources across a network. Some TCP/IP suite protocols are used for transferring files between computers, sending mail, or determining who is logged in on another computer.

TCP is a connection-oriented protocol (acknowledgements sent by receiver to the originator), whereas UDP is a connectionless protocol (no acknowledgements are used).

The key to TCP/IP networking is found in the IP addressing, currently IPv4 (IP version 4). IPv4 addresses consist of a 32-bit number. When the Internet was commercially introduced it was broken down into smaller networks. Network classes were the mechanism that broke down the address space in line with these smaller networks.

Class A networks have network addresses from 1.0.0.0 through 127.0.0.0. The network number is the first octet, being from 1 to 127. That number uniquely identifies the class A destination network. The rest of the address, three octets, uniquely identifies a machine within that network.

Class B networks have addresses from 128.0.0.0 through 191.255.0.0. The network number is the first two octets, being from 128.0 through 191.255. The number uniquely identifies which class B network is the destination of the packet. The rest of the address uniquely identifies a machine on that network.

Class C networks have addresses from 192.0.0.0 through 223.255.255.0. The network number is the first three octets, being from 192.0.0 through 223.255.255. Each class C network can have one octet worth of hosts.

Class D networks have addresses from 224.0.0.0 to 239.255.255.255. Class D network addresses are used for multicast protocols.

Class E networks have addresses from 240.0.0.0 to 255.255.255.255. Class E networks are reserved for future use.

Frequently Asked Questions (FAQ)

1 Does IP protect data on the network?

IP itself does not guarantee data delivery. IP leaves all data protection issues to the transport protocol. Both TCP and UDP have mechanisms that guarantee that the data they deliver to an application is correct.

IP does try to protect the packet's IP header, the relatively small part of each packet that controls how the packet is moved through the network. It does this by calculating a checksum on the header fields and including that checksum in the transmitted packet. The receiver verifies the IP header checksum before processing the packet. Packets whose checksums no longer match have been damaged in some way and are simply discarded.

2   What is IPv6?

IP Version 6 (IPv6) is the newest version of IP, sometimes called IPng for "IP, Next Generation." IPv6 is defined but is not yet widely deployed. The main differences between IPv6 and the current version of IP (IPv4) are these:

- IPv6 uses larger addresses (128 bits instead of 32 bits in IPv4) and can support many more devices on the network.

- IPv6 includes features like authentication and multicasting that had been bolted on to IPv4 in a piecemeal fashion over the years.

3   What is IPSec?

IPsec stands for *IP Security*. The IPsec working group of the IETF has developed standards for cryptographic authentication and for encryption within IP, often used to enable secure VPNs across a public IP network, such as the Internet.

Case Study

An organization has been assigned the network number 193.1.1.0/24 and it needs to define six subnets. The largest subnet is required to support 25 hosts.

The first step is to determine the number of bits required to define the six subnets. Because a network address can be subnetted only along binary boundaries, subnets must be created in blocks of powers of two 2 (2^1), 4 (2^2), 8 (2^3), 16 (2^4), and so on. It is impossible to define an IP address block such that it contains exactly six subnets. For this example, the network administrator must define a block of 8 (2^3) and have two unused subnets that can be reserved for future growth.

Because 8 = 2^3, three bits are required to enumerate the eight subnets in the block. In this example, the organization is subnetting a /24 so that it will need three more bits, or a /27, as the extended-network-prefix. A 27-bit extended-network-prefix can be expressed in dotted-decimal notation as 255.255.255.224. This is illustrated in Figure 3-4.

Figure 3-4   *Defining the Subnet Mask/Extended-Prefix Length*

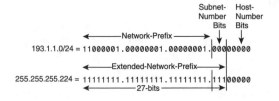

A 27-bit extended-network-prefix leaves 5 bits to define host addresses on each subnet. This means that each subnetwork with a 27-bit prefix represents a contiguous block of 2^5 (32) individual IP addresses. However, because the all-0s and all-1s host addresses cannot be allocated, there are 30 (2^5-2) assignable host addresses on each subnet.

The eight subnet numbers for this example are given in the following list. The italicized portion of each address identifies the extended-network-prefix, while the **bold** digits identify the 3 bits representing the subnet-number field:

```
Base Net: 11000001.00000001.00000001.00000000 = 193.1.1.0/24
Subnet #0: 11000001.00000001.00000001.000 00000 = 193.1.1.0/27
Subnet #1: 11000001.00000001.00000001.001 00000 = 193.1.1.32/27
Subnet #2: 11000001.00000001.00000001.010 00000 = 193.1.1.64/27
Subnet #3: 11000001.00000001.00000001.011 00000 = 193.1.1.96/27
Subnet #4: 11000001.00000001.00000001.100 00000 = 193.1.1.128/27
Subnet #5: 11000001.00000001.00000001.101 00000 = 193.1.1.160/27
Subnet #6: 11000001.00000001.00000001.110 00000 = 193.1.1.192/27
Subnet #7: 11000001.00000001.00000001.111 00000 = 193.1.1.224/27
```

An easy way to check whether the subnets are correct is to ensure that they are all multiples of the Subnet #1 address. In this case, all subnets are multiples of 32: 0, 32, 64, 96, etc.

The broadcast address for Subnet #2 is the all-1s host address:

```
11000001.00000001.00000001.010 11111 = 193.1.1.95
```

Note that the broadcast address for Subnet #2 is exactly one less than the base address for Subnet #3 (193.1.1.96). This is always the case—the broadcast address for Subnet #n is one less than the base address for Subnet #(n+1).

The broadcast address for Subnet #6 is the all-1s host address:
11000001.00000001.00000001.110 **11111** = 193.1.1.223. Again, the broadcast address for Subnet #6 is exactly one less than the base address for Subnet #7 (193.1.1.224).

This chapter covers the following topics:

- Servers and Workstations
- Communication Equipment
- LAN CPE
- Analog Equipment

CHAPTER 4

Customer Premise Equipment (CPE)

Customer Premise Equipment (CPE) is any hardware that is physically located at a customer site. For example, each of the following is considered CPE:

- Servers
- Workstations
- Communication hardware (CSU/DSUs, modems)
- LAN equipment (hubs, bridges, switches)
- WAN equipment (routers)

This chapter describes each of these items.

Servers and Workstations

The word *server* can refer to both the hardware and software or just the software that performs the service, such as File Transfer Protocol (FTP). *Workstation* refers to any local area network (LAN) host (a computer) that enables a user to interface with LAN resources.

Servers

Servers are computers in a network that are shared by multiple users. The server *serves* the required or requested information to the user's client. Following is a list of the more common server types found in networks:

- **Application servers**—computers in a network environment that perform the necessary data operations to process and deliver information for clients.
- **File servers**—computers in a network that act like remote disk drives in that they store programs and data files shared by users. The difference between a file server and an application server is that the file server stores programs and data, and the application server runs the programs and processes the data.
- **Intranet servers**—computers dedicated to providing Internet-like services to private network users (such as hosting a corporate intranet).

- **Mail (SMTP/POP) servers**—computers in a network that store incoming mail for distribution and forward outgoing mail.

- **Network access servers**—computers in a network dedicated to authenticating users who log on. (*Authentication* is the process of verifying that users are who they say they are, similar to a person "showing ID." Authentication does not play a role in a user's access rights to a system, however.)

- **Remote Access Servers**—work much the same as Network Access Servers with the exception that remote access users, such as remote dial, virtual private network (VPN) dial, and so on, are verified and/or authenticated.

- **Print servers**—computers (or other dedicated hardware devices) in a network that controls one or more printers. Print servers enable printers to be located anywhere on a network and remain accessible to users on that network.

- **Proxy servers**—computers that serve as a liaison between a sender and receiver. All input is received on one port and forwarded out a different port, closing a straight path between two networks and preventing intruders from accessing a private network. Proxy servers are one way to build a firewall between public and private networks.

- **Terminal servers**—computers used to connect multiple dumb terminals to a network or host computer. (*Dumb terminals* are output devices—such as display monitors— that have no processing capabilities, but only accept data from the CPU and display it to the user.)

- **Web servers**—computers that provide World Wide Web services on the Internet. If a Web server is used internally and not by the public, it is known as an *intranet server*.

Cisco Note

The Cisco LocalDirector series offers a solution that balances user traffic load across multiple Transmission Control Protocol/Internet Protocol (TCP/IP) application servers, such as a WWW or FTP server. Cisco LocalDirector tracks network sessions and server load conditions in real time, directing each session to the most appropriate server. All physical servers appear as one virtual server, requiring only a single IP address and URL for an entire server farm. More information about LocalDirector can be found at `www.cisco.com/warp/public/cc/pd/cxsr/400/`.

Server Platforms

Table 4-1 shows you various server hardware with their associated central processing units (CPUs) and Network Operating Systems (NOSs).

Table 4-1   *Server Platforms (Abridged, Source: Computer Desktop Encyclopedia, 2001, The Computer Language Co., Inc.)*

Server Hardware	CPU & NOS
Intel (x86)	Lantastic-DOS
	NetWare
	OS/2-Lan Manager/Server
	Microsoft Windows NT, 2000, XP
	Solaris (UNIX)
	AIX (UNIX)
	SCO Open Server (UNIX)
	SCO UltraWare (UNIX)
	NeXTStep (UNIX)
	VINEs (UNIX)
	Interactive UNIX
Sun SPARCserver	Solaris (UNIX)
Motorola 680x0	Mac OS
	A/UX (UNIX)
PowerPC	Mac OS
	AIX (UNIX)
Unisys (x86)	UNIX SVR4
NCR (x86)	
IBM System/390 zSeries	MVS
	VM
	DS/390
	ZOS
IBM RS/6000 pSeries	AIX (UNIX)
IBM AS/400 iSeries	OS/400
Compaq Alpha	Digital UNIX
	OpenVMS
	Windows NT

continues

Table 4-1   *Server Platforms (Abridged, Source: Computer Desktop Encyclopedia, 2001, The Computer Language Co., Inc.) (Continued)*

Server Hardware	CPU & NOS
DEC VAX	VMS
	Ultrix (UNIX)
	Pathworks
HP (PA-RISC)	HP/UX (UNIX)
	MPE/ix (UNIX)
Tandem (MIPS)	NonStop Kernel

Clients and Workstations

Clients and LAN workstations are any host enabling a user to access and use network resources. Clients can be classified as any hardware or software that makes a request from a server, such as a file transfer request from a file server or a URL request from an intranet/Internet server.

Table 4-2 details the client hardware with associated CPU and operating system (OS) implementations.

Table 4-2   *Client Platforms (Abridged, Source: Computer Desktop Encyclopedia, 2001, The Computer Language Co., Inc.)*

Client Hardware	CPU & OS
Intel (x86)	Windows 3.1, 95/98, NT, 2000, ME and XP
Sun SPARCstation	Solaris (UNIX)
Motorola 680x0	Mac OS
	A/UX (UNIX)
PowerPC	Mac OS
	AIX (UNIX)
HP 9000 (PA-RISC)	HP/UX (UNIX)
IBM RS/6000	AIX (UNIX)
Silicon Graphics (MIPS)	IRIX (UNIX)
Compaq Alpha	Digital UNIX
	OpenVMS
	Windows NT
DEC VAX	VMS
	Ultrix (UNIX)

Communication Equipment

For servers and clients to communicate with each other, certain communications equipment is required. The communications equipment used depends on the method of data transmission.

The following sections discuss three types of communication equipment: multiplexers (muxes), Channel Service Unit/Data Service Units (CSU/DSUs), and modems.

Multiplexers

Multiplexing combines multiple (analog or digital) low-speed signals into a single high-speed signal for transmission over a communications line. Following are examples of different multiplexing methods:

- **Frequency Division Multiplexing (FDM)**—Each signal is assigned a different frequency. FDM allocates a portion of the bandwidth for use all the time.

- **Time Division Multiplexing (TDM)**—Each signal is assigned a fixed time slot in a fixed rotation. TDM allocations the entire bandwidth for a short amount of time.

- **Statistical Time Division Multiplexing (STDM)**—Time slots are assigned to signals dynamically to make better use of bandwidth.

- **Wavelength Division Multiplexing (WDM)**—Each signal is assigned a particular wavelength for use all the time. WDM is used only on optical fiber.

Multiplexers, also known as *muxes*, do the actual signal combination for transmission. The demultiplexer reverses the process by separating the high-speed signal into the original low-speed signals. The multiplexer and demultiplexer are often a single device capable of processing both outgoing and incoming signals, as illustrated in the Figure 4-1.

Figure 4-1   *Multiplexer Combining Four Low-Speed Lines into a Single High-Speed Line*

CSU/DSU

Channel Service Unit/Data Service Units are devices that terminate a digital signal on a customer's premise. CSU/DSUs perform line coding, line conditioning and equalization, and some (remote and local) test functions, such as loopback testing. CSU/DSUs terminate the local loop from the network service provider and translate the bipolar (WAN) digital signal into a unipolar (LAN) digital signal, as illustrated in Figure 4-2 and 4-3.

Figure 4-2 *CSU/DSU with Four-Wire Interface to the Telco and V.35/RS-232/449 Interface to the End-user Equipment*

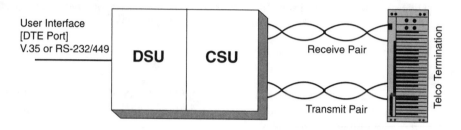

Figure 4-3 *Unipolar/Bipolar Digital Signal Conversion (by CSU/DSU)*

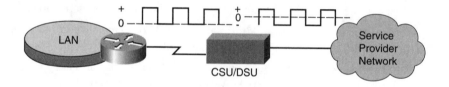

NOTE Some CSU/DSUs have built-in data compression; however, most IXCs/LECs do not support this compression. If a private (leased) line service is implemented in which a customer location is terminating both ends of the service, data compression can be implemented as the serving IXCs/LECs are passing the data through their networks (instead of terminating the service).

Figures 4-4 and 4-5 illustrate these compression and no-compression scenarios.

Figure 4-4 *Compression (Often) Not Supported by Service Provider*

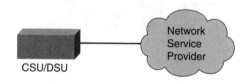

Figure 4-5   *Compression Supported*

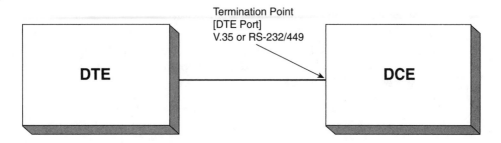

The CSU/DSU device performs two distinct functions, as detailed in Table 4-3.

Table 4-3   *CSU/DSU Functions*

Device	Function
CSU	Receives and transmits signals to and from the WAN line.
	Provides a barrier for electrical interference from either side of the unit.
	Echoes loopback signals from the service provider for remote testing purposes.
DSU	Manages line control and converts input and output signals between RS-232C, RS-449, or V.35 frames from the LAN (router or bridge interface) DS-x frames on the DS0/DS1/DS3 line.
	The DSU manages timing errors and signal regeneration.
	The DSU provides a modem-like interface between the computer as data terminal equipment (DTE) and the CSU.
	The DSU is often integrated with the CSU, is called a CSU/DSU, and is sometimes a component of a T1 WAN card (in a voice PBX or router).

DTE/DCE Interfaces

A DTE/DCE interface is the point of interconnection between the user DTE and the communications facilities. The *data circuit-termination equipment* (DCE) is the termination point and interface for these communications facilities.

The DTE/DCE components are described as follows:

- **DTE**—is the component that converts user information into signals for transmission and reconverts the received signals back into user information. A user interacts with the DTE, or the DTE may be the user. The DTE interfaces with the DCE.

- **DCE**—performs functions such as signal conversion and coding at the network end of the line between the DTE and the line. The DCE can be a separate or an integrated part of the DTE or the intermediate equipment.

DTE/DCE interfaces are often RS-232C/, RS-422/449, V.35, V.90, High-Speed Serial Interface (HSSI), or High Performance Parallel Interface (HIPPI/HPPI). DTE/DCE interfaces also have a direct impact in terms of supportable bandwidth and maximum distance between DTE and DCE.

RS-232C

RS-232C is a standard ("C" is the current version) that describes the physical interface and protocol for low-speed serial data communication between computers and related devices. RS-232 is used for both asynchronous (PC or terminal server) and synchronous data transfer (such as Frame Relay or SDLC/HDLC) DTE/DCE interfaces.

The RS-232 standards restrict transmission to 20 kbps or less and line lengths of 15 m (50 feet) or less. However, RS-232 is more robust than the traditional specified limits of 20 kbps over a 15 m line. Most 56 kbps DSUs are supplied with both V.35 and RS-232 ports because RS-232 can support speeds up to 200 kbps (over the same 50-feet distance).

NOTE   The 15 m limitation for RS-232C cable length can be stretched to about 30 m for ordinary cable, if it is well screened and grounded, and about 100 m if the cable is of low capacitance (ratio of electrical charge to potential in a conductor).

RS-422/449

The RS-422/449 standards are designed to replace the older RS-232 standard because they support higher data rates and distances (2 Mbps at 200 feet). RS-422/449 also provides for greater immunity to electrical interference, or *crosstalk*, than does RS-232.

NOTE   Crosstalk is a disturbance caused by electromagnetic interference along a circuit or a cable pair. Telecommunications signals can disrupt a signal in an adjacent circuit, causing the signals to become confused and cross over each other, resulting in crosstalk. Crosstalk is similar to two people talking over each other during the course of a conversation; the signals (in this case, the words from each speaker) talk over each other, resulting in a conversation that neither party can understand.

V.35

V.35 is a standard for high-speed data transmission (up to 2.048 Mbps). In the U.S., V.35 is the interface often used by routers and CSU/DSUs to connect to T1/E1 services.

V.90

V.90 is an asymmetrical transmission standard in which upstream transmission (keystroke and mouse-click commands) are sent at speeds up to 33.6 Kbps; and downstream transmission is sent at speeds up to 53.3 Kbps.

NOTE   V.90 modems receive data at speeds of up to 56 Kbps; however, due to Federal Communications Commission (FCC) rulings on maximum permissible transmit power levels during down load transmissions, speeds of 53.3 Kbps are the maximum allowed. The actual data speeds achieved vary depending on line conditions.

HSSI

The *HSSI* is a DTE/DCE interface that enables transmission rates of up to 52 Mbps. HSSI was developed by Cisco Systems and T3plus Networking to address the need for high-speed communication over WAN links.

HSSI can handle the T3 speeds (45 Mbps) of many WAN technologies, such as High-Speed Frame Relay and Asynchronous Transfer Mode (ATM), as well as the Office Channel-1 (OC-1) speeds (52 Mbps) of the synchronous digital hierarchy (SDH).

HIPPI/HPPI

HIPPI, previously called HPPI is a DTE/DCE standard enabling speeds of 800 Mbps or 1.6 Gbps (simplex or full-duplex). HIPPI is used for short distances (up to 10 km depending on cable type) to interconnect DTE/DCE devices, such as a high-speed server with an ATM switch in a data-center.

LAN CPE

LAN CPE is the collection of LAN communications devices, which include the following:

- Hubs
- Bridges

- Routers
- Switches

Each of these items is discussed in the following sections.

Hubs

Hubs are multiport repeaters that connect devices on a shared LAN. Because only two devices can be connected with LAN cables, a hub is needed to interconnect two or more devices on a single LAN. Hubs repeat every LAN signal received on a single port out all ports, propagating the signal to every device on the LAN. The cable termination points are the hub and the LAN device (host).

Bridges

Bridges connect LAN segments, lengthening the diameter (across a distance) of the LAN as well as segmenting, or breaking up, collision domains. These are the four types of LAN bridges:

- **Transparent**—Used in Ethernet LAN environments only
- **Source-Route**—Used in Token Ring LAN environments only
- **Source-Route Translational (Mixed-Media)**—Used to mix Ethernet and Token Ring LAN environments
- **Source-Route Transparent**—Used to mix Ethernet and Token Ring LAN environments

Routers

Routers enable communications between LANs and/or wide-area networks (WANs). Routers are protocol specific in that they must support the network-layer protocol used by each data packet. For example, for a router to support Internet connections, the router must be able to support Internet Protocol (IP) traffic. To support of a Novell Netware implementation, the router must support IPX.

LAN Switches

Switches carry network traffic by receiving data frames from a source host (connected to a switch port) and forwarding these frames through a different switch port (based on the frame header information).

Analog Equipment

Because you cannot pass an analog signal directly to a digital device or vice versa, you need analog-digital (A-D) and digital-analog (D-A) converters.

The modem is a classic example of an A-D/D-A converter. The modem converts a digital signal into an analog audio signal when sending (originating) data over a phone line. It then converts the signal from analog to digital for the terminating (receiving) end of the line.

Modem is an abbreviation for MOdulator-DEModulator. A *modem* is a device connected to a PC that enables the PC to transmit data over a telephone line. Modems convert digital signals (from the PC) to analog signals for transmission across a phone line. Wireless modems convert digital data into radio signals and vice versa.

Modems came into existence in the 1960s as a way enabling communication terminals to connect to computers over telephone lines. A typical arrangement is illustrated in Figure 4-6.

Figure 4-6   *Modem Operation (with Terminal and Mainframe)*

As faster modems were invented and deployed, the concept of gradual degradation was introduced. *Gradual degradation* is the modem's capability to test the phone line and fall back to slower speeds if the line cannot support the modem's fastest possible speed. Gradual degradation is why a 56 Kbps dial-up modem will sometimes connect at 53.3 Kbps or 48 Kbps, and 33.6 Kbps other times.

The next step in modem evolution was the asymmetric digital subscriber line (ADSL) modem. This is called *asymmetric* because these modems send data faster in one direction than the modem sends in the other. ADSL modems operate over dedicated copper facilities between the residence/business and the Local Exchange Carrier's DSL Access Multiplexer (DSLAM).

Technical Note: DSL Modems

DSL modems function by sharing, or dividing, the frequency spectrum. The phone line's bandwidth between 24,000 hertz and 1,100,000 hertz is divided into 4000-hertz bands, and a virtual modem is assigned to each band. Each of these 249 virtual modems tests its band and does the best it can with the slice of bandwidth it is allocated. The aggregate of the 249 virtual modems is the total speed of the pipe.

Summary

CPE is any hardware that is physically located at a customer site. For example, each of the following is considered CPE: servers, workstations, communication hardware (CSU/DSUs, modems), LAN equipment (hubs, bridges, switches), and WAN equipment (routers).

Servers refer both to the hardware and software or just the software that performs the service, as FTP. *Workstation* refers to any LAN host (computer) that enables a user to interface with LAN resources.

Before a LAN can connect to a network service provider's access line, a CSU/DSU or multiplexer must be used on both ends of the access line (one by the customer and the other by the network service provider).

For analog service, such as low-speed asynchronous lines (such as those used with radio relay or voice automatic ring-down services), you must perform an A-D conversion. Because analog signals (such as voice) cannot be transmitted directly over a digital network, modems are required to perform both the A-D conversion from the sending side and the D-A conversion on the receiving side of the line.

Frequently Asked Questions (FAQ)

1 What is COAM?

COAM is an acronym for Customer Owned And Maintained. COAM is often used by service providers to identify who is responsible either for a certain piece of equipment or for the customer, the service provider, or a third party vendor (designated by the customer or the service provider depending on service contract terms).

2 If 56K (V.90) modems can't really connect at 56 K, why are they called 56K?

Calling V.90 modems 56 K modems is an unfortunate misnomer. The FCC (Part 68) limits legal speed on the telephone network to 53.3 Kbps. Actual speeds vary according to your phone line conditions. The FCC limitations were designed in the late 1960s when 300 bps was the norm and 53.3 Kbps was considered both high-speed and the most power the copper facilities used in the Public Switched Telephone Network (PSTN) could support. Japan has deployed 64 Kbps dial-up service and as of this writing, FCC Part 68 is under review for amendment to include 64 Kbps service in North America.

This chapter covers the following topics:

- LAN Topologies
- Ethernet
- Token Ring
- FDDI
- LAN Transmission
- LAN Hardware

CHAPTER 5

Local Area Networks (LANs)

This chapter discusses local area network (LAN) topologies, associated equipment, and transmission environments.

LAN Topologies

LAN topologies are dependant upon the LAN technology in use, such as Ethernet or Token Ring. The LAN technology used in turn depends upon user applications, such as file sharing, Web hosting, or mainframe data centers.

There are four LAN topologies:

- Star (Hub-and-Spoke)
- Bus
- Ring
- Tree

Each of these is discussed in the following sections.

NOTE   *LAN hosts* are any device attached to a LAN; for example, workstations, servers, printers, routers, and so on.

Star (Hub-and-Spoke)

In a *star*, or *hub-and-spoke*, topology, the LAN hosts are connected by point-to-point links to a central hub. Several different cable types can be used for these point-to-point links, such as shielded twisted-pair (STP), unshielded twisted-pair (UTP), and fiber optic. Wireless transmission media also can be used for these point-to-point links.

The advantage of a hub-and-spoke topology is that no cable segment is a single point of failure. If one of these cables fail or develops a problem only that LAN host is affected, all other hosts remain operational.

The disadvantage of a hub-and-spoke topology is the central hub itself. This central hub is a single point-of-failure in that if it fails, every attached host is impacted; that is, out of service.

Figure 5-1 illustrates a hub-and-spoke topology with a file server, printer, and two workstations. As is shown here, if a cable to one of the LAN hosts fails, the rest of the devices are unaffected, unless they need to access the "disconnected" host. If the central hub fails, however, all attached hosts are affected and the LAN is considered down, or out-of-service.

Figure 5-1   *Star (Hub-and-Spoke) Topology*

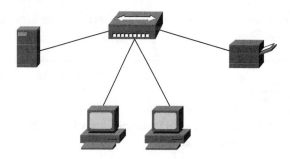

Hub-and-spoke topologies are often found in small office/home office (SOHO) environments where there are a small number of LAN hosts.

Bus

The *bus* topology is a simple design using a single length of cable with attached LAN hosts sharing the cable segment. Every host on this segment sees transmissions from every other host on the cable segment. This operation categorizes bus topologies as broadcast medium. The LAN hosts are endpoints to the cable segment and are known as *bus network termination points*.

This bus cable segment is a single point of failure. If the cable is broken, no LAN host will have connectivity and the LAN is out-of-service.

Ethernet (IEEE 802.3) best represents the bus topology, which is illustrated in Figure 5-2.

Bus topologies are similar to hub-and-spoke topologies and are often found in SOHO environments.

Figure 5-2   *Bus Topology*

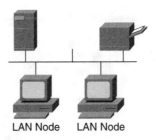

LAN Node   LAN Node

Ring

Ring topologies are the most redundant of network topologies. All hosts in a ring topology are considered repeaters and are enclosed in a loop. Unlike the star topology, there are no endpoints in a ring topology. The repeater in a ring topology is the LAN host's network interface card (NIC).

The NIC in a LAN host repeats any signal that is on the network, whether it is destined for that particular host or not. If for any reason, a NIC fails to perform this repeater function, the entire network could come down. The NIC controller recognizes and handles the problem of a defective repeater by pulling itself off the ring, allowing the ring to stabilize and continue operation.

Token Ring (IEEE 802.5) best represents a ring topology, albeit physically cabled in a star topology, as illustrated in following Figure 5-3 and 5-4.

Fiber Data Distributed Interface (FDDI) is another example of a ring topology implementation. Like Token Ring, FDDI rings are physically cabled in a star topology. FDDI hosts are configured either as a single-attached station (SAS) or as a dual-attached station (DAS). Single-attached stations are connected to one of the two FDDI rings, whereas dual-attached stations are connected to both rings by an A and B port on the FDDI stations and concentrator.

The significant advantage of ring topologies is the inherent redundancy; if a cable or NIC fails on one side of a LAN host in a ring, data traffic will traverse the other side of the failure.

Ring topologies are found in environments where high-availability and redundancy are critical components of a LAN segment.

Figure 5-3   *Ring Topology (Logical)*

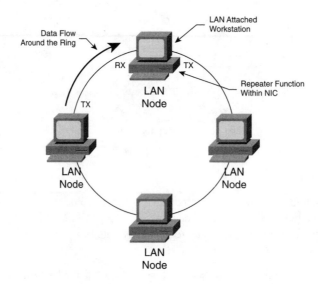

Figure 5-4   *Ring Topology (Physical)*

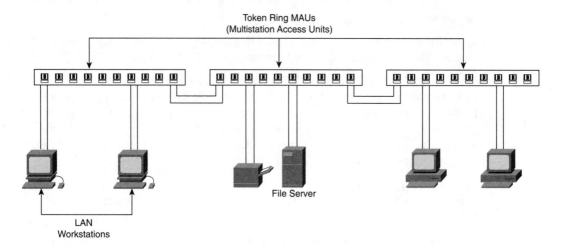

Tree

The *tree* topology is a logical extension of the bus topology and is best described as multiple interconnected bus networks. Tree topologies enable a network to expand dynamically with only one active data path between any two-network endpoints (hosts). The tree topology is illustrated in Figure 5-5.

Figure 5-5   *Tree Topology*

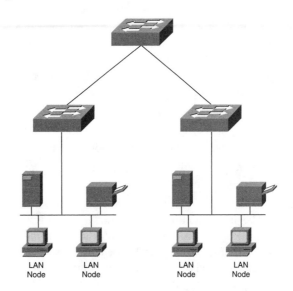

A tree network is one that does not employ loops in its infrastructure. An example of a tree network is one using the Spanning Tree Algorithm, often found with Ethernet (IEEE 802.3) networks. The Spanning Tree Algorithm prevents loops and ensures only one active path exists between any two LAN hosts.

Tree topologies are often found in larger enterprise or campus environments.

Ethernet

Ethernet LANs are covered by the IEEE 802.3 standard and are deployed in approximately 85 percent of the world's LANs. The IEEE 802.3 standard also defines the Carrier Sense Multiple Access/Collision Detect (CSMA/CD) protocol.

Ethernet can operate in either *half-duplex* or *full-duplex* mode. Fast Ethernet and Gigabit Ethernet (discussed later in this chapter) operate in full-duplex mode. Half-duplex communication is when the host sends and receives data over the same wire, but not at the same time; for example, the host can send or receive, but not simultaneously. Full-duplex communication is when the host can send and receive data over the same wire at the same time.

Technical Note: CSMA/CD

The CSMA/CD protocol was developed as a means by which two or more hosts could share a common media in a switch-less environment. In this shared environment, the CSMA/CD protocol does not require central arbitration, access tokens, or assigned time slots to indicate when a host will be allowed to transmit. Each Ethernet NIC determines when it will be allowed to send a frame based on sensing a data carrier on the network medium.

The CSMA/CD access rules are as follows:

Carrier sense (CS)—Each Ethernet LAN host listens for traffic on the medium to determine when gaps between frame transmissions occur.

Multiple access (MA)—LAN hosts can begin transmitting any time they detect that the network is quiet, meaning that there is no traffic across the wire.

Collision detect (CD)—If two or more LAN hosts in the same CSMA/CD network, or collision domain, begin transmitting at the same time, the bit streams from the transmitting hosts will interfere (collide) with each other, and both transmissions will be unreadable. Each host stops transmitting as soon as it has detected this collision and then waits a random length of time (as determined by a back-off algorithm) before attempting to retransmit the frame. In this event, each transmitting host will transmit a 32-bit jam signal alerting all LAN hosts of a collision before running the backoff algorithm.

In other words, in a room full of people, if everyone tried to talk at the same time, no one would be able to communicate. With CSMA/CD, each person would wait to ensure that the medium (in this case, air) was clear (meaning that no one else was talking) before speaking. If two people started to talk at the same time, each would stop talking, wait a random period of time, and start talking again.

In a half-duplex (traditional) Ethernet LAN environment, collisions are part of normal operation. Collisions occur more frequently in a heavily used network, resulting in network performance decreases (as traffic load increases). If the Ethernet LAN experiences traffic load in excess of 30 percent, it is considered to be saturated and it is then worthwhile to consider redesign and/or LAN segmentation initiatives.

Fast Ethernet

Fast Ethernet (100 Mbps) is a high-speed LAN technology that provides increased bandwidth to desktop users, as well as to servers and server clusters (server farms) in data centers.

Fast Ethernet networks support *autonegotiation* (as an optional feature). Autonegotiation enables a network device and a hub to exchange information about their capabilities.

Autonegotiation functions by working through a list of supported configurations until a matching configuration is found. Autonegotiation supports the following capabilities:

- Speed matching for network devices that support both 10- and 100-Mbps operation
- Full-duplex operation mode
- Automatic signaling configuration differing Ethernet network hosts

There are several implementations of Fast Ethernet found today:

- Deployed to the desktop in large organizations with multimedia, Computer Assisted Design/Computer Assisted Modeling (CAD/CAM) or large data requirements, such as database updates
- Small data center implementations, providing faster access to server farms and other storage devices
- Inter-Switch Link (ISL) implementations, where single (100 Mbps) or multiple (up to 800 Mbps) Fast Ethernet channels are bundled together, providing backbone trunks between 10/100 Mbps Ethernet switches, as illustrated in Figure 5-6.

Figure 5-6   *Ethernet ISL*

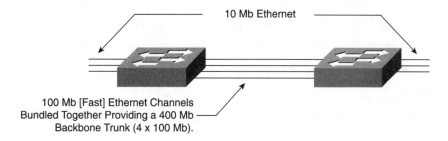

100 Mb [Fast] Ethernet Channels
Bundled Together Providing a 400 Mb
Backbone Trunk (4 x 100 Mb).

Gigabit Ethernet

Gigabit Ethernet (GigE) is Fast Ethernet with an extra zero added, and like Fast Ethernet, Gigabit Ethernet often is deployed to the desktop in larger organizations with multimedia, CAD/CAM, or large data requirements, such as large database updates or medical imagery storage, where Fast Ethernet does not provide enough bandwidth for efficient operation. Gigabit Ethernet also is found in larger data center implementations to provide faster access to server farms and other storage devices.

Like Fast Ethernet, Gigabit Ethernet can be deployed in ISL implementations where Gigabit Ethernet channels of 2 Gbps to 8 Gbps can be bundled to provide backbone trunks between 10/100 Mbps Ethernet switches.

10 Gigabit Ethernet

10 Gigabit Ethernet was recently standardized in the IEEE 802.3ae specifications. 10 Gigabit Ethernet is full duplex, operating like Fast Ethernet and Gigabit Ethernet with no inherent distance limitations.

10 Gigabit Ethernet matches the speed of the fastest WAN backbone technology today, OC-192. (OC-192 runs at approximately 9.5 Gbps.) 10 Gigabit Ethernet has applications across LANs, metropolitan area networks (MANs), and wide area networks (WANs).

NOTE   OC-768 (approximately 40 Gbps) is nearing widespread deployment, in turn pushing OC-192/10 Gigabit Ethernet to the network edge as an access medium.

10 Gigabit Ethernet fits well in these network environments:

- Server interconnection for server clusters
- Aggregation of multiple Gigabit Ethernet segments into 10 Gigabit Ethernet downlinks
- Switch-to-switch links for very high-speed connections between switches in the same data center, in an enterprise backbone, or in different buildings

Token Ring

Token Ring refers to both IBM's Token Ring and IEEE 802.5 network implementations. IBM originally developed the Token Ring network in the 1970s and Token Ring is still IBM's primary LAN technology. IEEE 802.5 is a related specification and is completely compatible with IBM's Token Ring network implementations.

NOTE   The IEEE 802.5 specification was modeled after IBM's Token Ring specification, and the IEEE continues to follow IBM's research and developmental work with Token Ring.

Token Ring is considered a half-duplex network implementation because only one host can transmit at any given time. Token Ring's full-duplex network implementation is known as *Dedicated Token Ring (DTR)*. In DTR implementations, LAN hosts connect to a DTR concentrator or switch and have all available link bandwidth to use for data transmission and reception.

Token Ring and IEEE 802.5 are two of the three chief examples of token passing networks; the third being FDDI. Token passing networks move a small frame, the token, around the network. Possession of the token by a host gives that host the right to transmit data. If a host receiving the token has nothing to send, it passes the token to the next host downstream in the ring. Each host can hold the token for a maximum period of time, called the *Token Holding Time* (THT), and the default is 10 ms.

If a host possessing the token has something to send, it seizes the token, alters one bit of the token to turn it into a start-of-frame (SOF), adds the data, and sends the complete frame (SOF and data). This frame is sent to the next host on the ring, known as the *downstream neighbor*, as illustrated in Figure 5-7.

Figure 5-7   *Token Ring Host B is the Downstream Neighbor of Host A*

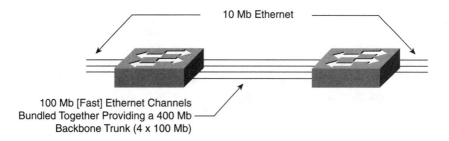

10 Mb Ethernet

100 Mb [Fast] Ethernet Channels
Bundled Together Providing a 400 Mb
Backbone Trunk (4 x 100 Mb)

While the data frame is circling the ring, no token is on the network, unless the ring supports early token release. If the ring does not support early token release, other hosts wanting to transmit must wait. If early token release is supported, a new token can be released when frame transmission is completed. If early token release is not in use, collisions cannot occur in Token Ring network implementations.

The data frame circles the ring until it reaches the intended destination host, which copies the information for further processing. The data frame continues to circle the ring and is removed when it reaches the originating host. The originating host then checks the returning frame, determining whether the frame was seen and copied by the destination.

Unlike Ethernet, Token Ring networks are *deterministic*, meaning that it is possible to calculate the maximum time that will pass before any host will be capable of transmitting. This deterministic nature makes Token Ring networks ideal for applications in which delay must be predictable, such as SNA-based (mainframe) applications.

FDDI

FDDI LANs were introduced in the mid-1980s as ANSI standard X3T9.5 and operate in a similar fashion to Token Ring LANs. FDDI LANs are a popular choice for LAN backbones because they have the following characteristics:

- **Operate at high speeds**—Data is transmitted around a FDDI ring at 100 Mbps.

- **Reliable**—Servers, workstations, or other network devices can be connected to dual rings. After a ring failure, a usable path on the other ring is automatically available.

- **Support a large network diameter**—Dual fiber-optic rings can have a network diameter of up to 100 kilometers each.

FDDI LANs are similar to Token Ring LANs because both are made up of a series of point-to-point links that connect a host to a host, a host to a concentrator, or a concentrator to a concentrator. FDDI specifies the use of fiber optic cabling for its infrastructure, but copper was later introduced and is supported by the Copper Distributed Data Interface (CDDI) specifications (similar to FDDI).

Figure 5-8 illustrates a FDDI LAN with single-attached stations (SAS), dual-attached stations (DAS), and FDDI concentrators (used to connect multiple stations to the FDDI LAN). To provide external access to a WAN, a router with dual-attached FDDI ports (ports A and B) is attached to the FDDI ring. Separate fibers are used in both transmit and receive directions, providing both an input and output point on each FDDI station.

Dual Homing

In an FDDI LAN environment *dual homing* is a fault-tolerant technique used for critical network devices, such as mainframes, server farms, or other mission-critical devices. In a dual-homed implementation, the host is attached to two FDDI concentrators, as illustrated in Figure 5-9.

Figure 5-8   *FDDI Topology*

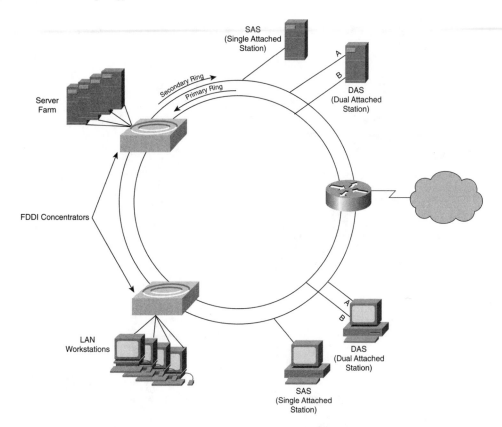

Primary and Secondary Rings

FDDI trunks consist of two rings, known as a *dual ring*. During normal operation, traffic flows on the primary ring, where the secondary ring is the backup in the event the primary ring fails. In the instance of a primary ring failure, the systems adjacent to the break automatically reconfigure the ring path and create a new path that is a combination of both the primary and secondary rings, as illustrated in Figure 5-10.

Figure 5-9 *FDDI Dual Homing Topology*

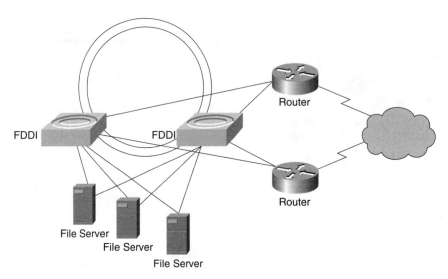

Figure 5-10 *FDDI Ring with Failed Primary Ring*

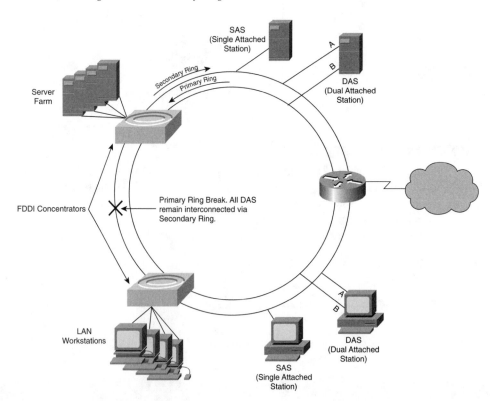

The path length around the ring is limited to 200 kilometers. It is this limitation that restricts the LAN circumference of the dual-ring to 100 kilometers. If one of the rings fails, the dual-ring becomes a single large ring, combining the circumference distances of both the primary and secondary rings.

LAN Transmission

There are three categories of LAN transmission:

- Unicast
- Multicast
- Broadcast

Each of these is discussed in the following sections.

Unicast

In a *unicast* environment, data is sent from the source to a single destination on the network (such as LAN and WAN). The source host addresses the data with the address of the destination host, forwards the data to the network, where it is carried to its destination. Figure 5-11 illustrates a unicast environment.

NOTE   Physical topology and transmission environments are independent of each other. For example, whether the LAN is hub-and-spoke or ring LANs has no bearing on whether the application environment is unicast, multicast, or broadcast.

Figure 5-11 *Unicast Network*

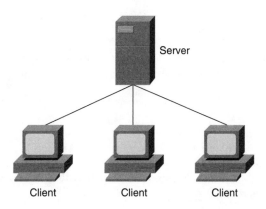

Some examples of unicast applications are person-to-person e-mail, file transfer, or print services.

Multicast

In a *multicast* environment, as illustrated in the Figure 5-12, the data is forwarded to a specific group of hosts on the network. The source host addresses the packet by using a multicast address; for example, the TCP/IP Suite uses 224.0.0.0–239.255.255.255. The multicast packets then are sent to the network, which forwards copies to each registered host in the multicast address group.

Figure 5-12 *Multicast Network*

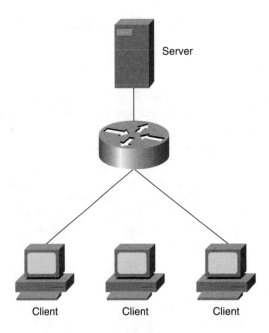

Server

Client   Client   Client

Some examples of multicast applications are videoconferencing or video broadcast applications, where some, but not all, users receive a streaming video feed from a source host.

Broadcast

Broadcasts often are found in LAN environments and will not traverse a WAN unless the router is configured with a *helper-address* to direct broadcasts to a specified network address often across a WAN.

In a broadcast environment, as shown in Figure 5-13, the data packets are sent to all hosts on the network. In broadcast environments, the source host addresses the data with the broadcast address, such as 255.255.255.255 (used in the TCP/IP suite). These data packets then are forwarded to every host on the network.

Figure 5-13 *Broadcast Network*

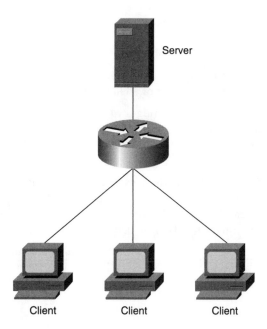

Some examples of broadcast applications are Novell's Get Nearest Server (GNS) requests or TCP/IP's Dynamic Host Configuration Protocol (DHCP).

NOTE   DHCP supports LAN hosts that are not statically (manually) configured with network (IP) addresses. When these hosts join a LAN, a DHCP request is sent to all hosts on the LAN in the hope that the DHCP server will receive the request and return the host configuration information.

Technical Note: Broadcast-based Networks

Broadcast-based networks are not preferred network implementations because every network device on the broadcast network must expend CPU cycles to process each data frame and packet to determine whether that device is the intended recipient. Data broadcasts are a necessary evil of LAN environments and usually have minimal impact because the data frames traversing the network typically are small. Broadcast storms can cripple a network in no time because the broadcasting device uses all available bandwidth on the network.

LAN Hardware

Four hardware devices are used in LANs:

- **Hubs**—multiport repeaters. Hubs work at the Physical layer (Layer-1) of the OSI Model, repeating signals out of all hub ports.

- **Bridges**—multiport hubs. Bridges work at the Physical layer (Layer-1) of the OSI Model and operate at the Data-Link layer (Layer-2). Bridges forward data frames based on the destination MAC address using the spanning tree algorithm for path determination.

- **LAN switches**—multiport bridges. LAN switches connect common broadcast domains, providing frame-level filtering and dedicated port-speed to end-users. LAN switches create Virtual LANs, or VLANs. Like bridges, LAN switches use the spanning tree algorithm for path determination.

- **Routers**—found at the edge of a LAN providing the interface to a WAN, such as a Frame Relay network or the Internet. Routers operate at the Network layer (Layer-3) of the OSI Model.

Hubs

Hubs connect devices on one shared LAN, as illustrated in Figure 5-14. Because only two devices can be connected with LAN cables, a hub is needed to interconnect two or more devices on a single LAN. The cable termination points are the hub and the LAN device (host).

Figure 5-14 *Hub-based Network*

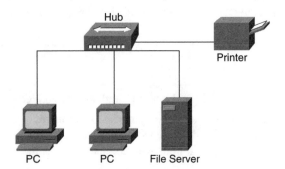

Hubs are not smart devices, meaning that they only repeat the data sent from a network host on one port to all other hub ports, without examining the data frame or the frame header. When network hosts are connected by a hub, each hubbed host will hear all conversations across the LAN. Each host examines the message header to determine whether it is the intended recipient.

Backbone hubs are deployed to connect other hubs into a single termination, or root, point. This is known as a *multi-tiered* design and is illustrated in Figure 5-15.

Figure 5-15 *Backbone, or Multi-Tiered, Hub Network*

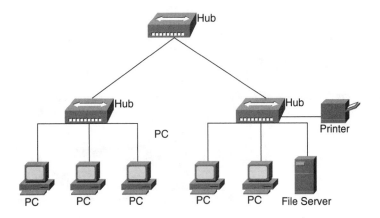

A couple benefits are derived from multi-tiered designs:

- They provide interdepartmental connections between hubs.
- They extend the maximum distance between any pair of hosts on the network.

Bridges

Bridges connect LAN segments, lengthening the diameter (across a distance) of the LAN as well as segmenting, or breaking up, collision domains. The four types of LAN bridging are listed here:

- **Transparent bridging**—Ethernet bridging (see Figure 5-16) connects two or more LAN segments and is transparent to end-devices.

Figure 5-16 *Transparent Bridge Connecting Two Ethernet LAN Segments*

- **Source-route bridging**—Token Ring bridging (see Figure 5-17) connects Token Ring LAN segments, whereby frames are sent from the originating host with the source-to-destination route, or path, included.

Figure 5-17 *Source-Route Bridge (SRB) Connecting Two Token Ring LAN Segments*

- **Source-route translational bridging**—Also known as *mixed-media bridging*, connects networks of two different media (see Figure 5-18), such as Ethernet and Token Ring.

Figure 5-18 *Source-Route Translational Bridge Connecting One Ethernet LAN Segment and One Token Ring LAN Segment*

- **Source-route transparent bridging**—Token Ring bridging (see Figure 5-19) that will either source-route or transparently bridge a frame depending on the Routing Information Indicator (RII) field.

Figure 5-19 *Source-Route Transparent Bridge Connecting Two Token Ring LAN Segments*

Cisco Note: Cisco Specific Bridging Solutions

Cisco has developed five alternative solutions to the previously discussed bridging options. These five are as follows:

- **Concurrent Routing and Bridging (CRB)**—Specific protocols can be bridged out from specific interfaces and routed out other interfaces. However, the protocols in question do not interconnect, or "mix."

- **Integrated Routing and Bridging (IRB)**—Unlike CRB, IRB enables bridged and routed traffic of the same protocol to be interchanged by creating a logical interface, called the Bridge Virtual Identifier (BVI).

- **Virtual Rings for Multi-Port Source Route Bridges**—Where standard Token Ring bridges have only two ports, Cisco routers can be configured as a multi-port source-route bridge by creating a virtual-ring within the router.

- **Remote Source Route Bridging (RSRB)**—Instead of forwarding Token Ring frames from one physical interface to another through a virtual-ring, RSRB forwards Token Ring frames from physical Token Ring interfaces to interfaces connected to an IP cloud through a virtual-ring. RSRB provides a method for performing source route bridging over a WAN, such as Frame Relay or ATM.

- **Data-Link Switching Plus (DLSw+)**—DLSw+ is backwards compatible with Remote Source Route Bridging (RSRB). DLSw+ performs the same functions as RSRB with additional options supported. DLSw+ enables interconnection of transparent bridging (TB), source-route transparent bridging (SRT), source-route translational bridging (SR/TLB), and SDLC-to-LAN Conversion (SDLLC) over an IP backbone.

Spanning-Tree Protocol (IEEE 802.1d)

The Spanning-Tree Protocol (STP) is the protocol used in a bridged or switched environment enabling these devices (bridges and switches) to communicate LAN management information with each other. When multiple bridges or switches are interconnected with multiple paths, a *looped topology* can be formed. A looped topology often is desirable to provide redundancy, but looped traffic is undesirable and bridged traffic is especially vulnerable to broadcast loops. The STP, IEEE 802.1d, was designed to prevent broadcast loops from being formed. The STP originally was developed for bridges; however, today it also is applied to LAN switch topologies. By applying the STP to a looped bridged or LAN switch topology, all bridged segments will be reachable, but any points where loops can occur will be blocked.

Technical Note: Spanning Tree Port States

The IEEE 802.1d specification defines five port states (in order) for STP:

- **Disabled**—The port has either been disabled by the switch itself because of physical problems or security, or it has been manually disabled by the network administrator.

- **Blocking**—The port only listens for BPDUs from other bridges; it does not forward any data frames. In this state, the bridge assumes that it's the root until it exchanges BPDUs with other bridges.

- **Listening**—The port listens for frames to detect available paths to the root bridge but will not take any source MAC addresses of end-stations and place them into the bridge's address table. Also in this state, the bridge will not forward any user frames.

- **Learning**—The port examines data frames for the source MAC address and places these addresses in the bridge's address table. Like the listening state, no user data frames are forwarded while the port is in this state.

- **Forwarding**—The port is now placed into a forwarding state, where the bridge performs its normal functioning. The bridge learns source MAC addresses, updates the bridge's CAM table, and forwards frames through the bridge itself.

When a bridge or LAN switch port is activated, it proceeds through three spanning tree states: listening, learning, and forwarding. If the port is the highest cost path to the root bridge in a looped topology, it enters the blocking state. By default, all bridge ports go through the first two states: learning and listening. Based on the information obtained during these states, the interface enters either the forwarding or blocking state.

The spanning tree algorithm takes 50 seconds to calculate a new topology. The transition time for each state is as follows:

- From blocking to listening—20 seconds
- From listening to learning—15 seconds
- From learning to forwarding—15 seconds

Latency, in addition to normal operation, is incurred when the ports go through the different states due to a network change, such as a failed path, addition of a new bridge or switch, or enabling a bridge or switch port. Cisco uses a default value of 15 seconds for the Forward Delay time, which is used to measure the time a port stays in a specific state.

Switches

LAN switches connect common broadcast domains and provide frame-level filtering as well as dedicated port speed to end-users. Some switches have limited routing capabilities and can provide Layer-3 routing functions at the most basic level. Some benefits of using switches are higher bandwidth to the desktop and ease of configuration. Switches are deployed often to replace hubs and bridges as more bandwidth-intensive applications are implemented within an organization.

NOTE   Virtual LANs (VLANs) are implemented in switched environments and can keep broadcast traffic within a specific domain of network users.

Switch Operations

Switches carry network traffic by receiving data frames from a source host (connected to a switch port) and forwarding these frames through a different switch port (based on the frame header information). Traditional Layer-2 switching works by looking at the Media Access Control (MAC) address information in the data frame's header and forward the data according to the switch, or Content Addressable Memory (CAM) table. If the switch looks at the MAC address information and cannot determine which port to send the frames, the switch will broadcast (flood) the frames out from all ports. This broadcast process is known as *flooding* and is used to determine the destination port of a host (based on the destination information in the frame header). When the destination address is found, the associated port information is added to the switching table for future reference.

Switches give network users the ability to transfer data traffic in a network environment without collisions or bandwidth contention. Deploying LAN switches in an existing network environment requires minimal configuration and no changes to existing wiring closets, hubs, LAN cabling, or NICs.

There are several types of switching technologies that enable quick and scalable network transmission.

Switching Types

These four types of LAN switching are found today:

- **Store and Forward Switching**—This is one of the two common types of LAN switching. A Store and Forward switch works by reading and copying the entire data frame into its buffers. The switch performs error checking, looks up the destination address in the MAC address table, and forwards the frame to the appropriate destination.

- **Cut-through Switching**—This is the other common LAN switching type. A Cut-through switch copies the destination address and a small portion of the frame into its buffers before checking for the destination address interface in its MAC address table. When the destination port is determined, the frame is sent out the appropriate switch port. Cut-through switching increases switching speed because the switch does not copy the entire frame to the switch buffers.

- **Fast Switching**—This is the process of copying data frames into a memory buffer. The switch determines the switching path to the destination port by looking up the location of the destination port in the fast-switching cache. After the destination host path is determined, subsequent data frames use that switching path, thereby reducing path determination time.

- **Layer-3 Switching**—This uses routing functions, such as network layer addressing. Switches can be configured like routers regarding an addressing mechanism, but are still bound by a flat-network addressing scheme (no hierarchical addressing is supported). Switches that operate at Layer-3 currently do not support special features such as path optimization and load balancing.

NOTE	Layer-3 switching differs from the traditional Layer-2 switching by enabling data frames to be switched based on network addressing information. Traditional Layer-2 switching will look at the frames for the MAC address information for the destination address.

Routers

Routers are hardware devices that enable communications between networks. Routers are protocol-specific in that they must support the network-layer protocol used by each data packet. For example, for a router to support Internet connections, it must be able to support IP traffic; or for support of a Novell Netware implementation, the router must support IPX.

Routers often are found connecting a LAN to a WAN, such as a Frame Relay network or to the Internet. Routers can support multiple networks, limited only to the number of network interfaces (serial ports) that are available on the particular unit in question.

Routers are available in several sizes, for example:

- SOHO (Cisco 700/1600 Series)
- Small (Cisco 26xx Series)
- Medium (Cisco 3600/4500 Series)
- Large (Cisco 7x00 Series)
- Very Large (Cisco 12000 Series)

Routers examine and evaluate each packet arriving from and/or sending to each of the networks to which the router is attached. The router decides which network provides the best path, or route, to the packet's intended destination. The router can make this decision because the router has direct knowledge about each network to which it is connected and the protocols each network supports.

Routers forward packets by maintaining a list of each network and its connected hosts. This list is called a *routing table* and is maintained (and updated) by the use of routing protocols. *Routing protocols* are a suite of protocols, such as Open Shortest Path First (OSPF); Border Gateway Protocol, version 4 (BGP4); or Routing Information Protocol (RIP). These routing protocols each use a different method to learn the routes to networks and hosts. In the event there are multiple routes to a specific network/host, each routing protocol uses a different algorithm to determine which route is the best choice to the targeted destination network/host.

Summary

LAN topologies are dependant upon the LAN technology in use, such as Ethernet or Token Ring. The LAN technology in turn depends on the user applications, such as file sharing, Web-hosting, or mainframe data centers.

There are four LAN topologies:

- Star (Hub-and-Spoke)
- Bus
- Ring
- Tree

The two most prevalent LANs deployed today are Ethernet and Token Ring. Ethernet LANs are covered by the IEEE 802.3 standard and are deployed in approximately 85 percent of the world's LANs. The IEEE 802.3 standard also defines the CSMA/CD protocol.

Token Ring (and FDDI) networks are deterministic, meaning that it is possible to calculate the maximum time that will pass before any host will be capable of transmitting. This deterministic nature makes Token Ring networks ideal for applications in which delay must be predictable, such as SNA-based (mainframe) applications.

Hubs connect devices on one shared LAN. Bridges connect LAN segments, lengthening the diameter (across a distance) of the LAN as well as segmenting, or breaking up, collision domains. LAN switches connect common broadcast domains and provide frame-level filtering as well as dedicated port speed to end-users. Some switches have limited routing capabilities and can provide Layer-3 routing functions at the most basic level. Routers are hardware devices that enable communications between networks. Routers are protocol-specific in that they must support the network-layer protocol used by each data packet. Routers often are found connecting a LAN to a WAN, such as a Frame Relay network or to the Internet. Routers can support multiple networks, limited only to the number of network interfaces (serial ports) that are available on the particular unit in question.

Frequently Asked Questions (FAQ)

1   Does the LAN topology affect the WAN?

No, the LAN topology is independent of the WAN. LAN applications can affect the WAN, however, especially in multicast and broadcast environments. It is not uncommon to find LAN broadcasts unnecessarily traversing the WAN, impacting WAN traffic and possibly costing more money in WAN costs supporting this unnecessary LAN traffic.

2   Can unicast, multicast, and broadcast applications be mixed?

Yes, because the traffic type is associated with the application. For example, a LAN could support video (multicast), e-mail and print (unicast), and DHCP (broadcast) applications. As long as there is sufficient LAN bandwidth to support user applications, there is no issue.

3 Which is better of the following topologies: star, bus, ring, or tree topology?

The answer to this question is the same answer to any design question: "It depends." The LAN topology depends on several variables, such as applications in use, traffic load and patterns, geographic location of the LAN hosts (within a single room or spread across a campus), and redundancy requirements, to name a few.

4 Can LAN topologies be mixed?

Yes.

5 Can routers run multiple routing protocols simultaneously?

Yes, dependant upon the router's Internetwork Operating System (IOS). For example, with the proper IOS a router can simultaneously maintain and update routes and connections to IP, IPX, and AppleTalk networks.

Case Study

Figure 5-20 illustrates the RomaNet network. RomaNet is a large enterprise organization with several remote (SOHO) offices, a few campus locations, and a data center (hosted at the corporate headquarters).

The remote offices deployed Ethernet and support a small number of users without a need for network redundancy. If this office were to go offline—for example, lose WAN access—there is minimal impact to the enterprise network.

The campus locations also deployed Ethernet, but with more users requiring more bandwidth. Fast Ethernet and GigE are deployed here with a Fast/GigE implementation, and these bandwidth needs are met with a Fast/GigE Ethernet Switch providing the campus connectivity, including connectivity to the routers for WAN access. Because the campus locations have higher connectivity requirements, these sites are dual-homed to the WAN with the deployment of two access lines and routers.

The corporate headquarters site deployed a FDDI LAN in support of the organization's database server farms, network management, and mainframe applications. The FDDI LAN is used because of the organization's high availability and redundancy requirements of the dual-attached LAN servers and workstations. The HQ location, like the campus locations, is dual-homed to the WAN, providing redundancy to the WAN.

Figure 5-20 *RomaNet Case Study Topology*

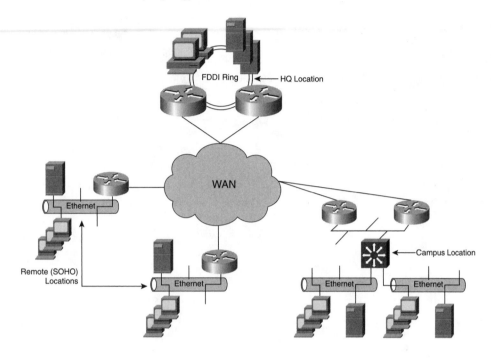

This chapter covers the following topics:

- Dedicated Local Access Configuration
- Switched Local Access Configuration
- Local Exchange Carrier (LEC) Central Office (CO) Configuration

CHAPTER 6

Local Access

Access to a network service provider's (NSP) services requires a physical connection (landline or wireless) to that NSP's office. This physical connection between the customer site and the NSP office is known as the *network local access*. This local access, also known as the *local loop* or the *last mile*, supports both dedicated and switched services.

NOTE   A *landline* is a cable that is attached to the ground between two end-points—for example, a telephone line between telephone poles. Landlines can be suspended, as is the case with telephone poles, or they can be (and often are) buried underground.

Dedicated access is a permanent connection terminating (from the customer's perspective) at either the local exchange carrier's (LEC) or Interexchange Carrier's (IXC) central office (CO). Examples of dedicated access circuits are DS0, DS1/DS3, or OC-x. Switched access is not a permanent connection, requiring the customer/end-user to initiate a call setup process. Examples of switched access are POTS/PSTN or ISDN-BRI/PRI service.

NOTE   *Plain old telephone service (POTS)*—the telephone system we know and use today. POTS runs across the public switched telephone network (PSTN).

Integrated services digital network (ISDN), an international communications standard for sending voice, video, and data over digital telephone lines or normal telephone wires. ISDN is available in two offerings: Basic Rate Interface (BRI) at 144 Kbps (2B + D) and PRI at 1536 Kbps (23B + D). The B(earer) channels are 64 Kbps and carry the signal (voice/data), and the D(ata) channel carries the signaling: 16 Kbps for BRI, and 64 Kbps for PRI.

Dedicated Local Access Configuration

Two forms of dedicated local access exist, based on the network-side termination point: *LEC dedicated* or *IXC dedicated*. LEC dedicated access terminates at the customer site and the LEC CO, and IXC dedicated access terminates at the customer site and the IXC CO (passing through the LEC CO). Each configuration provides certain advantages, depending on the customer's networking requirements (for example, local dial-tone, IntraLATA data service, or InterLATA data services). Regardless of where the local loop terminates (LEC or IXC), the local loop can be copper, coaxial, or fiber optic cabling.

NOTE   *Local Access and Transport Area* (LATA) is a U.S. term referring to a geographic region assigned to one or more telephone companies. These telephone companies provide communication services within these geographic areas.

An *intraLATA* connection is made between two telephone companies within the same region. An *interLATA* connection is established between two local exchange carriers in different regions. This is also known as *long-distance service*.

Provisions guiding the use of LATAs are outlined in the Telecommunications Act of 1996.

Figure 6-1 illustrates local access terminating at the LEC CO.

Figure 6-1   *Dedicated Access Terminating to LEC CO*

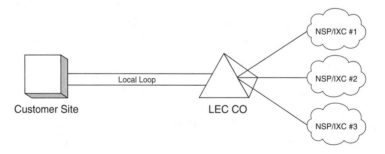

This configuration is implemented when any one (or more) of the following customer communications requirements are needed:

- Local dial-tone (voice services)
- IntraLATA data services
- Any LEC-provided services, such as LEC-provided Internet access
- Multiple IXC data services

Figure 6-2 illustrates local access terminating at an IXC CO.

Figure 6-2   *Dedicated Access Terminating to IXC CO*

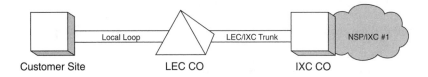

This configuration is implemented when any one or more of the following customer communications requirements are needed:

- Long distance (LD) dial-tone (voice service)
- InterLATA data services
- Any other IXC-provided services, such as IXC-provided Internet access

NOTE   Note that in both configurations (Figures 6-1 and 6-2), the facilities between the LEC CO and the customer site are referred to as the *local loop*, or the *last mile*. These terms are understood to refer to the portion of the access circuit terminating at the customer premise.

Customer Premise Configuration

Whether the local access terminates at the LEC or IXC CO, a network interface unit (NIU), also referred to as a *network termination unit* (NTU), is required at the customer premise to terminate the other end of the access circuit. Figure 6-3 illustrates the placement of the NIU or NTU.

Figure 6-3   *NIU (or NTU) Placement*

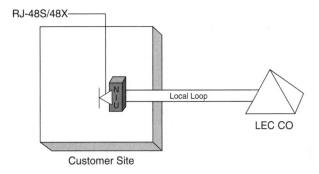

A modular jack is required for customers to connect their communications equipment to the NIU, in turn accessing the service provider network. For digital service, this jack is either an RJ-48S or RJ-48X. The difference between the RJ-48S and the RJ-48X is that when it is unterminated, meaning nothing is plugged into the jack, the RJ-48X is in a hard loop facing the network. This jack also provides a clear demarcation (demarc) point, defining the hand-off between the customer and the network service provider.

Technical Note: Loopback Testing

Loopback testing is a means by which a circuit can be tested remotely. One end of the circuit sends a test pattern down the line. When this test pattern terminates on the other end of the circuit, the loopback causes this test pattern to be returned to the sender. The sending side compares what was sent to what was received, looking for differences (errors). These errors indicate that there is an issue with the line affecting transmission (voice or data).

There are three types of loopback testing:

- **Soft loop**—Initiated remotely and drops immediately when there is no test pattern being sent; also known as an *alternating loopback*.

- **Hard loop**—Must be physically made at the loop point and can only be physically removed as well.

- **Latch loop**—Similar to a hard loop in that the loop must be manually put up and taken down. However, latch loops are remotely established by sending a specific code (bit pattern) down the line to the device.

Often the customer's communications equipment is in another space, separated from the NIU. In these instances, the demarc is extended from the NIU to the desired termination point. If this distance exceeds the maximum distance limitations for the cabling used, one or more repeaters can be installed to extend the signal reach.

This extended demarc can be installed by the customer or the LEC and can take the form of patch panels, punch-down blocks, or an RJ-jack (RJ-48S/48X). If the LEC extends the demarc, the extension becomes the responsibility of the customer after 30 days because it is then considered to be in-house wiring. An exception to this 30-day rule exists if the customer and the LEC have a separate agreement for wiring maintenance.

NOTE   Although an extended demarc can be ordered from the LEC, often the end customer will perform this extension in-house.

Punch-Down Blocks (66-blocks)

Punch-down blocks, also known as *66-blocks*, were the predecessors to distribution frame patch panels. A 66-block is a punch-down block with type 66 connectors; hence the name. These blocks are used to terminate and cross-connect telephone cabling. 66-blocks are used when there is a single incoming line from the LEC/IXC, but connections are required to several different offices within a building.

Figure 6-4 illustrates a 66-block.

Figure 6-4   *66-block*

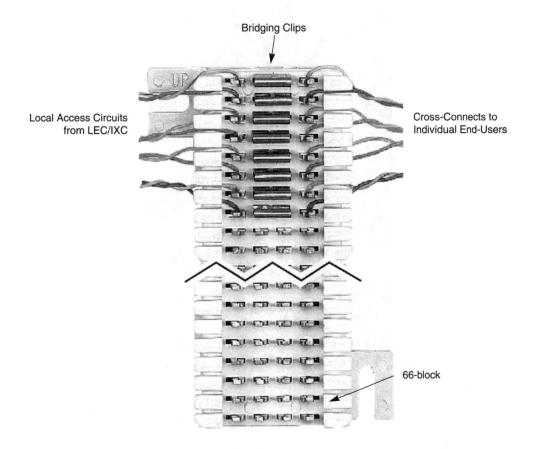

In this figure, columns 1 and 2 are connected, as are columns 3 and 4. These column pairs (1/2 and 3/4) are often prewired. Each of the four columns is connected to one of the four pins on a phone connector. Column 1 is the often used as the "incoming" column and column 4 is used as the "outgoing" column, with each row connected to a pin on a cable leading to an office drop.

Bridge clips are little metal clips used to wire "straight through," for example, to connect columns 2 and 3. If it is necessary to crosswire a circuit, you cannot use bridging clips to connect a wire from column 2 in one row to column 3 in a different row; in that case, the connection must be wired. This arrangement has made 66-blocks very popular in telephone and network cable management.

Figure 6-5 illustrates what a 66-block installation would look like at a customer premise.

Figure 6-5   *Customer Premise 66-block*

Figure 6-6 illustrates a complete dedicated circuit termination at the customer premise, with a 66-block used to extend the demarc from the NIU to the CSU/DSU.

Figure 6-6   *End-to-End Access Circuit (with Extended Demarc)*

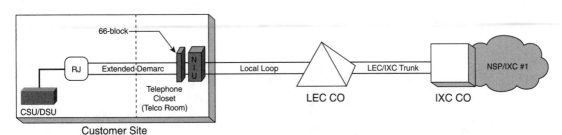

Switched Local Access Configuration

Switched local access to a network requires a call setup process, such as that found with POTS/PSTN or ISDN-BRI/PRI service. Access to the service provider's network is dependent on the dialed digits of the end-user or programmed PBX.

The customer can access a NSP's LD network in one of two ways, using either a Prescribed Interchange Carrier (PIC) or Carrier Identification Code (CIC). The PIC code is the IXC the customer/end-user designates to carry all 1+10-digit long-distance calls. The CIC is used when the customer/end-user wants to tell the LEC which carrier to use for 1+ service, either via presubscription or casual dialing. *Casual dialing* is when the customer/end-user dials the 7-digit CIC prior to the 1+10-digit dialed number, such as dialing 10-10-228-1-703-555-1212.

Appendix A "PIC Codes," lists the PIC/CIC codes available for use as of 6/1/2002.

LEC CO Configuration

Local access circuits have two termination points: the customer premise and the LEC CO. Figure 6-7 illustrates a common CO infrastructure.

Figure 6-7 *Typical Service Provider POP/CO Infrastructure*

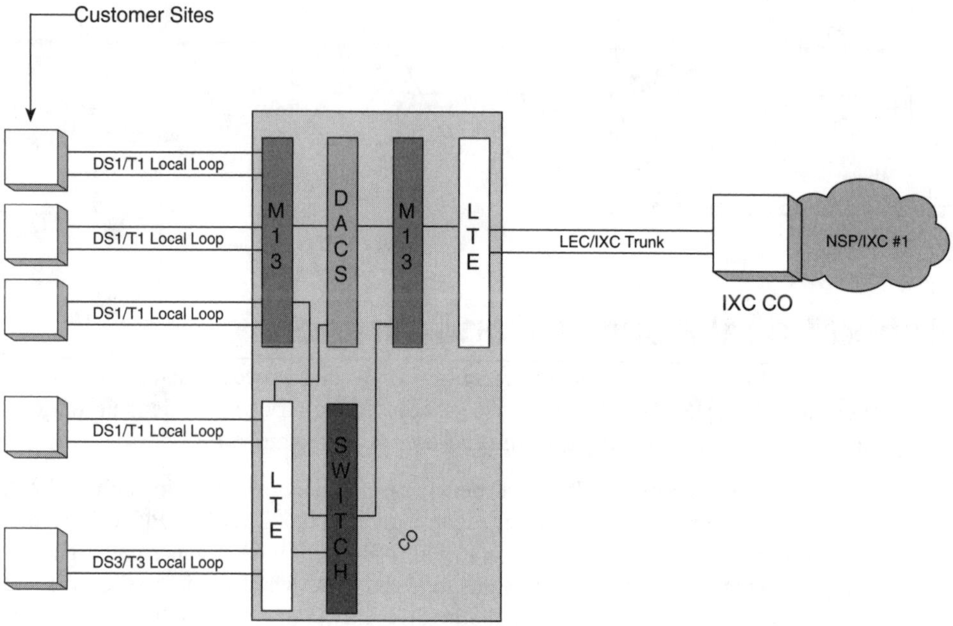

The equipment illustrated here is identified as follows:

- **Light Termination Equipment (LTE)**—Fiber-optic transmissions terminate here, often in the form of fiber or lightwave multiplexers (muxes). LTE can be used to terminate fiber-optic signals from a customer site or for interconnection of fiber-optic signals between LEC/IXC COs. LTE cannot terminate copper facility-based signals; M13's are used for these terminations.

- **Multiplexer DS1/DS3 (M13), pronounced "M-One-Three"**—Performs both multiplexing and demultiplexing functions. Multiplexes 28 DS1 signals into a single DS3 signal for transmission, often terminating to the LTE. Demultiplexes DS3 signals into 28 DS1 signals, often terminating into a DACS (DXC) or voice/data switch. M13s terminate copper-based signals; LTE (Fiber muxes) are used to terminate fiber-optic signals found in "fiber-to-the-curb" (FTTC) implementations.

- **Digital Cross Connect System (DACS or [DXC])**—They electronically switch the DS0s within each DS1, or DS1s within each DS3. DACS can also be used to provide network timing for dedicated T1 service. Optical DACS are used to switch fiber optic signals, switching DS1/DS3s within higher bandwidth transport, such as OC-x (OC3, OC12, etc.).

- **Switch**—This could be a voice or data (ATM or Frame Relay) switch. The switch is an interface to the respective network for which it provides service, such as voice or data.

Summary

Customer site access to network services (from a NSP) requires a physical connection, often in the form of landline facilities (as opposed to wireless facilities) to the NSP CO or point-of-presence (POP). This local access, also known as the *local loop* or the *last mile*, can support both dedicated and switched services, including voice, data, fax, or video services. This local access can be either a copper or fiber-optic based facility, depending on the customer's requirements and the cost and expense of laying new facilities (if necessary).

There are two types of access circuits:

- **Dedicated**—DS0, DS1/DS3, OC-x
- **Switched**—POTS/PSTN, ISDN-BRI/PRI

Dedicated access circuits provide permanent connectivity to a network service provider, whereas switched access circuits provide on-demand connectivity. Switched access requires a call-setup procedure, often in the form of dialing a PIC/CIC from the user interface, unless otherwise programmed into the customer premise PBX or voice switch.

The following components are fundamental to a local access circuit:

- CSU/DSU or other signal termination device (for example, WAN interface card (WIC) in a Cisco Series Router
- RJ Jack
- (Extended) Demarc point
- Punch-down block (also known as 66-block)
- NIU/NTU
- Local Loop (Copper or Fiber)
- LEC CO
- LEC/IXC trunk between the LEC CO and the IXC CO (depending on the subscribed service; for example, long-distance voice or data service)

The following components are fundamental to a LEC/IXC CO:

- LTE—Light termination equipment
- M13—Multiplexer DS1/DS3
- DACS (or DXC)
- Voice or data switch

Frequently Asked Questions (FAQ)

1 Is there a difference between switched and dedicated voice service?

Yes. The difference often resides in the cost-per-minute (CPM) charged by the NSPs. Dedicated access services are more efficient to maintain than switched access services and therefore these efficiencies can be passed on to the customer. There is a break-even point in the dedicated versus switched access debate. This break-even point is based upon the customer site call volume and the CPM.

For example, if a customer's call volume is 10,000 minutes a month (444 minutes a day, based on 10,000/22.5 = 444.4, 22.5 days in a standard business month), and the CPM is five cents (0.05), the total cost for switched service is $1000/month. If this same customer secures dedicated service from a service provider at a cost of $500/month and a CPM of three (0.03) cents, there is a $200/month cost savings over the $1,000/month based on switched access. The calculation here is 10,000 minutes ∞ $0.03/min = $300.00, + $500.00 (dedicated access) = $800/month.

Case Study

RhymeNReason Company is a small organization with offices in two buildings: a main building and an annex building approximately 100 feet away. RhymeNReason is a small service organization requiring dedicated Internet access, long-distance, and local service. RhymeNReason leased three DS1s from NSP#1; one DS1 for dedicated Internet service, one for dedicated long-distance voice service, and the third servicing the annex building's requirements for Internet connectivity. The main building has also installed several local switched access lines to NSP#2 to meet the local voice service requirement.

Figure 6-8 illustrates RhymeNReason Company's configuration.

Figure 6-8   *RhymeNReason Company Case Study*

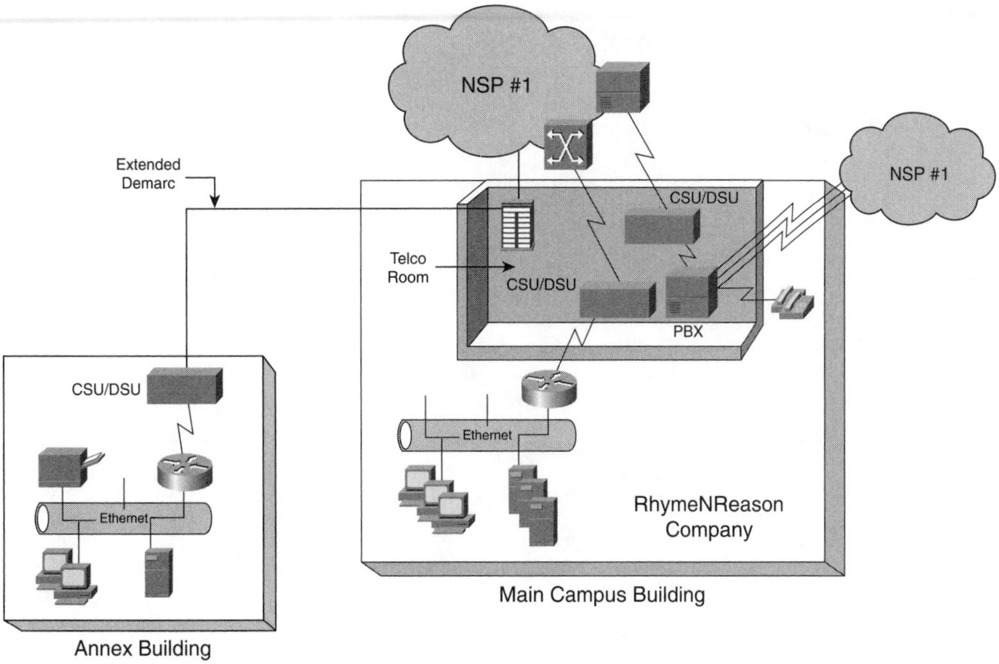

NOTE	There are several configurations that would meet these requirements; this configuration represents the concepts presented in this chapter.

This chapter covers the following topics:

- Digital Subscriber Line
- Cable Access Technologies

CHAPTER 7

DSL and Cable Modem Networks

DSL and cable modem network access are two alternative ways to connect to a network service provider without the use of more expensive dedicated service, such as Frac-T1/T1. DSL and cable modem networks achieve the same result of providing dedicated access to a network service, often the Internet, but each do so using differing technologies. This chapter discusses what DSL and cable modem technologies do and how they do it.

Digital Subscriber Line

Digital subscriber line (DSL) technology is a modem technology using existing twisted-pair telephone lines to carry high-bandwidth applications, such as multimedia and video. The term *xDSL* covers a number of DSL technologies, such as Asymmetrical Digital Subscriber Line (ADSL), Symmetrical Digital Subscriber Line (SDSL), Hi-Speed Digital Subscriber Line (HDSL), HDSL-2 (HDSLv2), ITU DSL standard (G.SHDSL), ISDN Digital Subscriber Line (IDSL), and Very-High-Data-Rate Digital Subscriber Line (VDSL).

xDSL services are dedicated point-to-point network access over twisted-pair copper wire on the local loop (last mile) between a network service provider's (NSP) central office (CO) and the customer site. xDSL also can be deployed in intra-building and intra-campus environments, as illustrated in Figure 7-1.

xDSL offers two chief benefits over dial-up service:

- Dial-up service is limited to 53.3 Kbps, whereas xDSL service can enable up to 6.122 Mbps.
- Dial-up service is initiated "on-demand" by the end-user, but xDSL service is a dedicated connection, meaning that it is "always on."

Figure 7-1 *Intra-Building and Intra-Campus/Inter-Building*

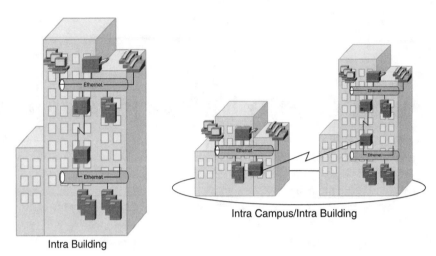

Intra Campus/Intra Building

Intra Building

The following sections discuss ADSL. ADSL is often deployed in the small office/home office (SOHO) environment and is the traditional DSL service for residential deployment. The asymmetry is ideal in these environments because the majority of upstream bandwidth is consumed by Internet requests; for example, users navigating through web sites. These upstream requests are small compared to the downstream response, such as the web site fulfilling the user's request.

ADSL

ADSL technology makes more bandwidth available downstream, from a NSP central office (CO) to the customer site, than it makes available upstream, from the customer site to the CO. Figure 7-2 illustrates an example of an ADSL connection.

Figure 7-2 *ADSL Connection*

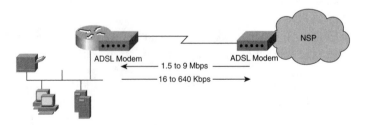

The asymmetry of ADSL, combined with always-on access (which eliminates call setup), makes ADSL another solution for Internet/intranet surfing, video-on-demand, and remote LAN access because users of these applications often download more data than they upload.

ADSL Architecture

ADSL circuits connect ADSL modems on each end of a twisted-pair telephone line, creating three data channels:

- **A high-speed downstream channel**—Ranges from 1.5 to 9 Mbps.

- **A low-speed upstream channel**—Ranges from 16 to 640 Kbps.

- **A basic telephone service channel**—The basic telephone service channel is split off from the digital modem by filters or plain old telephone service (POTS) splitters, providing uninterrupted basic telephone service.

NOTE   The upstream and downstream bandwidth ranges depend upon the distance between the customer site and the DSL provider's CO; the greater the distance, the lower the bandwidth capacity.

Figure 7-3 illustrates the architecture of an ADSL network.

Figure 7-3   *ADSL Architecture*

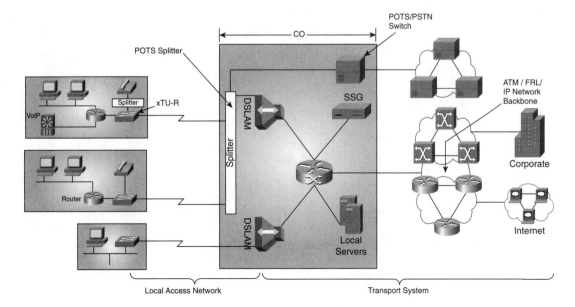

ADSL architecture is made up of the following components:

- **Transport System**—Provides the carrier backbone transmission interface for the DSLAM system. This device can provide service specific interfaces such as T1/E1, T3/E3, OC-1/3, and STS-1/3.

- **Local Access Network**—Uses the local carrier Inter-CO network as a foundation, providing connectivity between multiple service providers and multiple services users, often with Frame Relay or ATM switches.

- **Digital Subscriber Line Access Multiplexer (DSLAM)**—Concentrates data traffic from multiple DSL loops onto the backbone network for connection to the rest of the network.

- **DSL Transceiver Unit-Remote (xTU-R)**—The customer site equipment for service connection to the DSL loop.

- **POTS Splitters**—Optional device at both CO and service user locations, enabling the copper loop to be used for simultaneous DSL and transmission and single line telephone service. POTS splitters come in two configurations:

  — Single splitter version for mounting at the residence

  — Multiple splitter version for mass termination at the CO

  POTS splitters are either passive or active. *Active* splitters require an external power source, and *passive* splitters require no power and often have a higher mean time between failure (MTBF) than the active splitter. Passive splitters enable lifeline services, such as 911, in the event of a DSLAM or xTU-R power loss; active splitters require backup power.

ADSL Data Rates

Downstream bandwidth depends on a number of factors:

- Length of the copper line
- Wire gauge of the copper line
- Presence of bridged taps
- Presence of cross-coupled interference

NOTE   *Bridged taps* are any cable pair spliced into the main pair. Many unused bridged taps remain from the early days when party lines were the norm and two or more taps were made on every line. Bridged taps cause undesirable reflection that can distort the high-frequency signals in modern transmission technologies.

Line attenuation increases with line length and frequency, and decreases as wire diameter increases. Ignoring bridged taps, ADSL performs as shown in Table 7-1.

Table 7-1   *ADSL Rates (Ignoring Bridged Taps)*

Rate (Mbps)	Wire Gauge (AWG)	Distance (feet)	Wire Size (mm)	Distance (km)
1.5 or 2	24	18,000	0.5	5.5
1.5 or 2	26	15,000	0.4	4.6
6.1	24	12,000	0.5	3.7
6.1	26	9000	0.4	2.7

Customer sites beyond the previously listed distances can be reached with fiber-based digital loop carrier (DLC) systems, as illustrated in Figure 7-4.

Figure 7-4   *ADSL with and Without Fiber-based DLC*

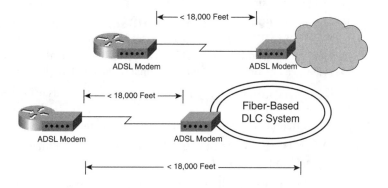

| | |
| NOTE | xDSL service will not work over fiber-to-the-curb (FTTC) implementations. *FTTC* is the installation of optical fiber to within a thousand feet of the home or office. Fiber-to-the-home (FTTH) is the installation of optical fiber from the carrier directly into the home or office. |

ADSL Standards and Associations

The American National Standards Institute (ANSI) Working Group T1E1.4 approved an ADSL standard at rates up to 6.1 Mbps (DMT/ANSI Standard T1.413). The European Technical Standards Institute (ETSI) contributed an annex to T1.413 reflecting European requirements including a single terminal interface at the premise side of the access circuit.

The ATM Forum and the Digital Audio-Visual Council (DAVIC) have both recognized ADSL as a physical layer transmission protocol for unshielded twisted pair (UTP) media.

NOTE	UTP is a popular type of cable consisting of two unshielded wires twisted around each other. Because UTP cabling is cost efficient, it is used extensively for local-area networks (LANs) and telephone connections. UTP cabling does not offer the high bandwidth or protection from interference that is found with coaxial or fiber optic cables; however, UTP is less expensive and easier to work with than coaxial or fiber-optic.

Other xDSL Technologies

There are several xDSL implementations in addition to ADSL. These are as follows:

- **Single-lined digital subscriber line (SDSL)** — A rate-adaptive version of Hi-speed digital subscriber line (HDSL) which like HDSL is symmetric. SDSL enables equal bandwidth downstream from a network service provider CO to the customer site as upstream from the customer site to the CO. SDSL supports data only (maximum of 1.544 Mbps) on a single line and does not support analog calls.

- **High-data-rate digital subscriber line (HDSL)** — Developed by Bellcore, high bit-rate DSL (HDSL)/T1/E1 technologies have been standardized by ANSI in the United States and by ETSI in Europe. HDSL is a more cost-efficient method of installing T1 service to a customer site than traditional dedicated DS1 service.

- **HDSL 2** — Standard enabling symmetric service at T1 speeds using a single-wire pair rather than the two pairs of HDSL service. HDSL-2 also was developed as a standard by which different vendors' equipment can interoperate.

- **G.SHDSL (ITU HDSL Standard)** — A standards-based, multirate version of HDSL-2, which offers symmetrical service.

- **Integrated services digital network (ISDN) digital subscriber line (IDSL)** — A cross between ISDN and xDSL, using a single-wire pair to transmit full-duplex data at 128 kbps.

- **Very-high-data-rate digital subscriber line (VDSL)** — Transmits high-speed data over short reaches of twisted-pair copper telephone lines, with a range of speeds depending on actual line length. The maximum downstream rate under consideration is between 51 and 55 Mbps over lines up to 1000 feet (300 m). Downstream speeds as low as 13 Mbps over lengths beyond 4000 feet (1500 m) also are in consideration.

Cable Access Technologies

Cable television (CATV) is a unidirectional medium carrying broadcast analog video channels to the most customers possible at the lowest possible cost to the CATV service provider. Since the introduction of CATV more than 50 years ago, little has changed beyond increasing the number of channels supported.

Fearing loss of market share when DSL was introduced (in the 1990s) and recognizing the need to offer advanced services to remain economically viable, key multiple system operators (MSOs) formed the Multimedia Cable Network System Partners, Ltd. (MCNS). The goal of the MCNS was to define a standard product and system capable of providing data and future services over the CATV infrastructure. MCNS partners included Comcast Cable Communications, Cox Communications, Tele-Communications Inc., Time Warner Cable, MediaOne, Rogers CableSystems, and Cable Television Laboratories (CableLabs).

The MCNS defined the Data Over Cable Service Interface Specification (DOCSIS) 1.0 standard, which was in turn accepted as the North American standard. These key MSOs defined upgrade and construction programs to provide two-way functionality to the end-user over the CATV infrastructure.

Cable Access Architecture

To deliver data services over a cable network, one television channel (50 to 750 MHz range) is allocated for downstream traffic to homes and another channel (5 to 42 MHz band) is used to carry upstream signals.

Figure 7-5 illustrates the architecture of a cable access network for both CATV and cable modem services.

Figure 7-5   *Cable Access Architecture*

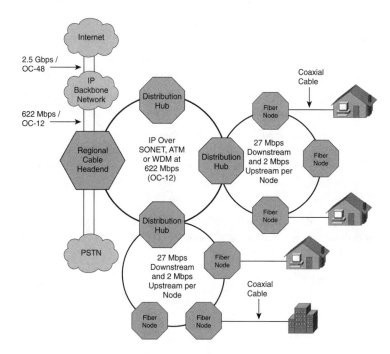

The following list details the cable access network architecture:

- Residential and business end-users are connected to fiber nodes by coaxial cables. Users attach to this cable through an Ethernet network interface card (NIC) installed in the PC, in turn connected to a cable modem, as illustrated in the Figure 7-6.

Figure 7-6   *Cable Modem Access*

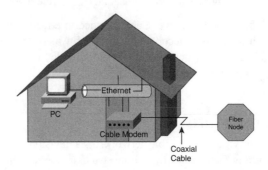

- The fiber nodes house the cable modem termination system (CMTS) at the head-end, communicating with the cable modems at the end-user premise. This communication creates a LAN connection between the end-user and the cable modem service provider.

- Most cable modems are external hardware devices connecting to a PC through a standard 10Base-T Ethernet card or Universal Serial Bus (USB) connection.

- These fiber nodes are connected by fiber rings (such as SONET) to the distribution hubs, which are in turn connected by fiber rings to a regional cable head-end.

- The cable head-end then forwards the traffic to the appropriate network—the PSTN for VoIP applications and the public Internet for all other IP traffic.

A single downstream 6 MHz television channel can carry up to 27 Mbps of downstream data throughput from the cable head-end; upstream channels can deliver 500 Kbps to 10 Mbps from home and business end-users. This upstream and downstream bandwidth is shared by other data subscribers connected to the same cable network segment, which is often 500 to 2000 homes on a modern network.

An individual cable modem subscriber can reach speeds from 500 Kbps to 1.5 Mbps or more, depending on the network architecture (for example, oversubscription ratio) and traffic load.

NOTE   Although other users on the network segment affect cable modem speed, the CATV-signal does not affect this speed because each signal (CATV and cable modem) uses a different frequency on the line. This means that your cable modem connection will not be slower if you are watching TV.

NOTE   When you are surfing the World Wide Web, your system's performance can be affected by Internet backbone congestion. The local access provider has no direct management control over this backbone congestion; it's the Internet.

DOCSIS Standards, Signaling Protocols, and Applications

Data Over Cable Service Interface Specification (DOCSIS) is a set of standards for transferring data by CATV and cable modems. The DOCSIS interface specifications enable multivendor interoperability for transporting Internet Protocol (IP) traffic. The DOCSIS layers are compared with the OSI Reference Model layers in Figure 7-7.

Figure 7-7   *OSI Layers and DOCSIS Layers*

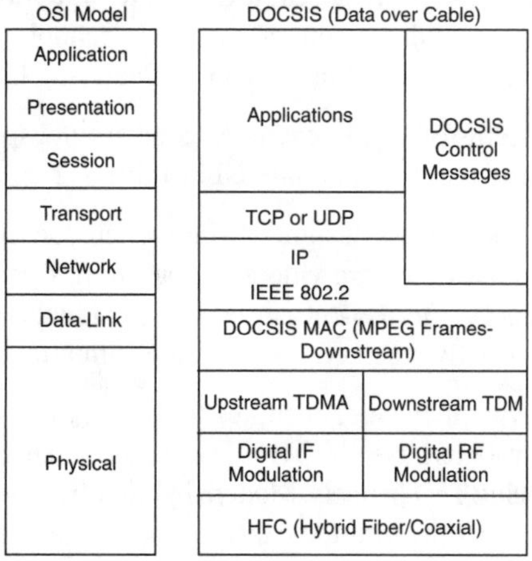

OSI Model	DOCSIS (Data over Cable)	
Application	Applications	DOCSIS Control Messages
Presentation		
Session		
Transport	TCP or UDP	
Network	IP	
	IEEE 802.2	
Data-Link	DOCSIS MAC (MPEG Frames-Downstream)	
Physical	Upstream TDMA	Downstream TDM
	Digital IF Modulation	Digital RF Modulation
	HFC (Hybrid Fiber/Coaxial)	

The following list details the correlation between the OSI Reference Model and the DOCSIS standard:

- TCP/IP support:
  - IP services at the network layer (OSI Layer 3)
  - TCP/UDP services at the transport layer (OSI Layer 4)
- Data-link layer:
  - Logical Link Control (LLC) sublayer conforming to Ethernet standards
  - Link security sublayer for basic privacy, authorization, and authentication
  - Media Access Control (MAC) sublayer supporting variable-length protocol data units (PDU)
- Physical (PHY) layer comprised of the following:
  - Downstream convergence layer conforming to MPEG-2
  - Physical Media Dependent (PMD) sublayer for downstream and upstream data transmission; through Time Division Multiplexing (TDM).

Summary

DSL and cable modem network access are two alternate ways to connect to an NSP without the use of more expensive dedicated service. DSL technology is a modem technology using existing twisted-pair telephone lines capable of carrying high-bandwidth applications.

There are several forms of xDSL, each designed around specific goals and needs of the marketplace. Each of these is summarized in Table 7-2.

Cable systems originally were designed to deliver broadcast television signals efficiently to subscribers' homes. Downstream video programming signals begin around 50 MHz, the equivalent of channel 2 for over-the-air television signals. The 5 MHz to 42 MHz portion of the spectrum is usually reserved for upstream communications from subscribers' homes.

Each standard television channel occupies 6 MHz of the Radio Frequency (RF) spectrum. Traditional cable systems have 400 MHz of downstream bandwidth, capable of carrying the equivalent of 60 analog TV channels. Modern hybrid fiber/coax (HFC) systems have 700 MHz of downstream bandwidth, with the capacity for approximately 110 channels.

The MCNS defined the DOCSIS 1.0 standard, which in turn was accepted as the North American standard.

Table 7-2 *DSL Service Summary*

DSL Type	Description	Data Rate Downstream; Upstream	Distance Limit	Application
ADSL	Asymmetric digital subscriber line	1.544 to 6.1 Mbps downstream; 16 to 640 Kbps upstream	1.544 Mbps at 18,000 feet; 2.048 Mbps at 16,000 feet; 6.312 Mbps at 12,000 feet; 8.448 Mbps at 9,000 feet	Used for Internet and web access, motion video, video on demand, remote LAN access.
HDSL	High-data-rate digital subscriber line	1.544 Mbps duplex on two twisted-pair lines; 2.048 Mbps duplex on three twisted-pair lines	12,000 feet on 24-gauge wire	T1/E1 service between server and phone company or within a company; WAN, LAN, server access.
SDSL	Single-line digital subscriber line	1.544 Mbps duplex (U.S. and Canada); 2.048 Mbps (Europe) on a single duplex line downstream and upstream	12,000 feet on 24-gauge wire	Same as for HDSL but requiring only one line of twisted-pair.
VDSL	Very-high digital subscriber line	12.9 to 52.8 Mbps downstream; 1.5 to 2.3 Mbps upstream; 1.6 Mbps to 2.3 Mbps downstream	4500 feet at 12.96 Mbps; 3000 feet at 25.82 Mbps; 1000 feet at 51.84 Mbps	ATM networks; Fiber to the Neighborhood.

DSL and cable modem network access is not available in all parts of the country or even to every house and business within a city. Before planning on deploying either of these services, it is imperative to discuss these plans with the local DSL/Cable NSP. In the event these services are not available for connectivity, you need to consider the more traditional Frac-T1/T3, ISDN, or dial-up services.

Frequently Asked Questions (FAQ)

1 Which is better: DSL or cable modem?

There is no clear choice between the two because each service offers its own advantages and disadvantages.

The main disadvantages of cable modems, when compared to DSL service, is the shared bandwidth to the cable head-end; end-users and their neighbors share the same cable. The Internet access point tends to be the congestion point, as well as the Internet itself. Another disadvantage is the end-user cannot choose the Internet Service Provider (ISP). Cable TV lines do not have "common-carrier" status as do phone lines.

DSL solutions provide the end-user with a dedicated line to the ISP; there is no bandwidth sharing with other users on the same access network. Like cable modem implementations, the Internet access point tends to be the congestion point, as well as the Internet itself.

2 Does Cisco manufacture or sell xDSL solutions?

Yes, Cisco provides DSL equipment for NSP and enterprise environments, as well as network management for a DSL platform. More information regarding Cisco's product and solution offering can be found at
`www.cisco.com/warp/public/44/solutions/network/dsl.shtml`.

3 Does Cisco manufacture or sell cable solutions?

Yes, Cisco provides cable equipment for head-end and customer premise environments, as well as network management for a cable platform. More information regarding Cisco's product and solution offering can be found at
`www.cisco.com/warp/public/44/jump/cable.shtml`.

4 Can a television be connected to the cable modem line?

Yes. In most cases this configuration will work as long as a splitter is used to "split" the television signal apart from the cable modem (data) signal. It is imperative to discuss this configuration with the CATV provider to ensure that no adverse effects to the TV or data signal are experienced by the end-user.

Case Study

HB & J, Inc. is an organization with a corporate campus and several remote SOHO users. HB & J, Inc. has outsourced file storage to a server farm hosted by an off-site data center company. HB & J, Inc. decided to forego traditional Frame Relay service and implemented an IP-VPN, with the public Internet as the transport medium. The topology of the HB & J, Inc. network is illustrated in Figure 7-8.

Figure 7-8   *HB & J, Inc.*

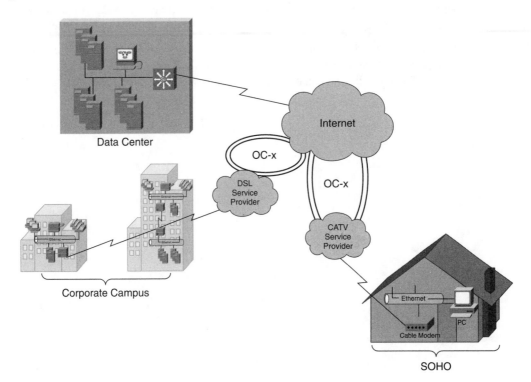

HB & J, Inc. is using SDSL between their two campus buildings—the main building and the annex building. SDSL is implemented by the deployment of a pair of SDSL modems on each side of an existing copper facility. The main building of the HB & J, Inc. campus is using HDSL, provided by the local NSP, to connect to the Internet.

HB & J, Inc.'s SOHO users have deployed cable modem access (where available) for connectivity to the Internet. These SOHO users are using a virtual private network (VPN) client to establish a secure communications tunnel across the Internet to the HB & J, Inc. Corporate Campus and the Data Center server farms. The VPN client must interoperate and be supported by the Corporate Campus and the Data Center in order to establish the secure tunnel across the Internet.

The Data Center has deployed a dedicated service to the Internet (likely DS3 or higher) to meet the demands of their large, high-volume customer base.

DSL and cable modem service provide HB & J, Inc. a more cost-efficient connectivity method than traditional dedicated service. For new locations where DSL or cable modem service may not be available, HB & J, Inc. will need to install dedicated Internet service.

If HB & J, Inc. decides at some time to add traditional Frame Relay or ATM service to support remote users, the Corporate Campus also will need to implement a Frame Relay/ATM connection so that connection can be established with these users as well.

This chapter covers the following topics:

- WAN Switching Services
- Network Interfaces
- WAN Architecture

CHAPTER 8

WAN Basics

Wide area network (WAN) connectivity enables individuals and organizations to take advantage of internetworking services such as Frame Relay, Asynchronous Transfer Mode (ATM), and the Internet. Local area networks (LAN) enable communication and resource-sharing within an enterprise or campus setting. WANs connect two or more LANs.

NOTE   The "wide" in wide area network implies a geographic separation between network sites; however, this separation is not always the case. By definition, a WAN is a government (FCC)-regulated public network or privately owned network that crosses into the public network environment. If the geographical separation crosses over a public thoroughfare, a WAN is required to make the connection.

A number of telecommunications services are used for WAN communications, such as a switched (shared) or dedicated service. For the LAN user, these LAN and WAN services and components combine, creating the illusion of one large end-to-end virtual network. Because of this virtual network illusion, the WAN is often represented as a cloud, as shown Figure 8-1.

Figure 8-1   *A WAN "Cloud"*

WAN Switching

There are three basic types of WAN transmission technologies:

- **Circuit-switched WANs (public switched telephone networks [PSTNs])** create a dedicated circuit, or channel, which is used for the duration of the transmission.

- **Packet-switched WANs (Frame Relay, Internet, IP Virtual Private Networking [IP VPN])** separate messages into variable-length segments and send these segments across dynamic connections.

- **Cell-switched WANs (ATM)** separate messages into fixed-length cells and send these cells across dynamic or permanent connections.

Each of these circuit types is discussed in the following sections.

Circuit-Switched WANs

Circuit-switched WANs, the most prevalent example of which is the PSTN, are designed for analog voice transmission and have the following characteristics:

- Circuit-switched networks are connection-oriented, requiring call setup before information can be exchanged. This temporary connection is known either as a *circuit* or *channel*.

- The circuit bandwidth is constant and dedicated throughout the duration of the call.

- There is no error recovery because circuit-based switches maintain small buffers.

- Circuit-switched network providers charge customers for the duration of the connection in a cost-per-minute (CPM) fashion.

Packet-Switched WANs

Packet-switching, which divides messages into smaller packets for transmission, was developed for the purpose of sending data over unreliable analog circuits. The Internet is a packet-switched network in which web pages, e-mail, and file transfers are broken down into smaller packets that are reassembled at the destination.

Packet-switched networks have the following characteristics:

- Packet-switched networks are connection-oriented, meaning that the receiving host must acknowledge the sending host before communication can begin.

- Packet-switched connections do not require call setup because each packet contains a destination address that is used to route the packet through the network. This dynamically routed connection is known as either a *virtual circuit* or *virtual channel (VC)*.

- Dynamic routing results in flexible use of bandwidth and network resources, enabling the network service providers to share backbone bandwidth across several subscribed customers.

- Packet-switched network service providers charge based on subscribed bandwidth and usage instead of the CPM model of a circuit-switched network.

Cell-Switched WANs

Cell-switching divides messages into small, fixed-length cells for transmission. ATM WANs are the most prevalent use of cell-switching, using cells 53 bytes in length (48 bytes for user payload, and 5 bytes for the cell header). Cell switching combines the guaranteed bandwidth of a circuit-switched network and the bandwidth-sharing and prioritization capabilities of a packet-switched network.

Cell-switched WANs have the following characteristics:

- Like packet-switched networks, cell-switched networks are connection-oriented, meaning that the receiving host must acknowledge the sending host before communication can begin.

- Cell-switched (ATM) WANs do not require call setup because each 53-byte cell contains the destination address used to forward the cell through the network.

- Cell-switched networks enable both dynamic (on-demand) and permanent connections. Dynamic connections are known as *switched virtual circuits* (SVC) and permanent connections are known as *permanent virtual circuits* (PVCs).

- The logical (virtual) circuits of a cell-switched network enable network service providers to guarantee Quality of Service (QoS) connections to their customers.

- Like packet-switched services, cell-switched network service providers charge based on subscribed bandwidth and usage instead of the CPM model of a circuit-switched network.

Network Interfaces

Regardless of the WAN in use—ATM, Frame Relay, or IP VPN—a network interface is required. This interface is either a user-to-network interface (UNI), connecting a customer to a service provider's network, or a network-to-network interface (NNI), connecting two networks whether they are two customer or two service provider networks.

UNI

A UNI is used in ATM and Frame Relay (FRL) networks to describe the interface between the ATM/FRL end-user and the network service provider ATM/FRL network access switch.

The term UNI can also describe the interface between a private ATM switch and the public
network service provider ATM network.

Figure 8-2   *UNI*

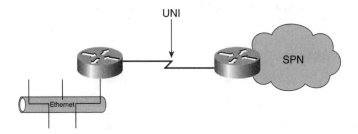

NNI

An NNI is created when two disparate networks require interconnection, such as two Frame
Relay WANs from different service providers. This scenario is best used when clients are
migrating from one service provider to another, they use different network service
providers, or they need to use two or more network service providers.

The building of the Transcontinental railroad in 1870 serves as a good example of the first
NNI and the way an NNI operates. In 1870, the Denver and Río Grande Railway Company
was chartered to build a railway from Denver, Colorado to El Paso, Texas. This line reached
Pueblo by 1872, and the company built a branch west from there to coal mines at Cañón
City. The choice was made early on to construct the railroad on a three-foot gauge—not the
four-foot, eight-inch gauge of its chief competitor, the Atchison, Topeka, and Santa Fe.

In 1881, the Río Grande Railway Company had extended its narrow-gauge tracks throughout the mountains of Colorado. The tracks crossed the Continental Divide in five places,
over mountains and across gorges. On the track from Denver to Pueblo, the Río Grande
Railway Company bowed to increasing use of standard gauge rolling stock. A third rail was
added to accommodate both sizes of trains. If this third rail had not been added, another
solution would have been possible.

These two railroads are independent networks requiring an interconnection to complete the
Transcontinental Railroad. The additional solution would involve the Western and Eastern
Railroad meeting at a point in the country where both the Eastern track and the Western
track could find a common point of connection: a railroad station, as shown in Figure 8-3.

This railroad station would be constructed so that both the Eastern and Western Railroad
tracks were connected to the station. The station, acting like an NNI, provided a means for
which passengers and goods could be offloaded from the railcars of one railroad—for
example, Western—and loaded onto the railcars of the other railroad—for example, Eastern
(see Figure 8-4).

Figure 8-3   *Two Railroads Representing Networks*

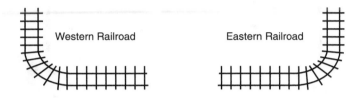

Figure 8-4   *The Train Station Provides a "Railroad NNI"*

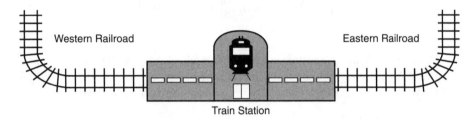

When this passenger/goods transition was completed, the journeys of the two trains could continue across the other railroad network, as shown in Figure 8-5.

Figure 8-5   *The Eastern and Western Railroads Interconnect Through a Train Station, or an NNI*

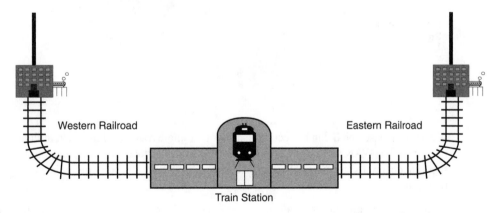

If you replace the train station with a router or switch and you consider this the customer premise, you'd achieve the concept of an NNI, as shown in Figure 8-6.

Figure 8-6 *Railroad vs. WAN NNI*

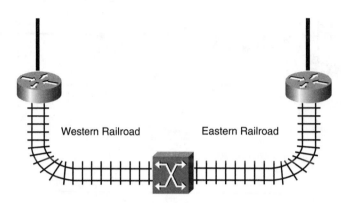

Figure 8-7 illustrates a customer-based NNI, with a LAN switch providing connectivity to two WAN routers: one router is connected to Network Service Provider #1's network, and the other router is connected to Network Service Provider #2's network.

Figure 8-7 *Customer WAN NNI*

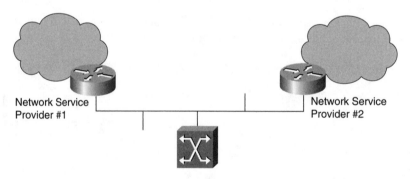

A customer-based NNI can be accomplished with a single router, as illustrated in Figure 8-8. However, two WAN Interface Cards (WICs) or serial interfaces, each connecting to a separate channel service unit/data service unit (CSU/DSU) and subsequent local loop, are required.

Some NSPs can provide NNI service to other network service providers, as illustrated in Figure 8-9. This scenario is used when customers requires WAN connectivity to some locations where their primary providers cannot provide service.

Figure 8-8   *Customer WAN NNI (with One Router)*

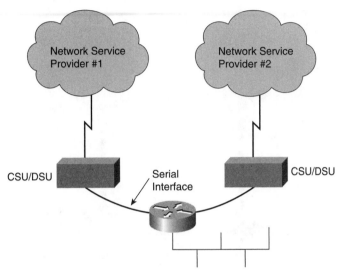

Figure 8-9   *Network Service Provider NNI*

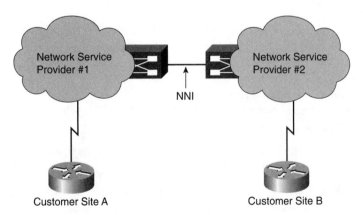

WAN Architecture

The architecture of a WAN is much like the interstate highway system, with multiple sites interconnected by multiple paths and exchanges, as shown in Figure 8-10.

Figure 8-10 *An Interstate Highway System That Looks Like a WAN*

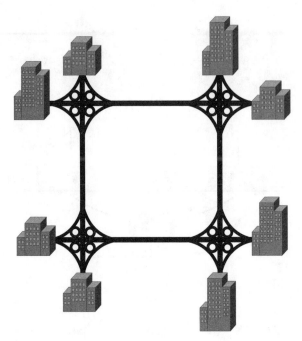

Highway on-ramps (local access loops) provide direct access from each city or town (in a WAN, the town would be the customer site) to the system, or network of interstate highways. The highway system works much the same way as a WAN, where WAN switches provide points where traffic "changes direction." Highway clover leafs enable the same operation to take place. The WAN, illustrated in Figure 8-11, enables communications transport between customer sites much like the highway enables vehicular transport between each city or town.

WAN connectivity is enabled by the transport components within the network core. This network core is comprised of the following elements:

- **Multiplexers**—Merge several low-speed transmissions into one high-speed transmission (and vice versa). Multiplexers are found both at the network access and core, aggregating low-speed signals (for example, DS3) into a single high-speed signal (such as OC-12). The most prevalent multiplexer used in the NSP network is the M13 (Multiplexer DS1/DS3, pronounced "M-One-Three"). The M13 performs both multiplexing (combining) and demultiplexing (separating) functions. M13s multiplex 28 DS1 signals into a single DS3 signal for transmission, often terminating to the Fiber Optic Light Terminating Equipment (LTE), and demultiplex DS3 signals into 28 DS1 signals, often terminating into DACS (DXC) or voice/data switches.

Figure 8-11 *A WAN*

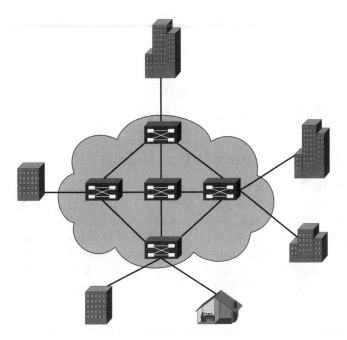

NOTE	When we are discussing multiplexing, *low-speed* identifies the multiplexer input and *high-speed* identifies the multiplexer output, regardless of the actual bandwidth speeds in discussion.

- **WAN switches**—Connect network links in order to transport traffic throughout the WAN. WAN switches dictate the service provided by the WAN service provider, such as ATM, Frame Relay, and Internet (IP).

- **Repeaters**—Physical Layer devices that amplify or regenerate analog and digital signals across a physical link. Repeaters are used for long-distance transmission, such as a fiber optic cable across a large geographic area.

- **A Digital Access Cross-Connect Switch (DACS or DXC)**—Electronically switches the DS0s within each DS1. A DACS can provide network timing for dedicated T1 service, provided that the DACS (and customer's T1 CSU) are configured for such. In order for a DACS to provide network timing, the DACS port must be groomed as "T1 Intact."

- **ATM Data Exchange Interface (ATM DXI)**—Enables existing non-ATM routers to support ATM cells by providing a direct interface between a network service provider router and the customer CSU/DSU.

Summary

WAN connectivity enables individuals and organizations to take advantage of internet-working services such as Frame Relay, ATM, and the Internet. LAN enable communication and resource-sharing needs within an enterprise or campus setting. WANs connect two or more LANs.

This chapter covered the following WAN topics: switching, network interfaces, and architecture.

Frequently Asked Questions (FAQ)

1 Is one WAN technology better than another?

There is no one WAN technology—for example, ATM, Frame Relay, SMDS, IP VPN, etc.—that is the best choice. As with all network design questions, the answer is "It depends." ATM is better suited for applications where a consistent QoS is required, such as supporting voice/video applications. Frame Relay is better suited for bursty data applications, such as e-mail, file transfer, or LAN-to-LAN communication not requiring a QoS Service Level Agreement (SLA) with the NSP.

2 How is a WAN accessed?

Most WAN implementations use dedicated (DS0/DS1/DS3) access to the NSP. The access bandwidth depends on customer application requirements. For example, video conferencing requires approximately 112 K to 384 Kbps for one conversation (depending on the desired quality), whereas e-mail and other data transfers might require only 56 Kbps of bandwidth.

3 Where do IP VPNs fit into wide area networking?

IP VPNs are a relatively new technology, and several challenges are being addressed; most notably, the requirement for QoS. Several network service providers provide this QoS for IP VPNs with an underlying ATM backbone core. IPv6 (IP version 6) is designed to address QoS in native IP networks, but has yet to gain rapid acceptance due to the wide deployment of IPv4 (IP version 4). Some network service providers do provide for IPv4/IPv6 conversion at the network access point; however, IPv6 remains to be implemented in a ubiquitous fashion.

Case Study

The network topology shown in Figure 8-12 represents Drolrevo Enterprises WAN architecture.

Figure 8-12 *Drolrevo Enterprises WAN*

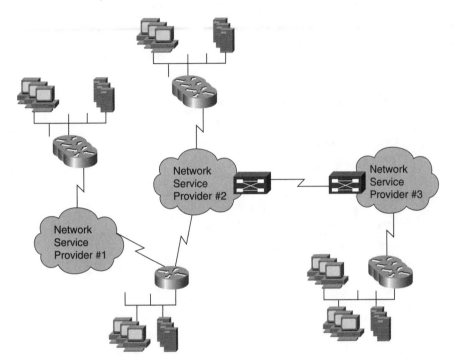

The Drolrevo customer sites serviced are being migrated from Network Service Provider #1 (NSP#1) to Network Service Provider #2 (NSP#2). The customer router is configured with two serial interfaces, each interconnected with a respective network service provider; NSP#1 and NSP#2. Drolrevo Enterprises has implemented an NNI at their main site so that their remote sites, interconnected to either NSP#1 or NSP#2, can communicate with each other through the headquarters site.

NOTE *Routing tables* provide the routing information to the headquarters and remote sites so that each site knows how to reach its intended destination.

Drolrevo Enterprises has sites in very remote parts of the world where there is no direct access to their new network service provider. However, NSP#2 does have a NNI agreement with NSP#3 that services these remote locations. It is through this service provider NNI that Drolrevo Enterprises can establish communication with these remote sites.

The following topics are covered in this chapter:

- ATM Wide Area Networks (WANs)
- ATM WAN Interfaces
- ATM Connections
- Virtual Paths
- Cell Transmission
- ATM Traffic Parameters
- ATM Service Classes
- Quality of Service (QoS) Parameters
- ATM WAN Architecture
- ATM Traffic Contract and Negotiation

CHAPTER 9

Asynchronous Transfer Mode (ATM) Introduction

Many enterprise customers and some service providers consider Asynchronous Transfer Mode (ATM) a mature, legacy technology. ATM supports the need for a low-cost wide-area networking (WAN) alternative to point-to-point, high-bandwidth, dedicated services. In addition to providing dedicated point-to-point services, ATM also enables switch-to-switch trunking, which supports legacy Time Division Multiplexed (TDM) Private Branch Exchange (PBX) networks, and public circuit switching networks used to support public switch telephone network (PSTN) voice services.

ATM is primarily used in the areas of a network service provider's (NSP's) WAN core and for inter-networking services provided to enterprise customers. Today, most service providers are migrating away from future deployments of ATM technologies or attempting to augment their existing ATM networks with incremental investments in related Edge, IP, and MPLS technologies.

There is much complexity and many concepts and acronyms to learn within ATM technologies. This chapter discusses these ATM concepts, acronyms, and technologies.

ATM is the most widely implemented network backbone technology in the NSP market. ATM is an Open System Interconnection (OSI) standards-based transport medium and is widely used within the core (network backbone) and the network access edge, enabling data, video, and voice communication at high (broadband) speeds. Although ATM WANs often are found in service provider backbones, with the rise in converged voice and data broadband applications, ATM also can be found in the large enterprise space.

ATM WANs

ATM WANs are made up of a set of ATM switches under control by the same network administration. Figure 9-1 illustrates an ATM WAN supporting direct access by routers, PBXs (with Voice-over-ATM [VoATM] modules), file servers, and a video server.

Figure 9-1 *ATM WAN*

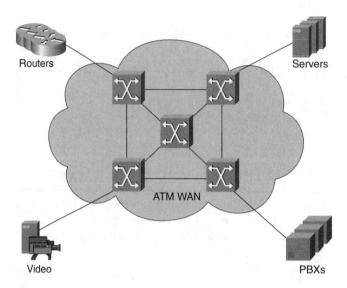

ATM WANs are a connection-oriented service, meaning that a communications path must be provisioned between endpoints prior to the exchange of traffic across the circuit. ATM WANs also can be set up as a connectionless service with the use of Switched Virtual Circuits (SVCs), using X.121 or E.164 addressing for device addressing. ATM SVC service operates in a similar fashion to SMDS (Switched Multimegabit Data Service), a similar dial-on-demand broadband access technology.

ATM works by transmitting all traffic as fixed-length, 53-byte cells, shown in Figure 9-2. These fixed-length cells enable very fast switches to be built, because it is much faster to process a known datagram (packet or cell) size than to figure out the start and end of variable-length datagrams. These small ATM cells ensure that voice and video can be inserted into the stream often enough for real-time transmission.

ATM networks are made up of switches, interfaces, and endpoints (often customer sites). ATM interfaces are the connection points between two ATM switches. These interswitch connections are called *Network-to-Network interfaces* (NNI). Connections between an ATM switch and an endpoint (customer site) are called User Network Interfaces (UNI). UNIs and NNIs can be privately owned by customers or publicly owned by NSPs. These private and public connections are known as private or public UNIs and NNIs. When two network service providers interconnect ATM switches, a broadband intercarrier interface (B-ICI) is used.

Figure 9-2 *ATM Cell*

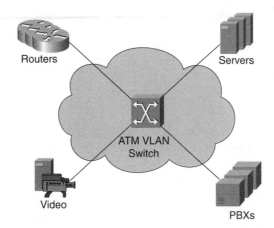

ATM WAN Interfaces

ATM WANs can support any of the following five interface types:

- **ATM UNI**—Defines the interaction between the following:

  - ATM endpoint device and a private network switch

  - ATM endpoint device and a public network switch

  - A private network switch and a public network switch

  The UNI specifications also include physical layer specifications, Integrated Local Management Interface (ILMI), and parameters to control quality of service elements of the ATM connection; for example, to govern traffic management.

- **ATM NNI**—Signaling used between ATM switches across NNI links.

- **ATM Data Exchange Interface (DXI)**—Enables communication with a DXI-enabled router via the router's serial interface. ATM DXI requires an ATM data service unit (ADSU), which receives data from the router in ATM DXI format over a High-Speed Serial Interface (HSSI) from the ATM switch/router. The ADSU converts the data into ATM cells and transfers them to the ATM network over a DS-3/E3 line.

- **ATM Private Network Node Interface or Private Network-to-Network Interface (PNNI)**—Enables different switch vendors to interoperate across an ATM WAN. Vendors can implement proprietary ATM signaling between their own switches, and often do, using PNNI to manage the inter-vendor connections. PNNI lets the switches inform each other about network topology so that appropriate forwarding decisions can be made. PNNI is based on the OSPF (Open Shortest Path First) protocol, but also measures line capacities and delays rather than just the cost metrics measured by OSPF. It is this PNNI operation that enables ATM switches to reroute packets dynamically, based on current line conditions.

NOTE   Cisco Systems, Inc. implements PNNI 1.0.

- **ATM B-ICI**—Describes PNNI interface points enabling the interconnection of public ATM networks.

ATM Connections

ATM is a connection-oriented technology supporting point-to-point (unicast) and point-to-multipoint (multicast) connections. Regardless of the application or the upper-layer protocols (such as TCP/IP), ATM cells are received in the same order in which they are sent.

ATM does not guarantee data delivery across the WAN because of possible congestion in the network backbone. ATM determines the handling of such congestion issues based on the Class of Service (CoS) to which the customer is subscribed.

There are two types of ATM connections: virtual paths (VPs), which contain virtual channels (VCs). A virtual channel connection (VCC) (or virtual circuit) is the basic unit, which carries a single stream of cells, in order, from user to user. A collection of virtual circuits can be bundled together into a virtual path. VPs can be created end-to-end across an ATM WAN. In this case, the ATM network does not route cells belonging to a particular virtual circuit. All cells belonging to a particular virtual path are routed the same way through the ATM network, thus resulting in faster recovery in case of major failures.

VPs

ATM VPs are made up of bundled multiple VCCs with the same origination/termination endpoints. This bundling of virtual channels into a single VP simplifies the provisioning and implementation of large numbers of VCs, provided they share common endpoint pairs. Figure 9-3 illustrates VP and VCs.

ATM point-to-point connections are a pair of simplex connections; one connection from Site A → Site B, and one connection from Site B → Site A. Each connection pair is made up of a VCC.

Figure 9-3 *ATM VPs and VCs*

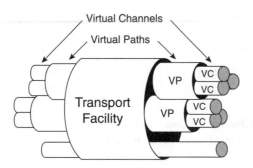

Cell Transmission

Prior to data transmission, an end-to-end path needs to be established through the ATM WAN. Once this path has been provisioned, either on a Permanent (PVC) or Switched (SVC) basis, the following steps are performed:

1 At the sending side, the data is broken down into small, fixed-sized cell payloads (message data) for transmission. Each cell header provides the VPI/VCI (Virtual Path Identifier/Virtual Channel Identifier) values for the destination endpoint.

2 Each ATM switch along the path examines the cell header to determine the appropriate egress interface.

3 Cell payloads are extracted at the destination endpoint and transported data is passed on to upper-layer protocols or applications.

Figure 9-4 illustrates four ATM nodes using VPs and VCs to communicate across the ATM WAN. The ATM NSP is switching the VCs based on the VPI/VCI pairs in the ATM cell header.

Figure 9-4 *ATM WAN with VPs and Virtual Switching*

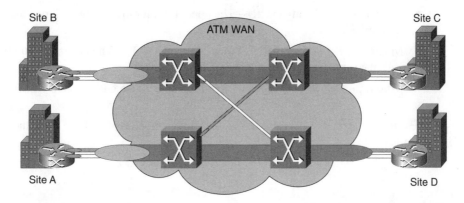

ATM Traffic Contract Parameters

Before ATM data traffic can be sent across the network, the customer and NSP must agree on traffic characteristics and on the kind of service the network is to deliver. This agreement, called the traffic contract, consists of four parts:

- **Source traffic descriptor**—Uses four attributes to describe user traffic: peak cell rate (PCR), sustainable cell rate (SCR), maximum burst size (MBS), and minimum cell rate (MCR).

- **Conformance definition**—Defines which traffic the network will accept at what rate and at what burstiness (traffic in excess of subscribed average) a user is allowed to send traffic.

- **Cell Delay Variation Tolerance (CDVT)**—Is a safety margin that absorbs delay variations in premises equipment.

- **Quality-of-Service (QoS) parameters**—Must be guaranteed by the network. The following are examples of Quality-of-Service parameters:

  - **Cell Transfer Delay (CTD)**—CTD is the delay experienced by a cell between network entry and exit points. CTD includes network propagation delays, queuing delays at various intermediate switches, and service times at queuing points.

  - **Cell Delay Variation (CDV)**—A measure of the variance of the CTD. High variation implies larger buffering for delay-sensitive traffic such as voice and video.

  - **Cell Loss Ratio (CLR)**—The percentage of cells not delivered at their destination because they were lost in the network, often because of network congestion or buffer overflow.

ATM Service Classes use one or more of the following service parameters, depending on the CoS implemented, such as Constant Bit Rate (CBR) or Variable Bit Rate-Real Time (VBRrt):

- **Peak Cell Rate (PCR)**—The maximum bit rate that can be transmitted.

- **Sustainable Cell Rate (SCR)**—The upper limit for the average cell rate that can be transmitted.

- **Maximum Burst Size (MBS)/Burst Tolerance (BT)**—The maximum number of cells the source can transmit at the PCR.

- **Minimum Cell Rate (MCR)**—The minimum cell rate guaranteed by the ATM network.

These traffic parameters combine in specific combinations to provide a QoS to the network customer.

Technical Note: Leaky Bucket

Leaky Bucket is an informal term for the Generic Cell Rate Algorithm (GCRA). The concept behind the Leaky Bucket/GCRA is that there is a finite queue serving as a door between the sending host and the ATM network. When the host wants to send an ATM cell, the cell must go through the door, which resembles a bucket with a hole in the bottom (the "leaky bucket"). This "bucket" holds as many cells to be transmitted as it can until it overflows. The bucket will transmit cells from the leakage at a constant rate with the overflow cells being discarded.

The Dual Leaky Bucket operation is described as follows:

- "Leaky Bucket 1"—Enforces the PCR commitment and ensures that the PCR is not exceeded for a given service category by measuring and enforcing the rate at which cells are sent to the network switch by the CPE. Cells exceeding the PCR are discarded at the ingress switch.

- "Leaky Bucket 2"—Ensures that the sending CPE adheres to the SCR for the appropriate service category. Cells which exceed the average SCR over a period of time are tagged CLP=1 (Discard Eligible) by the ingress switch. The burst tolerance is provided by the MBS parameter.

The Dual Leaky Bucket is illustrated in Figure 9-5.

Figure 9-5   *Dual "Leaky Bucket"*

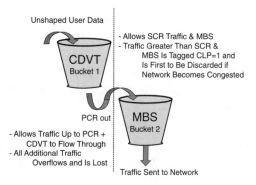

ATM Service Classes

ATM Service Classes represent a class of ATM connections that have uniform characteristics in terms of traffic pattern and QoS requirements. The following sections discuss the different ATM Service Classes implemented and their respective traffic parameters.

CBR

CBR is used by connections that need a fixed amount of bandwidth that is always available during the connection lifetime. The source can send cells at or below this fixed rate at any time and for any duration. ATM cell traffic is policed by the network ingress ATM switch according to the PCR, and cells presented in excess of the PCR are discarded.

CBR is ideal for use by real-time applications; that is, those applications requiring tightly constrained CTD and CDV, such as voice, video, or Circuit Emulation Services (CES).

VBRrt

VBRrt is for time-sensitive applications (that is, those requiring tightly constrained delay and delay variation), such as voice and video applications. Sources are expected to transmit at a rate that varies with time, which can best be described as "*bursty*" traffic.

NOTE   Voice and video applications can be supported either by CBR or VBRrt service. Most often the determining factor is cost and Service Level Agreements/Service Level Guarantees (SLAs/SLGs) by the network service provider.

Traffic parameters for VBRrt are as follows:

- PCR
- SCR
- MBS

Cells that are delayed beyond the CTD threshold are presumed to be of less value to the application and can be dropped. Real-time VBR service may support statistical multiplexing of real-time sources. ATM traffic is policed by the network ingress (incoming from the customer) ATM switch according to the PCR and the SCR.

Policing is accomplished in a two-stage process: In stage one, cells presented in excess of the PCR are discarded. In stage two, cells which exceed the average SCR over a period of time are tagged CLP=1 by the ingress switch. If the sending CPE switch has been idle for a period of time, it is permitted to burst to port speed at MBS without having cells tagged CLP=1. If this burst exceeds MBS, however, cells are marked CLP=1 and are therefore eligible for discard in case of network congestion.

Variable Bit Rate (Non-Real-Time) (VBRnrt)

VBRnrt is intended for use by applications having bursty traffic characteristics without tight constraints on delay (CTD) and delay variation (CDV).

Like VBRrt, VBRnrt traffic parameters are as follows:

* PCR
* SCR
* MBS

For those cells that are transferred within the traffic contract, the application expects a low CLR. For all cells, a bound on the CTD by the NSP is expected.

Available Bit Rate

Available Bit Rate (ABR) is for sources with the capability of dynamically reducing or increasing the sending data rate. This dynamic sending rate enables the source to exploit the changes in the ATM network, such as available bandwidth.

Traffic parameters for ABR are as follows:

* PCR
* MCR

No specific QoS parameter (PCR, MCR) is negotiated with ABR; however, it is expected that the end-system will adapt traffic shaping based on network conditions. This traffic shaping will enable the ABR traffic stream to experience a low cell loss ratio (CLR) and obtain a fair share of the available bandwidth. ABR service is not intended to support real-time applications.

Unspecified Bit Rate

Unspecified Bit Rate (UBR) is a "best effort" service used for non-critical applications. By their nature, these non-critical applications do not require controlled delay and delay variation, or a specified QoS. UBR sources are expected to transmit non-continuous bursts of cells and are often used to "fill in" gaps in the traffic stream created by other CoS having no traffic to send. ATM Cells that exceed the MCR are marked discard-eligible. Discard-eligible cells are allowed to pass through the network if bandwidth is available. If network congestion is encountered, these cells are discarded. ATM cells that exceed the PCR are immediately discarded by the network ingress ATM switch.

QoS Parameters

QoS is the ability to define a level of performance in a data communications system. For example, ATM networks specify modes of service ensuring optimum performance for traffic such as real-time voice and video.

The QoS parameters selected to correspond to a network performance objective can be negotiated between the end-systems and the network—for example, through signaling procedures—or can be taken as default. These QoS parameters are often enabled on a per-connection basis and are listed here:

- **CDV**—Measured in microseconds. CDV is the distortion caused by change in arrival times between cells, also known as *jitter*.

- **Max CTD**—Sum of the fixed-delay component across the link or node and the CDV. Max CTD, or MCTD, is a required metric for CBR and VBRrt service categories; it is an optional metric for VBRnrt.

- **CLR**—The ratio of lost cells to total cells transmitted on a link or node:

  ```
  CLR= Lost Cells/Total Cells
  ```

Two CLR attributes are calculated: CLR0 and CLR0+1. The cell loss priority portion of CLR0 considers only CLP=0 traffic; for CLR0+1, both CLP=0 (No discard) and CLP=1 (Discard Eligible) traffic are considered in the calculation.

ATM WAN Architecture

ATM WAN architecture uses two traffic control parameters and mechanisms for congestion control: Connection Admission Control (CAC) and Usage Parameter Control (UPC). The primary role of these traffic control parameters is to protect the network and the end-users so that network performance objectives are met.

ATM CoS relate quality requirements and traffic characteristics to network behavior parameters and mechanisms. ATM CoS must be declared when the connection with the network service provider is initially provisioned. CoS categories apply to both VCCs and Virtual Path Connections (VPCs); for example, a VP cannot be provisioned as UBR and carry VCs that are provisioned for Constant Bit Rate.

CAC and UPC are used within the ATM switch for each Service Category, guaranteeing the provisioned CoS.

CAC

CAC is the process the ATM network uses during the VP/VC setup to determine whether a connection can be made. If available, network resources (port bandwidth and buffer space) are reserved for the incoming connection at each ATM switch in the connection path. CAC maintains the end-to-end connection QoS of an ATM connection, ensuring the QoS of other network connections is not compromised by the new connection.

UPC

UPC, or policing, is the ATM network process monitoring and controlling the traffic at the UNI. UPC is a requirement for any ATM network supporting multiple CoS. UPC has the primary purpose to protect network resources from malicious and unintentional misbehavior, which can affect the QoS of other established connections. Traffic shaping can be applied to each cell arrival to assess conformance to the traffic contract for each ATM connection. Violations of negotiated parameters are either discarded or tagged for possible discard.

ATM Traffic Contract and Negotiation

A *traffic contract* specifies the negotiated characteristics of a VP/VC connection at the ATM UNI (either Private or Public UNI). The traffic contract at the Public UNI consists of a connection traffic descriptor and a set of QoS parameters for each ATM connection, including the definition of a compliant connection. The values of the traffic contract parameters are specified either by ATM network default rules or explicit definitions during connection setup.

Summary

ATM WANs are a connection-oriented service, meaning that a communications path must be provisioned between endpoints prior to the exchange of traffic across the circuit. Interfaces to these ATM WANs are categorized as any one of the following five types: UNI, NNI, PNNI, DXI, and B-ICI.

ATM WAN connections are classified by their CoS, defined in Table 9-1.

Table 9-1   *ATM CoS Description*

QoS	Description and Application Use
CBR	Provides constant bandwidth across the virtual connection. Used for private line emulated services, such as multimedia, CAD/CAM, or medical imaging.
VBRrt	Provides a specified average bandwidth across the virtual connection. Used for transporting delay-sensitive applications, such as voice or video.

continues

Table 9-1   *ATM CoS Description (Continued)*

QoS	Description and Application Use
VBRnrt	Provides a specified average bandwidth across the virtual connection. Used for transporting non-delay-sensitive applications, such as data information.
UBR	Best-effort service, meaning no bandwidth is specified across the connection or delivery of service guaranteed.
ABR	Best-effort service implemented in a different fashion than UBR. This service provides continuing feedback indicating how much bandwidth is available for use. By throttling back as necessary, sending hosts avoid network congestion, preventing traffic from being sent, but thrown away before it reaches its intended destination. Used to support data applications where delivery is important, but not necessarily in a near-real-time environment.

Table 9-2 demonstrates user applications with the most appropriate ATM CoS to support communications for these applications.

Table 9-2   *Application Areas for ATM Service Categories*

Application Area	CBR	VBRrt	VBRnrt	ABR	UBR
Critical Data	••	•	•••	•	- - -
LAN Interconnection/LAN Emulation	•	•	••	•••	••
Data transport/Internetworking (IP/Frame Relay)	•	•	••	•••	••
Circuit Emulation (PBX)	•••	••	- - -	- - -	- - -
POTS/ISDN – Video Conference	•••	•	•	- - -	- - -
Compressed Audio	•	•••	••	••	•
Video Distribution	•••	••	•	- - -	- - -
Interactive Multimedia	•••	•••	••	••	•

Legend:

••• = Optimum   •• = Good   • = Fair   - - - = Not Suitable

ATM CoS are defined by one (or more) of the following parameters, dependant on the CoS implemented (for example, CBR, VBRrt, etc.):

- **PCR**—Maximum bit rate that can be transmitted
- **SCR**—Upper limit for the average cell rate that can be transmitted

- **MBS/Burst Tolerance (BT)**—Maximum number of cells the source can transmit at the Peak Cell Rate (PCR)
- **MCR**—Minimum cell rate guaranteed by the ATM network
- **CDVT**—Tolerance in CDV (referred to as the *PCR*)

ATM WAN Architecture uses two traffic control parameters and mechanisms for congestion control: CAC and UPC. CAC is the process the ATM network uses during the VP/VC setup to determine whether a connection can be made. UPC, or policing, is the ATM network process monitoring and controlling the traffic at the UNI.

Frequently Asked Questions (FAQ)

1 The number 53 may be the first time a binary number is not used in networking, so how did ATM cells come to be 53 bytes in length?

   During the standardization process, a conflict arose within the CCITT as to the payload size within an ATM cell. The U.S. wanted 64-byte payloads; the Europeans and Japanese wanted 32 payloads. The 48-byte payload plus the 5-byte header was the compromise.

   The 5-byte header was chosen because 10 percent of payload (5 bytes) was perceived as the upper bound on the acceptable overhead.

2 What is ATM LANE?

   ATM LAN Emulation (LANE) enables an ATM network to be used as a LAN backbone for hubs, bridges, and switches. ATM LANE enables LAN hosts connected to "legacy" LANs to communicate though a LAN-to-ATM hub/bridge/switch with an ATM-attached device (a file server, for example) without requiring the traffic to pass through a router. The purpose of LANE is to enable common protocols, such as IP, IPX, AppleTalk, and DECnet, to ride over an ATM backbone.

   LANE does not replace routers or routing, but provides a LAN switching solution in the wiring closets of large LANS.

3 What is "traffic shaping"?

   Traffic shaping is forcing traffic to conform to a certain behavior, often in one of two scenarios:

   - **Worst case**—An application will generate 10 Mbps of data for a maximum burst of 5 seconds; for example, streaming multimedia, bulk file transfer.
   - **Worst case plus average case**—An application will generate 10 Mbps of data for a maximum burst of 5 seconds and its average over any 10 second interval will be no more than 5 Mbps; for example, several users accessing a corporate intranet simultaneously.

Traffic shaping can be performed by any one (or more) of the following three functions:

- **Acceptance**—Each ATM switch is configured with the option of accepting a virtual circuit request based on the traffic parameters declared by the customer/end-user.

- **Policing**—Each ATM switch ensures that the customer/end-user equipment keeps its promises and does not consume more bandwidth than agreed upon at initial connection setup.

- **Traffic Shaping**—Occurs in the CPE using information about the policing functions in order to change the traffic characteristics of the traffic stream to get the lowest CLR possible.

For example, an IP router attached to an ATM network might delay some cells in order to reduce the peak rate and rate variance without affecting throughput. An MPEG codec that was operating in a situation where delay wasn't a problem might operate in a CBR mode.

4   What is the difference between QoS and CoS?

QoS refers to the network mechanisms that determine which packets have priority. CoS refers to feature sets, or groups of services, that are assigned to users based on company policy. If a feature set includes priority transmission, CoS is implemented in QoS functions within the network routers and switches.

Case Study

The following case study illustrates a four-node ATM WAN enabling multiple CoS in support of the customer's voice, video, and data applications. Figure 9-6 illustrates an ATM-based network backbone that an NSP might implement. The ATM WAN backbone depicted here is carrying Frame Relay, ATM, and IP traffic.

The Barker and Brown ATM WAN, illustrated in Figure 9-7, depicts what a customer ATM-based WAN might look like, enabling multiple CoS between several locations. In this scenario, CBR service is being used to carry voice and video traffic from the New York office to Seattle and Paris. VBRnrt service is used to carry corporate intranet services, such as file transfer, between the New York, Seattle, and Sydney offices. UBR service is used between the New York and Seattle/Sydney offices to "fill in" the remaining available bandwidth between these offices, enabling non-mission critical data applications.

Figure 9-6   *Network Service Provider ATM Backbone Network*

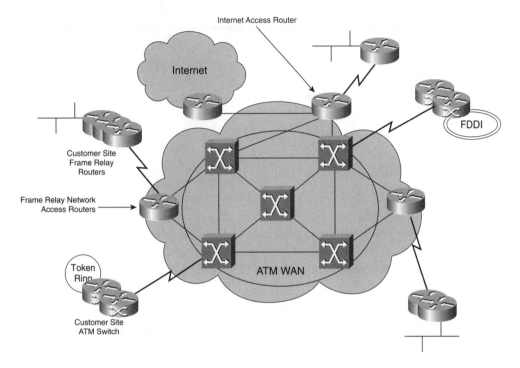

Figure 9-7   *Barker and Brown ATM WAN*

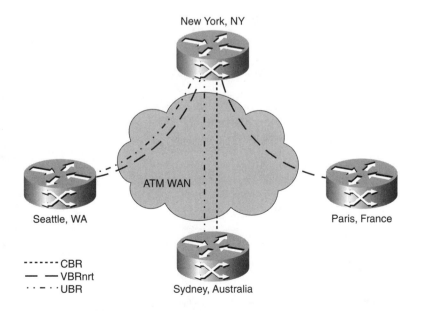

The following topics are covered in this chapter:

- Frame Relay Components
- Frame Relay Error Handling
- Frame Relay Local Management Interface

CHAPTER 10

Frame Relay Introduction

Frame Relay is a Layer-2 (Data-Link) wide-area networking (WAN) protocol operating at both Layer-1 (Physical) and Layer-2 (Data-Link) of the Open System Interconnection (OSI) model (see Figure 10-1). Frame Relay WANs are often deployed as a cost-effective replacement for point-to-point leased line services. Where point-to-point customers incur a monthly fee for local access and long-haul connections, Frame Relay customers incur the same monthly fee for local access but have only a fraction of the long-haul connection fee.

Frame Relay was standardized by two standards bodies—internationally by the International Telecommunications Union (ITU-T) and domestically by American National Standards Institute (ANSI).

Figure 10-1 *Frame Relay WAN*

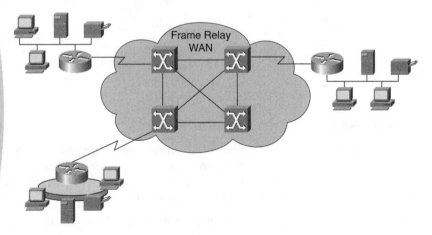

Frame Relay Components

Frame Relay WANs are made up of four functional components:

- Access Router or Frame Relay Access Device (FRAD)
- Local access loop to the service provider network
- Frame Relay network switch access port (Link Management Interface [LMI] parameters are defined here)
- Frame Relay virtual circuit between Frame Relay User Network Interface (UNI) switch ports

Each of these components is discussed in the following sections.

Frame Relay Router/FRAD

The *Router/FRAD* is located at the customer premise, shown in the Figure 10-2, and is either a dedicated FRAD or a router. Cisco routers can support multiple WAN interface cards (WICs), each connecting to a separate WAN, such as those provided by separate Frame Relay network service providers.

Figure 10-2 *FRAD*

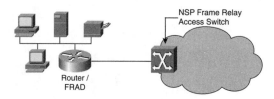

Local Access Loop

The *local access loop* is the physical wiring interconnecting the customer premise router/FRAD and the network service provider's Frame Relay switch access port. The local loop is one of the following types of services: DS0, DS1, NxDS1, DS3 service, or some fraction of DS1/DS3 service (for example, Frac-T1).

The local loop terminates into a Network Interface Unit (NIU) at the customer premise (see Figure 10-3), with subsequent connection to the customer data communication equipment (DCE) device, such as a channel service unit/data service unit (CSU/DSU). The data termination equipment (DTE) port of this CSU/DSU, often an RS-232/V.35 port, provides connectivity to the router/FRAD.

Figure 10-3 *Frame Relay Local Access Loop*

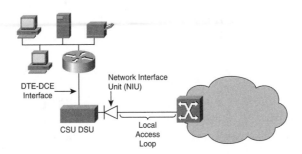

Frame Relay Virtual Circuits

A *virtual circuit* is a logical communications path between two physical devices, such as a Frame Relay switch/router. Frame Relay is a connection-oriented service using data-link connection identifiers (DLCIs) to identify the virtual circuit between the originating and terminating sites, as shown in Figure 10-4. This path, or virtual circuit, is a bidirectional logical (network-based) connection across the WAN between two end-nodes.

NOTE   Sometimes the originating node of a virtual circuit is annotated as Site A and the terminating node of a virtual circuit is annotated as Site B or Site Z.

Figure 10-4 *Frame Relay WAN with Virtual Circuit and DLCI*

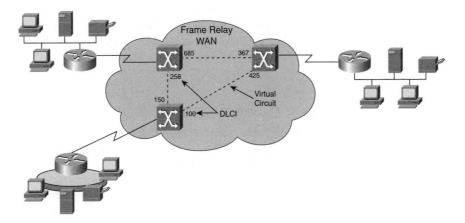

The heart of a Frame Relay network is the virtual circuit, which can be either permanent (PVC) or switched (SVC). It is this virtual circuit that traverses the Frame Relay WAN backbone, interconnecting Frame Relay sites. DLCIs identify which virtual circuit a Frame Relay datagram (frame) must take to reach its intended destination.

DLCIs

DLCIs identify the PVC transporting the data traffic. DLCIs are of local significance, unless an agreement has been made with the network service provider to deploy global DLCIs. *Local significance* means that DLCIs are of interest to the local Frame Relay networking device; for example, the router or FRAD. Frame Relay DLCIs are analogous to an organization's telephone network using speed-dial functions. The most common deployment involves the use of local DLCIs because there is a network size limitation regarding the use of global DLCIs.

Technical Note: Global DLCI Addresses

Global DLCI addresses are assigned so that each DLCI has universal significance, meaning that the DLCI number is pointed to the same destination (termination point) regardless of the origination point.

The intent behind global DLCI addressing is to simplify frame relay network addressing administration; however, there is an inherent limitation with global addressing in that no more than 992 DLCIs can be used, which is 1,024 DLCIs less the 32 reserved DLCIs. In a Frame Relay network of more than 992 sites, global addressing will not work.

Use of global DLCIs requires that each DLCI be preassigned (often these assignments are negotiated between the customer and the network service provider) and can be used only once throughout the network. (If two sites had the same DLCI, the network would not know which site is the intended destination). The Frame Relay switch within the service provider's network will have tables that route the traffic between each origination and termination pair.

Suppose that an organization has deployed the following speed-dialing scheme (illustrated in Figure 10-5):

- Ian speed-dials "37" to talk with Deborah.
- Ian speed-dials "71" to talk with Tom.
- Deborah speed-dials "47" to talk with Tom.
- Deborah speed-dials "61" to talk with Ian.

- Tom speed-dials "98" to talk with Ian.
- Tom speed-dials "106" to talk with Deborah.

Figure 10-5 *Telephone Speed-dial Network*

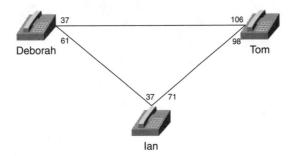

The following table provides another view of this example Telephone Speed-Dial network.

Table 10-1 *Telephone Speed-Dial Configuration Table*

Site A	Site B	A → B Speed Dial	B → A Speed Dial
Deborah	Tom	37	106
Deborah	Ian	61	37
Ian	Tom	71	98
Ian	Deborah	37	61
Tom	Ian	98	61
Tom	Deborah	106	37

In order for Ian to speak with Deborah, Ian will press speed-dial "37" on the telephone set. However, Deborah will see speed-dial "61" on the telephone because that is the local speed-dial assignment given to Ian. The speed-dial "37" local assignment on Deborah's telephone set is assigned to Tom.

If Deborah presses speed-dial "37," Tom will answer the phone; and speed-dial "106" will show on the Marketing VP's phone because that is the local assignment given to Deborah.

This same speed-dialing concept applies to Frame Relay DLCIs; the DLCI assignment is locally significant. The distant-end of the virtual circuit is unaware of this number because it has its own local DLCI assignment to identify the distant-end node. The DLCI local significance is illustrated in Figure 10-6.

Figure 10-6 *Frame Relay Network with DLCI Assignment*

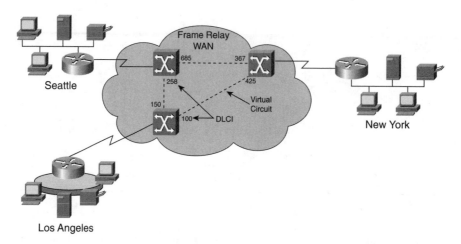

In this example, in order for Los Angeles to send traffic to New York, the Frame Relay Access Device (FRAD) will map the network layer information—for example, the IP address—to the Data-Link Connection Identifier (DLCI), which in this case, is 100. New York will see traffic arrive on DLCI 425 and will be able to identify within its Frame Relay mapping tables that this traffic has arrived from Los Angeles.

The following table provides a summary of the Frame Relay network shown in Figure 10-6.

Table 10-2 *Frame Relay DLCI Table for Figure 10-6*

Site A	Site B	A → B DLCI	B → A DLCI
Los Angeles	New York	100	425
Los Angeles	Seattle	150	258
Seattle	New York	685	367
Seattle	Los Angeles	258	150
New York	Seattle	367	685
New York	Los Angeles	425	100

DLCI values are discussed in further detail in the "Frame Relay Virtual Circuit Parameters" section later in this chapter.

PVCs

PVCs are permanently established virtual circuit connections; Frame Relay PVCs use DLCIs for connection addressing. PVCs, are used for frequent communication, such as file sharing, file transfer, and computer aided design/computer aided manufacturing (CAD/CAM) imaging between Frame Relay sites. PVCs operate in one of two modes:

- **Idle**—The connection between end-nodes is active albeit with no data transfer occurring. PVCs are not terminated or "taken-down" when in an idle state.
- **Data Transfer**—Data traffic is being transmitted between end-nodes over the virtual circuit.

Even though PVCs often are discussed as being full-duplex, PVCs are simplex connections, each with its own DLCI/CIR (committed information rate) assignment. For more information on DLCI/CIR assignments see the "Frame Relay Virtual Circuit Parameters" section later in this chapter.

NOTE	The three duplex modes are as follows: - **Full-duplex**—Originating and terminating points are sending and receiving at the same time; full-duplex is a two-way communication at all times. - **Half-duplex**—Originating and terminating points are sending and receiving, but not at the same time. Only one flow of traffic is allowed across the connection; half-duplex is a two-way communication that moves in one direction at a time. - **Simplex**—Originating or terminating point is sending, transmitting, or receiving; simplex is a one-way communication only.

Switched Virtual Circuits

Unlike PVCs, switched virtual circuits (SVCs) require a call setup process. SVCs are temporary connections used when communication between Frame Relay sites is infrequent or sporadic, such as Voice over Frame Relay (VoFr) applications.

NOTE	Frame Relay SVCs use E.164 or X.121 addresses for connection addressing.

The SVC call setup process is defined as follows:

1 **Call setup**—Establishes the virtual circuit between Frame Relay end-nodes. Call setup includes negotiation of virtual circuit parameters, such as CIR.

2 **Data transfer**—Data traffic is transmitted between end-nodes (originating and terminating) across the virtual circuit.

3 **Idle**—When the virtual circuit is idle (no data traffic), the connection between end-nodes remains active and available for communication. Unlike PVCs, which do not terminate the connection, however, an SVC terminates the connection if it is in an idle state for a configured time period.

4 **Call termination**—The virtual circuit between Frame Relay sites is terminated, or "taken down."

Frame Relay Virtual Circuit Parameters

Frame Relay Virtual Circuits, both PVC and SVC, have three configurable parameters that must be agreed upon between each site and the Frame Relay network service provider. For example, if the originating site is configured for one DLCI and the network service provider is expecting another, communication will not occur across the virtual circuit.

These parameters are as follows:

- Committed Information Rate (CIR)
- Discard Eligibility (DE)
- Data-Link Connection Identifiers (DLCIs) for PVCs
- X.121/E.164 addresses for SVCs

Frame Relay Committed Information Rate

The CIR is the amount of bandwidth that will be delivered as "best-effort" across the Frame Relay network backbone. Network service providers often have provisions in their tariffs guaranteeing delivery of CIR traffic at some percentage. For example, a tariff may state a guarantee delivery rate of 99.9 percent CIR-marked traffic.

CIR is measured in bits per second, over a period of time, expressed as T_C. T_C is often measured as one second. B_C is the committed burst rate across the virtual circuit for that second (T_C). B_c is represented by the following formula:

$$B_C = CIR \times T_C$$

B_c is the maximum number of bits that a Frame Relay network is committed to accept and will transmit at the CIR. Traffic in excess of CIR is measured as B_e (Excess Burst Rate). B_E is the number of bits that a Frame Relay network will attempt to transfer after B_c is accommodated, and it is marked as Discard Eligible (DE). T_C is the time period over which B_C and B_E are measured. The T_C interval counter starts at zero when data begins to enter the Frame Relay network and ends when data is no longer entering the network. When a new data stream enters the network, the T_C counter restarts at zero.

Frame Relay PVCs often are discussed as being two-way, but these PVCs are simplex (one-way) connections, each virtual circuit is configured with its own CIR. The Frame Relay network service provider provisions these PVCs in pairs: A → B and B → A. This means that an A → B PVC could be configured for 64 Kbps CIR, and a B → A PVC could be configured with a 32 Kbps CIR. It is up to the network designer or engineer to determine the proper amount of CIR required, often based on user and application traffic.

Frame Relay Discard Eligibility

Frame Relay uses a bit in the frame header indicating whether that frame may be discarded in the event congestion is encountered during transmission. The Discard Eligibility (DE) bit can be set by the sending Frame Relay site to prioritize the frame to show that it has a lower priority than other outgoing frames. If the network becomes congested, frames with the DE bit marked will be discarded before frames that do not have the DE bit marked to relieve this network congestion.

The following flowchart (see Figure 10-7) illustrates the process each Frame Relay network service provider's switch runs when receiving a frame for transmission.

Figure 10-7 *Frame Relay Data Frame Transmission Flowchart*

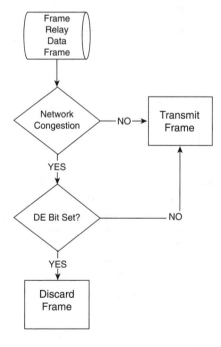

Discard eligibility means that in the event the frame encounters congestion while traversing the network, it is eligible to be discarded from the network, in part relieving the network congestion. Some networks take no action when the DE bit is set. When a DE frame is discarded, it is up to the upper-layer protocols, such as TCP (of the TCP/IP suite), to determine the loss and make corrective actions, such as retransmission.

NOTE	The DE bit can be used to determine which frames should be dropped first or which frames have lower time sensitivity. DE lists can be created within Cisco routers to identify those frames eligible for discarding, and DE groups can be specified to identify the DLCI that is affected.

PVC DLCIs

DLCI values can be 10, 16, or 23 bits in length—10-bit DLCIs are the norm and have become the *de facto* standard for Frame Relay WAN implementations.

The 10-bit DLCI values, as recommended by the Frame Relay Forum, and are defined as shown in Table 10-3.

Table 10-3   *Frame Relay Forum 10-bit DLCI Recommendations*

DLCI Value	Function
0	FRF—In-channel signaling
1 to 15	Reserved
16 to 1007	Available for VC endpoint assignment
1008 to 1022	Reserved
1023	Local Management Interface (LMI)

The 10-bit DLCI values, as recommended by both the ANSI (T1.618) and the ITU-T (Q.922) are defined as shown in Table 10-4.

Table 10-4   *ANSI (T1.618) and ITU-T (Q.922) 10-bit DLCI Recommendations*

DLCI Value	Function
0	In-channel signaling and management (LMI)
1 to 15	Reserved
16 to 991	Available for VC endpoint assignment
992 to 1007	Frame Relay bearer service Layer-2 management
1008 to 1022	Reserved
1023	Reserved for in-channel layer management

NOTE	The number of DLCIs configurable per port varies depending on the traffic level. All 1000 may be used; however, in common use, 200 to 300 is a typical maximum. If the DLCIs are used for broadcast traffic, 30 to 50 are more realistic due to CPU overhead caused by broadcast generation.

SVC X.121/E.164 Addressing

Where PVCs use DLCIs, Switched Virtual Circuits (SVCs) use X.121 for virtual circuit addressing. X.121 is a hierarchical addressing scheme and was originally designed to number X.25 nodes. X.121 addresses are up to 14 digits in length and are structured as follows:

- **Country Code:** 3 digits

  The first digit is a zone number that identifies a part of the world. For example, Zone 2 covers Europe and Zone 3 covers North America. These codes are found in ITU-T Recommendation X.121.

- **Service Provider:** 1 digit
- **Terminal Number:** Up to 10 digits

E.164 is a hierarchical global telecommunications numbering plan, similar to the North American Number Plan (NANP). E.164 addresses are up to 15 digits in length and are structured as follows:

- **Country Code:** 1, 2, or 3 digits

  This code is based on the international telephony numbering plan. (The international telephony numbering plan can be found in any phone book).

- **National Destination Code and Subscriber Number:** Up to 14, 13, or 12 digits in length (maximum length depends on the length of the Country Code).

- **Subaddress:** Up to 40 digits

NOTE	ITU-T is the designation for the International Telecommunications Union Telecommunications Standardization Sector.

Frame Relay Error Handling

Frame Relay performs error detection (and therefore handling) by using the Cyclic Redundancy Check (CRC) method, which determines whether the receiving device (router/FRAD) received the frame error-free. There is an important distinction in that

Frame Relay services perform error detection rather than error checking; error detection is based on the premise that the network media carrying the traffic is reliable. Error correction is left to the upper-layer protocols, such as the Transmission Control Protocol (TCP) of the TCP/IP protocol suite.

Frame Relay LMI

The Frame Relay LMI is a set of Frame Relay specifications. The original LMI was developed in 1990 by the Gang of Four (Cisco, DEC, Nortel and StrataCom). The LMI specifications include support for the following:

- **Keepalive mechanism**—Verifies the data flow across the UNI (User-Network Interface)

- **Multicast mechanism**—Provides the network server with local and multicast DLCI information

- **Global addressing**—Gives DLCIs global rather than local significance

- **Status mechanism**—Provides on-going status reports of each known DLCI on the network service provider's switch

Figure 10-8 illustrates the end-points for LMI Status Messages.

Figure 10-8 *LMI Status Message End-points*

The original LMI specification enables a number of enhancements to the original Frame Relay protocol for managing Frame Relay networks. The most noteworthy LMI extensions enable support for the following:

- **Global addressing**—Giving Frame Relay DLCI values a global, rather than local, significance. These global DLCI values become Frame Relay networking device addresses that are unique in the Frame Relay WAN.

- **Virtual circuit status messages**—Provide communication and synchronization between FRADs and the network service provider switches. These status messages report at regular intervals the up/down status of configured PVCs.

- **Multicasting**—LMI extension supports the assignment to and management of multicast groups. Multicasting conserves bandwidth by enabling routing updates and address-resolution (for example, ARP, RARP) messages to be sent only to specific router groups.

There are three LMI types found in Frame Relay WAN implementations. These three types are listed here:

- **ANSI T1.617, (Annex D)**—Maximum number of connections (PVCs) supported is limited to 976. LMI type ANSI T1.627 (Annex D) uses DLCI 0 to carry local (link) management information.

- **ITU-T Q.933, (Annex A)**—Like LMI type Annex-D, the maximum number of connections (PVCs) supported is limited to 976. LMI type ITU-T Q.933 (Annex A) also uses DLCI 0 to carry local (link) management information.

- **LMI (Original)**—Maximum number of connections (PVCs) supported is limited to 992. LMI type LMI uses DLCI 1023 to carry local (link) management information.

NOTE   The LMI (Original) type is annotated as LMI type "Cisco" within the Cisco IOS.

Summary

Frame Relay was intended for LAN-to-LAN internetworking over the WAN. Frame Relay WANs are deployed as a cost-effective replacement for point-to-point leased line services. Frame Relay WANs are made up of four functional components:

- Access Router or Frame Relay Access Device (FRAD)
- Local access loop to the service provider network
- Frame Relay network switch access port
- LMI parameters are defined here

Frame Relay devices fall into the following two general categories:

- DTEs, which include terminals, personal computers, routers, and bridges
- DCEs, which transmit the data through the network and often are carrier-owned devices (although, increasingly, enterprises are buying their own DCEs and implementing them in their networks)

Frame Relay networks transfer data using one of the following two connection types:

- PVCs are permanent connections between two Frame Relay sites. PVCs use DLCIs for addressing.

- SVCs are temporary connections created for each data transfer and are terminated when the data transfer is complete. SVCs use X.121 addresses for connection addressing.

The DLCI is a value assigned to each virtual circuit and DTE device connection point in the Frame Relay WAN. Two different connections can be assigned the same value within the same Frame Relay WAN, one on each side of the virtual connection.

A set of Frame Relay enhancements called LMI offer a number of features (referred to as *extensions*) for managing complex internetworks, including the following:

- Global addressing
- Virtual circuit status messages
- Multicasting

Frequently Asked Questions (FAQ)

1 What is oversubscription of Frame Relay ports?

Because data connections tend to be idle as much as they are used, oversubscription of a Frame Relay port is often used as a strategy for achieving more cost-effective WAN connectivity. Oversubscription is another tool network designers use when designing WANs. Designers can "play the averages" by assigning a total committed information rate (CIR) greater than the port speed.

Oversubscription is attractive for saving money on the port connection and is measured in percentages. For example, four 32 K bit/sec permanent virtual circuits (PVC)—a total CIR of 128 K bit/sec—attached to a 64 K bit/sec port represents a 200 percent subscription. Two 32 K bit/sec PVCs attached to a 64 K bit/sec port equals 100 percent subscription, which represents no oversubscription.

A network configuration consisting of 24 (DLCIs/PVCs) × 56 Kbps (CIR per PVC) = 1.344 Mbps is well within the T1 bandwidth limitation of 1.344/1.536 Mbps (depending on physical line coding; AMI = 1.344 Mbps; B8ZS = 1.536 Mbps). This configuration is not oversubscribing the interface because there is sufficient bandwidth available to support the traffic requirement (1.344 Mbps _ 1.344/1.536 Mbps).

A network configuration of 50 (DLCIs/PVCs) × 56 Kbps (CIR per PVC) = 2.800 Mbps far exceeds the maximum bandwidth supported by a T1 limitation of 1.344/1.536 Mbps (depending on physical line coding; AMI = 1.344 Mbps and B8ZS = 1.536 Mbps). This configuration is oversubscribing the interface because there is not sufficient bandwidth available to support the traffic requirement (2.800 Mbps _ 1.344/1.536 Mbps).

2 Can Frame Relay carry voice traffic?

Yes. Voice over Frame Relay (VoFr) is enabled with the use of a VFRAD. Voice Frame Relay access devices (VFRADs) integrate voice into the data network by connecting the router and the PBX at each site in the corporate network to the Frame Relay network.

The VFRADs' prioritization schemes "tag" different applications according to their sensitivity to delay, assigning a higher priority to voice. The VFRADs let the higher priority voice packets go first, keeping the data packets waiting. This prioritization has no negative impact on the queued data traffic because voice transmissions are relatively short and require very little bandwidth (because of voice compression).

The Frame Relay Forum has issued an implementation agreement regarding Voice over Frame Relay. You can read the implementation agreement (FRF.11.1) or downloaded it at `www.frforum.com/5000/5000index.html`.

3 Can a Frame Relay site "talk" to an ATM site?

Yes. Frame Relay to ATM Service Interworking (FRASI) virtual circuits are available by most network service providers. The Frame Relay Forum has issued several implementation agreements regarding FRASI: FRF.5, FRF.8.1, and FRF.18. You can read and download these implementation agreements at `www.frforum.com/5000/5000index.html`.

Case Study

ReitCo is an organization with three offices: New York, Seattle, and Los Angeles, (see Figure 10-9). The majority of the company's employees are in the New York and Seattle offices, with the Los Angeles office hosting ReitCo's database and web servers. In an effort to cut their long distance costs between the Seattle and New York offices, ReitCo deployed VoFr cards on their Frame Relay access routers. The additional bandwidth necessary to carry the voice traffic is still significantly lower than the long distance charges, based on comparing the cost-per-Megabits (Frame Relay) usage and cost-per-minute (long distance).

ReitCo deployed Cisco 3640s at all three locations to support the data and voice requirements. Frame Relay Wan Interface Cards (WICs), VoFr WICs, and 10/100-Mbps Ethernet LAN cards were deployed for the Seattle and New York locations. The Los Angeles location deployed their Cisco 3640 with the Frame Relay WIC and 16-Mbps Token Ring LAN card.

Figure 10-9 *ReitCo Case Study*

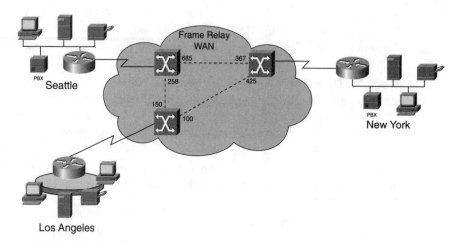

ReitCo/Seattle is using the following DLCIs in their router:

- DLCI 685 → New York
- DLCI 258 → Los Angeles

ReitCo/New York is using the following DLCIs in their router:

- DLCI 367 → Seattle
- DLCI 425 → Los Angeles

ReitCo Los Angeles is using the following DLCIs in their router:

- DCLI 150 → Seattle
- DLCI 100 → New York

For example, if data is to be sent across the Frame Relay WAN from Los Angeles to New York, the router identifies this traffic to the network service provider by using DLCI 100 in the header of the Frame Relay message. The New York router sees the traffic arriving from DLCI 425 because "425" is the DLCI New York has identified with Los Angeles.

This chapter covers the following topics:

- Routing Components
- Routing Algorithms
- Network Protocols

CHAPTER 11

Understanding Routers and Routing

Routing is the process of moving information across an internetwork from source to destination. *Routers* are network devices using routing protocols to make decisions regarding where to send network traffic. Routing differs from bridging in the way in which the path determination is made. Although routing and bridging both move traffic across a network, bridging occurs at the data-link layer (OSI Layer 2), whereas routing occurs at the network layer (OSI Layer 3).

Routing Components

Routing involves two functions: determining the best routing path, and transporting data traffic in the form of packets across the best path through an internetwork. The routing process also is referred to as *packet switching*. Even though packet switching is straightforward, determining the path for the traffic to take to its intended destination can be complex.

Path Determination

Routing protocols use metrics to measure and determine which path is the best for a packet to travel through an internetwork. Metrics are standards of measurement, such as path bandwidth, used by routing algorithms to determine the best path to a destination network or host. To determine the best path to a destination host/network, routing algorithms build and maintain routing tables which contain route information for each available path. The information in these routing tables varies depending on which routing algorithm is used.

Destination/next hop associations tell a router that a particular destination can be reached by sending the packet to a particular router, representing the "next hop" on the way to the final destination. When a router receives an incoming packet, it checks the destination address against its routing tables and associates this address with a next hop if available.

If there is no next hop available in the routing table, the router sends the packets to the default gateway. The default gateway is considered the path of last resort in that if the router doesn't know what to do with a packet it forwards it out the default gateway interface to the associated attached network. Not all default gateways are pointed to an attached network; there are instances where the default gateway represents what is called a "bit bucket," or null interface. The null interface is a logical interface where the packet is sent and subsequently dropped from the router.

Routing tables can contain other information, such as data about path desirability. Routers compare the metrics of each path in its routing table to determine optimal routes. These metrics differ depending on the design of the routing algorithm used. Metrics are discussed in the "Routing Metrics" section of this chapter.

Routers communicate with one another and maintain their routing tables through the exchange of *routing update messages*. The routing update message consists of all, or a portion, of a routing table. By analyzing routing updates from other routers in the network, a router can build a detailed picture of the network topology. *Link-state advertisements (LSAs)* are another example of routing update messages exchanged between routers. LSAs inform other routers in the network of the state of connected network links. This link information is used to build a complete picture of network topology, enabling routers to determine the best path to a network destination.

In most cases, a router determines that it must send a packet to another router in the network so the packet can reach its intended destination. The next router in the packet's path is known as the *downstream neighbor*, or the next hop router. The router knows the physical (MAC) address of this next hop router, (learned through other means), and forwards the packet to this next hop router with both the physical (MAC) and logical (network) addresses.

As the router examines the packet's destination network address, the router determines that it either does, or does not, know how to forward the packet to the next hop. If the router knows how to forward the packet, it changes the packet's destination physical (MAC) address to that of the next hop and sends the packet. If the router does not know how to forward the packet, it is often configured to drop the packet.

The next hop might be the ultimate destination; if not, the next hop is often another router in the network, which in turn executes the same routing decision process. As the packet moves through the internetwork, its physical (MAC) address changes, but its logical (network) address remains constant.

The International Organization for Standardization (ISO) developed a hierarchical terminology useful in describing the process of forwarded packets between source and destination. The ISO hierarchical terminology is as follows:

- **End systems (ES)**—Network devices without the ability to forward packets between sub-networks.

- **Intermediate systems (IS)**—Network devices with the ability to forward packets between subnetworks are called *intermediate systems (ISs)*. ISs are further divided into those that can communicate within routing domains (*intradomain ISs*) and those that communicate both within and between routing domains (*interdomain ISs*).

- **Autonomous systems (AS)**—Routing domains under common administrative authority regulated by a particular set of administrative guidelines. Routing domains can be divided into areas, but intradomain routing protocols are used for routing within and between these areas.

Routing Algorithms

Routing algorithms are differentiated based on several key characteristics. These are as follows:

- The particular goals of the routing algorithm design affect the operation of the resulting routing protocol.
- Various types of routing algorithms exist with each algorithm having a different impact on network and router resources.
- Routing algorithms use a variety of metrics affecting route calculation.

The following sections discuss these routing algorithm attributes.

Design Goals

Routing algorithms have one or more of the following design goals:

- **Optimality**—Refers to the ability of the routing algorithm to select the best route, depending on the metrics and metric weightings used to make the calculation. For example, a routing algorithm might use a number of hops and network delay, but the algorithm might put more weight on the delay variable than the hop count in the path calculation.
- **Simplicity and low overhead**—The routing algorithm must offer its functionality with a minimum of software and utilization (CPU) overhead. Efficiency is important when the software implementing the routing algorithm runs on a computer with limited physical resources, such as memory (RAM).
- **Robustness and stability**—Means the routing protocol should perform in the face of changing network conditions, such as hardware failures, high load conditions, or network outage. Because routers are located at network junction points and provide the internetwork connection, the router can cause considerable issues if there is a failure. The best routing algorithms are those that are stable under a variety of network conditions and topologies.
- **Rapid convergence**—Convergence is the process of agreement, by all routers, on optimal routes within an internetwork. When a network event causes routes to fail or become available, routers distribute routing update messages, propagating through all

attached networks, causing each internetwork router to recalculate optimal routes, in turn causing all routers to agree on these new routes. Routing algorithms converging slowly can cause routing loops or network outages.

- **Flexibility**—The routing algorithm quickly and accurately adapts to changes in a network environment. If a network segment fails, many routing algorithms learn of the problem and will select the next-best path for all routes otherwise using the failed segment. Routing algorithms can be programmed to adapt to changes in network bandwidth, router queue size, and network delay.

Figure 11-1 illustrates the construction of a routing loop.

Figure 11-1 *Construction of a Routing Loop*

The following steps show you how a routing loop forms:

1 A packet arrives at Router 1.

2 Router 1 has already been updated and knows that the best (optimal) route to the destination (Network B) calls for Router 2 to be the next hop.

3 Router 1 forwards the packet to Router 2, but because Router 2 has not yet been updated to reflect a link failure to the destination (Router 3 attached to Network B), Router 2 believes that the best next hop is Router 1 because Router 1 is advertising a path to Router 3, albeit through Router 2.

4 Router 2 forwards the packet back to Router 1, and the packet continues to bounce back and forth between the two routers until Router 2 receives its routing update or until the packet has exceeded the maximum number of hops allowed (often a destination is considered unreachable at 16 hops).

Algorithm Types

Routing algorithms are classified by type with the following key differentiators:

- Static versus dynamic
- Single-path versus multipath
- Flat versus hierarchical
- Host-intelligent versus router-intelligent

- Intradomain versus interdomain
- Link-state versus distance vector

Each of these is discussed in the following sections.

Static Versus Dynamic

Static routing algorithms are table mappings (routes to destination networks) established by the network administrator before the beginning of routing. These mappings do not change without manual intervention, such as by a network administrator. Algorithms using static routes work well in environments where network traffic is predictable and where network design is simple.

Because static routing algorithms cannot react to network changes, static routing algorithms are considered unsuitable for large changing networks. Most of the routing algorithms used are *dynamic routing algorithms*, which adjust to changing network conditions by analyzing and evaluating routing update messages. If the update message indicates a network change, the routing software recalculates routes and sends out new routing update messages to attached routers. These messages propagate throughout the network, causing attached routers to rerun their algorithms and change their routing tables as deemed necessary.

Single-Path Versus Multipath

A single path is the only path that can be used to reach a destination network. However, a single path is not necessarily a static route because the best route to that network can change based on changes in the network.

Some routing protocols enable multiple paths to the same destination and are often used in load-sharing environments. Unlike single-path algorithms, multipath algorithms permit load-sharing over multiple links to the same destination.

Flat Versus Hierarchical

Some routing algorithms operate in a flat space, while others use routing hierarchies. These are described as follows:

- **Flat routing system**—The routers are peers (equal) of all others.
- **Hierarchical routing system**—Some routers are logically grouped to form a routing backbone.

Packets from nonbackbone routers travel to the backbone routers, where these packets are sent through the network backbone until they reach the destination network. Upon arrival at the destination network, these packets travel from the last backbone router throughout one or more nonbackbone routers to the final destination subnetwork or host.

Routing systems often designate logical groups of nodes, called *domains*, *autonomous systems*, or *areas*. In hierarchical systems, some routers in a domain can communicate with routers in other domains, while others can communicate only with routers within their own domain. In very large networks, additional hierarchical levels can exist, with routers at the highest hierarchical level forming the routing backbone, as illustrated in Figure 11-2.

Figure 11-2 *Hierarchical Networks*

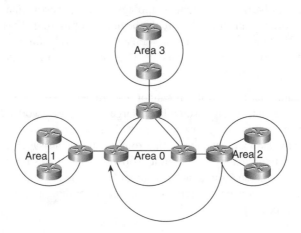

In this figure, routers in Area 1, Area 2 and Area 3 can communicate directly with other routers within the same area. If a router in Area 2 needs to communicate with a router in Area 3, then all traffic exchanged between the two routers must go through the network backbone area—in this case, Area 0.

An advantage of hierarchical routing over flat routing is that hierarchical routing can mimic the organization of most enterprises, providing a method to manage traffic patterns within the network. Most network communication occurs within small enterprise organizations (domains). Because intradomain routers need to know only about other routers within their domain, these intradomain routing algorithms can be simplified and routing update traffic between intra- and interdomain routers can be reduced.

Host-Intelligent Versus Router-Intelligent

Some routing algorithms presume that the source host will determine the entire route; this is referred to as *source routing*. These are host-intelligent algorithms. In source-routing systems, routers act as store-and-forward devices, sending the packet to the next hop without examining the contents of the packet header. In this case, the hosts have the routing intelligence.

Router-intelligent algorithms presume that hosts know nothing about routes and the routers determine the path through the internetwork based on their own calculations. In this case, the routers have the routing intelligence.

Intradomain Versus Interdomain

Some routing algorithms work only within domains. These are called *intradomain algorithms*. Other routing algorithms, called *interdomain algorithms*, work within and between domains. The nature of these two algorithm types is different in that the best intradomain-routing algorithm is not necessarily the best interdomain-routing algorithm.

Link-State versus Distance Vector

Link-state algorithms, also known as *shortest path first* (SPF) algorithms, flood routing information to all routers in the internetwork. Each router sends only the portion of the routing table that describes the state of its own links. Routers running link-state algorithms build a picture of the entire network in their routing tables.

Distance vector algorithms, also known as Bellman-Ford algorithms, require each router to send all or some portion of its routing table only to its neighbors, not to all routers in the internetwork.

Link-state algorithms send small updates everywhere in the internetwork, while distance vector algorithms send larger updates only to neighboring routers. Distance vector algorithms know only about their neighbors.

Because link-state algorithms converge quicker than distance-vector algorithms, link-state algorithms often are less prone to routing loops than their distance vector algorithm counterparts. Link-state algorithms require more router CPU power and memory than distance vector algorithms, however, making link-state algorithms potentially more expensive to implement and support. The trade-off here is that link-state protocols (based on link-state algorithms) are more scalable than distance vector protocols.

Technical Note: Distance Vector Routing Protocols

The following routing protocols are classified as distance-vector routing protocols:

- Routing Information Protocol/RIPv2 (RIP / RIPv2)
- Interior Gateway Routing Protocol (IGRP)
- Enhanced Interior Gateway Routing Protocol (EIGRP)

The following routing protocol is classified as a link-state routing protocol:

- Open Shortest Path First (OSPF)

The following routing protocols are classified as hybrid routing protocols:

- Border Gateway Protocol (BGP)

- EIGRP—EIGRP is a Distance-Vector/Link-State Hybrid

Routing Metrics

Routing tables contain information used by routers to select the best route to a destination network/host. Routing tables are built by the routing algorithms (protocols) in use by the router. Routing algorithms can base route selection on a single metric, such as hop count, or on multiple metrics, combining them in a single (hybrid) metric.

The following list identifies metrics used by routing protocols in making path determinations; however, not all of these metrics are used by every routing protocol:

- **Path length**—The most common routing metric. Some routing protocols allow network administrators to assign arbitrary costs to each network link. In this case, path length is the sum of the costs associated with each link traversed. Other routing protocols define hop count, a metric specifying the number of passes through network routers that a packet must take from source to destination.

- **Reliability**—Refers to the dependability, often described in terms of bit-error rate (BER), of each network link. After a network failure, certain network links might be repaired quicker than other links, for whatever reason. Any reliability factor can be taken into account in the assignment of a reliability rating. Reliability is an arbitrary numeric value often assigned to network links by network administrators.

- **Delay**—Refers to the length of time required to move a packet from source to destination through the internetwork. Delay depends on many factors:

  — Bandwidth of intermediate network links

  — Port queues at each router along the way

  — Network congestion on all intermediate network links

  — Physical distance to be traveled

  Because delay is a collection of several variables, it is a common and useful metric.

- **Bandwidth**—Refers to the available traffic capacity of a network link. All other things being equal, a 10 Mbps Ethernet link is preferable to a 64 kbps leased line. Although bandwidth is a rating of maximum attainable link throughput, routes through links with greater bandwidth do not always provide better routes than routes through slower links. For example, if a faster link is busier, the actual time required to send a packet to the destination could be greater.

- **Load**—Refers to the degree to which a network resource, such as a router, is busy. Load can be calculated in a variety of ways, such as CPU utilization or packets processed per second. Monitoring router resources on a continual basis can be resource-intensive in itself. Because of this Cisco does not recommend using the router IOS *debug* command unnecessarily.

- **Communication cost**—It's important to acknowledge communication cost because some organizations are concerned about performance as much as they are concerned about operating expenditures. Although line delay might be longer, organizations might send packets over their own lines rather than through the public lines that cost money for usage time. An example would be a network deployment where a 56K Frame Relay link might be more cost-effective to deploy to a small office/home office (SOHO) environment than several dial-up links.

NOTE   When multiple routing protocols are used, the administrative distance determines the primary route used by the router. *Administrative distance* is the value used to reflect the desirability of a learned path to a neighbor router. The lower the administrative distance, the better the path, because the route is considered to be more believable.

You can think of each of these routing metrics as an aspect of taking a family road trip. There are several factors you need to weigh in a certain order to get from Point A (home) to Point B (vacation spot).

- The first metric is path length, or in this case, the number of highway junctions and/or stop lights encountered during the trip.

- There is the question of reliability of each of the available roads; perhaps one of the roads tends to flood during heavy rain or the like.

- Delay is another metric you need to consider. Are any of the considered roads to the destination experiencing delays, such as those caused by traffic accidents or construction?

- Link bandwidth is comparable to the number of lanes available on each road; it is fair to say that a four-lane highway can carry more vehicular traffic than a two-lane highway.

- What is the traffic load on each road being considered? The four-lane highway might be able to accommodate more vehicles, but the consideration here is the number of vehicles on that road when the family vehicle is using the same highway.

- Then there is the cost of each road; perhaps the two-lane highway is not as congested, but you can weigh the number of tolls to be paid against the additional time the trip would take over another road that had no tolls but more vehicles.

Routing protocols, like the vacation driver, can weigh certain metrics over others. For example, the driver might opt to take the four-lane highway, disregarding the number of other cars using the same road, and possibly congesting the route. Some routing protocols might put an additional weight on the bandwidth metric, discounting the delay metric in the total metric calculation.

NOTE   The network administrator has the ability to change manually the metric valuables in whatever routing protocol is used, although letting the routing protocol use its default options is recommend.

Network Protocols

Routed protocols are transported by routing protocols across an internetwork. These routed, or network, protocols perform functions required for communication between user applications in source and destination hosts, and these functions can differ among protocol suites. Network protocols occur at the upper five layers of the OSI reference model: the network layer (3), the transport layer (4), the session layer (5), the presentation layer (6), and the application layer (7).

Routed protocols and routing protocols are two different types of protocols, as detailed in the following list:

- *Routed protocols* are protocols that are routed over an internetwork. Examples of such protocols are as follows:
    - Internet Protocol (IP)
    - DECnet
    - AppleTalk
    - Novell NetWare
    - OSI (Open Systems Interconnection), not to be confused with the OSI Reference Model
    - Banyan VINES
    - Xerox Network System (XNS)
- *Routing protocols* are protocols implementing routing algorithms. They are used by intermediate systems to build routing tables used in path selection of routed protocols. Here are some examples of these protocols:
    - IGRP, Cisco Proprietary
    - EIGRP, Cisco Proprietary
    - OSPF

— EGP

— BGP

— Intermediate System-to-Intermediate System (IS-IS)

— Routing Information Protocol (RIP)

Summary

Routing is the process of moving information across an internetwork from source to destination. Routers are network devices using routing protocols to make decisions regarding how to forward traffic across an internetwork.

Routing involves two functions: determining the best routing path and transporting data traffic in the form of packets across the best path through an internetwork. Routing protocols use metrics to measure and determine which path is the best for a packet to travel through an internetwork. Metrics are standards of measurement, such as path bandwidth, used by routing algorithms to determine the best path to a destination network or host.

Routing algorithms are classified by type, as listed here:

- Static versus dynamic
- Single-path versus multipath
- Flat versus hierarchical
- Host-intelligent versus router-intelligent
- Intradomain versus interdomain
- Link-state versus distance vector

There is no right or wrong routing protocol to use when implementing a routed network. Certain routing protocols are more beneficial in certain network implementations; for example, RIP would serve a small network well, whereas a larger network might benefit from OSPF or EIGRP.

The network designer/administrator must take several factors into account when deciding which routing protocol to use, such as the protocol convergence rate in recovering from a disaster scenario like a network link failure.

Frequently Asked Questions (FAQ)

1 If a router is running multiple routing protocols, how does it know which one to use?

The administrative distance is used to determine the preferred route. The following table lists the administrative distance values for each routing protocol. These are automatically calculated values and can be manually changed in the router configurations.

Table 11-1 *Routing Protocol Administrative Distance Values*

Protocols	Distance Value
Connected Interface	0
Static routes	1
EIGRP Summary routes	5
EBGP	20
Internal EIGRP	90
IGRP	100
OSPF	110
IS-IS	115
RIP	120
EGP	140
External EIGRP	170
Internal BGP	200
Unknown	255

2 What is route redistribution?

Redistribution is the process by which routes learned through one routing protocol are distributed into another routing protocol.

Figure 11-3 illustrates two networks with the following routing protocols:

- A,B,C – EIGRP
- A,E,D – OSPF

Router A is configured to redistribute EIGRP routes into the OSPF cloud so that Routers D and E have visibility into the EIGRP cloud and can connect with Routers B and C. Router A also is configured to redistribute OSPF routes into the EIGRP cloud so that Routers B and C can connect with Routers D and E.

Figure 11-3 *Routing Protocol Redistribution*

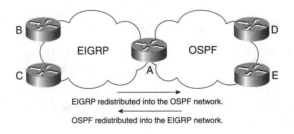

EIGRP redistributed into the OSPF network.

OSPF redistributed into the EIGRP network.

3 Can a router run multiple routing protocols at the same time?

Yes. A router operating as a network-to-network interface (NNI), connecting two (or more) networks, can run a separate routing protocol for each network.

Another scenario in which a router can run multiple routing protocols simultaneously would be in support of a migration from one routing protocol to another. For example, suppose that a network initially implemented a distance vector protocol (such as RIP), and as the network has grown, the decision was made that a link-state protocol (such as OSPF) would better suit the internetwork environment. In order to minimize user disruption during this routing protocol migration, the network administrator can enable both routing protocols on each router in the internetwork until the migration is complete. When the migration is complete, the "old" protocol (no longer being used) can be removed from the router, freeing up router resources for the "new" protocol.

Case Study

The following case study illustrates the point that there is no right or wrong choice to use when deciding which routing protocol to use as each has its own advantages and disadvantages. It is up to the network administrator to make the determination based on the best information available at the time.

Figure 11-4 illustrates a five-node, fully-meshed, wide area network (WAN).

Figure 11-4 *Routing (Full-Mesh) Topology*

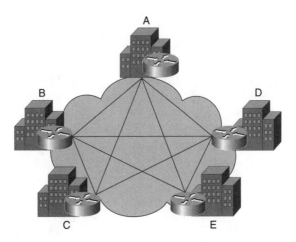

The network administrator can elect one of two routing protocol types to use here: distance vector or link-state.

A distance vector protocol is a viable option because the network is small enough that the routes are manageable with this protocol in that the hop count does not exceed 15 hops (a destination network is considered unreachable at 16 hops). If one or more links were to fail, the amount of time it would take each WAN router to converge on the new network can result in significant delay and dropped sessions. Network stability/reliability can be used to determine whether distance vector should be used in this network.

A link-state protocol is a viable option if the network administrator questions network stability/reliability. If the network administrator feels that stability/reliability is an issue, the convergence time of link-state protocols would better serve the users in that the likelihood of significant delay and dropped sessions is reduced.

This chapter covers the following topics:

- VLAN Memberships
- VLAN/WAN Integration

CHAPTER 12

Virtual LAN (VLAN) Introduction

VLANs create logically separate LANs on the same physical switch. VLANs also can be used to group physically separate LANs so they behave as though they are on the same physical network segment (wire). Each switch port switch is assigned to a VLAN and in the case of the Cisco Catalyst, VLAN operation is performed at Layer-2 (OSI Model Data-Link Layer), requiring a Layer-3 (Network) device (such as a router, to move traffic between VLANs). You configure VLANs through software rather than hardware, which make VLANs flexible in their implementation. The biggest advantage of a VLAN is that when you move a workstation to another location, it can stay on the same VLAN without any hardware reconfiguration. VLANs are used in both EtherNet and Token Ring LAN configurations.

NOTE

VLANs support Ethernet, Token Ring, and FDDI LAN implementations.

Figure 12-1 illustrates a VLAN implementation, with two VLANS: VLAN 100 and VLAN 200.

The LAN switch is the core component of the VLAN—for example, Cisco Catalyst 2900/3500/6500 Series switches. The following list details the significant benefits of using VLANs over traditional LAN implementations (for example, shared media):

- **Reduction in the cost of handling user moves and changes**—Any node can be moved or added quickly and conveniently from the network management console rather than the wiring closet. VLANs provide a flexible, easy, and less costly way to modify logical groups in changing environments.

- **Forming "virtual workgroups"**—VLANs provide independence from the physical network topology by enabling physically diverse workgroups to be connected logically within a single broadcast domain. If an organization expands or relocates, it is more efficient to add ports in new locations to existing VLANs.

- **VLANs can increase network performance**—By reducing the number of collision (Ethernet) domains, VLANs increase performance. Forming logical networks improves network performance by limiting broadcast traffic to users within defined workgroups.

- **VLANs can enhance network security**—In a switched network, frames are delivered only to the intended recipients and broadcast frames only to other members of the VLAN. This containment enables network managers to segment users who require access to sensitive information into VLANs separate from the general user community.

Figure 12-1 *VLAN Implementation with Two VLANS (100 and 200)*

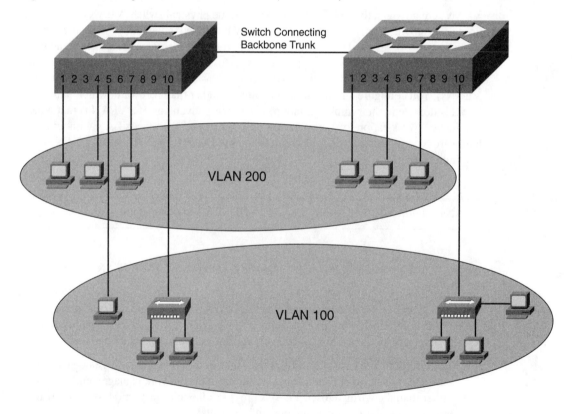

Another VLAN application is web-hosting centers. Hosting center customers sometimes prefer to avoid accessing their servers in these hosting centers across the public Internet because of security concerns. VPNs give you one way to address these concerns, and VLANs provide another, depending upon the customer's bandwidth requirements for file transfer in and out of the data center. A WAN component is required in the VLAN method, such as Frame Relay or ATM. Frame Relay is discussed in more detail in Chapter 10, "Frame Relay Introduction," and ATM is discussed in more detail in Chapter 9, "Asynchronous Transfer Mode (ATM) Introduction."

Data centers can reduce their investments by using VLANs to create a separate dedicated LAN to each customer's server with the same physical LAN infrastructure. Because each VLAN uses its own IP subnet, the customer's private address spaces also can be preserved.

VLAN Memberships

VLAN members can communicate with other members only on the same VLAN; for example, a member from VLAN 100 cannot communicate with a member from VLAN 200. Inter-VLAN communication is possible only with the addition of routing functionality, either with a route-switching module (RSM) in the VLAN switch, or a router external to the VLAN switch.

NOTE   The RSM provides Layer-3 switching at more than one million packets per second (pps) between switched VLANs.

VLAN members are assigned one of three ways, depending upon the VLAN implementation. These are:

- **Port based VLAN**—The systems manager (or administrator) assigns each port of a switch to a VLAN. For example, ports 6 through 10 might be assigned to the R&D VLAN, ports 1 through 4 to the Marketing VLAN, and ports 4 through 6 to the Sales VLAN. The main drawback of VLANs defined by port is that the systems manager must reconfigure VLAN membership when a user moves from one port to another.

- **MAC address-based VLANs**—Membership is defined by the source or destination MAC (hardware address). The advantage of this model is that you do not need to reconfigure the VLAN switch when a user makes a move to a different port. The issue with MAC address-based VLANs is that a single MAC address cannot be a member of multiple VLANs without extensive effort and configuration.

- **Layer-3 VLANs**—Based on Layer-3 (OSI Model Network Layer) information, take into account the protocol type (IP, NetBIOS) and the Layer-3 addresses when you are determining VLAN membership. One of the benefits of this method is that users can move their workstation without having to reconfigure their network addresses. The issue with Layer-3 VLANs is that Layer-3 gives you slow performance.

VLAN/WAN Integration

You can add WAN routers to a VLAN, providing VLAN connectivity across a Frame Relay WAN (or the like), as illustrated in Figure 12-2.

Figure 12-2 *VLANs Across a WAN*

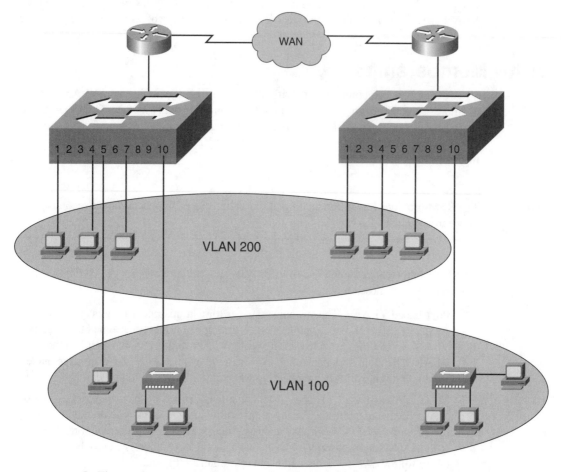

In Figure 12-2, two geographically diverse sites share resources across a Frame Relay WAN. Workstations within the same VLAN can communicate with each other across the WAN via the Frame Relay routers attached to each VLAN switch.

Summary

This chapter discussed how to use VLANs to create logically separate LANs on the same physical switch. VLANs also are used to group physically separate LANs so that they behave as though they are on the same physical network segment (wire). Each switch port switch is assigned to a VLAN. For the Cisco Catalyst, VLAN operation is performed at Layer-2 (OSI Model Data-Link Layer), requiring a Layer-3 (Network) device, such as a router, to move traffic between VLANs.

These are the benefits of using VLANs over traditional LAN implementations. These include the formation of virtual workgroups, reduced cost of handling user moves and changes, increased performance, and enhanced security.

Port-based VLANs, MAC address-based VLANs, and Layer-3 VLANs are used to establish membership to a VLAN. For port-based VLANs, the administrator assigns each port of a switch to a VLAN; for MAC address-based VLANs, the source or desination MAC (hardware address) defined the membership; and finally, for Layer-3 VLANs, the membership is based on the Layer-3 (Network) address of the host.

Frequently Asked Questions (FAQ)

1 Are VLANs standardized?

Yes, with the caveat that the switch vendors do deploy proprietary implementations. Before VLANs were standardized by the IEEE, each vendor developed its own unique and proprietary VLAN solution and product. Switches from one vendor, implementing the vendor's proprietary solution, will not necessarily interoperate with VLANs from other vendors.

However, the IEEE has defined the 802.1q standard for VLAN implementations to ensure the interoperability of VLAN implementations between switches and NICs from different vendors. A second IEEE specification, 802.1p, defines the use of priority bits, which are part of the explicit VLAN tag as defined in 802.1q. Two different VLAN models are specified in the 802.1q specification: the shared model and the independent model.

Geographically diverse sites can share VLAN resources across a WAN. Workstations within the same VLAN can communicate with each other across the WAN through the network (edge) routers attached to each VLAN switch.

Case Study

Figure 12-3 illustrates an organization called ELBCo that uses three VLANS: 101, 102, and 204. ELBCo has three departments within a single building: Sales, Research and Development (R&D), and IS/IT Support. Each department is assigned a VLAN as follows:

Department	VLAN
Sales	102
R&D	204
IS/IT Support	101

Figure 12-3 *The ELBCo VLAN*

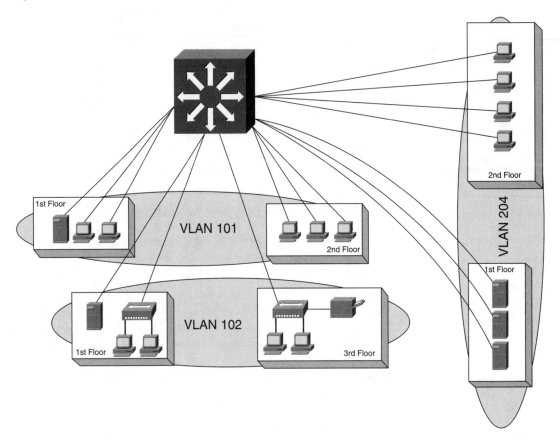

As shown here, resources for each of these departments are spread across three floors of a building. With the implementation of a VLAN, physical location is not an issue for the users requiring access to resources. For example, the R&D users can sit at their desks on the second floor and access their server farm on the first floor without contending with other users on the LAN for bandwidth. Likewise, the Sales and IS/IT departments do not need to be concerned about the high-bandwidth network applications the R&D department is using interfering with their network usage.

In the ELBCo VLAN implementation, the VLAN provides for both an efficient use of network resources and physical workspace.

This chapter covers the following topics.

- ATM
- Frame Relay
- Internet Protocol
- MPLS and MPLS-TE
- DiffServ

CHAPTER 13

Quality of Service Introduction

Quality of service (QoS) refers to the capability of a network to provide better service to selected network traffic over various networking technologies. Network service providers (NSPs) implement QoS in customer wide-area networking (WAN) technologies, such as Asynchronous Transfer Mode (ATM), Frame Relay, IP/IP-VPN (IP-based Virtual Private Networks), and MPLS, which can use any of these underlying technologies. The primary goal of QoS is to provide priority to customer traffic across a network by dedicating bandwidth, controlling jitter and latency (required by some real-time and interactive traffic), and improving loss characteristics.

The abbreviations *QoS* and *CoS* (class of service) often are used interchangeably in discussions about transport technologies. These terms are different, however, as the following definitions show:

- **QoS**—A measure that is inviolable. It is absolute in that when QoS is implemented in a network, the service provider guarantees that they will deliver measurable performance characteristics as defined by the QoS statements in the service level agreement (SLA) between the provider and the customer.

- **CoS**—A relative measure defined by the NSP and is unrelated to quality measurements. For example, a service provider could advertise the following transmission Classes of Service:

    — Great

    — Good

    — Fair

    — Poor

    — Carrier pigeon

Technical Note: Analyzing Network Traffic Patterns

In determining which applications require QoS, the first step is to establish which applications are mission-critical. Netflow Accounting, Network-based Application Recognition (NBAR), or QoS Device Manager (QDM) can be used to analyze the network traffic patterns, as you see here:

- NetFlow Accounting provides network traffic detail and can be used to capture traffic classification or precedence associated with each flow.

- NBAR is a classification tool that can identify traffic up to the application layer, providing per-interface, per-protocol, and bi-directional statistics for each traffic flow traversing an interface.

- QDM is a Web-based network management application that provides a graphical user interface (GUI) for configuring and monitoring advanced IP-based QoS functionality in routers.

This chapter discusses QoS networking technologies found in ATM, Frame Relay, IP, and MPLS.

ATM

One of the biggest advantages of ATM over other LAN/WAN technologies, such as Frame Relay or Fast Ethernet, is that ATM supports QoS levels, enabling ATM service providers to guarantee to their customers some sort of end-to-end latency. The ATM Forum has defined four ATM Layer service classes, each with scalable QoS levels:

- **Class A, defined as constant bit rate (CBR)**—Traffic is characterized by a continuous stream of bits at a steady rate, such as Time Division Multiplexer (TDM) traffic. Class A traffic is low-bandwidth traffic that is sensitive to delay and intolerant to cell loss.

- **Class B and C, defined as variable bit rate (VBR)**—Traffic has a bursty nature and can be characterized by voice or video applications using compression.

  — Class B traffic is real-time VBR (RT-VBR), in which end-to-end delay is critical (for example, interactive video conferencing).

  — Class C is not real time (VBR-NRT) traffic and delay is not as critical (video playback, training tapes, and video mail messages are examples).

- **Class D, defined as available bit rate (ABR) and unspecified bit rate (UBR)—** Classes are for bursty LAN traffic and data that is more tolerant of delays and cell loss.

  — UBR is a "best-effort" service that does not specify bit rate or traffic parameters and has no QoS guarantees. Originally devised as a way to make use of excess bandwidth, UBR is subject to increased cell loss and the discard of whole packets.

  — ABR, like UBR, is also a best-effort service, but differs in that it is a managed service based on minimum cell rate (MCR) and with a low cell loss. No delay variation guarantee is currently envisioned for either UBR or ABR service classes, making this service unsuitable for voice or video applications.

Frame Relay

Frame Relay supports QoS only through a preset committed information rate (CIR) that allows packets to be designated as either "committed" or "excess." Frame Relay QoS often is found supporting Voice applications; for example, Voice over Frame Relay (VoFr). QoS is achieved within a Frame Relay network by artificially creating a fixed data stream. Frame Relay is designed for bursty data traffic, with the length of Frame Relay frames varying up to 4095 bytes (4 KB). VoFr applications truncate this variable-length frame to a fixed size; for example, 2 KB, providing the ability for sending and receiving equipment to clock the signal at regular intervals.

NOTE   Clocking enables the sending and receiving devices to synchronize with each other, ensuring a smooth transition state from idle to active and vice versa. In a VoFr application, clocking provides a "smoothing" of the signal so that voice conversations aren't clipped. (*Clipping* in voice conversations results in words being cut off or conversations sounding choppy; that is, with a lot of starting and stopping.)

VoFr often is used within converged enterprise networks; for the most part, VoFr is used for point-to-point virtual tie lines within an organization. VoFr traffic is marked as CIR, assuring no throughput delays affect voice signal quality. FRF.13 (*Frame Relay Forum Implementation Agreement #13—Service Level Definitions Implementation Agreement—August 1998*) specifies the range of QoS parameters and SLAs that can be measured. FRF.13 also details how delay, frame delivery, data delivery and service availability should be calculated.

NOTE	A converged network is one supporting multiple and diverse applications across a single backbone with the same technology, such as a network carrying voice and data with a single protocol; for example, IP or Frame Relay.

IP

Internet Protocol (IP) is based on the notion that datagrams with source and destination IP addresses can traverse a network of (IP) routers without the help of the sender or receiver. The Internet was built on this concept of a dumb network, with the intelligence provided by the sender and receiver.

IP provides a best-effort service; making no guarantees about when and how data arrives at the destination. IP provides the following features:

- **Network addressing**—Enables independent handling of each IP datagram across the network.

- **Datagram fragmentation and reassembly (by the sending and receiving routers)**—Enables carrying of traffic across different network media, such as Ethernet and Token Ring, each supporting different datagram sizes.

Being a best-effort protocol, IP does not provide reliable data delivery. Routers can discard IP datagrams in transit without notifying sender or receiver. IP relies on upper-level protocols, such as Transmission Control Protocol (TCP), to track datagrams and retransmit as required. These "reliability" mechanisms can assure only the delivery—not the timeliness—of data delivery and do not provide any throughput guarantees.

This issue of "data delivery without guarantee" is not a problem for traditional Internet applications such as Web browsing, e-mail, or file transfer. New applications, such as streaming video and audio, demand high throughput capacity in the form of bandwidth requirements and have low-latency demands when used in two-way communications, such as conferencing and telephony.

Three solutions to the "data delivery without guarantee" issue have yielded the following proposed methodologies:

- **Differentiated QoS**—IETF standards (RFC 2474, 2475) define a differentiated services (DiffServ) field for IPv4 and IPv6 headers. This DiffServ field provides classes of service that can be assigned to specific types of voice, video, or data applications.

- **Resource Reservation Protocol (RSVP)**—IETF standard (RFC 2205) provides for guaranteed, on-time delivery of data over an IP network. RSVP works in cooperation with the DiffServ standard by reserving bandwidth in response to client requests.

- **IEEE 802.1p**—Defines frame format extensions for Ethernet, Token Ring, FDDI, and other data-link layer protocols. This frame format extension carries extra bits used to specify the priority of the packet; priority ranges from 0 (lowest) to 7 (highest).

MPLS and MPLS-TE

Multiprotocol Label Switching (MPLS) is a specification for Layer 3 switching from the IETF. Similar to Cisco's tag switching, MPLS uses labels, or tags, containing forwarding information. These labels are attached to IP packets by the router sitting at the edge of the network and are known as *label edge routers* (LERs). The routers in the core of the network are known as *label switch routers* (LSRs) and examine the label more quickly than looking up destination addresses in a routing table, which provides for greater network efficiency.

NOTE	MPLS also is an acronym for Multiprotocol Lambda Switching. In an optical networking system, MPLS is the ability to route a data transmission based on the wavelength of light that carries it. The routing device analyzes only wavelengths (light frequencies) to make its forwarding decision rather than inspecting fields within each packet. The correct spelling of this term is with the Greek "L" for Lambda.

MPLS-Traffic Engineering (TE) increases network utilization by creating a uniform distribution of traffic throughout the network, avoiding congestion on any one path. Traffic engineering does not automatically select the shortest path between two devices; for two-packet data flows, it is possible these packets can take different paths through the network, even if these packets share the same originating and destination sites. This distribution method can use the less-exposed or less-used network resources, enabling the support of differentiated services across the network.

MPLS-TE does not, in itself, provide for QoS to applications. MPLS-TE provides a means to transport this QoS traffic by using traffic engineering to set up paths between originating and destination nodes, in turn meeting service level guarantees (SLGs).

DiffServ

Differentiated Services (DiffServ) is an Internet Engineering Task Force (IETF) method, defined in RFC 2475, for adding a QoS aspect to IP networks. DiffServ works only at Layer 3 (Network layer) of the OSI Reference Model, using per-hop behavior (PHB). The PHB is specified in the DiffServ code point (DSCP), found in the IP type of service (TOS) field in the IPv4 header as the DiffServ byte (DS byte), and the Traffic Class byte in the IPv6 header.

NOTE	It is expected that network service providers will use MPLS within the network backbone and use DiffServ at the network edge for QoS classification and path assignment.

DiffServ is a best-effort service and is currently supported only in IP networks. Where traditional IP networks can be likened to bulk mail in the post office—no single item is given preferential treatment or handling over another—DiffServ provides for classification of the traffic, similar to First Class mail, Express Mail, and so forth.

DiffServ provides QoS guarantees for aggregates of traffic. Traffic *aggregates* are made up of a set of packets with the same DSCP, going in the same direction over a given link. DiffServ traffic is separated into classes characterizing their QoS needs; for example, one class is "real-time traffic" and another class is "loss or delay sensitive traffic."

Summary

QoS is the ability to define a specified level of network performance, enabling certain (customer specified) applications to have better service than others. QoS provides priority to customer traffic across a network by dedicating bandwidth, controlling jitter and latency (required by some real-time and interactive traffic), and improving loss characteristics.

CoS differentiates traffic based on priority. Labels or tags can be added to the packets to identify such classes, but CoS does not guarantee traffic delivery; whereas QoS does provide for such a guarantee.

There are currently four WAN technologies that have some provisions for QoS/CoS:

- ATM
- Frame Relay
- IP
- MPLS/MPLS-TE

Each of these technologies enables QoS/CoS support in different ways that are specific and limited to the constraints of the technology itself. For example, IP does not provide for a CIR in the way that Frame Relay does or for the several Classes of Service that ATM provides.

Frequently Asked Questions (FAQ)

1 What is congestion, delay, and jitter?

A network experiences congestion when it is presented with more traffic than it can handle. Network congestion points are strong candidates for quality of service (QoS) mechanisms. Figure 13-1 shows an example of typical congestion points:

Figure 13-1 *Network Congestion Points*

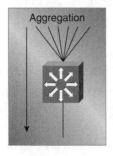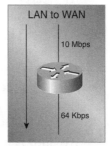

Network congestion causes delay, caused in turn by transmission propagation and networking hardware. Both network delay and jitter must be controlled and minimized to enable real-time, interactive traffic to be transported across the network.

Voice and video traffic is more sensitive than data to jitter in a network connection. Minimal jitter in a data network is often not cause for concern because the receiving devices are still able to recognize the signal incoming from the network. Jitter can result in static or clipping of voice conversations or video streams, resulting in a less-than-clear signal.

2 What is the difference between MPLS and DiffServ?

Differentiated services (DiffServ) and Multiprotocol Label Switching (MPLS) are two separate standards, each claiming to solve the issue of quality of service (QoS) in an IP network.

DiffServ works at Layer 3 only and does not deal with lower layers. DiffServ uses the IP TOS (type of service) field, renaming it the DS byte, and uses this field to carry information about IP packet service requirements.

MPLS specifies which Layer 3 traffic can be mapped to connection-oriented Layer 2 transports, such as ATM and Frame Relay. MPLS adds a label containing specific routing information to each IP packet and allows routers to assign explicit paths to various classes of traffic. MPLS also offers traffic engineering capabilities whereas DiffServ does not.

DiffServ relies on traffic conditioners at the edge of the network, indicating each packet's requirements. MPLS requires capital investment in a network of label-switching routers (LSRs) that can read header information and assign packets to specific paths; for example, virtual circuits on a switched network.

3 Why is queuing discussed with QoS/CoS?

Queuing accommodates temporary congestion on a network device's interface by storing excess packets in buffers until bandwidth becomes available. Queuing is used to assign packets to a particular class of service (CoS) prior to transmission. For example, traffic can be sorted based on destination IP address, with certain addresses having first claim to network bandwidth over others.

Cisco IOS routers support several queuing methods meeting bandwidth, jitter, and delay requirements of different applications. These queuing algorithms are as follows:

- **First In/First Out (FIFO)**—Stores packets when the network is congested and forwards these packets in order of arrival when the network is no longer congested (Cisco IOS default).

- **Weighted Fair Queuing (WFQ)**—A flow-based queuing algorithm that does two things simultaneously:
  - Schedules interactive traffic to the front of the queue to reduce application response time
  - Shares the remaining bandwidth fairly between high bandwidth flows

- **Class-Based Weighted Fair Queuing (CBWFQ)**—Extends standard WFQ functionality to provide support for user-defined traffic classes. For example, traffic classes are defined based on match criteria including protocols, access control lists (ACLs), and router input interfaces.

- **Low Latency Queuing (LLQ), which is CBWFQ with a Priority Queue (PQ) (known as PQCBWFQ)**—Provides strict priority queuing for CBWFQ, reducing jitter in voice conversations.

- **Priority Queuing (PQ)**—Gives strict priority to important traffic ensuring that important traffic gets the fastest handling at each point where PQ is used. PQ can prioritize according to network protocol (such as IP, IPX, or AppleTalk), incoming router interface, packet size, or source/destination address.

- **Custom Queuing (CQ)**—Reserves a percentage of a router interface's available bandwidth for each selected traffic type. If a particular type of traffic is not using it's reserved bandwidth, other traffic types can use the remaining reserved bandwidth.

4 What is Cisco doing regarding QoS/CoS implementations?

QoS/CoS implementations and improvements often are made and new techniques are discovered. Cisco System's QoS Technical Assistance Center (TAC) page, found at `www.cisco.com/pcgi-bin/Support/PSP/psp_view.pl?p=Internetworking:QoS_General` is a good source to use to keep up with QoS changes.

Case Study

QualityCorp, Inc. is a small company with two sites (New York and Florida), each with LAN workstations, file servers, Voice over IP (VoIP), and Video over IP implementations. New York and Florida also have a connection to the Internet for external e-mail and World Wide Web (WWW) access. QualityCorp, Inc.'s network topology is illustrated in Figure 13-2.

Figure 13-2 *QualityCorp, Inc.*

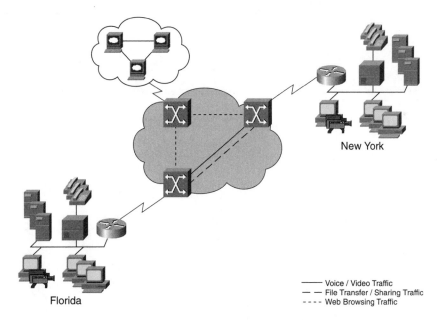

QualityCorp, Inc. has dedicated IP lines to the NSP, and is using DiffServ to classify each traffic flow (the DiffServ code points are defined in IETF RFC 2474, which you can read at `www.ietf.org/rfc/rfc2474.txt?number=2474`), ensuring that each class of traffic is handled accordingly by the NSP. These code points are shown in Table 13-1.

Table 13-1   *Code Points*

Application Traffic	Code Point
Voice/Video	7
File Transfer/Sharing	4
Web Browsing	1

The NSP is carrying this DiffServ IP traffic over an ATM backbone, mapping the code points as shown in Table 13-2.

Table 13-2   *Code Points Mapped to ATM CoS*

Code Point	ATM CoS
7	CBR
4	VBRnrt
1	UBR

The following topics are covered in this chapter:

- Network Devices
- Hierarchical Network Model
- WAN Oversubscription

CHAPTER 14

Network Architecture Introduction

Networks can be broken down into four categories, depending on the geographic relation of the network components. These four network categories are as follows:

- **Wide Area Network (WAN)**—WANs use interconnections that span geographically separate networks. Figure 14-1 illustrates a WAN.

Figure 14-1 *WAN*

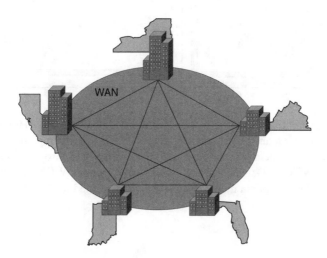

- **Campus Area Network (CAN)**—CANs interconnect local area networks (LANs) within a limited geographical space, such as a school campus or a military base. CANs are illustrated in Figure 14-2.

Figure 14-2 *CAN*

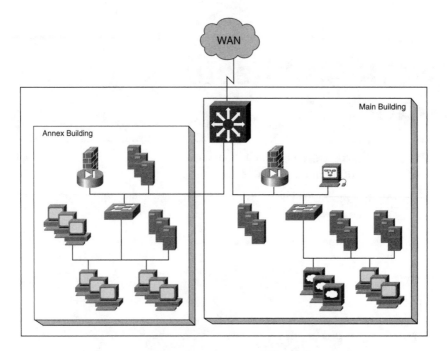

- **Metropolitan Area Network (MAN)**—MANs are designed for a town or city. MANs are larger than LANs, but smaller than WANs. MAN implementations often involve the deployment of fiber optic facilities, such as Synchronous Optical Network (SONET) or Dense Wave Division Multiplexing (DWDM) to interconnect several buildings within a metropolitan area, as illustrated in Figure 14-3.

Figure 14-3 *MAN*

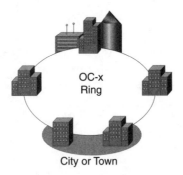

- **Local Area Network (LAN)**—LANs span a relatively small area; a LAN is illustrated in Figure 14-4.

Figure 14-4 *LAN*

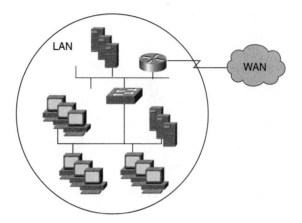

Often LANs are confined to a single building or group of buildings, creating a CAN. However, one LAN can be connected to other LANs over any distance via network service provider connections, which in turn creates a WAN.

Network Devices

Four basic types of networking hardware are used in an internetwork:

- **Hubs (LAN)**—Hubs connect multiple LAN hosts and users to a single device, which in turn is connected to the network.

- **Bridges (LAN)**—Bridges logically separate network segments within the same network and operate at the Data-Link layer of the OSI Reference Model.

- **Switches (LAN/WAN)**—Similar to bridges, switches provide a unique network segment on each switch port, separating LAN collision domains (in turn minimizing LAN congestion).

- **Routers (LAN/WAN)**—Routers interconnect different networks and separate broadcast domains. Routers are protocol-dependant and operate at the Network layer of the OSI Reference Model.

Each of these network devices performs internetworking functions in accordance with their location within the hierarchical network model, not to be confused with their geographic location within the network.

Hierarchical Network Model

Network architecture is broken down into a three-tiered hierarchical model, as illustrated in Figure 14-5.

Figure 14-5 *Three-tiered Hierarchical Network Model*

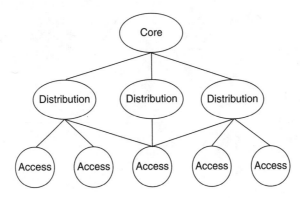

The following lists the three layers, or tiers, in the three-tiered hierarchical network model:

- **Core**—The backbone layer providing (optimal) transport between sites
- **Distribution**—The layer providing policy-based connectivity
- **Access**—The layer providing site/user access to the network

These three layers—core, distribution, and access—need not exist in a clear and distinct physical fashion. These layers are defined to aid in network design, representing the network functionality that must exist. Each layer can exist in distinct and separate router or switch deployments, physical media, or they can be combined into a single device. For example, a Cisco Catalyst 6000 Series Switch can provide services for all three layers; the core layer is represented by the Multilayer Switch Feature Card (MSFC), providing WAN functionality. The distribution layer is represented by the switch backplane, and the access layer is represented by each switch port.

Core Layer

The core layer is the high-speed switching backbone designed and engineered to move packets through the network as quickly as possible. The core layer should not perform any manipulation of packets because the flow of packets would be slowed. An example of packet manipulation is access-list filtering.

NOTE   Access lists can be configured for all routed protocols, such as IP, IPX, or AppleTalk. They are used to prevent certain traffic from entering or exiting a network.

Some examples of Cisco equipment often found in the core layer are as follows:

- Cisco 720x Series Routers
- Cisco Catalyst 6000 Series Switches

The following features enable core (backbone) services in a hierarchical network:

- **Path Optimization**—A logical environment where optimal traffic paths are selected based on routes learned from configured routing protocols. The key in selecting which routing protocol to implement often depends on how quickly the routing protocol can converge when there is an issue in the network backbone.

- **Traffic Prioritization**—The router prioritizes traffic flows, enabling policy-based routing and ensuring that mission-critical traffic takes precedence over other less time-sensitive traffic. Traffic prioritization is different from quality of service (QoS) in that traffic prioritization determines which traffic leaves the router first and QoS guarantees the bandwidth for that traffic across the network backbone.

  Traffic prioritization is enabled through the implementation of one of the following queuing algorithms:

  - **Priority Queuing**—Enables network administrators to prioritize traffic. Priority classifications are high, medium, normal, or low.

  - **Custom Queuing**—Enables network administrators to ensure that each protocol is ensured a minimum level of service, preventing higher priority traffic from dominating a network link. A maximum of 16 queues can be built with custom queuing, enabling the network administrator to assign a percentage of network bandwidth to each protocol.

  - **Weighted Fair Queuing**—Uses the time-division multiplexing (TDM) model to divide available network bandwidth among all protocols using the interface. Queues are serviced in a round-robin fashion, with each queue getting a fair share of network bandwidth (if every queue has the same weighting). Weighting enables a network administrator to ensure time-delay-sensitive traffic is guaranteed bandwidth leaving the router (entering the WAN), providing consistent response time under heavy traffic loads.

- **Load Balancing/Sharing**—Routers provide built-in load balancing for up to four paths to a destination network. Some routing protocols require that each path have an equal cost metric. Load balancing implies that each path has identical metrics so that there is no differentiator; in an NSP environment, this is not always possible. To emulate load balancing, equal cost load sharing is implemented, providing network administrators a way to adjust the cost metrics so that each router believes each path to be equal and identical.

NOTE   In networking, *load* refers to the amount of data (traffic) being carried by the network. *Load sharing* is the sharing of network traffic across multiple network connections, but not necessarily an equal load; for example, 65 percent of the load might traverse one network link and the remaining 35 percent would then traverse another link. Load balancing is the equal sharing of network traffic across multiple network connections—50 percent load across two links, 33.3 percent load across three links, etc.

NOTE   Cisco's IGRP and EIGRP provide unequal-cost load balancing.

- **Alternative Paths**—These are redundant network links that are available for use when primary end-to-end network links are unavailable.
- **Switched Access**—Provides the capability to enable a WAN link on an as-needed basis through automated router functions. Switched links often are used as dial backup lines for network sites. These dial backup lines are carried by the public switched telephone network (PSTN) and can automatically be established by the router using Cisco's Dial-on-Demand Routing (DDR).

    Figure 14-6 illustrates an end-to-end dial backup implementation between two network sites.

Figure 14-6 *Switched Access DDR*

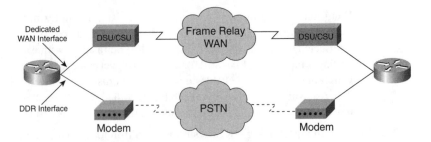

- **Encapsulation (Tunneling)**—Takes packets/frames from one network system and places them inside packets/frames from another network system, as illustrated in Figure 14-7.

Figure 14-7 *IPX Tunneled Through an IP Network*

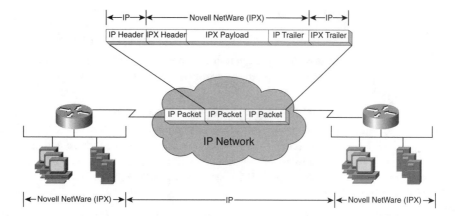

For example, if Internet Protocol (IP) is used for network transport, but IPX is used on the LAN on each side, the IPX traffic is tunneled through the IP network by having each IPX packet encapsulated by an IP packet.

Encapsulation is the solution to use when multiple protocols need to traverse a single protocol backbone; for example, when AppleTalk and IPX users at multiple sites are interconnected by an IP backbone.

Distribution Layer

The distribution layer is the demarcation point between the core and access layers, helping define and delineate between network access and backbone functions. The distribution layer provides policy-based connectivity in the form of packet manipulation services for the core layer, such as access-list filtering. The distribution layer also provides for the following services:

- Network address aggregation/summarization
- Departmental workgroup access
- Broadcast/Multicast domain definition
- Virtual LAN (VLAN) routing
- Network media transition/conversion (such as Frame Relay access to an ATM backbone)
- Network security services (such as firewall services)

Some examples of Cisco equipment often found in the distribution layer are as follows:

- Cisco 450x Series Routers
- Cisco 36x0 Series Routers
- Cisco Catalyst 400x Series Switches
- Cisco Catalyst 35xx Series Switches

The following features enable distribution services in a hierarchical network:

- **Backbone Bandwidth Management**—Enabled by router performance tuning features, such as priority queuing, custom queuing, weighted fair queuing, and routing metrics.

- **Area and Service Filtering**—Traffic filters based on area or service are the primary tools used at the distribution layer to provide policy-based access control into the network backbone (core). These filters are used to enforce the selective sending of traffic based on network address, such as IP or IPX address, or specific protocol services, such as Simple Mail Transfer Protocol (SMTP) or HTTP (Web browsing) services.

- **Policy-Based Distribution**—Based on the premise that different groups or departments within an organization might have different traffic dispersion policies based on a set of rules implemented by the network administrator. These policies often are implemented to minimize unnecessary traffic from being sent into the network backbone.

  One of the more common policy-based implementations is found in Novell NetWare implementations where Novell's Service Advertising Protocol (SAP) broadcast traffic is contained to the LAN and is not carried across the WAN.

- **Gateway Services**—Part of each router's standard software implementation. Gateway services enable a router to connect to multiple networks with different network addressing and facilitate communication between these network hosts by translating the network address as necessary.

- **Route Redistribution**—Routers can provide gateway services for routing protocols, redistributing information from one routing protocol into another. For example, Figure 14-8 illustrates a routing redistribution that interconnects two networks.

Figure 14-8 *Routing Protocol Redistribution*

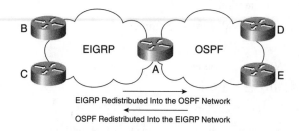

In the figure, one network is using Open Shortest Path First (OSPF) as its routing protocol, and the other is using Enhanced Interior Gateway Routing Protocol (EIGRP). In order for the OSPF routed sites (D and E) to communicate with the EIGRP routed sites (B and C), router A must redistribute routes from each network into the other so that Routers B and C can "see" Routers D and E, and vice versa.

- **Media Translation**—Translates frames from one network system into frames of another, such as translating frames between an Ethernet and a Token Ring network, as illustrated in Figure 14-9.

Figure 14-9 *Media Translation*

The router here is providing translation between Ethernet and Token Ring LANs, specifically between the Ethernet Transparent Bridging (TB) and the Token Ring Source-Route Bridging (SRB). Without the router between and connecting these two networks, users and network resources on either LAN would not be able to internetwork with each other.

Access Layer

The access layer is the point of entry into the network for local users. The access layer also can provide for policy-based services, such as access-list filtering. The access layer also provides for the following services:

- Bandwidth sharing
- Bandwidth switching

- MAC layer filtering
- Micro-segmentation

The following list provides some examples of Cisco equipment often found in the access layer:

- Cisco 260x Series Routers
- Cisco 170x Series Routers
- Cisco Catalyst 25xx Series Switches

The following features enable access services in a hierarchical network:

- **Value-Added Network Addressing**—Uses protocol specific *helper-addressing* to ensure that traffic is sent through a network that might not otherwise carry the traffic, as illustrated in Figure 14-10. Site C hosts the Dynamic Host Configuration Protocol (DHCP) server for Site A and Site B, without the use of a helper-address. LAN users at Site A and Site B would not be configured with an IP address because the router at these respective sites would not forward the DHCP request to Site C, because DHCP is a broadcast, which routers do not forward without a helper-address.

Figure 14-10 *DHCP with Helper-Address*

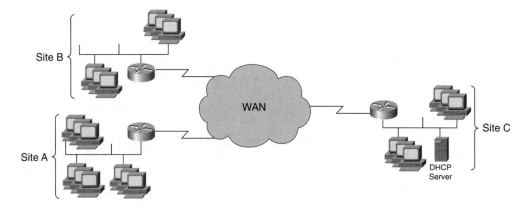

When DHCP is used, each LAN workstation is assigned an IP address when powered on and booted up. This LAN workstation sends a DHCP broadcast across the network requesting an IP address. If the DHCP server is on the same LAN, the request is received and an IP address is sent back to the requesting LAN workstation. If the DHCP server is on another network, however, the request will not be seen because routers do not forward broadcasts; routers break up broadcast domains by not forwarding broadcast traffic across the network. The helper-address tells the router that if certain broadcast traffic is received—in this case, DHCP traffic—it should be forwarded to a specified address.

- **Network Segmentation**—Splits a network into smaller, more manageable pieces (segments). Local-access routers implement local access policies limiting unnecessary traffic from traversing the network, consuming network bandwidth and other resources.

- **Broadcast/Multicast Capabilities**—Routers stop the propagation of broadcasts across a network, but can be configured to forward both broadcasts and multicasts to a single network address or group of network addresses. Broadcasts are messages sent to all network destinations; multicasts are messages sent to a specific group of network destinations.

- **Naming, Proxy, and Local Cache Capabilities**—Three key router capabilities reducing network traffic. Routers can act as Domain Name System (DNS) servers, resolving network names to network addresses (for example, resolving www.cisco.com to 198.133.219.25). Routers can act as proxy servers for a name server and as a name cache for NetBIOS implementations.

- **Media Access Security**—Routers keep local traffic from reaching the network backbone and keep network backbone traffic from entering into a local department or workgroup network, preventing possible security violations and inappropriate file and resource access.

- **Router Discovery**—The process of finding routers in a network by a LAN host. The following are router discovery protocols:

  - **Routing Information Protocol (RIP)**—A routing protocol common on IP hosts. Many hosts use RIP to find the address of a router on a LAN.

  - **Address Resolution Protocol (ARP)**—Uses broadcast messages to determine the MAC-layer address of an interface based on a known network address. For example, a host knows the router's Ethernet interface is 10.52.217.16, but does not know the MAC-address (required for Ethernet addressing). The LAN host sends an ARP (broadcast) request, destined for 10.52.217.16. The router will receive this request, recognize it is the intended recipient (based on the IP network address), and respond to the requesting host, thereby providing the requested MAC address of the router's interface.

WAN Oversubscription

Because data connections tend to be used on an intermittent basis (for example, "bursty data"), oversubscription of a WAN (most often Frame Relay) port can be effective for achieving more economical network connectivity in an enterprise organization. Oversubscription lets network designers "play the averages" by designing and provisioning a total committed information rate (CIR) to a given port that is greater than the port speed. For example, a Frame Relay port might be provisioned for 56 Kbps, with the total CIR measuring 112 Kbps.

Oversubscription is often measured as a percentage, such as, 200 or 400 percent oversubscription. For example, four 32 Kbps permanent virtual circuits (PVCs)—a total CIR of 128 Kbps—attached to a 64 Kbps port represents a 200 percent subscription.

This 200 percent, or 2:1, oversubscription rate is illustrated in Figure 14-11.

Figure 14-11   *200 Percent (2:1) Oversubscription*

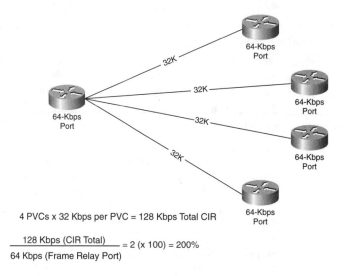

4 PVCs x 32 Kbps per PVC = 128 Kbps Total CIR

$$\frac{128 \text{ Kbps (CIR Total)}}{64 \text{ Kbps (Frame Relay Port)}} = 2 \text{ (x 100)} = 200\%$$

If two 32-Kbps PVCs were attached to a 64-Kbps port, the total CIR equals the size of the attached port: 2 ∞ 32 Kbps = 64 Kbps, 64 Kbps/64 Kbps equals 1, or a 100 percent (1:1) subscription rate, representing no oversubscription.

Summary

Networks are defined as one of the following four categories, depending on the geographic relation of the network components:

- **Wide Area Network (WAN)**—Interconnection spanning geographically separate networks.

- **Campus Area Network (CAN)**—Interconnection of local area networks (LANs) within a limited geographical space.

- **Metropolitan Area Network (MAN)**—Designed for a town or city; larger than LANs and smaller than WANs.

- **Local Area Network (LAN)**—Spans across a small area; often within a building or on a single floor within a building.

These network components are broken down into one of the following four basic types of internetworking hardware:

- **Hubs (LAN)** — Connect multiple LAN hosts/users to a single device, in turn connected to the network.

- **Bridges (LAN)** — Logically separate network segments within the same network.

- **Switches (LAN/WAN)** — Similar to bridges, switches provide a unique network segment on each switch port, separating LAN collision domains.

- **Routers (LAN/WAN)** — Interconnect different networks and separate broadcast domains.

Internetworks are made up of the following three-tiered hierarchical model:

- **Core** — The backbone layer providing (optimal) transport between sites.

- **Distribution** — Layer providing policy-based connectivity.

- **Access** — Layer providing site/user access to the network.

Oversubscription of a WAN port can be effective for achieving more economical network connectivity in an enterprise organization because data connections tend to be bursty, or used intermittently.

Oversubscription is often measured as a percentage; for example, 200 or 400 percent oversubscription. For example, four 32 Kbps permanent virtual circuits (PVCs) — a total CIR of 128 Kbps — attached to a 64-Kbps port represents a 200 percent subscription.

Frequently Asked Questions (FAQ)

1 What is the difference between a router and a switch?

Routers "think" before forwarding; switches just forward.

When a switch receives a datagram (frame) on one of its ports, the switch tries to find the destination device (host) by looking up the MAC address in its Content Addressable Memory (CAM) table, and forwards the frame out of the appropriate port. The destination device must reside on the same local area network because a switch will not send datagrams to hosts on different network segments.

When a router receives a datagram (packet), the router tries to find the destination device (host) by looking up the network address (for example, the IP address) in its routing tables (built by the routing protocol). If the destination computer is not on the same network segment or LAN, the router tries to determine where the intended host is located and then sends the datagram to that network (with the attached destination host).

2 How much can a WAN port be oversubscribed?

A port can be oversubscribed without causing too high a risk to your application performance. There is no hard and fast recommended ratio because it all depends on the traffic characteristics. It is common to find that in many applications, a ratio concentration of 2:1 or 4:1 is acceptable and causes few application issues because most data applications are bursty, not requiring 100 percent of the bandwidth at all times.

To determine an appropriate oversubscription rate, it is necessary to measure network usage. Measurements and related performance data can be collected from CSU/DSUs, WAN probes, the NSP, or from the WAN router itself.

3 Does network architecture require core, distribution, and access layers?

Yes. The lines between these three hierarchical layers can be blurred, for example a router or switch can perform both access and distribution services. The three-tiered hierarchical model defines the services a network device needs to perform, depending on where the device is placed within the network architecture.

Case Study

The following (two) case studies illustrate the network hierarchical model first from the customer perspective, and then from the network NSP perspective.

Figure 14-12 illustrates a customer LAN/WAN internetwork architecture.

Figure 14-12 *Enterprise Customer LAN/WAN Architecture*

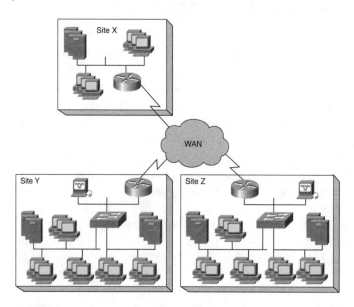

The following list details the hierarchy found in this LAN/WAN internetwork:

- Core functionality is represented by the WAN; providing site interconnectivity through Frame Relay, ATM, or IP VPN.

- Site X represents a remote office LAN, with severs, workstations, and a WAN router. Distribution and access functionality is represented by the WAN router.

- Site Y represents a medium site, using a LAN switch (for example, Cisco 3550/4000 Series Switches) to interconnect multiple LAN segments, as well as enabling WAN connectivity (through the WAN router). Distribution functionality is provided by the WAN router and access functionality is provided by the LAN switch in place. These LAN switches also can provide distribution functionality within the CAN/LAN environment.

- Site Z represents a large site, also using a LAN switch (such as Cisco 3550/4000/6000 Series Switches) to interconnect multiple LAN segments, as well as enabling WAN connectivity (through the WAN router). Distribution functionality is provided by the WAN router and access functionality is provided by the LAN switch in place. These LAN switches also can provide distribution functionality within the CAN/LAN environment.

Figure 14-13 illustrates a NSP architecture.

Figure 14-13 *NSP Architecture*

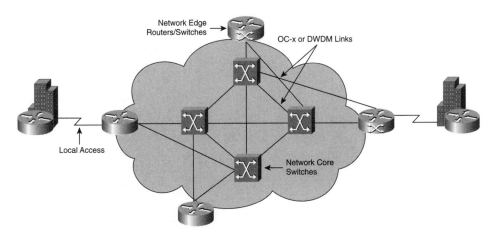

The three-tiered hierarchy of this network is defined in the following list:

- Core functionality is represented by the WAN switches in the core of the NSP's net-work backbone. These WAN switches are interconnected with high-speed dedicated lines, such as an OC-48/192 (2.5 Gbps/10 Gbps) SONET implementation or DWDM 2.5 Gbps/10 Gbps wavelengths.

- Distribution functionality is represented by the network edge routers/switches, connected to two core switches for link redundancy.
- Access functionality is represented by the customer WAN router.

The following topics are covered in this chapter:

- Network Threats
- Network Attack Methods
- Proxy Servers and DMZ
- Firewalls
- Intrusion Detection Monitoring
- Network Security Architecture

CHAPTER 15

Network Security Basics

The goal of network security is to provide users with access to the resources they need on a network or system, while preventing access to resources they don't need, which protects the system against known and unknown threats. This chapter looks at network security threats and shows how to protect against them.

Network Threats

In order to design an effective security solution, it is important to understand the types of network threats that exist. These threats to a network or system are categorized as follows:

- Denial-of-Service (DoS)
- Unauthorized Access
- Illicit Command Execution
- Confidentiality Breaches
- Destructive Behavior

Each of these threats is discussed in the following sections.

Denial-of-Service (DoS)

DoS attacks are considered to be both the most dangerous threat and the most difficult to address. The premise of a DoS attack is the attacker sends more requests to a host (for example, a web server) than the host can handle. For example, if a host can answer 20 requests per second and the attacker is sending 50 requests per second, the host is unable to service all of the requests, much less any legitimate requests, such as hits on a web site from legitimate users or customers.

DoS attacks are considered the most dangerous threat because DoS attacks are easy to launch, difficult (sometimes impossible) to track, and it is not an easy task refusing attacker requests for service without refusing legitimate service requests.

The following list offers things that can be done to reduce the risk of being a target of a DoS attack:

- Avoid running visible-to-the-world servers close to capacity, leaving room for a flood of service requests.

- Use packet filtering to prevent forged packets from entering into the network. *Forged packets* are those that claim to come from one of the network hosts; for example, addresses reserved for private networks (defined in RFC 1918) and the loopback network (127.0.0.0).

- Maintain up-to-date security-related patches on host operating systems.

Each of these possible solutions has an associated implementation and management cost. It is this cost that must be weighed versus the risk of lost service.

Unauthorized Access

Unauthorized access is a high-level term referring to a number of different sorts of attacks. The goal of an unauthorized access attack is for the attacker to access some host resource that would not otherwise be available. For example, a host could be a web server, and therefore should provide anyone with requested Web pages. However, the web server should not provide command line access to someone without ensuring that the requestor is someone who should have such access, such as a local administrator.

Illicit Command Execution

It is undesirable for an unknown and/or an unauthorized person to be able to execute commands on an organization's servers. There are two main severity classifications of this problem:

- **Normal user access**—A normal user can do a number of things on a host, such as read files or send e-mail that an attacker should not be able to do. This access might be all the access that an attacker needs to create havoc impacting the network.

- **Administrator access**—With administrator privileges, an attacker can make host configuration changes, such as changing its IP address or putting a start-up script in place to cause the machine to shut down every time it's started.

Confidentiality Breaches

Confidentiality breaches are based on the model that certain information could be damaging if it fell into the wrong hands, such as those of a competitor, an enemy, or the public. In these cases, it is possible that the compromise of a normal user account on the host can be enough to cause damage, resulting, perhaps, in bad publicity for the organization or access to information that can be used against the company.

Destructive Behavior

Two major categories of destructive break-ins and attacks are used:

- **Data Diddling**—Considered the worst sort of attack because the break-in might not be obvious. The attacker could do any number of things, such as the following:

  — Change numbers in spreadsheets

  — Change dates in a project plan

  — Change the account numbers for direct deposit of paychecks

  It is rare that something wrong is immediately identified. An accounting procedure might turn up a discrepancy in the books three or four months later. Once the problem is discovered, the question "How can any numbers from that time period be trusted?" is raised.

- **Data Destruction**—Attackers are deleting data, resulting in something comparable to a fire or other disaster caused the host or server to be destroyed.

Network Attack Methods

Attackers can access or abuse unprotected networks or hosts (computers) many different ways, including these:

- **Remote login**—Someone is able to connect to a computer and control it in some form. This control can range from being able to view or access files to running programs on the computer.

- **Application back doors**—Some programs have special features enabling remote access. Others programs contain bugs that provide a "back door," or hidden access, providing some level of control of the program.

- **SMTP session hijacking**—SMTP is the most common method of sending e-mail over the Internet. By gaining access to a list of e-mail addresses, a person can send unsolicited junk e-mail (spam) to thousands of users. This spamming is done by redirecting the e-mail through the SMTP server of an unsuspecting host, making the actual sender of the spam difficult to trace.

- **Operating system bugs**—Like applications, some operating systems have back doors. Other applications provide remote access with insufficient security controls or have bugs an experienced attacker can use to gain advantage.

- **DoS**—This type of attack is nearly impossible to counter. When the server responds with an acknowledgement to a user (attacker) requesting to establish a connection, it cannot find the system that made the request. By inundating a server with these unanswerable session requests, an attacker causes the server to slow to a crawl or crash.

- **E-mail bombs**—An e-mail bomb is often a personal attack. Someone sends the same e-mail hundreds or thousands of times until the recipient's e-mail system cannot accept any more messages and sometimes crashes as a result.

- **Macros**—To simplify complicated procedures, many applications enable the creation of a script of commands the application can run; this script is known as a *macro*. Attackers take advantage of this scripting capability to create their own macros that, depending on the application, can destroy data or crash a computer.

- **Viruses**—A *virus* is a small program that can copy itself to other computers. This self-replication enables the virus to spread from one system to the next. Viruses range from displaying harmless messages to erasing all of a machine's data.

- **Spam**—*Spam* is the electronic equivalent of junk mail but can be dangerous. Quite often, spam contains links to web sites outside the protected network. These web sites might use these cookies to provide an attacker a back door to the computer. (*Cookies* are messages given to a web browser by a web server. The message is then sent back to the server each time the browser requests a page from the server.)

- **Redirect bombs**—Hackers can use ICMP to change (redirect) the path information follows by sending it to a different router. Redirect bombs are one of the ways that a denial of service attack is initiated.

- **Source routing**—In most cases, the path a packet travels over a network (such as the Internet) is determined by the routers along that path. The source providing the packet can specify the route that the packet should travel. Attackers can take advantage of this to make information appear to come from a trusted source or even from inside the network. By default, most firewalls disable source routing, which in turn prevents this type of attack.

Firewalls are an effective solution against most of these attacks because they can stop an attacker outside the network from logging into a computer inside the network. Firewalls alone will not prevent all of these attacks. Firewalls with an Intrusion Detection System (IDS) and a virus monitor combine for an effective network security solution. You learn more about firewalls later in this chapter.

Proxy Servers and DMZ

A *proxy server* is a function often combined with a firewall. The proxy server is used to access web pages by other computers on the network, as illustrated in Figure 15-1.

When a user requests a web page, it is retrieved by the proxy server and then sent to the requesting computer. The result of this action is that the remote computer hosting the web page never comes into direct contact with anything on the home network other than the proxy server.

Figure 15-1 *Proxy Server*

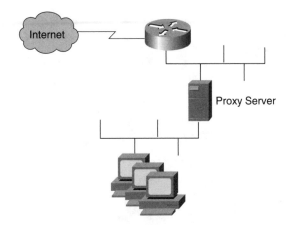

Proxy servers also can make Internet access more efficient for an organization. If a user accesses a web page, it is cached (stored) on the proxy server, meaning that the next time that same page is requested, it does not have to load again from the web site; instead the page loads from the proxy server.

There are times that remote users will require access to resources on a network. Here are some examples of such access:

- Organization Intranet site
- Online business
- FTP download and upload area

In cases like this, a demilitarized zone (DMZ) should be created. The DMZ is a part of the network that is outside the firewall, similar to the front yard of a house. It belongs to the network (in this case, the house) and some things can be left there (in the yard), but it is not advisable to leave anything valuable in this part. A common DMZ implementation is illustrated in Figure 15-2.

- The Internet access router on the public side of the DMZ provides the first line of defense for the private network.
- The DMZ hosts public access servers, such as an e-commerce store or corporate Web site.
- The firewall and router protect the private network from public users. In order for a user to gain access to a resource on the private network, the user must first be granted access through the firewall.

Figure 15-2 *A Common DMZ Implementation*

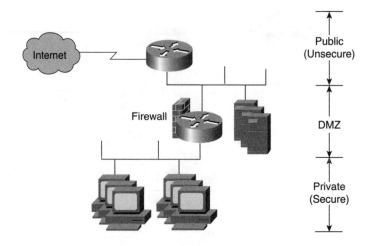

Firewalls

A *firewall* is a system controlling network traffic flow between a local area network (LAN) and a public network like the Internet (see Figure 15-3).

Figure 15-3 *Firewall*

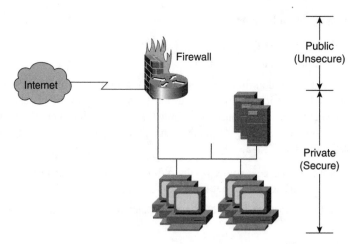

Firewalls enforce the security policy of a particular network site and can provide a more efficient method of securing hosts on a network than securing each host individually. On networks protected by a firewall, each host does not need to be 100 percent secure because the firewall makes access to those hosts from outside nearly impossible.

Firewalls can prevent unwanted traffic generated by unsuccessful attacks against the network to which the firewall is protecting. In addition to protecting network resources from attackers, firewalls can log Internet traffic, eavesdrop on communication (as appropriate or necessary), and create virtual private network (VPN) connections.

Firewalls cannot protect against viruses, prevent attacks occurring from within the network, or protect against undiscovered threats. Firewalls can prevent and protect against only known threats. An attacker can discover a new threat, such as a bug in a server program, and exploit the bug to attach the system.

Intrusion Detection and Monitoring

Intrusion detection is the detection of inappropriate, incorrect, or anomalous activity. An intrusion can include a network attack from the outside (intruder) or from an internal network user (misuse). IDSs monitor network systems detecting these types of attacks. IDSs collect information from several points within networks and analyze this information for signs of intrusion and misuse.

Intruders are unauthorized users, and they are classified as follows:

- **External**—Users not authorized to use the system, also known as *intruders*. External intruders are the focus of physical security and firewalls.

- **Internal**—Users not authorized to use some resources, often referred to as *misuse*.

- **Masquerades**—Users who impersonate other users.

- **Clandestine**—Users who evade auditing and are a threat to weak operating systems and mismanaged systems.

- **Misfeasors**—Users who misuse their privileges.

IDSs must protect network and system integrity from several different types of attacks and users. All users are considered possible threats, regardless of origin or how the users were authenticated.

IDSs use various techniques to trace unauthorized use of network and system resources. These techniques include the analysis of audit trail data and network traffic, either real-time or off-line (after-the-fact). The goal of intrusion detection is catching the intruder in the act. Real-time testing and monitoring of audit data is the most prevalent technique used to catch intruders.

Intrusion Detection System Methodologies

IDSs use two methodologies to detect unauthorized use of a network or system:

- Signature analysis matches network traffic against known rules containing known attack traces and protocol uses. If a match is detected, the traffic is flagged for notification to the network administrator or security manager.

- Statistical profiling is performed on host-based intrusion detection systems. Statistical profiling monitors the characteristics of the users using the system, developing sophisticated profiles over time.

  Characteristics of users include the following:

  — Application

  — Amount of data

  — Time of usage

  — Protocols used

  — Source and destination addresses

  Once a profile is completed, subsequent uses are compared to the user's original profile. If the system detects a change in user activities, the user is flagged by the system. For example, a user who regularly edits documents in Microsoft Word, but opens UNIX <u>vi</u> to edit a remote host password file, should be flagged.

  Statistical profiling also can be performed at the network level by developing the activity profiles of web servers. For example, if a web server begins receiving remote commands and file uploads, these are not normal processes and are thus flagged.

IDS Implementation

IDSs are implemented in one of two ways: host-based or network-based.

Host-Based Intrusion Detection

Detection software is loaded on the host the IDS will be monitoring, and data is audited from this single host. Each network host will need the intrusion detection software running in order to be effective in identifying attacks. Host-based IDSs monitor system, event, and security logs on Windows NT and syslog in UNIX environments. If any changes in these files are detected by the IDS, the IDS compares the new log entry with attack signatures to see whether a match exists. If a match is found, the system alerts the administrator.

There are two classes of host-based intrusion detection software:

- **Host wrappers/personal firewalls**—Configured to look at all network packets, connection attempts, or login attempts to the monitored machine. Personal firewalls can detect software on the host that may be trying to connect to the network as well.

- **Agent-based software**—Monitors access, changes to critical system files, and changes in user privilege.

Network Intrusion Detection Systems (NIDS)

Packets on the network and audit data from several hosts are monitored on the particular segment the NIDS is covering. As the packets pass the sensor, they are examined for their similarities to a signature. NIDs are primarily concerned with remote intrusion from an external source outside of the network. If an attack is detected, the NIDS will notify the administrator, terminate the connection, and/or record the session for forensic analysis and evidence collection.

NOTE   More information regarding Cisco Systems IDS (formerly NetRanger) platform can be found at `http://www.cisco.com/warp/public/cc/pd/sqsw/sqidsz/index.shtml`.

Signatures

Signatures represent an activity pattern required to gain access to a computer network or system. Signatures enable the IDS to verify whether the monitored sequence of events is a threat to the integrity of the network or system.

The following is a list of signatures monitored by IDSs:

- **Attack, or string signatures**—Look for specific and well-known patterns of activity logged by the system, indicating malicious or suspicious intent. The most common attack signatures include these:
  - **Reconnaissance**—Made up of the following attacks:
  - **Ping sweeps**—Pinging a range of IP addresses
  - **TCP scans**—Probes for open (listening) TCP ports
  - **UDP scans**—Sending garbage UDP packets revealing open ports
- **OS identification**—Sending of illegal/strange ICMP or TCP packets identifying the OS by the way in which the OS responds to the packets.
- **Account scans**—Look for accounts with no passwords, common word passwords, or passwords that are the same as the user name.
- **Exploits**—Intruders will take advantage of hidden features, holes, or bugs to gain access to the system. Common exploits include:
  - CGI scripts
  - Web server attacks
  - Web browser attacks
  - SMTP attacks
  - IP spoofing

— Buffer overflows

— DNS attacks

- **DoS attacks**—The intruder attempts to crash a service or host machine, overload network links, overloaded the CPU, or fill up the disk, preventing legitimate users from accessing services. Common DoS attacks include:

  — Ping-of-Death

  — SYN Flood

  — WinNuke (targeting older Microsoft Windows 95/NT machines)

NOTE   The Web site `http://www.jtan.com/resources/winnuke.html` can be used to test a PC for vulnerability to the WinNuke attack.

- **Port signatures**—Look for connection attempts to well-known and frequently attacked ports.

- **Header condition signatures**—Look for illogical or dangerous combinations in packet headers.

As you can see, the list of signatures for which IDSs watch is quite extensive. Network attackers change and/or update their attack methods on a continuing basis, in turn requiring IDS vendors to update their signature databases to watch for these attacks.

Network Security Architecture

There are many possible places for an enterprise to place the IDS. Three of the most common and effective include the following:

- **Network perimeter**—Includes all that is internal to the network against all that is external. The perimeter equipment includes:

  — **Firewalls**—Connect the internal network to the external network. Firewalls also can create firewalls within firewalls, blocking off various resources to other areas, for example, blocking certain human resource services from employees.

  — **Access servers and modems**—Enable the users entry point into the network.

  — **Network service provider links**—The points between the proprietary wiring and commercial services; for example, direct connection to the Internet.

Figure 15-4 illustrates the network perimeter.

Figure 15-4 *Network Perimeter*

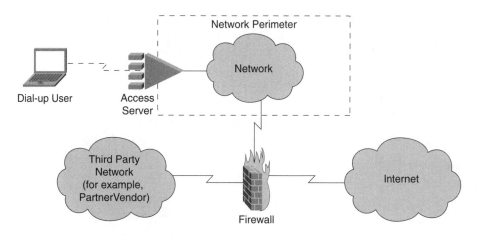

In this scenario, a network-based IDS should be placed at every entry point on the network perimeter; in this case, at the Access Server and firewall points.

- **Server farms**—The server farms are the segments of the network that host the servers; no client workstations exist in the server farm environment.

Figure 15-5 illustrates a server farm layout.

Figure 15-5 *Server Farm*

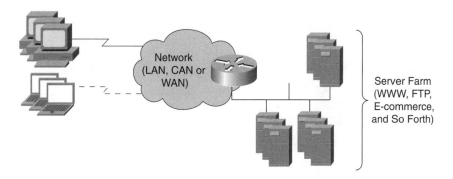

The *server farm* is a network concentration of servers providing resources to users, such as World Wide Web hosting, FTP servers, organization file servers, e-commerce servers, etc.

In this scenario, a network-based IDS should be placed at the entry point for both dedicated and dial-in users, as well as the entry point to the server farm. Further protection is afforded by placing host-based IDS systems on each server in the server farm.

- **Network backbone**—The network backbone provides access to various network areas. They can be low- or high-bandwidth, depending on the implementation. Avoiding backbone links may eliminate some network delay. Intruders would be looking for important systems on this type of network. Anomalous traffic such as port scanning and IP spoofing attempts should encourage a flag for the administrator to investigate.

Figure 15-6 illustrates regional network connections, with all traffic crossing a backbone as the traffic is forwarded from one region to the next.

Figure 15-6 *Network Backbone*

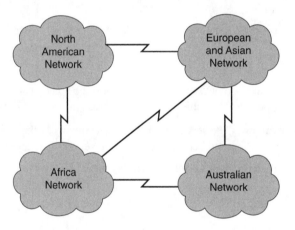

In this scenario, a network-based IDS should be placed at the entry point for each regional network in the network backbone.

Summary

The goal of network security is to provide users with access to necessary network resources, while preventing access against known and unknown, internal and external, threats. Network or system threats are categorized as follows:

- **Denial-of-service (DoS)**—The attacker sends more requests to a host (such as a web server), than the host can handle.

- **Unauthorized Access**—The attacker accesses host resource that would not otherwise be available to that person.

- **Illicit Command Execution**—Unauthorized persons executing commands on an organization's servers.

- **Confidentiality Breaches**—Access to certain, potentially damaging, information through the compromise of a normal user account.

- **Destructive Behavior**—There are two types destructive attacks: changing the data and destroying the data

There are many ways that attackers can access or abuse unprotected networks or hosts (computers), the most popular being via the introduction of macros or viruses to a network system.

Firewalls are an effective solution against most network attacks because they can stop an attacker outside the network from logging into a computer inside the network and wreaking havoc on network resources. Intrusion Detection Systems (IDSs) are another effective solution against most network attacks. IDSs detect the inappropriate, incorrect, or anomalous activity impacting network and its resources. An intrusion can include a network attack from the outside (intruder or unauthorized user) or from an internal network user (misuse).

IDSs are implemented in one of two ways:

- **Host-based**—Detection software is loaded on the host the IDS will be monitoring.

- **Network-based (NIDS)**—Packets on the network and audit data from several hosts are monitored on a particular network segment.

Firewalls and IDSs can be placed anywhere within a network, but the most common and effective placements are at the network perimeter, the network backbone, and network server farms.

Frequently Asked Questions (FAQ)

1 Are IDSs similar to firewalls?

Intrusion Detection is considered to be a complement to network firewalls because they extend the security management capabilities of system administrators/managers to include things like the following:

- Monitoring and analysis of user and system activity

- Auditing of system configuration and vulnerabilities

- Assessing the integrity of critical system files and data files

- Recognizing patterns of activity that reflect known attacks

- Statistical analysis for abnormal activity patterns

- Operating system audit trail management, with recognition of user activity that violates company policy

2 Which is the preferred IDS: Host-based or network-based?

Network-based IDSs are the recommended solution because they protect every device on the network, detect problems quickly, and are not vulnerable to attack. Host-based IDSs are an effective solution in small networks where it is more cost-efficient to deploy multiple host-based IDSs rather than a single network-based IDS.

Case Study

Figure 15-7 illustrates the security architecture for ABC, Inc.

Figure 15-7 *ABC, Inc.*

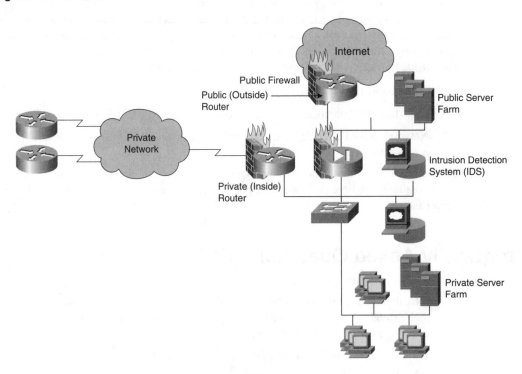

The security components implemented are detailed as follows:

- Public firewall and the public (outside) router provide the first line of defense against network attackers. This "first line of defense" protects against well-known attacks on the network and its systems.

- The public server farm hosts World Wide Web sites, public file sharing servers (FTP), e-commerce servers, etc.

- A network-based intrusion detection system (NIDS) is placed on the public (outside) network segment augmenting the outside firewall and router in protecting the network and its systems.

- A second firewall (Cisco PIX, in this case) connects the outside (public) and inside (private) network segments. This firewall provides more stringent control regarding who can enter the private network—in this case, only those users authorized by the organization to access private network resources, such as partner vendors and telecommuters.

- The private (inside) router provides routing services for the protected (internal) network.

NOTE	A firewall can be coupled with this private router to provide network and system isolation from other private network segments, such as other organizational sites, vendor partners, etc. This firewall implementation lends itself to a "watch those we trust" mentality.

- A second NIDS is placed on the internal network segment to monitor for internal intrusion or misuse activities.

- The private server farm hosts organizational intranet resources, such as corporate e-mail servers, intranet servers, database and accounting servers, etc.

This chapter covers the following topics:

- VPN Basics
- Authentication
- Tunneling Protocols
- Encryption
- PGP
- PKI
- MD5
- IPSec
- IKE
- LAN-to-LAN VPN
- VPN Architecture

CHAPTER 16

Remote Access Virtual Private Networks (VPNs)

Remote access is best defined as providing access to fixed site resources for users who are not at a fixed workstation at that same site's Local Area Network (LAN). The largest remote access user community is mobile or telecommuting users, such as a sales force or field engineering team. Figure 16-1 illustrates a traditional remote access network using the Public Switched Telephone Network (PSTN) or the Integrated Services Digital Network (ISDN).

Figure 16-1 *Traditional Remote Access (PSTN/ISDN Transport)*

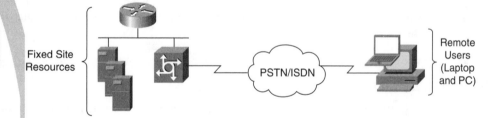

Traditional remote access connectivity is achieved with users dialing into a dedicated PSTN/ISDN modem pool, maintained either by a corporate IS/IT staff or by the network service provider. A secure alternative to traditional remote access is IP-based Virtual Private Networking (IP-VPN). With IP-VPNs, all connections to corporate intranets are calls to a local ISP, carried by the Internet to a corporate VPN gateway.

VPNs

A virtual private network (VPN) is a public network being used for private communication. The VPN connection is an authenticated and encrypted communications channel, or tunnel, across this public network, such as the Internet. Because the network is considered insecure, encryption and authentication are used to protect data while in transit. VPN service is considered to be independent, in that client operation (for example, encryption) is transparent to the user and that all information exchanged between the two hosts World Wide Web [WWW], File Transfer Protocol [FTP], e-mail, and so on) is transmitted across the encrypted channel.

VPN Basics

Before a VPN can be established, certain requirements must be met. These include the following:

- Each network site must be set up with a VPN-capable device (router, firewall, or some other VPN dedicated device) on the network edge.

- Each site must know the IP addressing scheme (host, network, and network mask) in use by the other side of the intended connection.

- Both sites must agree on the authentication method and, if required, exchange digital certificates.

- Both sites also must agree on the encryption method and exchange the keys required.

VPNs are used to replace both dial-in modem pools and dedicated wide area network (WAN) links. A VPN solution for remote dial-in users can reduce support costs because there are no phone lines or 800-number charges. A VPN solution offers advantages over a dedicated WAN environment when sites are geographically diverse or mobile, saving the cost of dedicated facilities and hardware. VPNs provide security and reliability to what would otherwise be an insecure connection through a private network. A VPN is made up of three technologies that when used together form the secure connection; authentication, tunneling, and encryption.

Authentication

Authentication is the first major component of a VPN. Authentication is the process of identifying the entity (user, router, or network device) requiring access. This authentication is often done by means of a cryptographic function, such as with challenge/response algorithms; for example, "I ask you a question and you give me the right answer."

The following sections discuss the other authentication methods:

- Point-to-Point Tunneling Protocol Password Authentication Protocol/Challenge Handshake Protocol (PPTP-PAP/CHAP)

- Digital certificates

- Smart cards and hardware tokens/PKCS #11

- RADIUS servers

- Terminal Access Controller Access Control System Plus (TACACS+)

NOTE   PKCS #11 is Public-Key Cryptography Standard (PKCS) #11, defining a technology-independent programming interface called Cryptoki for cryptographic devices such as smart cards and PCMCIA cards.

PPTP-PAP/CHAP

Password Authentication Protocol (PAP) is the most insecure authentication method available today because both the username and password are sent across the link in clear text. Anyone monitoring the connection could collect and use the information to gain access to the network.

NOTE   Using PAP for authentication is not advisable.

The Challenge Handshake Authentication Protocol (CHAP) works as follows:

1 The client establishes a connection with the server and the server sends a challenge back to the client.

2 The client then performs a hash (mathematical) function, adds some extra information, and sends the response back to the server for verification.

3 The server looks in its database and computes the hash with the challenge.

4 If these two answers are the same, authentication succeeds.

While CHAP eliminates a dictionary attack, the hashing functions could still be attacked. CHAP also supports the (user transparent) periodic challenge of the client username/ password during the session to protect against wire-tapping.

Technical Note: Dictionary Attacks

A *dictionary attack* is a threat to all passwords. An attacker obtaining some password-derived data, such as a hashed-password, performs a series of computations using every possible guess for the password; a *brute-force* attack. Because passwords are small by cryptographic standards, the password often can be determined by this brute-force method. Depending on the system, the password, and the skills of the attacker, such an attack can be completed in days, hours, or a few seconds.

The term *dictionary attack* initially referred to finding passwords in a specific list, such as an English dictionary. Today, a brute-force approach can compute common passwords, such as all five-letter combinations, on-the-fly instead of using a pre-built list. Because these threats are equivalent, the term dictionary attack is used in the broader sense to include all brute-force attacks.

Digital Certificates

Digital certificates include information about the owner of the certificate; therefore, when users visit the (secured) web site, their web browsers will check information on the certificate to see whether it matches the site information included in the URL. A digital certificate could be likened to a security driver's license.

NOTE   Certificates are issued by Certificate Authorities (CAs).

The contents of a digital certificate are shown here:

- The certificate holder's identity
- The certificate's serial number
- A valid, unchangeable date for the transaction
- The certificate's expiration dates
- A copy of the certificate holder's public key for encryption and/or signature
- Group name
- City and state

Smart Cards and Hardware Tokens/PKCS #11

Smart cards are credit card-sized plastic cards with small chips embedded in them to store user information. Smart cards provide data portability, security, and convenience. A smart card is an access control device supporting different applications; it allows users to access personal and business data.

Like smart cards, hardware tokens are tamper-resistant, credit-card sized or smaller devices (a type of smart card) that users hold in their possession. An LCD on the card consists of six to eight digits, often changing every 60 seconds.

NOTE   The term *software token* identifies an application emulating a hardware token device.

RADIUS servers

Remote Authentication Dial-In User Service (RADIUS) is a distributed system securing network remote access and network resources against unauthorized access.

RADIUS authentication includes two components:

- **Authentication server**—Installed at the customer's site and holds all user authentication and network access information
- **Client protocols**—RADIUS works on the client sending authentication requests to the RADIUS server, and the client acts on server acknowledgements sent back to the client.

NOTE   RADIUS is not limited to dial-up service; many firewall vendors support a RADIUS server implementation.

TACACS+

With Terminal Access Controller Access Control System Plus (TACACS+), when the user attempts to log in, the network access server (NAS) asks the security server what to do instead of forwarding the name/password to some central server. The security server tells the network access server to initiate a command, such as prompt for the username/password. After the username/password combination has been entered, the TACACS+ server sends a permit or deny message to the NAS.

NOTE   Cisco Systems developed the TACACS+ protocol.

Tunneling Protocols

Tunneling is the second major component of a VPN. With the growth of dial-up services and the availability of many different protocols, a method was required to create a virtual dial-up scenario in which these non-IP protocols could take advantage of Internet connectivity. Cisco defined the concept of *tunneling*, which means the encapsulation of non-IP packets. Tunneling is used to encapsulate network protocols (TCP/IP, Novell IPX/SPX, AppleTalk, and NetBEUI) into an IP packet that can travel across the Internet.

Tunneling is similar to sending an envelope with a postage stamp using an overnight service. The overnight service won't accept the first-class stamp for postage, so the envelope is packaged within an overnight envelope, which the overnight service will accept. Tunneled protocols operate in the same fashion. An AppleTalk or Internet Packet Exchange (IPX) packet cannot be sent across the Internet without being tunneled because the Internet is an IP network. Figure 16-2 illustrates what this tunneled packet looks like.

Figure 16-2 *AppleTalk or IPX Packet Tunneled within an IP Packet*

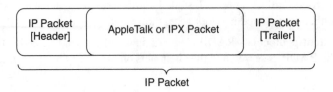

NOTE	TCP/IP could travel across the Internet on its own, but it would not be a part of the tunnel or the VPN, which means that it would be left unsecured.

Technical Note: PPP

Tunneling protocols require an underlying infrastructure protocol, which is often the Point-to-Point Protocol (PPP). PPP is one of the most common access protocols in use today and is the default for most desktop operating systems.

PPP is a suite of standardized protocols, much like TCP/IP, that provides the following features:

- Data encapsulation (tunneling)
- Data compression
- Multiplexing (multilink), combining two or more WAN links
- Network configuration negotiation

PPTP

The *Point-to-Point Tunneling Protocol* (PPTP) enables remote users to dial into a local Internet Service Provider (ISP) and tunnel across the public Internet to their respective corporate intranet server. PPTP uses PPP to establish the dial-up connection. Because of the reliance on PPP, PPTP uses encryption algorithms (PAP/CHAP) to provide encryption.

L2F

Cisco Systems developed Layer 2 Forwarding (L2F) to be used in combination with Microsoft's PPTP. After the PPP connection to the local ISP is made, L2F connects users to their corporation's intranet servers.

L2F enables the following:

- Protocol independence (IPX, SNA)
- Authentication (PPP, CHAP, TACACS)
- Address management (assigned by destination)
- Dynamic and secure tunnels
- Accounting
- Media independence (L2F over ATM, Frame Relay, X.25)
- Both L2F tunneling and local Internet access

L2TP

Layer 2 Tunneling Protocol (L2TP) is to replace PPTP as the tunneling protocol of choice by such vendors as Cisco, Microsoft, 3Com, and others. L2TP is based on PPTP and the L2F protocol. L2F was designed by Cisco supporting the encapsulation of additional protocols, such as AppleTalk and IBM's Systems Network Architecture (SNA).

Like PPTP, L2TP relies on PPP to establish a dial-up connection; but unlike PPTP, L2TP defines its own tunneling protocol. L2TP uses PAP/CHAP for user authentication and allows for transportation of non-IP protocols (such as AppleTalk, SNA, or IXP).

NOTE	L2TP is optimized for dial-up connections rather than site-to-site implementations.

Encryption

Encryption is the third major component of a VPN. Encryption is an extra measure that protects data as it moves through the tunnel. Data is encrypted before it is tunneled (encapsulated); this reduces the risk of someone tampering with the data if the tunnel is breached.

PGP

Pretty Good Privacy (PGP) is a hybrid cryptosystem, enabling the best of both worlds — public, and private key algorithms. To the user, PGP acts like any other public-key cryptosystem, using the RSA Laboratories public-key algorithm and the IDEA encryption engine for encryption. A single IDEA key is used to encrypt the message, and the same key is used to decrypt the message (symmetric encryption). RSA is used to encrypt the IDEA key used for encryption with the recipient public key (asymmetric). The receiver uses a private key to decrypt the RSA-encrypted IDEA key. Then the decrypted IDEA key is used to decrypt the rest of the message.

PGP is freely distributed in versions that run on a variety of platforms, including DOS/Windows, UNIX, and Macintosh. PGP was not developed, nor controlled by, any government or standards organization. PGP supports the use of digital signatures, message encryption, compression, e-mail compatibility and segmentation (to accommodate protocol message size limitations).

PKI

The Public Key Infrastructure (PKI) is a system of digital certificates, certificate authorities, (both commercial and governmental), certificate management services, and directory services (LDAP, X.500) that verify the identity and authority of each party involved in any transaction over the Internet. PKI is the framework that provides for privacy and digital signature services in support of international commerce, balancing government oversight while ensuring privacy for users.

PKI can be used for authentication and authorization, privacy and confidentiality, data integrity, and nonrepudiation. Nonrepudiation provides a way for one party to be sure that the other party has indeed sent the message. Without such a guarantee, financial house, banking, and sales transactions could not occur. The guarantee lies in that nonrepudiation prevents a sending party from "denying" that any transmission occurred.

Public/Private Key Infrastructure can be likened to a telephone book. The sending party looks up the recipient's encryption-key (public) in the "phone book," encrypts and sends the message across a public network. The recipient uses a private key, the only key that will work, to decrypt the message so that it can be read.

MD5

Developed by RSA Labs, Message Digest 5 (MD5) is a hash function that takes a string of arbitrary length and produces a fixed-length output of 128-bits. Hash algorithms turn a variable-sized amount of text into a fixed-sized output (hash value) and are used in creating digital signatures.

IPSec

The Internet Engineering Task Force (IETF) has a working group called IP Security Protocol (IPSec), which is responsible for defining Internet security standards and protocols. IP-VPNs use the IPSec standards as part of their security measures.

IP packets have no inherent security and as such it can be considered easy to forge the source and destination addresses of IP packets, modify the contents of IP packets, replay old packets, and inspect the contents of IP packets in transit. There is no guarantee that IP messages received are:

- From the sender (the source address in the IP header),
- They contain the original data the sender placed in them,
- Or that the original data was not inspected and/or copied by a third party while the packet was in transit.

IPSec is a collection of cryptography-based services and protocols, providing authentication as well as encryption to an IP-VPN connection using L2TP. IPSec protects IP message traffic by providing data origin authentication, connectionless data integrity authentication, data content confidentiality, anti-replay protection, and limited traffic flow confidentiality.

NOTE   IPSec provides an IP-only tunnel (not multiprotocol without L2TP or PPTP) or straight IP connection between two endpoints.

IKE

Internet Key Exchange (IKE) is a good general-purpose security exchange protocol which can be used for policy negotiation and establishment of authenticated keying material. The specification of what IKE is being used for is done in a Domain of Interpretation (DOI). The IPSec DOI can be found in RFC 2407 (www.ietf.org/rfc/rfc2407.txt?number=2407), defining how IKE negotiates IPSec Security Association (SA).

NOTE   SAs are used with IPSec to define the processing done on a specific IP packet.

LAN-to-LAN VPN

The LAN-to-LAN VPN is tied to the IPSec standard—where the remote dial-up user VPN uses protocols such as PPTP, L2F, and L2TP, IPSec concentrates on LAN-to-LAN. In a typical LAN-to-LAN design, not all traffic is encrypted. Two types of communication are possible:

- **Web server access**—When a user connects to the web server on another network, the HTTP traffic is unencrypted. There is no requirement for the VPN device to encrypt this traffic.

- **VPN server access**—When a user connects to the VPN server on another network, the VPN device recognizes that it is a VPN request and encrypts the packets.

The Data Encryption Standard (DES) supporting 56-bit encryption also can be used for LAN-to-LAN encryption. Symmetric-key systems are simpler and faster; however, their main drawback is that the two parties must somehow exchange the encryption key in a secure way. Public-key encryption avoids this problem because the public key can be distributed in a non-secure way, and the private key is never transmitted.

NOTE   DES is the most popular symmetric-key system and cannot be used for export.

DES and Triple-DES (3DES, 168-bit encryption) both can be used to support cryptographic requirements between routers for Intranet communication, as long as both cryptographic endpoints are in the United States.

NOTE   LAN-to-LAN VPN configurations also are used in a dial back-up scenario, where a site's dedicated WAN access has failed and the WAN router will initiate a VPN dial session to reestablish communication until the dedicated connection is restored.

VPN Architecture

Several VPN network architectures are deployed by enterprise organizations for VPN services. The following list of remote access VPN network architectures is discussed in the following sections:

- Firewall based
- Black-box based
- Router based
- Remote-access based

Firewall-Based VPNs

With firewall-based VPNs, it is considered a safe presumption that a firewall will be used and placed at the network perimeter, as illustrated in Figure 16-3.

This presumption leads to a natural extension that this device also can support the VPN connections, providing a central point of management of both the firewall and network access security policies. A drawback to this combined firewall/VPN-access method is performance. On a single "box," a busy Internet circuit with multiple VPNs could overload the system.

Figure 16-3 *Firewall-Based VPN*

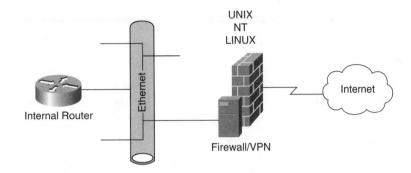

Black-Box-Based VPNs

In the black-box scenario, a vendor offers just that, a black box; a device loaded with encryption software to create a VPN tunnel. Black-box VPN vendors should be supporting all three tunneling protocols—PPTP, L2TP, and IPSec. Specific vendors need to be thoroughly researched, however, because they don't all provide the same level of tunneling protocol support.

The black-box VPN sits behind or with the firewall, as illustrated in Figure 16-4.

Figure 16-4 *Black-Box-Based VPN*

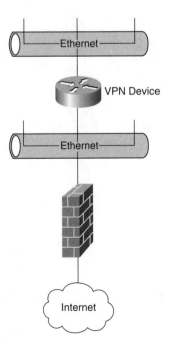

The firewall provides security to the organization, not the data, whereas the VPN device provides security to the data, but not the organization. If the firewall is in front of the VPN device, a rule-based policy on that firewall will need to be implemented.

Router-Based VPNs

Router-based VPNs are for an organization that has a large capital investment in routers and an experienced IT staff. Many router vendors support router-based VPN configurations. There are two ways to go about implementing router-based VPNs:

- Software is added to the router to allow an encryption process to occur.
- An external card from a third-party vendor is inserted into the router chassis. This method is designed to off-load the encryption process from the router CPU to the additional card.

Some vendors support hot swapping (replacing hardware) and redundancy (backup solutions), which are built into their router-based VPN products. Performance can be an issue with router-based VPNs because of the addition of an encryption process to the routing process; a heavier burden may be added to the router CPU, more than ever if the router is handling a large number of routes or implementing an intensive routing algorithm. Figure 16-5 illustrates a router-based VPN, where packets are encrypted from source to destination.

Figure 16-5 *Router-Based VPN*

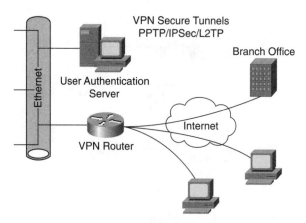

The drawback to a router-based VPN is security. Routers are considered to be poor at providing network security compared to a firewall. It is possible that an attacker will spoof traffic past the router, in turn fooling the firewall because the firewall will interpret these packets as originating from the other side of the VPN tunnel. This spoofing allows the attacker to gain access to services that are not visible from other locations on the Internet.

Summary

Remote access solutions are deployed by enterprise organizations to provide access to fixed site resources to remote users (not at a fixed workstation) at a site's LAN. A virtual private network (VPN) is a public network being used for this private and secure communication between the remote (telecommuting or mobile) user and the organization's LAN. This VPN connection is authenticated and encrypted across the public network. Often times this public network is the Internet.

A VPN is made up of three technologies, used together, to form a secure connection. These three technologies are as follows:

- **Authentication**—The process of identifying the entity (user, router, network device) requiring access. Some examples of authentication are those schemes using PAP/CHAP or RADIUS.

- **Tunneling**—Used to encapsulate network protocols (TCP/IP, IPX/SPX, AppleTalk, and NetBEUI) into an IP packet that can travel across the Internet. Some examples of tunneling protocols are PPTP, L2TP, or L2F.

- **Encryption**—An extra measure protecting the data through the tunnel. Data is encrypted before it is tunneled (encapsulated). Some examples of encryption are PGP, MD5, or IPSec (if configured to provide encryption).

The following list provides several VPN network architectures deployed by enterprise organizations for VPN services:

- Firewall based (for example, Cisco PIX)
- Black-box based (for example, any VPN vendor proprietary implementation)
- Router based (for example, Cisco 36x0/75xx Series routers)
- Remote-access based (for example, Cisco 300x Series VPN Concentrators)

Frequently Asked Questions (FAQ)

1 Will IP-VPNs replace traditional WAN services, such as ATM or Frame Relay?

Although VPNs do offer flexibility for communications planners, they also enable the consumer to retain better control of security and communications policy management, rather than turning those controls over to a third-party as is the case with Frame Relay networks. The feature that attracts most consumers to VPNs in WANs is the low cost.

The concern with widespread acceptance of IP-VPNs replacing traditional WAN services is twofold:

a. The Quality of Service (QoS), Service Level Agreements (SLAs), and QoS Service Level Guarantees (SLGs) of the IP Network Service Providers carrying the IP traffic and whether the providers will have these levels of quality and meet the service agreements. Currently, customers aren't willing to accept the replacement of WAN services with VPNs because they aren't convinced that ISPs are providing QoS, SLAs, and SLGs.

b. The VPN parameters themselves (authentication, tunneling, and encryption) must be agreed upon by all VPN network sites.

These concerns are being addressed by IP-VPN vendors, network service providers, and customers alike and it is expected that widespread acceptance and use of IP-VPNs will coincide with the same widespread acceptance of IP, version 6 (IPv6). IPv6, originally called IP Next Generation (IPng), increases the address space from 32 to 128 bits, providing for a nearly unlimited (2^{128}, or 3.4028236692093846346337460743177e+38, unique addresses) number of networks and systems. IPv6 enables QoS parameters for real-time audio and video.

2 What is QoS and why is it important?

QoS is the ability to define a level of performance in a network. For example, ATM networks specify modes of service that ensure optimum performance for traffic such as real-time voice and video. QoS is a major issue on the Internet as well as in enterprise networks, because voice and video are more often transported over IP-based data networks that were not designed for continuous speech or video. Thus, transmissions are broken into packets that can travel different routes and arrive at different times, causing "choppy" conversations.

There is no better QoS than that offered by the plain old telephone system (POTS), which provides the highest quality of service in the world for voice calls. This circuit-switched system provides a continuous channel between two parties until one hangs up.

It is important to realize the difference between QoS and Class of Service (CoS). QoS refers to the mechanisms in the network software that determine which packets have priority. CoS refers to feature sets, or groups of services, that are assigned to users based on an organization's policy.

3 Are there issues with router-based VPNs?

There are two concerns with router-based VPNs:

- **Interoperability**—If a connection to a suppliers' VPN is required, will both the site router and suppliers' router operate with one another and create the VPN?

- **Encapsulation**—Will non-IP protocols, such as IPX or SNA, be transported? Some router manufacturers only encrypt; they do not encapsulate.

Although processor load also is a concern, many routers now use application-specific integrated circuit (ASIC) hardware, enabling the router to dedicate certain processors for specific tasks, preventing any one router activity from overloading the router.

Case Study

KeyNet Enterprises is a small company that has deployed a remote access VPN to support their telecommuting sales force. This VPN is illustrated in Figure 16-6.

Figure 16-6 *KeyNet Enterprises Remote Access VPN*

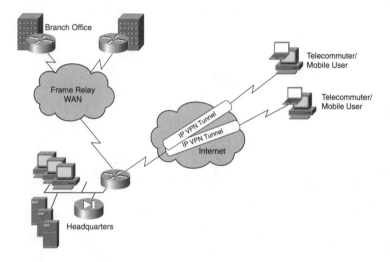

KeyNet's remote users dial into their local ISP and establish a VPN tunnel to corporate headquarters for access to corporate intranet functions. These remote users are using native IP communication, in turn using the VPN tunnel for encryption across the public Internet. Once these remote users are authenticated and are part of the organization's intranet, these users also can access branch office resources across the Frame Relay WAN. It is not automatic that these remote users can access branch office resources; this access depends on the network design, configuration, and management by the organizations IS/IT staff.

The following topics are covered in this chapter:

- Voice Network Access
- ANI
- Lines and Trunks

CHAPTER 17

Voice Networks

Voice switching and routing within a telecommunications network is based upon the automatic number identification (ANI). ANIs are constructed in accordance with the North American Numbering Plan (NANP), which you can find more information on at www.nanpa.com.

Before a network can rout a call, that network must first receive it, either through dedicated or switched access.

This chapter discusses the fundamental components of the Public Switched Telephone Network (PSTN) from a customer application point-of-view, such as network access and dial plans.

Voice Network Access

There are two methods available to support access from (and termination to) a customer premise to the PSTN—switched and dedicated.

- Switched access to the PSTN describes a customer implementation where a long-distance carrier either is pre-subscribed to by the caller or is identified by additional digits, called the Carrier Identification Code (CIC) to the dialed number. Switched access is beneficial to the customer in environments with small call volumes where dedicated access does not provide a cost-savings.

- Dedicated access to the PSTN describes a customer implementation where a dedicated circuit, or line, is provisioned between the customer site and the telephone switch. Dedicated access provides a cost-per-minute savings to the customer and is beneficial to the customer in environments with large call volumes.

NOTE   Dedicated access can terminate into either a local or long-distance telephone switch, depending upon the network service provider being a local or long-distance carrier.

Aside from switched and dedicated access, there are two additional distinctions regarding access to a long-distance, or interexchange, carrier; the CIC and Primary Interexchange Carrier (PIC), as described below:

- **CIC**—The CIC is a 4-digit code that controls the routing applied to a call by the originating switch. The CIC is also a numeric code assigned by the NANP Administrator for the provisioning of switched services. The CIC is unique to each carrier and is used by the telephone company to route a call to the trunk group designated by the CIC.

- **PIC**—The PIC is a code identifying a carrier chosen by a subscriber (a customer or end-user, for example) to be accessible via simplified dialing pattern, such as '8+Dialed Number' from a Private Branch Exchange (PBX).

Switched Access

Switched access to a long-distance IntereXchange Carrier (IXC) is dependant on the customer establishing a connection between themselves and the Local Exchange Carrier (LEC) and interconnecting trunks between the serving LEC and the IXC.

When the customer (end-user) places an outbound long-distance call, the LEC performs a database lookup to determine which long-distance carrier, or IXC, the route should be called to. The LEC's customer determines which IXC will carry the call by use of the Primary Interexchange Carrier Code (PIC). The LEC translates this PIC to a CIC determining which carrier will receive the dialed long-distance call from the end-user.

Figure 17-1 illustrates a typical switched access configuration. Switched access is physically a single 2- or 4-wire line from a telephone set directly connected to a LEC Central Office (C.O.) switch. It is possible for a customer premise to have several switched access lines, with groups of these switched access lines having different IXCs being selected as the primary carrier.

Switched access is typically found in a small office/home office (SOHO) environment where call usage is fairly low. The alternative to switched access is dedicated access, which is discussed in the next section.

NOTE   If a customer location has seven or more switched access lines it is worth considering a dedicated access option, such as a T1, to reduce costs.

Figure 17-1 *Switched Access*

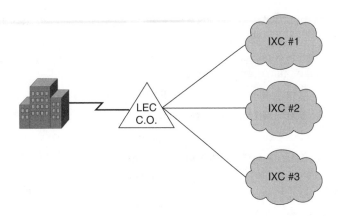

Dedicated Access

Dedicated long-distance access bypasses the LEC CO switch and connects the customer directly to the IXC. Dedicated access is typically seen in environments where call volume to a particular customer premise may be very high, such as large enterprise locations or call centers.

Because dedicated access is a straight-through facility as far as the LEC is concerned and not consuming switch capacity in the LEC voice switch, dedicated access tends to be more cost effective on a per-call basis. In a long-distance configuration, such as illustrated in Figure 17-2, the customer does not need to negotiate with the LEC at all. Instead the serving IXC will interface with the serving LEC on the customer's behalf.

Figure 17-2 *Dedicated Access*

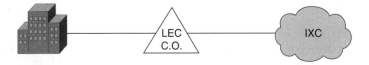

The physical connection in a dedicated access environment is typically DS1/DS3 between the customer premise and the IXC. In a dedicated environment only one IXC can support each physical line (DSx), however, the customer premise can have several physical lines going to several IXCs, with the PBX making the determination which IXC is to carry the call (based on PBX configuration).

ANI

ANI is a service that provides the telephone number of an incoming call. ANI is used for a variety of functions, such as:

- Telephone companies can direct a call to the proper long-distance carrier's equipment (based on the originating, or sending ANI)
- Help identify the caller's address for 911 calls
- Route 800# calls to the nearest vendor
- Call centers to identify the calling party to better service a customer

ANIs are constructed per the NANP. The NANP was designed to allow for quick and discreet connection to any phone in North America. The NANP is comprised of three elements:

- Area Code (NPA)
- Exchange CO Code (Nxx)
- Station Subscriber Number (xxxx)

Each of these is discussed in the following sections.

Area Code (NPA)

The Area Code, or Numbering Plan Assignment (NPA), identifies the calling destinations area. The first number of an NPA is 2-9, with 0 and 1 reserved. Zero (0) is reserved for operator access or operator services; One (1) is reserved for the local switching office to immediately set up a tandem switch connection for a long-distance toll call.

Certain NPAs have been set up for predefined or specific functions. These are:

- 456 Nxx
- 900/976 Nxx
- 500 Nxx
- 8xx (800/888/877/866/855)

456 NXX

Numbers within the 456 NPA are used to identify carrier-specific services. Carrier identification is provided within the dialed digits of the E.164 number; the prefix following 456 (456-NXX) identifies the carrier. Use of these numbers enables the proper routing of inbound international calls destined for these services into and between NANP area countries.

Current 456-NXX assignments are provided in Table 17-1:

Table 17-1   *456-NXX Assignments*

NXX	CARRIER
226	Teleglobe Canada
288	AT&T
289	AT&T
333	Startec, Inc.
624	MCI
640	Sprint
741	STSJ
808	Hawaiian Tel

900/976 Nxx

900 numbers are used to identify premium services, and the cost of calls to these services is billed to the calling party.

900 numbers are in the format of 900-NXX-XXXX. 900 service is not portable; the identity of the service provider is embedded in the number. The prefix (NXX) indicates the 900 service provider, and the line number (XXXX) indicates the particular premium service.

NOTE   When talking about telephone numbers "portable" means that the customer owns the number and can move the number to different carriers. When a number is not portable it means the carrier owns the number, not the customer.

500 Nxx

500 numbers are used for "follow me" personal communication services.

500 numbers are in the format 500-NXX-XXXX. 500 service is not portable; the identity of the service provider is embedded in the number. The prefix (NXX) indicates the 500 service provider, and the line number (XXXX) indicates the particular premium service.

8xx (800/888/877/866/855) Toll-Free Numbers

8xx toll-free is an automatic reverse-charge service. Instead of the caller paying for the cost of the call, it is automatically charged to the called number (the receiver). This includes surcharges, such as the payphone surcharge and toll-free directory assistance.

NOTE   Toll-free service in the U.S. is called Free-Phone in the rest of the world (ROW).

Toll-free numbers are commonly used by businesses so that their customers do not have to pay to call them. This free service is especially important today as more and more businesses are centralizing their support operations and are using interactive voice response (voice menu prompts) services.

Many non-business consumers have also found the toll-free numbers useful. These users will give the toll-free number to their family members so that when they are away from home, they can call without paying exceptionally high payphone, hotel, motel, and hospital rates.

Toll-free numbers have an associated "ring-to" (termination) number. This is commonly the main business telephone number or the primary telephone number at a residence. When someone calls the toll-free number, the telephone network looks up the toll-free number to find the carrier that handles the call and the ring-to number associated with the toll-free number and routes the call to the carrier for delivery.

Exchange CO Code (NXX)

This is the CO designator designator that lists the possible number of central office codes within each area code (NPA).

Certain NXXs have been set up for predefined or specific functions. These are:

- 555-xxxx
- 800-855-xxxx
- 555-Numbers (555-xxxx)

555 numbers are used to reach a wide variety of information services are reached by 555 numbers. For example, NPA-555-1212 will provide directory assistance information for the specified NPA.

555 numbers are in the format 555-XXXX, where the line number (XXXX) indicates the particular information service. The ATIS-sponsored Industry Numbering Committee assigns 555 numbers.

555 numbers may be assigned for either national or local use. A national assignment requires that the 555 number be implemented in at least 30 percent of all NPAs or states or provinces in the NANP Area. A local assignment is made for implementation in certain NPAs specified at assignment time.

800-855 numbers, in the format 800-855-XXXX, are used to access Public Switched Telephone Network services intended for use by the deaf, hard of hearing, or speech impaired. Such services include Telecommunications Relay Service and Message Relay Service.

Station Subscriber Number(XXXX)

This number identifies the service subscriber of the CO identified by the Nxx. There are no special or reserved XXXX numbers.

Lines and Trunks

A *line* is an end point from a CO or a PBX and carries a single conversation. A *trunk* interconnects two switching systems, such as between LEC central offices, or a LEC CO switch and a customer PBX. Trunks bundle several lines, carrying multiple simultaneous conversations and are used for call switching and routing.

Direct Inward Dialing

Direct Inward Dialing (DID), refers to a service whereby a caller can dial a 10-digit number from outside a switch and reach a specific individual without an operator (live or an automated attendant) intervention. In the context of a PBX, DID is a feature that must be configured to enable the direct dialing of an extension.

Direct Outward Dialing

Similar to DID, Direct Outward Dialing (DOD) enables a caller behind a switch or PBX to place outbound calls without an operator or automated attendant assistance. This was necessary in the early days of corporate telephone systems where operators screened incoming and outgoing calls, such as prohibiting employees from making international long-distance personal calls; these restrictions can now be configured on a corporate switch or PBX.

Tie Lines

Tie lines, or tie trunks, are dedicated private line, point-to-point, circuits used to connect two voice facilities; such as a dedicated trunk between two organization's PBXs, in different locations. There are no geographical limits to implementing tie lines, however, cost needs to be a consideration as most network service provider private line services are distance sensitive with a billable cost-per-mile.

Summary

Voice switching and routing within a telecommunications network, such as the PSTN, is based upon the ANIs. ANIs are constructed in accordance with the NANP (`www.nanpa.com`).

ANI (based on the NANP) provides the telephone number to the recipient of an incoming call. ANI is used for a variety of functions, such as:

- Telephone companies can direct a call to the proper long-distance carrier
- Identify the caller's address for 911 calls
- Customer call centers can route incoming 800# calls to the nearest support location

DID, DOD, and Tie Lines are the three common applications of line and trunk implementations. DID refers to a service whereby a caller can dial a 10-digit number from outside a switch and reach a specific individual without operator (live or an automated attendant) intervention. DOD, similar to DID, enables a caller behind a switch or PBX to place outbound calls without operator or automated attendant assistance. Tie lines, or tie trunks, are dedicated private line, point-to-point, circuits used to connect two voice facilities; such as a dedicated trunk between two organization's PBXs, in different locations.

Frequently Asked Questions (FAQ)

1 If a customer changes long-distance companies, do they have to change their 800/8XX number?

No, the number is assigned to the customer at the Service Management Systems (SMS), the main operations support system of the 800/8XX Data Base Service). When the customer changes long-distance companies, the number is "ported" by the SMS to your new company. This is where the term "800/8xx Portability" comes from.

2 What is a LATA?

Local Access and Transport Area (LATA), a term created by Judge Greene when he broke up Ma Bell in the early '80s into AT&T Long Distance and the original 7 regional Bell operating companies (RBOCs). Judge Greene tried to divide the U.S. telephone network into metropolitan areas that are used by the U.S. Department of Commerce for all government statistics. However, the telephone network didn't align with these boundaries, so the final set of defined areas are called LATAs.

There are several important aspects of LATAs. First, toll calls within a LATA are referred to as intraLATA toll calls, local toll calls, or regional toll calls. IntraLATA calls can be carried by the local telephone company or by a long-distance carrier.

Second, toll calls between LATAs are referred to as interLATA toll calls and state-to-state toll calls. However, not all interLATA toll calls are state-to-state because most states have several LATAs. The local telephone company is not permitted to carry interLATA toll calls. IXCs, or long-distance carriers, carry all interLATA toll calls.

3 What is 1+ service?

Most wireline telephone subscribers in the U.S. can presubsribe to the long-distance carrier of their choice for both intraLATA and interLATA calls. These calls are made by dialing a "1" plus the 10-digit telephone number, hence, "1+" is the popular way of referring to these calls.

4 What's the difference between a PIC and a CIC?

CIC, a four digit number that identifies a long-distance service provider. PIC is the long-distance provider used when a 1+ call is made.

There are currently two types of PICs: intra-LATA and inter-LATA. The inter-LATA PIC is also used for international calls (starting with "011," but not "0011").

A CIC is assigned to each PIC when a new number is assigned from the local telco (LEC) or when PICs are changed. Often both PICs are the same, but that need not be the case.

The current PICs of any given number can be determined by calling from that number as follows:

Intra-LATA: call 1-NPA-700-4141 where NPA is the first 3 digits or the 10 digit number.

Inter-LATA: call 1-700-555-4141.

Both numbers are toll-free and should result in a brief recorded message identifying the underlying carrier.

5 What is casual calling?

Casual Calling is using a 10-10 number to override the PIC selection. Using the 10-10 number only applies to the immediate call.

Although carriers advertise the casual calling as 10-10 followed by a 3-digit number, the actual casual calling is 101 followed by a 4-digit number (the CIC).

Case Study

The following case study (see Figure 17-3) demonstrates how switched and dedicated access to (one or more) voice networks can be used simultaneously in supporting a call center environment.

BrownCo has deployed dedicated voice network access to two IXC. Both dedicated lines support inbound and outbound calls, with IXC #2 designated the secondary carrier to IXC #1. In the event that BrownCo loses all dedicated access (for example access cable cut) then switched access to the serving LEC is in place to support the inbound/outbound calls. The LEC has trunks to IXC #1 and IXC #3. Which trunk to use (IXC #1 or IXC #3) is determined by the PIC/CIC. In the event that IXC #1 fails (such as switch or database outage), then IXC #2 will be used for dedicated inbound/outbound service and the switched access to the LEC can handle any overflow (calls the dedicated access do not have enough bandwidth to support, one call = one DS0 = 64 Kbps) by directing these switched calls to IXC #3.

Figure 17-3 *BrownCo Call Center Case Study (Voice Network Access)*

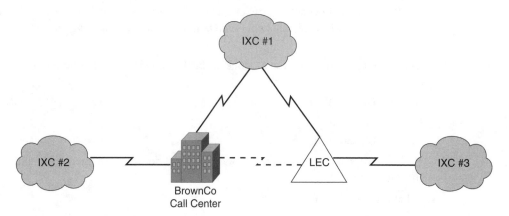

This chapter covers the following topics:

- FCAPS Model
- Network Management Architecture
- Network Management Protocols
- An Introduction to TMN

CHAPTER 18

Network Management Basics

Network management describes the methodology used to manage and maintain network operations and respond to user requirement changes. With the implementation of Simple Network Management Protocol (SNMP), local area network (LAN) and wide area network (WAN) components can be monitored and managed, often from what is called a central *Network Operations Center* (NOC) facility. The network management platform is an integrated suite of functions that can be implemented on one machine, or it can be implemented on several machines or databases spanning thousands of miles, supporting several organizations. Some examples of a network management platform are HP Openview or CiscoWorks 2000.

Network management can be segmented into two categories:

- **Tactical**—Tactical network management relates to proactive and reactive situations, such as network failures, congestion, and unacceptable service quality. The tasks include troubleshooting, configuration, and adjusting traffic flows.

- **Strategic**—Strategic network management involves a long-term perspective that is oriented toward adequate planning to avoid shortages as the network grows. Strategic tasks use information to adjust operations, optimize quality, and manage facilities to reduce overall operational costs.

This chapter discusses network management models that are both tactical and strategic. This includes a discussion of the following:

- FCAPS model
- Network management architecture
- Network management protocols
- Telecommunications Management Network (TMN)

FCAPS Model

The ISO FCAPS model is a major contributor to network management. It is similar to the OSI Reference Model used for internetworking (for more information regarding the OSI model, see Chapter 2, "OSI Reference Model").

The FCAPS model is made up of the following components:

- **Fault Management**—Detects, logs, notifies users of, and (if possible) automatically fixes network issues. Most fault management systems poll the managed objects for error conditions and present this information to the network manager.

  Fault management identifies and isolates network issues, proposes problem resolution, and subsequently logs the issues and associated resolutions. The testing of any fault resolutions should be performed on non-production systems prior to deployment in a "live" network.

- **Configuration Management**—Monitors network and system configuration information so that the impact on network operations (hardware and software elements) can be tracked and managed. Network changes, additions, and deletions need to be coordinated with the network management personnel, often in a NOC.

- **Accounting Management**—Measures network utilization parameters so that individual or group users on a network can be regulated, billed, or charged.

- **Performance Management**—Measures and makes network performance data available so that performance can be maintained at acceptable thresholds.

- **Security Management**—Controls access to network resources as established by organizational security guidelines. Most network management systems address security regarding network hardware, such as someone logging into a router.

Where FCAPS is a model for network management, the next section discusses the architecture for network management.

Network Management Architecture

The architecture of a network management platform is made up of a common set of relationships and structure that exists between managed devices and a management entity, as illustrated in Figure 18-1.

Figure 18-1 *Network Management Topology*

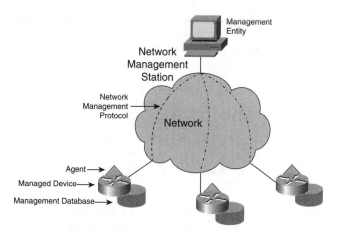

The following list details the components found in a network:

- **End stations**—Computer systems and network devices with software that enables the sending of alerts (to management entities) when network issues are identified; for example, any LAN server or user's workstation configured with network management software.

- **Management entities**—These entities are programmed to react to end-station alerts by executing a predefined set of actions, such as the following:
    - Event logging
    - System shutdown
    - Console notification
    - Automatic attempts to repair the system (such as reload or reboot)

The elements of a management system are as follows:

- **Network manager agents**—Integrate with network devices, platforms, and applications

- **Network manager applications**—Network management servers that collect network management data from the network manager agents and correlate the data for analysis by the network administrator/manager

Network management agents carry network management data and report network transmission problems to a network manager. The network manager controls a set of management agents and ensures that these agents collect the appropriate information.

Network management agents are software modules that compile information about the devices within which they reside and automatically or manually respond to all polls.

Agent information is conveyed to the management entity within the Network Management System (NMS) via a network management protocol, such as Simple Network Management Protocol (SNMP).

Network Management Protocols

Network management protocols carry network management data between the managed devices and the management console. The following network management protocols are defined by various Internet Engineering Task Force (IETF) standards:

- **SNMP**—The SNMP is used to communicate with a management "agent" in a network device. A remote manager collects status information and controls the remote device through the SNMP agent. There are three versions of SNMP:

  - **SNMPv1**—Reports only whether a device is functioning properly. In other words, it tells whether the device is "up" and running or "down."

  - **SNMPv2**—SNMPv1 with the addition of security and Remote Monitoring (RMON) Management Information Base (MIB) support. The RMON MIB provides continuous feedback to the network manager without having to be queried by the SNMP console.

  - **SNMPv3**—SNMPv2 with the addition of message level security. SNMPv3 also includes an MIB for remotely monitoring and managing the configuration parameters for the SNMPv3 Security Model.

- **SNMP MIBs**—The SNMP agent delivers the MIB information to the network manager. Each managed resource has an MIB, containing what can be known about the device and the device's capabilities. An MIB for a router contains information about each interface—bandwidth speed, protocols supported, and current status. An MIB for a server has information about the Central Processing Unit (CPU), operating system, memory, and disk usage space.

- **MIB2**—A standard MIB defining basic interface information such as bandwidth speed, numbers of packets sent and received by the interface, numbers of broadcast and unicast packets, and errors.

- **RMON**—An MIB that controls an agent monitoring a single LAN segment. Collects information as instructed by the network management console about traffic levels, which systems are talking, and specific conversations between two parties.

- **RMON2**—An MIB for controlling agents that monitor traffic across the network (LAN/WAN). RMON2 measures traffic flows between different parts of the network and identifies which protocols and applications are in use by each system.

- **Common Management Interface Protocol (CMIP)**—OSI standard protocol used with the Common Management Information Services (CMIS); CMIS defines a system of network management information services. CMIP provides improved security and better reporting of unusual network conditions. CMIP was proposed as a replacement for the SNMP but has not been adopted by the networking community for widespread implementation because of SNMP's incumbency.

An Introduction to TMN

TMN is the International Organization for Standardization (ISO) and International Tele-communications Union (ITU) standard detailed in the ITU-T Recommendation Series M.3000. The M.3000 series defines the framework for the planning, provisioning, installation, maintenance, operations, and administration of telecommunications networks and services. This framework is flexible, scalable, reliable, inexpensive to run, and easy to enhance. TMN provides for more capable and efficient networks by defining standard ways of doing network-management tasks and communicating across networks. TMN also allows processing to be distributed to appropriate levels for scalability, optimum performance, and communication efficiency.

NOTE   The full ITU-T M.3000 recommendation series can be found at www-comm.itsi.disa.mil/ tmn/tmn_itu.html.

The principles of TMN are incorporated into a telecommunications network, sending and receiving information and managing network resources. Telecommunications networks are made up of switching systems, circuits, terminals, etc. In TMN terminology, these resources are referred to as *network elements* (NEs). TMN enables communication between operations support systems (OSS) and NEs.

TMN architecture and interfaces build on existing open systems interconnection (OSI) standards, which include but not limited to the following:

- **CMIP**—Defines management services exchanged between peer entities (other network management devices).
- **Guideline for Definition of Managed Objects (GDMO)**—Provides templates for classifying and describing managed resources.
- **Abstract Syntax Notation One (ASN.1)**—Provides syntax rules for data types, such as those found in an MIB.
- **OSI Model**—Defines the seven-layer OSI Reference Model.

NOTE   The TMN standards work has been incorporated into the work by other standards bodies, such as the Network Management Forum (NMF), Bellcore, and the European Telecommunications Standards Institute (ETSI). The Synchronous Optical Network (SONET), SONET Interoperability Forum (SIF), and the Asynchronous Transfer Mode Forum (ATMF) are specifying TMN-compliant management interfaces.

Summary

The ISO FCAPS model is a major contributor to network management. It is similar to the OSI Reference Model used for internetworking. *FCAPS* is an acronym for Fault Management, Configuration Management, Accounting Management, Performance Management, and Security Management.

TMN is based on the OSI management framework. Management functions are performed by operations comprised of CMIS primitives.

Processes that manage the information are called *management entities*. A management entity can take on one of two possible roles: manager or agent. Network manager and agent processes send and receive information (requests and notifications) using CMIP.

The architecture of a network management platform is made up of a common set of management entities—end stations and manager stations (used for the analysis of collected network management data).

Frequently Asked Questions (FAQ)

1   Which is better, FCAPS, or TMN?

TMN has become separated into two parts: TMN as architecture for telecommunications management and TMN as a set of supporting protocols. Initial TMN proponents and implementations did not differentiate between architecture and protocol and often ran into adversity. The open-standards concept behind TMN was widely accepted, although the underlying protocols were not readily adopted.

The TMN model helps to categorize, prioritize, and specify the responsibilities of telecommunications management products and services. For the first years of TMN's existence, the industry was focused on standard protocol implementation, particularly at the element and network management layers. The future of TMN, however, is not in the protocol domain. TMN will continue as a framework for telecommunications management, but it will become less focused on defining protocols to support the TMN architecture.

FCAPS is the methodology used to implement the TMN standards for network management. Whereas TMN defines how networks, such as ATM, can be managed, FCAPS is the model used to implement the network management architecture.

There is no clear answer regarding which is better, FCAPS, or TMN. As the industry has evolved, TMN has found a niche within the FCAPS model.

2 Is it necessary to monitor and manage every network device?

No, it is not necessary to monitor and manage every device on a network. Device monitoring and management depends upon the mission-critical nature of that device. For example, it can be considered more worthwhile to an organization to monitor and manage a WAN router or corporate Internet/intranet servers rather than to monitor/manage individual workstations.

Although it is desirable to have visibility into and manage as much of the network as possible, even at the desktop level of granularity, there is a balance between the size and scale of the network and the network management organization itself. It is considered unreasonable for a single network manager to manage a large ATM WAN to the desktop level of granularity (such as routers, switches, servers, hubs, and LAN workstations), when management of the routers and servers is a huge task in and of itself.

Case Study

This case study illustrates how a network might be managed. Figure 18-2 depicts a simple three-node Frame Relay WAN. This Frame Relay WAN is managed by a third-party (neither the customer nor the network service provider) network management entity.

This third-party entity requires a Frame Relay Permanent Virtual Circuit (PVC) to each managed site so that it can have visibility into managed devices at those respective sites. The network manager uses SNMPv2 so that device status can be collected without having to be polled from the network management console, conserving network bandwidth by minimizing the amount of network management traffic and utilizing the manager console for data collection and analysis rather than as a polling server.

Figure 18-2 *Network Managed Frame Relay WAN*

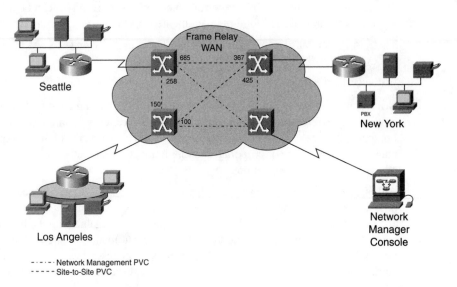

This same network manager console provides the network manager remote access to the managed devices at each site for change management, such as configuration or router software (IOS) upgrades.

The following topics are covered in this chapter:

- Measuring Network Availability
- Internetwork Reliability Options

CHAPTER 19

High Availability Networking

The term *high availability* can be nebulous to define because the term itself is considered subjective; what one person or network provider considers to be "high availability" does not necessarily mean the same for another person or network service provider.

High availability is a subjective interpretation of two network availability statistics:

- **Mean-Time-to-Repair (MTTR)**—Average time required to recover/restore from a network outage or repair a failed component.

- **Mean-Time-Between Failure (MTBF)**—Average time a network or component works without failure.

This chapter discusses measuring network availability and reliability in addition to the building of redundant networks.

Measuring Network Availability

Availability is expressed as a percentage and is measured by a ratio of two numbers: MTTR and MTBF. It is calculated using the following:

```
MTPF Availability = [MTBF / (MTBF + MTTR)] x 100%
```

The same availability number can be reached using the formula shown here:

```
Availability = [Uptime / (Uptime + Downtime)] x 100%
```

MTBF can be represented as the total uptime of a network, and MTTR can be represented as the total downtime of a network. For example, suppose that a car is available for use 24-hours a day for a full year, totaling 8760 hours. This car experienced some engine issues that kept the car from being used for three days, or 72 hours. Using these numbers, the availability of the car can be measured as shown here:

```
Uptime = (Total Hours - Downtime)
Uptime = (8760 - 72) = 8688
Availability Formula (Uptime)= [(8688) / (8688 + 72)] x 100% = 99.2%
```

Given the previous formula, the car's availability is measured at 99.2 percent.

Network availability is measured in the same fashion; the Uptime (or MTBF) is divided by the sum of the Uptime and the Downtime (MTBF + MTTR), and then multiplied by 100 for the percentage result.

Networks always available are measured as being available 100 percent of the time. This 100 percent goal is for all intents and purposes unattainable because of planned outages for network maintenance, unplanned outages such as a carrier network link or hardware failure, or for any other reason that a network or component can fail, such as a power outage. It is a function of the network designer to mitigate these situations as much as possible.

Network designers use the required availability given to them by the users, network administrators, or the applications themselves, to determine how much protection and redundancy to build into the network. Table 19-1 associates this availability requirement with an availability ratio, measured over the course of a 365-day year.

Table 19-1 *Network Availability Requirement Association*

Availability	24 × 7 Downtime	Single Shift Downtime
90%	36.5 days	2.5 working days
99%	87 hr, 40 min	20.8 hr (2.5 working days)
99.9% (Three 9s)	8 hr, 45 min	2 hr, 5 min
99.99% (Four 9s)	52.6 min	12.5 min
99.999% (Five 9s)	5 min, 15 sec	75 sec
99.9999% (Six 9s)	31.6 sec	7.5 sec

Consider the car example. The availability was measured for the entire car. If the mechanic wanted to improve the car's availability, it is necessary to analyze the cause of the car's downtime. This analysis is done by breaking the car into several components, such as the engine or transmission. The car's total availability then is measured by multiplying the availability of the individual components, as illustrated in the following formula:

$$\text{Availability}_{TOTAL} = (\text{Availability}_{ENGINE}) \times (\text{Availability}_{TRANSMISSION})$$

Using the earlier example of 72 hours downtime, engine-related issues caused 42 hours and transmission-related issues caused 30 hours of downtime, as shown here:

$$\text{Availability}_{ENGINE} = (8718) / (8718 + 42) \times 100\% = 99.5\%$$
$$\text{Availability}_{TRANMISSION} = (8730) / (8730 + 30) \times 100\% = 99.7\%$$

The following formula shows the total availability of the car based on the availability of the engine and transmission:

$$\text{Availability}_{TOTAL} = (99.5\%) \times (99.7\%) = 99.2\%$$
$$[\text{Availability}_{TOTAL} = ((.995) \times (.997) = .992) \times 100 = 99.2\%]$$

An automobile mechanic can drill down another level in the car to determine which engine and transmission components are affecting the car's availability, and then build in appropriate safeguards as necessary; that is, more frequent tune-ups, oil changes, and so on. Just as an auto mechanic can drill down into a vehicle's components, network administrators/designers can do the same to determine where to build in network safeguards.

The following two-node network (see Figure 19-1) is used to illustrate the following availability measurements.

Figure 19-1 *Two-Node Network*

Availability measurements can be taken from any of these points, as shown in Figure 19-2.

Figure 19-2 *Two-Node Network*

The total network availability for this "Two-Node Network" is measured as follows:

```
Availability_TOTAL = (Availability_ROUTERa)×(Availability_CABLEa)×(Availability_CSU/
DSUa)×(Availability_SERIALa)×(Availability_WAN)×(Availability_SERIALb)×(Availability_CSU/
DSUb)×(Availability_CABLEb)×(Availability_ROUTERb)
Availability_TOTAL = (.999)×(.9999)×(.9995)×(.98)×(.98)×(.98)×(.9995)×(.9999)×(.999)
Availability_TOTAL = (.9381) × 100
Availability_TOTAL = 93.8%
```

Up to this point, the equations have been based on linear networks; that is, networks with no redundant or backup components. Higher availability of a network can be achieved by adding redundancy at key points in the network (identified in the preceding equation) and deploying a backup solution, such as failover links or hardware.

For example, using the same two-node network illustrated in Figures 19-1 and 19-2, the network administrator decides that the 94 percent (.98 × .98 × .98) availability of the WAN and its serial links is not meeting availability requirements. The network administrator decides to add backup serial links on both sides of the network service provider's WAN, improving network access and uptime for users on each end.

Measuring the availability of a network with redundant components is a little bit different. The following network (see Figure 19-3) illustrates two (equal) paths between Router A and Router C.

Figure 19-3 *Availability with Redundant Components*

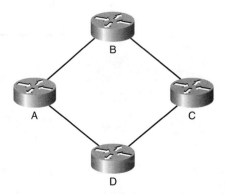

The following list details the availability percentage of each router shown in Figure 19-3.

Using this network, the following availability percentage is given:

- Router A = 99 percent (0.99)
- Router B = 97 percent (0.97)
- Router C = 98 percent (0.98)
- Router D = 95 percent (0.95)

```
AvailabilityABC = ((0.99) × (0.97) × (0.98)) × 100 = 94.1%
```

The availability of this network, without the redundant router (Router D) is 94.1 percent. However, this network has two paths between Router A and Router C; one path through Router B (Path ABC), the other path through Router D (Path ADC).

To compute the availability of the network with the redundant piece (Router D), the availability of Router B and Router D must be computed to determine a single variable. If the availability statistics for Router B and Router D were not combined, and the network availability was calculated linearly, the availability statistics are skewed, as the following demonstrates:

```
AvailabilityABCD = ((0.99) × (0.97) × (0.95) × (0.98)) × 100 = 89.4%
```

However, both Router B and Router D are not used simultaneously; Router D is the backup for Router B. To determine the availability of Router B and Router D combined, the following formula is applied:

```
AvailabilityB+D = 1 - ((1 - AvailabilityB) × ((1 - AvailabilityD))
AvailabilityB+D = 1 - ((1 - 0.97) × ((1 - 0.95))
AvailabilityB+D = 1 - ((0.03) × ((0.05)) = 1 - 0.0015 = 99.85
AvailabilityB+D = (99.85) × (100) = 99.85%
```

Now that the availability of the redundant piece has been computed, this is injected into the calculation for the entire network, as follows:

```
AvailabilityABCD = ((0.99) × (0.9985) × (0.98)) × 100 = 96.9%
```

NOTE

Adding redundant pieces to a network to improve availability works only if the redundant and primary devices do not share common failure points; for example, power supplies, local access, or routing across the network service provider backbone. To mitigate the risk of a network failure, end-to-end diversity must be maintained from customer entrance facility on one end of a circuit to the entrance facility on the other end.

This same principle of end-to-end diversity applies to local area networks (LANs) as well as wide area networks (WANs). LAN diversity is applied in the form of dual-NICs for servers and workstations, diverse media backbone (such as FDDI or dual-Ethernet), or dual routers or switches (with dual power supplies).

Internetwork Reliability Options

The level of application and network availability often is balanced against the cost of implementing the redundant/backup systems. It is not uncommon for the cost of making a network completely redundant or fault tolerant to be prohibitive. It is between this 100 percent network availability and the required availability (by the network applications) that the balance is determined.

Figure 19-4 illustrates a four-node nonredundant network design with two levels of hierarchy: Corporate HQ and three remote sites. There is no redundancy built into this network; if a site router fails, all users at that site have no network connectivity; if the Corporate HQ site fails, users at all remote sites have lost connectivity to corporate resources.

There are various approaches available to a network administrator/designer in creating a redundant internetwork, minimizing the impact a network-related outage has on network users. These approaches are as follows:

- Redundant WAN Links
- Meshed Network Topologies
- Redundant Power Systems
- Fault-Tolerant Media
- Hardware Backup

Each of these approaches is discussed in the following sections.

Figure 19-4 *Four-Node Nonredundant Network*

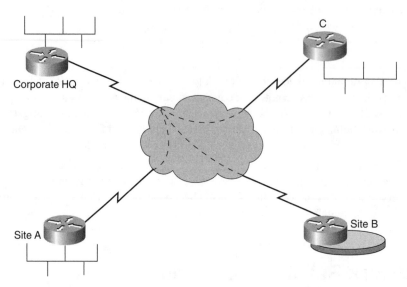

Redundant WAN Links

Redundant WAN Links are considered to be the least reliable component in an internetwork, often because of local loop issues. This suspect reliability, coupled with the importance of WAN links interconnecting LANs, make WAN links good candidates for redundancy and backup implementations.

The customer site implements a second WAN access link, either to the same network service provider via a diverse path from the primary link or to another network service provider, also via a diverse path from the primary link. Routers can automatically adjust for failed WAN links based on the routing algorithms (protocols) used, such as EIGRP, OSPF, or BGP. If a WAN link fails, these routing protocols will recalculate and converge on the new network topology.

Meshed Network Topologies

A *meshed network topology* enables interconnectivity of every node on a network with every other node. In large networks, full-meshed topologies can be difficult to manage, with the number of connections determined by this formula: $(N \times (N-1)) / 2$. For example, a network with 25 nodes yields 300 connections $((25 \times 24)/2) = 300$.

Meshed topologies often are more cost-efficient than redundant WAN links at every site. Consider the following three-node network (see Figure 19-5).

Figure 19-5 *Three-Node Network*

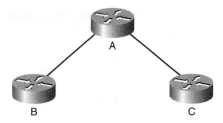

Presume that each WAN Link costs $1,000/month; therefore this network costs $2,000/ month in WAN charges (A →B = $1,000, A → C = $1,000). Given this $1,000/month charge for each WAN link, the following network (see Figure 19-6) would cost $4,000/month.

Figure 19-6 *Three-Node Network with Redundant WAN Links*

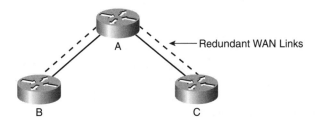

As an alternative to redundant WAN links at each site, a full-mesh WAN link topology can be used, as illustrated in Figure 19-7.

Figure 19-7 *Three-Node Network with Full-Mesh WAN Links*

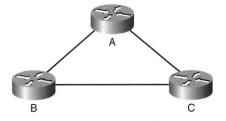

The cost for this network using the same $1,000/month model for WAN links totals $3,000/ month versus the $4,000/month cost for the redundant links. The network routing protocols will detect the failure of a WAN link and will converge on the new topology and reroute traffic as appropriate.

The meshed topology (see Figure 19-7) has three advantages over a redundant star topology (see Figure 19-6). These advantages are as follows:

- A meshed topology is often less expensive than the redundant star topology, at least by the cost of one WAN link.

- A meshed topology provides more direct communication between WAN sites, which can translate into improved application availability.

- A meshed topology enables distributed network operation, preventing network bottlenecks at the "root" or head-end of the network, often corporate headquarters.

Redundant star topologies, like the one illustrated previously in Figure 19-6, should be considered in either of the following situations:

- Little traffic travels between remote WAN sites.

- Traffic between the WAN head-end, often corporate office, and remote sites is delay-sensitive or mission critical. The additional WAN link (hop) might not be tolerable by such applications.

NOTE   The full-mesh topologies discussed here are physical links, such as WAN access. Logical network topologies, such as those created by Frame Relay or Asynchronous Transfer Node (ATM) Permanent Virtual Circuits (PVCs), can be considered more cost-efficient than both redundant star topologies and fully-meshed WAN links. There is no right or wrong way to provide redundant connectivity. The network administrator/designer must strike a balance between the organization's internetworking or communications needs and the cost incurred by the solution.

Redundant Power Systems

Power failures can be common in large-scale enterprise networks and can be caused by a wide range of actions: tripped circuit breakers, dislodged power cords, lightning strikes, brown-outs, or local power company failures. Because power failures are difficult to predict and preempt, each organization must assess their power needs, the probability of each type of power failure, and the impact of such a failure.

Large organizations can negotiate with their local power company for feeds from multiple power grids, similar to dual-access to a network service provider's WAN (see Figure 19-8).

Dual power feeds from the power company are not always available, and they can be cost-prohibitive. In these instances, an organization can install generators, as illustrated in Figure 19-9, to provide power to an entire facility or to mission-critical systems only.

Figure 19-8 *Dual Power Feeds*

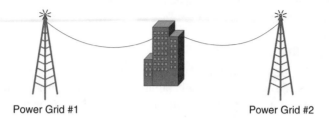

Power Grid #1 Power Grid #2

Figure 19-9 *Generator Backup*

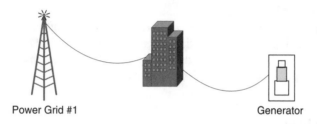

Power Grid #1 Generator

Another option for larger organizations is the deployment of Uninterrupted Power Supplies (UPS) to provide power to mission-critical equipment such as server farms and WAN networking equipment (see Figure 19-10).

Figure 19-10 *UPS*

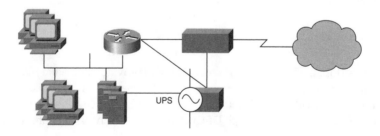

UPS

UPS systems run on charged batteries and, depending on the UPS deployed, the time that power is available can be measured in hours or minutes. UPS was developed to provide end-users with enough time to perform a graceful shutdown of their workstations in the event of a power outage, preventing corrupted data hard drives. More sophisticated UPS systems can provide power for a considerably longer period of time, but as with all things, this additional time comes with a financial cost that must be considered.

Fault-Tolerant Media

Media failure describes outages attributed to the media and its connections with network hardware. Some examples of media failure are network interface card (NIC) failures, attachment unit interface (AUI) cable failures, or LAN hub and transceiver failures.

A media failure often is the result of operator error and cannot always be easily eliminated. The impact of media failure on a network can be mitigated in one of two ways:

- Divide the network segment into smaller pieces, minimizing the effect of a network segment failure.

- Attach each LAN host to two different media segments via dual-NICs to a dual media backbone, such as Fiber Distributed Data Interface (FDDI) or dual-Ethernet segments. This approach can double the cost of a network implementation and should be considered only for mission-critical hosts.

Hardware Backup

The use of dual networking hardware devices, such as routers, switches, hubs, and bridges, can reduce the effect of a hardware failure on a network. If one of these devices fails, network discovery protocols can help the end-user workstations choose a new path to the internetwork. For example, in an environment with a primary and backup router, routing metrics can be used to ensure that the backup router is used only in the event the primary router fails.

Cisco Note: HSRP

Cisco's Hot Standby Routing Protocol (HSRP) provides automatic router backup when configured on Cisco routers running IP over Ethernet, FDDI, and Token Ring LANs. HSRP is compatible with Novell's Internetwork Packet Exchange (IPX), AppleTalk, and Banyan VINES, and is compatible with DECnet and Xerox Network Systems (XNS) in certain configurations.

HSRP allows changes in network topology to be transparent to network hosts, often taking no more than 10 seconds to converge on a topology change. For Internet Protocol (IP), HSRP enables one router to automatically assume the function of the second router if the second router fails. This is particularly useful when the users on one subnet require continuous access to resources in the network.

Summary

High availability is a subjective interpretation of two statistics:

- **MTTR**—Average time required to recover/restore from a network outage or repair a failed component.

- **MTBF**—Average time a network or component works without failure.

Network availability is measured by taking the uptime and dividing it by the uptime plus the downtime, then multiplying the result by 100, resulting in a percentage:

```
Availability = ((Uptime)/(Uptime + Downtime) × 100
```

Network designers use the required network availability to determine how much protection and redundancy to build into the network.

The level of application and network availability is balanced against the cost of implementing the redundant/backup systems. It is not uncommon for the cost of making a network completely redundant or fault tolerant to be prohibitive.

There are various approaches available to a network administrator/designer in creating network redundancy. These approaches are as follows:

- **Redundant WAN Links**—Multiple WAN access links providing local loop access redundancy.

- **Meshed Network Topologies**—Enables interconnectivity of every node on a network with every other node.

- **Redundant Power Systems**—Diverse power feeds or an extended-battery UPS.

- **Fault-Tolerant Media**—Dual-NICs preventing network media outages from taking down a network segment.

- **Hardware Backup**—Dual networking hardware devices, such as routers, switches, hubs, and bridges.

Frequently Asked Questions (FAQ)

1 Can I load-balance/load-share across redundant WAN access links?

Yes. It is the network administrator's preference to use both links in a simultaneous fashion or to leave the backup WAN link idle and in standby for failure of the primary WAN link. This decision often is based on the cost of the WAN link. For example, a dedicated WAN link might prove to be more cost-efficient by being used in a load-balance/load-share environment as opposed to letting the link sit there idle and unused.

2 Why is BGP the most often used routing protocol for redundant IP VPN WAN links?

BGP enables a customer site, or group of sites, to be treated as a single domain (autonomous system) and establish a peering relationship with the network service provider IP network. For ATM and Frame Relay WANs, any routing protocol can be used by the network administrator because the network service provider does not see customer routing protocols used across the WAN. The routing protocol detects and reacts to a link failure by the routing protocol provisions for metric weighting, enabling the network administrator to give one route preference over another route, either manually or through the use of the default metrics.

Case Study

Figure 19-11 illustrates a redundant LAN and WAN infrastructure.

Figure 19-11 *Redundant Network #1*

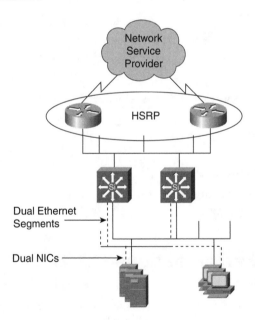

The redundant components in this configuration are as follows:

- Dual and diverse Ethernet network segments are used.
- Dual NICs are used, with each card attaching to one of the diverse Ethernet network segments.

- Each Ethernet network segment is attached to a Cisco Catalyst Switch; such as the 6000 Series.

- Each Catalyst switch is served by two WAN routers.

- Each WAN router is attached to the network service provider:

  — Cisco's HSRP creates a single (virtual) address to which the LAN devices connect, enabling two or more Cisco routers to be viewed as a single router interface to the LAN.

  — The same network service provider can be used for the redundant WAN link, or a second (diverse) network service provider can be used to provide this redundant link.

  — Both the primary and redundant WAN link can be connected to the same WAN router, but this configuration makes the WAN router a single point of failure and therefore should be carefully considered.

The following topics are covered in this chapter:

- WWW
- URL
- Internet Programming Languages
- Peering

CHAPTER 20

The Internet

The Internet is a computer network made up of thousands of such computer networks worldwide, with each computer communicating by using the Transmission Control Protocol/Internet Protocol (TCP/IP) suite.

In addition to using TCP/IP for communication, these Internet computers use client/server architecture, meaning that the server provides files and services to the end-user client, as illustrated in Figure 20-1.

Figure 20-1 *Client/Server Architecture*

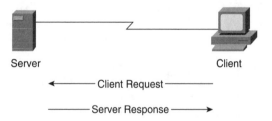

When a user views a web page, the web browser (client) requests information from the web server, which in turn fulfills the request by sending the web page back to the web browser.

An Internet user can access a variety of services, such as electronic mail (e-mail), file transfer/sharing, information resources, interest group membership, interactive collaboration, multimedia displays, real-time broadcasting, electronic commerce (e-commerce), news and current events, and so on. The most common Internet service is the World Wide Web (WWW).

WWW

"The Web," is a system of Internet servers interconnected across the world. The WWW provides a single interface for accessing Internet services, such as e-mail and file sharing.

The operation of the Web depends on *hypertext documents*, or pages, as the primary means of information retrieval. *Hypertext* is a document containing words connecting, or linking, to other documents. In the context of the Web, words or graphics can serve as links to other documents, images, video, and sound.

NOTE   A single hypertext document can contain links to several other documents, or pages, across the Internet. In Hypertext Markup Language (HTML) these links are known as *hyperlinks*.

Web pages are created using the HTML. With HTML, tags are placed within the text to format the document with visual features such as font size, italics, bold text and to create the hypertext links, using either text or graphics as the link's anchor (the source of the hypertext link). HTML is an evolving language, with each code release bringing new HTML tags enabling additional features for programmers to use when designing web pages.

NOTE   The World Wide Web Consortium (W3C) coordinates HTML standardizing efforts.

In addition to hyperlinked documents, or pages, the Web provides multimedia presentations, real-time collaboration, interactive pages, radio and television broadcasts, and the automatic push of information to a client computer. Programming languages such as Java, JavaScript, and Visual Basic are extending the capabilities of the Web. An increasing amount of information on the Web is served dynamically from content stored in databases. The Web is therefore not a fixed entity, but one that is in a constant state of flux.

The Web provides a single interface for accessing all these protocols. This creates a convenient and user-friendly environment. It is no longer necessary to be conversant in these protocols within separate, command-level environments. The Web gathers these protocols into a single system. Because of this feature, and because of the Web's capability to work with multimedia and advanced programming languages, the Web is the fastest-growing component of the Internet.

DNS

At the heart of the Web is the Domain Name Service (DNS), often referred to as DNS. DNS maps the names to Internet Protocol (IP) addresses for servers, such as web hosts, using the TCP/IP protocol.

All TCP/IP hosts (clients and servers) have an individual address, or IP number, such as 150.203.2.15 or 203.10.76.34. This IP address is used when an end-user connects to another computer also using TCP/IP. Because these numbers can be difficult for humans to remember each machine also has an individual name, such as www.cisco.com or www. whitehouse.gov. DNS is used to match up these names to their IP address. Figure 20-2 illustrates the DNS operation.

Figure 20-2 *DNS Operation*

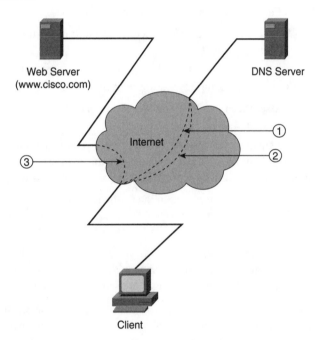

The following steps detail how DNS operates from an end-user perspective:

1 The web browser (client) queries the DNS server asking "What is the IP address for www.cisco.com?"

2 The DNS server looks in its database and finds the associated IP address to www.cisco.com: 198.133.219.25. The DNS server then sends this learned IP address to the requesting client.

3 The web browser (client) establishes an IP connection to the IP address learned from the DNS query.

Internet and WWW Applications

Almost every protocol type available on the Internet is accessible via the Web. Internet protocols are rule sets that enable communication between hosts across the Internet.

The following major protocols are accessible via the Web:

- **E-mail**—Uses the Simple Mail Transport Protocol (SMTP) to distribute electronic messages and files to one or more electronic mailboxes.
- **Telnet**—Facilitates login to a remote computer host to execute commands.
- **FTP**—Uses the File Transfer Protocol (FTP) to transfer text or binary files between an FTP server and client.
- **Usenet**—Uses the Network News Transfer Protocol (NNTP) to distribute Usenet news articles originating from newsgroup discussion boards.
- **HTTP**—Uses the HyperText Transfer Protocol (HTTP) to send and receive hypertext across the Internet.
- **Chat and Instant Messaging**—Uses several vendor specific protocols—such as America Online (AOL) and Microsoft— enabling Internet users to communicate with each other in real time by typing in a chat or instant messaging client.

Each of these protocols is discussed in the following sections.

E-mail

E-mail enables computer users to exchange messages across the Internet. Each e-mail user has a mailbox address to which messages are sent and received.

E-mail enables users to send and receive electronic files; these electronic files are referred to as *Multimedia Internet Mail Extension (MIME) attachments*. MIME was developed to enable e-mail software to handle a variety of file types. For example, a document created in Microsoft Word can be attached to an e-mail message and retrieved by the recipient, using the appropriate e-mail program.

Telnet

Telnet is a program enabling a user to log onto a computer on the Internet, such as an online database, library catalog, or chat services. To Telnet to a computer, the end-user must know its address, either the common name address (`locis.loc.gov`) or its IP address (140.147.254.3).

The most common web-based resources available through Telnet are library catalogs. For example, the Ohio State University library catalog can be reached via telnet by entering the following command at a command prompt: **telnet library.ohio-state.edu**. A link to a

Telnet resource often looks like any other command-line link, the difference being that a Telnet session is launched to establish the connection to the remote resource.

A Telnet client is required on the local host (computer) in order for the user to establish a Telnet session to a remote resource. Most operating systems, such as Unix, Linux, and Microsoft, include a Telnet client as part of the operating system (OS). For example, a Microsoft Windows user can access the Telnet client through a MS-DOS command prompt window by typing "**telnet**."

FTP

FTP is both a program and the protocol used to transfer files between computers. Anonymous FTP is an option enabling users to transfer files from host computers on the Internet to their personal computers without having to establish user accounts on the remote host. For example, anonymous FTP sites can house books, articles, software, games, images, sounds, multimedia, course work, and so on, for users to download to their computer for later review.

An FTP client is required on the local host (computer) in order for the user to access files from an FTP server. Most operating systems—such as Unix, Linux, and Microsoft Windows—include an FTP client as part of the OS package, which can be accessed with the command, "**ftp**." FTP transfers also can be done with a web browser, using the command "**ftp**" in the browser window rather than the normal "**http**" used when accessing a web site.

For example:

- The command http://www.cisco.com instructs the web browser to establish a connection with the web server using the HTTP.

- The command ftp://ftp.cisco.com instructs the web browser to establish an FTP connection with Cisco.com's FTP server.

NOTE   Not all sites have public FTP servers configured for use.

Usenet News and E-Mail Discussion Groups

Usenet News is a global electronic bulletin board system where computer users can exchange information regarding any topic. The major difference between Usenet News and e-mail discussion groups is that Usenet messages are stored on central computers, and users connect to these computers to read or download the messages posted to newsgroups. The distinction between Usenet and e-mail distribution is that with e-mail, messages are sent to an electronic mailbox for each user; newsgroup messages are sent to a central server for users to read and/or download.

Usenet itself is a set of machines that exchanges messages, or articles, from Usenet discussion forums, called *newsgroups*. Usenet administrators control their own sites and decide which newsgroups to sponsor and which remote newsgroups to allow as part of the system.

Chat and Instant Messaging

Chat programs enable users on the Internet to communicate with each other in real time by typing in a chat or instant messaging client. Chat is sometimes included as a feature of a web site, where users can log into a "chat room" to exchange comments about a particular topic.

Internet Relay Chat (IRC) is a service that allows users to communicate with each other on hundreds of channels based on specific topics. To access IRC, an IRC software program must be used.

A variation of chat is instant messaging (IM), where Internet users can communicate with other users on the same IM platform, such as America Online's Instant Messenger (AIM), Microsoft MSN Messenger (MSN), or ICQ.

URL

A Uniform Resource Locator (URL) specifies the Internet address of a file stored on a host computer connected to the Internet. Every file on the Internet, no matter what its access protocol (for example, HTTP or FTP), has a unique URL. Web software programs use the URL to retrieve the file from the host computer and directory in which the requested file resides. This file is then displayed in the client, most often the web browser.

NOTE   URLs are translated into IP addresses using the Internet DNS.

The format of a URL is as follows:

```
protocol://host/path/filename
```

For example, the URL for the meeting schedule of the House Committee on Agriculture of the U.S. House of Representatives can be found at the following address:

```
http://www.house.gov/agriculture/schedule.htm
```

The structure of this URL is as follows:

* Protocol: http

* Host computer name: www

- Second-level domain name: house
- Top-level domain name: gov
- Directory name: agriculture
- File name: schedule.htm

NOTE   The file extension .htm or .html indicates that the file is a HTML file.

Table 20-1 lists the top-level domains (TLDs) common in the United States.

Table 20-1   *Top-Level Domains (TLD)**

Domain Suffix	Domain Name
.com	Commercial Organization
.edu	Educational Institution
.gov	U.S. Government Organization
.mil	U.S. Military Organization
.net	Network Organizations (Access Providers)
.org	Nonprofit Organizations
.biz	Business Organizations*
.museum	Museums
.info	Unrestricted use*
.pro	Accountants, lawyers, physicians, and other professionals*
.name	For registration by individuals*
.aero	Air-transport industry
.coop	Cooperatives

*Indicates TLD is unsponsored.

An "unsponsored" TLD operates under policies established by the global Internet community through the Internet Corporation for Assigned Names and Numbers (ICANN) process; a "sponsored" TLD is a specialized TLD that has a sponsor representing the narrower community that is most affected by the TLD. The sponsor carries out delegated policy-formulation responsibilities over many matters concerning the TLD.

NOTE   More information regarding the status of unsponsored TLDs can be found at `http://www.icann.org/tlds/`.

Internet Programming Languages

The use of programming languages has extended the capabilities of the Web. The common programming languages found on the Internet are as follows:

- **CGI**—Common Gateway Interface (CGI) refers to a specification programs used to communicate with a web server.

  A CGI program, or script, is any program designed to accept from and return data to the end-user. The program can be written in any programming language, such as C, Perl, and Visual Basic Script. A common use for a CGI script is the processing of an interactive web page form.

- **ASP**—Active Server Pages (ASP) was developed by Microsoft. These are dynamically generated HTML web pages that include scripting and create interactive web server applications.

  The scripts run on the server, rather than on the web browser (such as with CGI), generating the HTML pages sent to browsers. Visual Basic and JScript (a subset of JavaScript) are often used for the scripting. ASPs end in the file extension .asp, rather than the .htm or .html of traditional web pages.

- **Java**—Java is an object-oriented programming language similar to C++. Developed by Sun Microsystems, the aim of Java is creating programs that are platform independent. A perfect Java program works on a PC, Macintosh, Unix, and so on, without any additional programming. Java can be used to write applications for both web and non-web use.

  Java *applets* are web-based Java applications called from an HTML page and can be downloaded from a web server to run on a Java-compatible browser (such as Netscape Navigator or Microsoft Internet Explorer).

- **VRML**—Virtual Reality Modeling Language (VRML) enables the creation of three-dimensional (3D) environments within the Internet browser.

  VRML produces a *hyperspace,* or *world*, a 3-dimensional space appearing on the display screen. The user can figuratively move within this space; that is, as the user presses keys to turn left, right, up, or down or go forwards or backwards, the images on the screen change to give the impression that the user is moving through a real space.

- **XML**—eXtensible Markup Language (XML) is a web page language that enables designers to create customized tags providing user-web page interaction not available with HTML. XML is a language of data structure and exchange, enabling developers to separate form from content.

Peering

Peering is a relationship between two or more Internet Service Providers (ISPs) in which the ISPs create a direct link and agree to forward each other's packets across this link instead of using the public Internet backbone (see Figure 20-3).

Figure 20-3 *Peering Interconnect between Two ISPs*

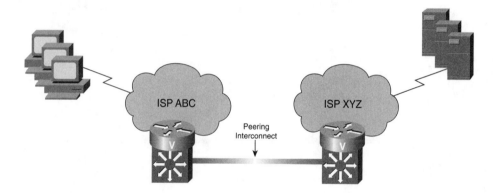

Suppose that a client of ISP ABC wants to access a web site hosted by ISP XYZ. If ABC and XYZ have a peering relationship, the IP packets travel across the direct connection between the two ISPs.

These peering interconnections result in more efficient access because there are fewer hops between client and server. These peering interconnections are more economical because the ISPs do not need to pay fees to a third-party network service provider (NSP).

Peering can involve more than two ISPs, in which case all traffic destined for any of the ISPs is first routed to a central exchange, or peering point, and then forwarded to the final destination, as illustrated in Figure 20-4.

This peering point operation is similar to, but on a smaller scale than, the Network Access Points (NAPs) managed by the NSPs. These peering points can be made across dedicated facilities, such as Synchronous Optical Network (SONET) or Dense Wavelength Division Multiplexing (DWDM), or cross-connected in co-located equipment rooms.

Figure 20-4 *NSP Peering Point*

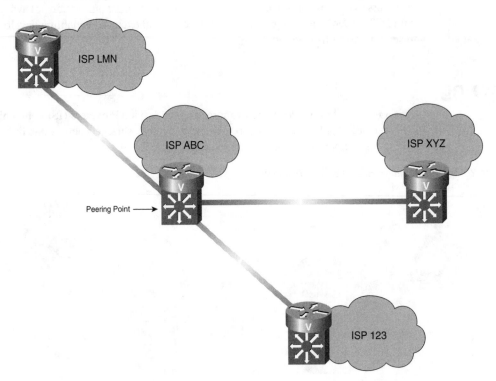

Peering Points

There are four official NAPs, considered the "heart" of the Internet. These four NAPs are as follows:

- San Francisco, CA
- Chicago, IL
- Washington, DC
- Pennsauken, NJ

These four NAPs establish the model that any network interconnected with at least one of these points can be interconnected with the rest of the public Internet. Private backbone operators or network service providers are not inclined to share customers by connecting their customers to another NSP.

The NSP customer requirement to be connected to the Internet forces the commercial network service providers to address network interconnection. The National Science

Foundation (NSF) defined the interconnection model by defining the Internet through its backbone and NAPs.

Metropolitan Fiber Systems, Inc. operates a series of Metropolitan Area Exchange (MAE) systems in large metropolitan areas across the country. MFS operates MAEs in San Jose (MAE West), Los Angeles (MAE LA), Dallas (MAE Dallas), and Chicago (MAE Chicago). MFS has two MAEs in Washington, D.C., the existing 10Mbps Ethernet MAE East, and a higher-speed 100Mbps Ethernet referred to as MAE East+. The two MAE-East NAPs and MAE West are *de facto* NAPs.

NOTE   Since the founding of the MAEs, MFS has been redefined through being acquired by UUNET in 1996. Since then, UUNET was in turn acquired by WorldCom, which also acquired MCI (in 1998).

The NAPs can be considered the "top" of the Internet, the heart of the Internet, or sometimes the "sweet spot of interconnection." The NAPs have also become the bottleneck of the Internet, however, not meeting the bandwidth of Quality of Service (QoS) demands of end-users. Some network service providers have been deploying more private peering points, and other NSPs are developing private NAPs and selling connectivity to those NAPs to divest themselves from the public peering points.

Summary

The Internet is a computer network made up of thousands of such computer networks worldwide, with each computer communicating by using TCP/IP suite. The Internet provides a home for the Web, a system of Internet servers interconnected across the world. The Web provides a single interface for accessing Internet services, such as e-mail, file sharing, etc.

Almost every protocol type available on the Internet is accessible via the Web; these include the following:

- E-mail
- Telnet
- FTP
- Usenet
- HTTP
- Chat and Instant Messaging

Web services are accessed via the URL. The URL specifies the Internet address of a file stored on a host computer connected to the Internet.

Web capabilities and services have been extended through the use of several programming languages:

- CGI
- ASP
- Java/Java Applets
- VRML
- XML

There are eleven major interconnection points: four official NAPs, three historical NAPs (CIX, FIX-EAST, FIX-West), and four *de facto* NAPs (MAEs). Any national backbone network service provider that has a peer connection at one or more of these interconnects is connected to the public Internet. Most of the national service providers are connected to all four official NAPs and most of the MAEs with some establishing their own private peering arrangements.

Frequently Asked Questions (FAQ)

1 How is the Internet managed and administered?

The Internet backbone, through which Internet traffic flows, is owned by private companies.

The Internet itself is governed by its members with the ultimate authority resting with the Internet Society (ISOC), a voluntary organization promoting information exchange worldwide using Internet technology. Technical management of the Internet is the responsibility of the Internet Architecture Board (IAB), appointed by the ISOC, which gives the go-ahead for standards and allocates resources such as addresses. Net users can influence opinion and initiate changes through the subgroup Internet Engineering Task Force (IETF), another volunteer organization that discusses operational and technical problems that anyone can join. Other organizations also have an influence.

2 What is a Level 2 or Tier 2 provider?

To form a rational image of the Internet, the following arbitrary levels were created and often overlap:

- NAPs are at the top of the pyramid, Level 1, where major backbone operators interconnect to establish the Internet core.
- Level 2 is made up of national backbone operators, often referred to as NSPs, and the network of networks spreads out from these service providers.

- Level 3 is made up of regional networks and the companies' operating regional backbones, often within a state or among several adjoining states, much like the national backbone operators. Level 3 providers connect to one or multiple national backbone providers to connect to the Internet. Some Level 3 providers do have a presence at a NAP where they then extend their network to smaller cities and towns in their areas.

- Level 3 providers connect businesses to those points with direct access connections and maintain dial-up terminal banks to offer 28.8 to 56KBps dial-up SLIP/PPP connections to consumers. In many cases, regional networks are more extensive than national backbones, but on a smaller geographic scale.

- Level 4 is the individual Internet service provider. These ISPs vary in size from small two- or three-person operations to large organizations, such as those with more than 100,000 dial-up customers. Level-4 providers often don't operate a backbone or regional network; leasing connections to a national backbone provider, or a regional network operator.

  Level 4 providers might offer service on a national basis, but using the points of presence (POPs) and backbone structure of their larger backbone partner(s). Several large providers, such as EarthLink and MindSpring, are Level 4 providers. These providers manage and operate an equipment room in a single area code, lease connections to a national backbone provider, and provide dial-up connections and leased connections to consumers and businesses in the local area.

  Level 4 providers tend to focus on customer service, configuration, and training at lower prices than a national ISP might provide.

- Level 5 is the consumer and business market, leasing a line from the customer office to an Internet service provider POP.

3 Who gives out Internet addresses and domain names?

Addresses and names are managed by a central authority, the InterNIC, to ensure global uniqueness in the assignment of names and addresses.

The InterNIC delegates portions of the address and name space to other international NICs and Internet Service Providers for further delegation to customers of those ISPs.

4 Is the Internet secure?

On a broad level, the Internet itself is not secure. On an individual basis, however, Internet access is as secure as each customer makes it. Internet users need to implement security options such as encryption and firewalls to protect data and internal networks.

5 What is the FIX and CIX?

FIX is the Federal Internet Exchange. There are two FIX points: FIX-East at the University of Maryland in College Park, MD and FIX-West at the NASA Ames Research Center at Moffet Field, CA (between Sunnyvale and Mountain View). CIX is the Commercial Internet Exchange. The CIX router is still operational in Santa Clara, CA and in Herndon, Virginia.

The FIX and CIX NAPs are overshadowed today by the MAEs, but they are still functional, serving more as historical legacy NAPs than as current influences.

This chapter covers the following topics:

- MPLS Terminology
- MPLS Operation
- MPLS-VPNs
- MPLS CE Routing

CHAPTER 21

MPLS Introduction

MPLS stands for *Multiprotocol Label Switching* and is a packet-forwarding technology. Where Internet Protocol (IP) networks, such as the Internet, use the network IP address to make routing and forwarding decisions, MPLS uses labels. MPLS was designed to give routers greater speed than Asyncronous Transfer Mode (ATM) switches for carrying IP traffic by enabling routers to make forwarding decisions based on labels, avoiding the packet-by-packet look-ups used in conventional routing. With MPLS, the Layer 3 header analysis is done once when the packet enters the MPLS network domain; label inspection determines subsequent packet forwarding. It is this operation that enables MPLS to provide for the following applications across a network backbone: Virtual Private Networking (VPN), Traffic Engineering (TE), Quality of Service (QoS), and ATM over MPLS (AToM).

MPLS is considered a mediator between Layers 2 and 3 (the Data-Link and Network layers, respectively) of the Open System Interconnection (OSI) Reference Model, as illustrated in Figure 21-1. MPLS is sometimes referred to as working at Layer 2.5 of the OSI Reference Model. As its name implies, MPLS can support multiple protocols, although the common implementation is IP over Point-to-Point Protocol (PPP)/ATM.

Figure 21-1 *MPLS Model (Multiprotocol)*

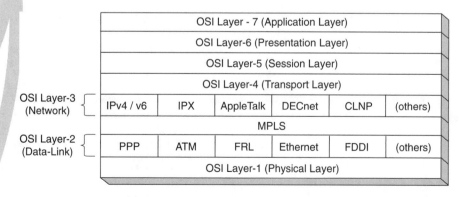

In addition to being a forwarding mechanism, MPLS provides for the (traffic) engineering of IP flows in a similar fashion to ATM Permanent Virtual Circuits (PVCs); in other words, MPLS moves the traffic engineering from layer 2 (ATM) to layer 3 (IP). MPLS Traffic

Engineering (MPLS-TE) is best described as being at Layer 2 to 2.5 of the OSI Reference Model, interworking IP with optical networks, such as Synchronous Optical Network (SONET) and Dense Wave Division Multiplexing (DWDM).

MPLS Terminology

Table 21-1 defines the terminology used with MPLS implementations.

Table 21-1   *MPLS Terminology*

Term	Definition
Label Switch Router (LSR)	The core device that switches labeled packets according to precomputed switching tables. This device also can be a switch or a router.
Label	The header used by an LSR to forward packets. The header format depends on network characteristics. In router networks, the label is a separate, 32-bit header. In ATM networks, the label is placed into the Virtual Path Identifier /Virtual Channel Identifier (VPI/VCI) cell header. In the core, LSRs read only the label, not the network layer packet header. One key to the scalability of MPLS is that labels have only local significance between two devices that are communicating. Local significance means that only the sender of the traffic cares what the labels are, not the receiver. For example, if a letter is received in your mailbox #17, you don't care that the postmaster put the same letter in the post office's outgoing mailbox #42.
Edge Label Switch Router (Edge LSR) or Label Edge Router (LER)	The edge device that performs initial packet processing and classification and applies the first label. This device can be either a router such as the Cisco 7500 or a switch with built-in routing, such as the Cisco MGX 8800.
Label Switched Path (LSP)	The path defined by all labels assigned between end points. An LSP can be dynamic or static. Dynamic LSPs are provisioned automatically using routing information. Static LSPs are explicitly provisioned.
Label Distribution Protocol (LDP)	Communicates labels and their meaning among LSRs. It assigns labels in edge and core devices to establish LSPs in conjunction with routing protocols such as Open Shortest Path First (OSPF), Intermediate System to Intermediate System (IS-IS), Routing Information Protocol (RIP), Enhanced Interior Gateway Routing Protocol (EIGRP), or Border Gateway Protocol (BGP).

Figure 21-2 illustrates the relationship between LSRs, LSPs, and Edge LSRs/LERs.

Figure 21-2 *MPLS Components*

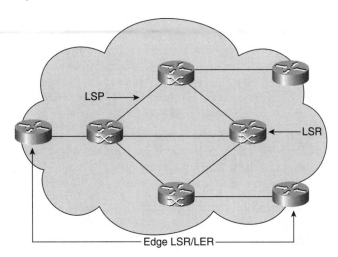

MPLS Operation

Figure 21-3 illustrates how MPLS operates in a service provider network.

Figure 21-3 *MPLS Operation*

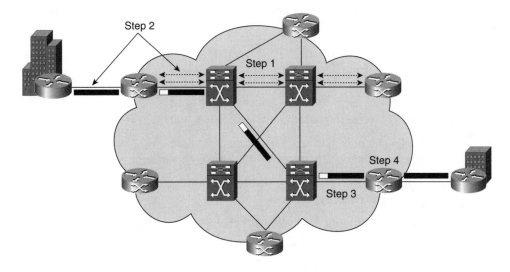

MPLS operation follows these steps:

1 The network routers and switches build routing tables as these same routers/switches participate in interior gateway protocols—for example, Operator Service Position System (OSPF)—throughout the service provider network. LDP creates label values between adjacent (connected) devices, using the routing topology in the LDP tables (learned from LDP). This operation creates LSPs between destination endpoints. Where ATM permanent virtual circuits (PVCs) require manual VPI/VCI, MPLS labels are automatically assigned via the LDP.

2 Packets enter the network where the ingress (point of entry) Edge LSR determines which Layer 3 services are required, such as QoS or bandwidth management. Based on these routing and policy requirements, the Edge LSR selects the labels and applies them to the packet headers before forwarding the packets across the network.

3 The LSR in the core reads each packet's label, replacing each label with a new one, and then forwarding the packet to the next hop in the path. These labels are maintained in the LSP tables.

4 The egress (point of exit) Edge LSR removes the packet's label, reads the packet header, and forwards the packet to its final destination.

The MPLS labels are looked up in the core network router/switch switching tables. These core network routers/switches hold Layer 3 (Network layer) information, enabling each switch to apply the required services to each IP packet. These switching tables are pre-calculated, not requiring packets to be reprocessed at each network hop. This only makes it possible to separate and classify traffic types, such as best-effort traffic from mission-critical traffic.

Figure 21-4 illustrates how packets are forwarded through an MPLS network.

Following are the packet forwarding steps shown in Figure 21-4:

1 A packet arrives at the (ingress) Edge LSR.

2 The LSR reads the packet for the destination prefix, 128.89.

3 The Edge LSR then looks up the destination address in the switching table and inserts the corresponding label 4; then forwards it out interface 1.

4 The LSR in the core receives the packet on interface 2 with Label 4 and looks up its match in its switching table.

5 The core LSR replaces label 4 with label 9 and forwards it out interface 0.

6 The egress LSR receives the packet on interface 1 and looks up the corresponding label (label 9) in its table.

7 The egress LSR table says to strip label 9 and forward the packet out interface 0.

Figure 21-4 *MPLS Packet Forwarding*

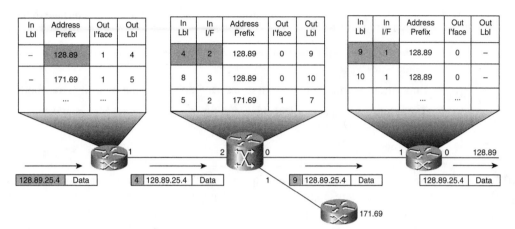

The sending and receiving customers are unaware of these MPLS label transitions while they are sending and receiving an IP packet to or from the network service provider. The customers are concerned about the network service provider meeting the promised Service Level Guarantees (SLGs), and it is MPLS that enables the service providers to meet these SLGs.

MPLS MPLS-VPNs

A VPN emulates a private wide area network (WAN) over the public network, namely the Internet. In offering VPN services to customers, a network service provider must solve the issues of data privacy and the use of non-unique, private IP addresses within a VPN. MPLS provides solutions to both these issues because MPLS makes forwarding decisions based on labels, not destination addresses.

NOTE   RFC 2547 (www.ietf.org/rfc/rfc2547.txt?number=2547) provides the following definition of a VPN, an intranet, and an extranet: "If all the sites in a VPN are owned by the same enterprise, the VPN is a corporate 'intranet.' If the various sites in a VPN are owned by different enterprises, the VPN is an 'extranet.' A site can be in more than one VPN; e.g., in an intranet and several extranets. We regard both intranets and extranets as VPNs. In general, when we use the term VPN we will not be distinguishing between intranets and extranets."

VPNs are constructed using four fundamental building blocks:

- **Firewalls**—Protect each user/customer site and provide a secure interface to the Internet

- **Authentication**—Verifies that each customer site exchanges data only with validated remote sites

- **Encryption**—Protects data from examination or manipulation as it is transported

- **Tunneling**—Encapsulation provides multiprotocol transport services and enables the use of private IP address space within the VPN

NOTE   Because IP addressing needs to be unique in order to communicate across an IP network, overlapping of IP address space can prevent communication between networks and their associated devices.

MPLS enables network service providers to offer VPN services by providing a VPN tunneling mechanism across the network backbone, as illustrated in Figure 21-5.

Figure 21-5 *MPLS VPN Tunnels*

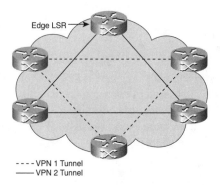

The following process describes how network service providers (NSPs) build and maintain MPLS-based VPNs:

- A network service provider can deploy VPNs by provisioning a set of LSPs providing connectivity among different VPN sites.

- Each VPN site advertises, or announces, to the network service provider a set of network prefixes for which the local site is responsible.

- The network service provider's routing protocol(s) distributes this information by either piggybacking labels in routing protocol updates or using a LDP.

- VPN Identifiers enable a single routing system to support multiple VPNs whose internal address spaces overlap with each other.

- Each ingress LSR places traffic into LSPs based on the packet's destination address and VPN membership information.

MPLS CE Routing

In order for customers to take advantage of multiple MPLS CoS tunnels, priority or custom-queues must be configured on the MPLS customer edge (CE) device (router/switch). Figure 21-6 illustrates an MPLS access link with three Classes of Service.

Figure 21-6 *MPLS IP-VPN*

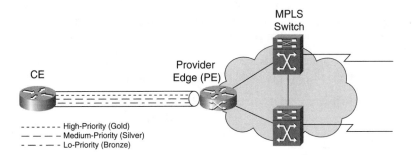

The CE router is configured with three queues:

- High Priority (Gold)
- Medium Priority (Silver)
- Low Priority (Bronze)

Each queue is provisioned with a percentage of the total bandwidth; for example, Gold = 40 percent, Silver = 40 percent, and Bronze = 20 percent. The CE router assigns packets to each queue based upon configured access-lists, using a Transmission Control Protocol (TCP)/User Datagram Protocol (UDP) port, source IP host/subnet, or destination IP host/subnet.

NOTE   *TCP/UDP port* refers to the well-known port numbers that are reserved for assignment by the Internet Corporation for Assigned Names and Numbers (ICANN) for use by IP application end points, using either the TCP or the UDP. Each application type has a designated, or "well-known," port number. For example, remote job entry applications have port number 5; Hypertext Transfer Protocol (HTTP) applications have port number 80; and Post Office Protocol Version 3 (POP3) applications (e-mail) have port number 110. When one application communicates with another application at another computer on the Internet, it specifies that application in each data transmission by using the appropriate port number.

Cisco IOS enables policing of these queues through Committed Access Rate (CAR) algorithms. CAR policies are often implemented on the CE device; however, under agreement, CAR policies can be implemented on the network service provider's PE device. CAR analyzes the packet and assigns a service class based on the packet's header information. CAR policies use access-lists to police against attributes such as source, destination, protocol, or application. CAR policies also can manage bandwidth allocation for specified traffic types; for example, ensuring that Gold classified traffic takes precedence over Silver traffic.

To enforce customer network policies, network managers configure Layer 3 thresholds based on the desired parameters, such as application or protocol. If a flow exceeds a given threshold, a variety of responses may be enacted, dropping excess packets or sending them at a lower service class (recoloring).

NOTE   CAR policies are used for packet classification and bandwidth management.

Summary

MPLS is a packet-forwarding technology using labels, instead of network addresses, to make routing and data forwarding decisions. MPLS implementations give routers greater efficiency than ATM switches for the forwarding of network traffic. MPLS enables routers to make forwarding decisions based on labels, avoiding the packet-by-packet look-ups used in conventional routing, such as those used on the Internet.

MPLS supports traffic engineering, enabling network service providers to eliminate multiple layers in the network backbone; for example, one network carrying ATM traffic and another network carrying IP traffic. Instead of running IP over ATM and configuring and maintaining both networks, MPLS enables the migration of ATM's functions to MPLS, possibly eliminating the underlying ATM protocol.

MPLS enables network service providers to segregate traffic, such as that from different customers, into separate VPNs. Although MPLS VPNs are not encrypted by the network service provider, the segregation of traffic provides a *de facto* separation of customer networks. MPLS gives network service providers better performance and better control over their networks.

In addition to VPN services, MPLS-TE, QoS and AToM.

MPLS is sometimes referred to as working at Layer 2.5 of the OSI Reference Model. As its name implies, MPLS can transport multiple network protocols across a network backbone, with the common implementation being IP over PPP/ATM.

In order for MPLS network customers to take advantage of multiple Class of Service (CoS) tunnels, priority or custom-queues must be configured on the customer's MPLS router/ switch. Cisco IOS enables policing of these queues through CAR algorithms. CAR policies are often implemented on the CE device but can be implemented on the network service providers PE device, with agreements between the network service provider and the customer.

Frequently Asked Questions (FAQ)

1 What is the status of the MPLS standard?

Most MPLS standards are in the "Internet Draft" phase, although several have moved into the RFC-STD (RFC Standard) phase. For more information on the current status of various Internet Drafts, see the IETF's MPLS Working Group home page at `www.ietf.org/html.charters/mpls-charter.html`.

2 What other protocols does MPLS support besides IP?

By definition, MPLS supports multiple protocols. At the Network Layer, MPLS supports IPv6, IPv4, IPX (Novell), and AppleTalk. At the Link Layer MPLS supports Ethernet, Token Ring, FDDI, ATM, Frame Relay, and Point-to-Point Links. MPLS can essentially work with any control protocol other than IP and layer on top of any link layer protocol.

3 What are the differences between MPLS and ATM?

MPLS brings the traffic engineering capabilities of ATM to packet-based networks. MPLS works by tagging IP packets with "labels" specifying route and priority. MPLS combines the scalability and flexibility of routing with performance and traffic management of Layer 2 switching and can run over nearly any transport medium, such as ATM, Frame Relay, Packet over SONET (PoS), and Ethernet.

4 Does MPLS replace ATM?

No, MPLS does not replace ATM but rather complements it. MPLS eliminates the complexity of mapping IP addressing and routing information directly into ATM switching tables. The MPLS label-swapping idea is the same that ATM switches use to forward ATM cells.

5 Are MPLS-VPNs secure?

VPNs are considered to be "encrypted" tunnels across a public network. Because MPLS-VPNs do not require encryption, many network engineers have expressed concern over using MPLS to tunnel non-encrypted traffic over a public IP network. There are a couple of points to consider:

- MPLS-VPN traffic is isolated by the use of tags, much in the same way ATM and Frame Relay PVCs are kept isolated in a public ATM/Frame Relay network. This implies that security of MPLS-VPNs is equivalent to that of Frame Relay or ATM public network services. Interception of any of these three types of traffic would require access to the service provider network.

- MPLS-VPNs do not prohibit security. If security is an issue, traffic can be encrypted before it is encapsulated into MPLS by using a protocol such as IPSec or SSL.

Customers comfortable with carrying their traffic over public ATM or Frame Relay services should have the same level of comfort with MPLS-VPN services. Customers requiring additional security should employ encryption in addition to MPLS.

6 What is "Generalized MPLS" or "GMPLS" (formerly MPL(ambda)S)?

Generalized MPLS extends MPLS to encompass time-division (such as SONET ADMs), wavelength (optical lambdas) and spatial switching (such as incoming port or fiber to outgoing port or fiber).

GMPLS represents an extension of MPLS to enable MPLS to be used as the control mechanism for configuring both packet-based paths and paths in non-packet based devices such as optical switches, TDM muxes, and SONET/ADMs (Add/Drop Multiplexers).

With GMPLS, providers can provision resources dynamically and provide the redundancy for implementing various protection and restoration techniques across the network backbone.

Case Study

Thirty-Seven Incorporated's headquarters is located in Seattle, WA, with virtual connections to regional offices in New York, NY, Miami, FL, and Albuquerque, NM. Buffalo is a supplier depot with a single virtual connection to the New York regional office. Figure 21-7 illustrates this VPN implemented by Thirty-Seven, Inc.

Figure 21-7 *Thirty-Seven, Inc. MPLS-enabled VPN*

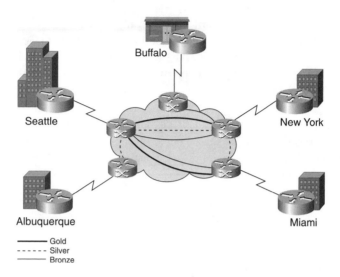

Thirty-Seven, Inc. is using an MPLS-VPN because the NSP has provided SLGs regarding the three Classes of Service provided by the NSP: Gold, Silver, and Bronze. Thirty-Seven, Inc. has several applications requiring WAN connectivity: e-mail, file sharing, file storage and data mining, and multimedia (voice and video applications).

MPLS enables the service provider to provide Thirty-Seven, Inc. the following Classes of Service to meet these application communication requirements (as detailed in the following table, Table 21-2).

Table 21-2 *Thirty-Seven, Inc. Application/Class of Service Implementation Chart*

Application	Class of Service
E-mail	Bronze
File sharing	Silver
Data mining	Silver
File storage	Bronze
Voice over IP (VoIP)	Gold
Video over IP	Gold

Thirty-Seven, Inc. has configured their Cisco routers with CAR policies to ensure that each CoS is queued in accordance with stated requirements. In this instance, the network service provider does not reclassify, or recolor, ingress traffic. Thirty-Seven, Inc. has decided that the VPN can be made more cost-efficient by recoloring outbound traffic from each site.

This recoloring enables Thirty-Seven, Inc. to take advantage of unused bandwidth in another CoS; for example, in the case Miami has exceeded the configured bandwidth queue for its Bronze connection to Seattle but has available bandwidth in its Gold connection. The Miami CE Router is configured to recolor this "extra" traffic to Gold so that it can be sent across the Gold virtual connection. In the event that Gold traffic is to be sent, the Bronze traffic is immediately dropped or buffered for transmission, depending on available resources in the Miami CE.

NOTE   If packets are dropped, it is up to the upper-layer protocols, such as TCP in the TCP/IP suite, to manage the retransmission of dropped packets.

The following topics are covered in this chapter:

- Optic Bands and Transmission Windows
- SONET
- DWDM

CHAPTER 22

Introduction to Fiber Optics

The foundation of any optical system is the fiber optic cabling. Basic fiber optic cables consist of the following components:

- **Silica core**—This is the center of the cable.
- **Cladding**—Cladding is also at the center of the cable; this and the silica core are used for carrying the optic, or lightwave (λ), signal
- **Coating, strength members, and a plastic jacket**—These enclose the fiber, providing the necessary tinsel and scratch resistance to protect the fibers.
- **Transceivers**—These are attached to both ends of the core for emitting and receiving the light pulses that form the information bits in the optical network. The capability of clear glass to contain light is the key behind optical transmissions and is based around the principle of total internal reflection.

Fiber optic transmission operates by injecting light at a specific angle. The glass cladding acts as a mirror, reflecting light within the fiber optic silica core. Significant in this light transmission is the Refractive Index (RI), or the change in the speed of light in a substance (in this case, silica) relative to the speed of light in a vacuum.

Light travels at about 300,000 kilometers (km) per second in a vacuum. When light moves from a substance of lower density to one of higher density—such as light moving from air to water—the light changes and is refracted. *Refraction* is the phenomenon that makes a stick appear to bend when one half is placed in water.

The "bending" of the light beam depends on two things:

- The angle at which light strikes the water
- The RI

At some point an angle is formed so that the light reflects off the water like a mirror. This angle is the critical angle, and the reflection of light is the total internal reflection.

This reflection principle determines how light propagates down a clear fiber. Fiber optic strands are manufactured so that the core contains a higher RI than the surrounding cladding. When light travels through the core and hits the cladding at a particular angle, it stays in the fiber. The exact size of the angle depends on the difference in RI; however, if a typical RI difference of 1 percent is assumed, all light striking the cladding at eight degrees or under will continue on in the fiber.

Optic Bands and Transmission Windows

The light used in fiber optic transmission is not the same as the light found in a flashlight or light bulb; optical network light sources are more precise. The ITU has specified six transmission bands for fiber optic transmissions. These bands are measured and represented in terms of wavelength (λ) sizes measured in nanometers (nm), one billionth of a meter, or microns (μm), one thousandth of a meter.

The six bands, or transmission windows, are these:

- O-Band (1260 nm to 1310 nm)
- E-Band (1360 nm to 1460 nm)
- S-Band (1460 nm to 1530 nm)
- C-Band (1530 nm to 1565 nm)
- L-Band (1565 nm to 1625 nm)
- U-Band (1625 nm to 1675 nm)

NOTE   The human hair is about 100 μm wide.

The higher the transmission window, the lower the signal degradation (attenuation); the tradeoff is more expensive electronics.

The reflective path taken by light in a fiber is considered the *mode*. Each mode has its own pattern of electromagnetic fields as it propagates through the fiber. From a cross section of the fiber, these modes can be viewed as multiple headlights beaming at you. In multimode fiber, multiple modes are generated, causing pulse dispersion at the receiving end.

There are two modes used in fiber optic networks:

- Multimode Fiber (MMF)
- Single Mode Fiber (SMF)

MMF

MMF optic cable is made up of multiple strands of glass fibers and has a larger core than single-mode fiber. MMF optic cables have a combined diameter of 50 to 100 microns, with each cable carrying independent signals. MMF has greater bandwidth capabilities than single-mode fiber due to its larger core size, which also leads to ease of coupling and interconnecting. MMF is used for specific applications where the distance limitation of two kilometers is not an issue.

To increase the range, manufacturers developed Graded Index (GI) fiber, an improved multimode fiber that operates in the second transmission window (band) at around 1,300nm. Graded Index fiber nearly eliminates modal dispersion by gradually decreasing the Refractive Index out toward the cladding where the modes are longest. Waves on the longer modes travel faster than on the shorter modes; therefore, the entire pulse arrives at the receiver at about the same time.

On distances over 2 km, Graded Index fibers need high-powered lasers introducing the issue of modal noise. With modal noise, the fiber and connectors interact so that there are power fluctuations at the receivers. This increases the signal-to-noise ratio in a link limiting the length of the fiber.

SMF

SMF uses a single glass strand with a smaller core than that of multimode fiber. Because single-mode fiber uses a smaller core of 8 μm to 10 μm, single-mode fiber enables only one mode of light to travel over the fiber. With a single mode, many multimode problems, such as modal noise and modal dispersion, are no longer an issue. SMF can reach as far as 100 to 200 kilometers before a fiber optic repeater, or amplifier, is required.

SMF is more expensive than MMF. The minute size of these cores demands that components have much tighter tolerance, which increases costs. These costs, however, are easily outweighed by the increased bandwidth and distances of 80 km and longer.

SONET

The Synchronous Optical Network (SONET) standard for fiber optic networks was developed in the mid-1980s and remains in widespread use today. SONET enables the interoperation of multiple technologies and vendor products by defining standard physical network interfaces.

SONET was designed for the public telephone network, where fiber optic cabling prevailed for long-distance voice traffic transmissions. The existing networks proved expensive to build and difficult to extend for so-called long-haul data and/or video traffic.

NOTE In Europe, the term *Synchronous Digital Hierarchy* (SDH) refers to essentially the same standard as SONET. This chapter uses the term *SONET* to refer to the common characteristics of SONET/SDH.

The American National Standards Institute (ANSI) devised SONET as the new standard for these applications. Like Ethernet, SONET provides a physical layer (OSI Layer-1) for internetworking. As such, SONET acts as a carrier of multiple higher-level application protocols. For example, Internet Protocol (IP) packets can be carried over SONET, such as Packet over SONET (PoS).

SONET transmits data at speeds between 155 Mbps (megabits per second) and 2.5 Gbps (gigabits per second). To build these high-bandwidth data streams, SONET multiplexes together channels as low as 64 Kbps) into SONET data frames sent at fixed intervals, such as Time Division Multiplexing (TDM).

SONET is most known for enabling ring topologies in an internetwork. Figure 22-1 illustrates the SONET ring concept.

Figure 22-1 *SONET Ring*

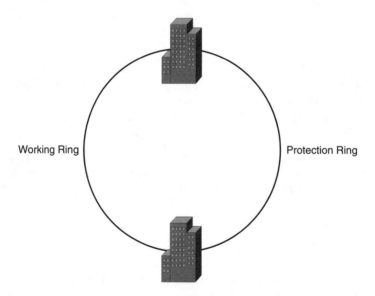

The working ring handles all data traffic while the protection ring is on standby. If the working ring fails, SONET enables the automatic failure detection and transfer control so the protection ring takes over as the working ring in a short period of time, often 50 to 100 ms. It is because of this working/protection ring design that SONET is described as a *self-healing network technology.*

SONET Operation

Communication between different networks requires multiplexing/demultiplexing and a coding/decoding process in converting the signal from one format to another format for transmission across multiple networks. To solve this problem, SONET standardizes the rates and formats, as illustrated in the Figure 22-2.

Figure 22-2 *SONET Multiplexing and Coding*

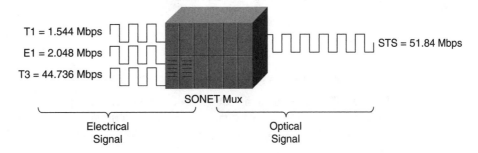

Different types of formats are multiplexed to form a single SONET 51.48 Mbits/s.

STS

The Synchronous Transport Signal (STS) is the basic building block of SONET optical interfaces, with a bandwidth rate of 51.84 Mbps. The STS consists of two parts:

- STS payload (carries data information)
- STS overhead (carries signaling and protocol information)

At the sending (origination) end of a communication system, signals of different rates and formats are converted to an STS frame, then multiplexed together to form a single STS signal (at 51.48 Mbps). This STS signal is carried by the SONET until the receiving (termination) end converts the STS frames back into the original user format (T1, T3, and so on.)

SONET Path Elements

Figure 22-3 illustrates the conceptual components of a SONET implementation.

Figure 22-3 *End-to-End SONET Elements*

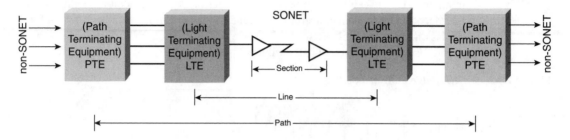

The following list describes the elements found in an end-to-end SONET connection.

- **PTE**—The STS path terminating equipment is the element multiplexing/demultiplexing the STS payload signal. The STS path terminating equipment assembles 28 DS1 signals and inserts path overhead forming the STS-1 signal (51.84Mbps).

- **LTE**—The LTE is the network element originating/terminating the optical (light) signal.

- **STE**—The STE is the network element that can modify, originate, regenerate, or terminate the STS signal.

SONET Layers

SONET has four optical interface layers, which are illustrated in Figure 22-4.

Figure 22-4 *SONET Layers*

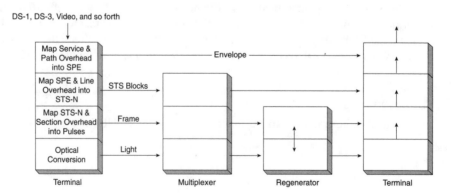

The following list describes each SONET layer:

- **Path Layer**—Manages the transport of services between the PTE. The path layer maps the signals into a format required by the line layer.

- **Line Layer**—Manages the transport of the path layer payload and its overhead across the physical medium. The line layer provides synchronization and performs multiplexing for the path layer.

- **Section Layer**—Manages the transport of an STS-N frame across the physical medium.

- **Photonic Layer**—Manages the transport of bits across the physical medium. The photonic layer converts the STS signal and OC signals.

DWDM

Dense Wave Division Multiplexing (DWDM), allows providers to enable services such as e-mail, video, and multimedia to be carried as IP data over ATM and voice carried over SONET/SDH. Despite these formats providing unique bandwidth management techniques, all three—IP, ATM, and SONET/SDH—may be transported over the optical layer using DWDM.

DWDM works by combining and transmitting multiple signals simultaneously at different wavelengths on the same fiber. In effect, one fiber is transformed into multiple virtual fibers. Eight OC-48 signals are multiplexed into one fiber, increasing the carrying capacity of that fiber from 2.5 Gbps to 20 Gbps. DWDM is protocol and bit-rate independent, meaning that DWDM-based networks can transmit data in IP, ATM, SONET, and Ethernet and handle bit-rates between 100 Mbps and 2.5 Gbps.

DWDM increases the capacity of existing fiber by assigning incoming optical signals to specific frequencies, or wavelengths (lambdas), and then multiplexing these signals into a single signal on a single fiber. Because incoming signals are never terminated in the optical layer, the interface is bit-rate and format independent; for example, IP, Ethernet, SONET, and so on.

DWDM contains multiple optical signals that are amplified as a group and transported over a single fiber increasing capacity. Each signal can carry different rates, such as OC-x (OC-3, OC-12, OC-48, etc.), and in a different format—SONET, ATM, and so on. Current DWDM systems can achieve capacity of over 40 Gbps, with future developments carrying 80 wavelengths of OC-48 (2.5 Gbps), totaling 200 Gbps, or 40 wavelengths of OC-192 (10 Gbps), totaling 400 Gbps.

The ITU has standardized channel separation of DWDM wavelengths at 100 GHz, although more vendors today are using 50 GHz or less to separate the wavelengths, yielding more capacity across the fiber.

DWDM Technology

The high-speed, high-volume transmission of DWDM is achieved by the *optical amplifier*. Optical amplifiers operate in a specific band of the frequency spectrum and are optimized for operation with existing fiber, making it possible to boost lightwave signals, extending their reach without converting them back to electrical form.

DWDM systems consist of multiple input lasers, LTE multiplexer, transport fiber, LTE demultiplexer, and receiving laser diodes. A DWDM system is illustrated Figure 22-5.

Figure 22-5 *DWDM Concept*

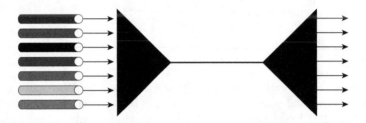

DWDM wavelengths are assigned a different frequency, or color, across the spectrum, with a minimal amount of frequency spacing between the "colored" wavelengths.

DWDM Capacity

The following table reflects current and future trends of DWDM implementations and the bandwidth enabled by each implementation.

Table 22-1   *DWDM Technology Timeline*

Wavelength	Timeline	Capacity
DWDM at OC-192 and 40λ	Current	40 wavelengths at 100 Ghz spacing, at 10 Gbps each, totaling 400 Gbps.
DWDM at OC-192 and 80λ	Current	80 wavelengths at 50 Ghz spacing, at 10 Gbps each, totaling 800 Gbps.
DWDM at OC-768 and 40λ	Current	This is current in that developmental work is being performed today. 40 wavelengths, at 40 Gbps per wavelength, totaling 1.6 Tbps (Terabits-per-second).
DWDM at OC-768 and 80λ	Future	(2002) 80 wavelengths totaling 3.2 Tbps.

Table 22-1   *DWDM Technology Timeline (Continued)*

Wavelength	Timeline	Capacity
DWDM at OC-192 and 160λ	Future	(2005) 160 wavelengths (with closer spacing) at 10 Gbps, totaling 1.6 Tbps.
DWDM at OC-768 and 160λ	Future	(2008-2009) 160 wavelengths at 40 Gbps, totaling 6.4 Tbps.

Technical Note: Optical Switching

Traditional electronic-based switching systems convert the wavelength from optical-electronic-optical; this conversion is not an ideal scenario because the electronic conversion process limits bandwidth capacity. Optical switching does not perform this conversion because all signals are "light," without any electrical signal conversion. Optical switching is a light-based form of a digital cross-connect. The digital cross-connect system, sometimes referred to as a Digital Access and Cross-Connect Systems, or Digital Cross-Connect System (DACS or DXC), is a switch designed to establish long-term "nailed-up" circuit paths.

Micro Electrical Mechanical Systems (MEMS) is the switching technology that Lambda (λ)-based systems use when deploying optical-based switching and routing devices. The following figure illustrates how MEMS performs optical switching. MEMS relies on micron-mirrors, which can be configured at various angles to ensure that incoming lambdas hit one fixed mirror, reflect from a movable mirror (Reflector) back to another fixed mirror, and then reflect back out another lambda.

Cisco Note: Cisco Optical Product Suite Notice

Cisco Systems announced the end of sales (EoS), end of life (EoL), and end of support for the Cisco ISR 3303/Cisco ONS 15303/4. The product is no longer orderable, and the support for the ISR 3303/ONS 15303/4 will end January 18, 2004. The Cisco ONS 15327 Metro Edge Optical Transport Platform is the recommended product to replace the Cisco ISR 3303/Cisco ONS 15303/4. The Cisco ONS 15327 delivers SONET, integrated optical networking, unprecedented multiservices on demand, and radical economics to the edge of metro networks. This platform enables the deployment of next-generation services more rapidly than traditionally available. In addition to the Cisco ONS 15327 and ONS 15454, Cisco offers an entire line of metro optical products including the Cisco ONS 15200 Metro DWDM family, the first solution to deliver instant wavelengths to buildings, premises, or points of presence (PoPs).

Figure 22-6 *MEMS*

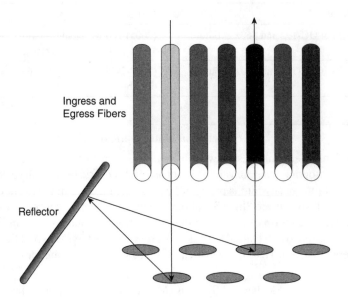

Ingress and
Egress Fibers

Reflector

Summary

The foundation of any optical system is the fiber optic cabling. Basic fiber optic cables consist of the following components:

- Silica core
- Cladding
- Coating, strength members, and a plastic jacket
- Transceivers

Fiber optic transmission operates by sending light at a specific angle down a fiber optic cable. This fiber optic cable is made up primarily of a silica core and glass cladding. It is this glass cladding that acts as a mirror, reflecting the light signal down the cable to its (destination) termination point.

The reflective path taken by light in a fiber is considered the mode. There are two modes used in fiber optic networks:

- **MMF**—Multimode fiber is used for specific applications where the distance limitation of two kilometers is not an issue.
- **SMF**—Single-mode fiber can reach as far as 100–200 kilometers before a fiber optic repeater, or amplifier, is required.

SONET enables the interoperation of multiple technologies and vendor products by defining standard physical network interfaces. SONET was designed for the public telephone network where fiber optic cabling prevailed for long-distance voice traffic transmissions.

DWDM is an optical technology used to increase bandwidth over existing fiber optic backbones. DWDM combines and transmits multiple signals simultaneously at different wavelengths on the same fiber, in effect creating several virtual fiber connections over a single physical connection. DWDM-based networks are protocol and bandwidth independent, capable of sending data in IP, ATM, SONET/SDH, and Ethernet frame formats. DWDM-based networks can carry different types of traffic at different speeds over an optical channel, such as bandwidth rates of between 100 Mbps and 2.5 Gbps.

SONET and DWDM are both viable options for network service providers to implement in the network backbone, with each providing its own advantages. SONET has the advantage over DWDM in regard to automatic ring protection; DWDM has the advantage over SONET when it comes to available bandwidth capacity.

Frequently Asked Questions (FAQ)

1 What is the difference between SONET and SONET Digital Hierarchy (SDH)?

The first level in the SDH hierarchy is Synchronous Transport Mode 1 (STM-1) and has a line rate of 155.52Mb/s. This is equivalent to SONET's STS-3c, STM-4 at 622.08Mb/s, and STM-16 at 2488.32Mb/s. The other difference is in the overhead bytes, which are defined differently for SDH. A common misconception is that STM-Ns are formed by multiplexing STM-1s. STM-1s, STM-4s and STM-16s that terminate on a network node are broken down to recover the VCs they contain. The outbound STM-Ns are then reconstructed with new overhead.

2 What is "dark fiber"?

Dark fiber refers to unused fiber-optic cable. Often companies lay more fiber lines than they need so that the company does not have to incur the cost of having to lay new fiber-optic cable. The dark strands can be leased to organizations that want to establish optical connections among their own locations.

In the case of a dark fiber deployment, the fiber is neither controlled by nor connected to the network service provider. Instead, the customer provides the necessary components to make the fiber functional; the network service provider provides only the path, or wavelength, to the organization.

3 What is "customer-owned dark fiber"?

With customer-owned dark fiber networks, the end customer owns and controls the actual fiber and decides to which service provider they want to connect for services such as telephony, cable TV, and Internet.

Professional third-party companies who specialize in dark fiber systems manage the installation and maintenance of the fiber on behalf of the customer.

4   What is Cisco COMET?

Cisco COMET is considered the next step in the evolution of IP+Optical networking by providing the following:

- Complete optical restoration, topology, and transmission support to maximize service velocity
- Multiservice delivery to maximize service density
- Edge support for all optical interfaces to maximize service variety
- Transport that is scalable and efficient to maximize service capacity throughout the network

Case Study

When deploying a fiber optic network, SONET and DWDM each offer advantages to the network service provider. Based on bit rate alone, DWDM has a fourfold advantage even over TDM (STM–64/OC–192). To compare the two technologies, however, it is necessary to review and outline the ideal technological solution for expanding network capacity. This review and comparison must be performed in a broad sense, recognizing that there are instances in which TDM may offer a better solution than DWDM.

When deciding to deploy SONET or DWDM within a network service provider backbone, the following items need to be considered:

- **Compatibility with Fiber Plant**—The majority of the legacy fiber plant cannot support high bit-rate TDM; it is expensive and can limit the ability of network service providers to migrate to the greater bandwidth available through DWDM at STM–16/OC–48 rates.

    DWDM implementations can use existing fiber, with necessary upgrades being accomplished by the swapping out of the LTE on both ends of the fiber optic cable.

- **Transparency and Interoperability**—The solution must be vendor independent, vendor interoperable, and conform to industry standards. The solution also must be capable of supporting mixed protocols and signal formats.

    DWDM systems provide this transparency and can be used with any SONET/SDH bit rates, as well as with asynchronous/PDH protocols; in essence, DWDM can carry SONET/SDH traffic.

- **Migration and Provisioning Strategy**—The solution must meet the following requirements:

  — Offer the network service provider the capability to expand the network with minimal cost

  — Capable of supporting differing bit rates and have channel upgrade capability

  TDM systems are nearing their technological barriers with the deployment of STM–64/OC–192. These TDM systems can represent a practical limit, exceeded only by DWDM.

- **Network Management**—The solution must meet international network management standards, interface with the network service provider's existing operating system, and provide direct connection for all of the network elements for performance monitoring, fault identification, fault isolation, and remedial action.

  SONET implementations provide automatic failover and protection against facilities (fiber) based network outages. The only instance SONET will fail during a network outage is if the working and protecting rings have both failed and/or are damaged in an outage (such as that caused by multiple fiber cuts).

- **Technical Constraints**—The systems deployed must be able to resolve some of the technical issues present in current lightwave systems: signal dispersion compensation, filtering and channel cross talk, nonlinear four-wave mixing, and physical equipment density.

  There is no clear technical advantage to either a SONET or DWDM implementation. These constraints can be improved only through continued research and development (R&D) by various vendors and technology labs.

PIC Codes

The following lists "10-10" codes only; other PIC codes ("10-15" and "10-16") can be found at http://www.dialxchange.com/pic_number.htm.

PIC Code	Company Name	Telephone Number
1010001	WorldCom Inc.	1-918-590-4581
1010002	WorldCom Inc.	1-918-590-4581
1010003	Frontier Communications Int'l, Inc.	1-716-777-8456
1010004	ATX Telecommunications Services	1-610-668-3000
1010005	EqualNet Corporation	1-281-529-4648
1010006	WorldCom Inc.	1-918-590-4581
1010007	TeleMarketing Communications Inc.	1-801-363-9600
1010008	WorldCom Inc.	1-918-590-4581
1010009	EqualNet Corporation	1-281-529-4648
1010010	Valley Telephone Long Distance	1-210-642-1160
1010011	WorldCom Inc.	1-918-590-4581
1010012	LCI International	1-614-798-6884
1010013	Access Services dba Pacific NW Telecom	Unavailable
1010014	Marathon Communications	1-206-286-5264
1010015	Hawaiian Telephone Company (GTE)	1-808-546-3616
1010016	TMC Long Distance dba Cherry Communications Inc.	1-708-449-7000
1010017	NCHE Telecommunications Network Inc.	1-703-352-2300
1010018	Sprint Local Telecommunications Division	1-913-624-6881
1010019	TMC Long Distance dba Cherry Communications Inc.	1-708-449-7000
1010020	Innovative Telecom Co.	1-603-889-8411
1010021	WorldCom Inc.	1-918-590-4581

continues

PIC Code	Company Name	Telephone Number
1010022	MCI	1-972-729-5166
1010023	IDS Long Distance, Inc.	1-305-620-1620
1010024	Primus	1-703-848-4628
1010025	International Exchange Communications (Pacific Gateway Exch.)	1-214-742-7439
1010026	NET-tel Corporation	1-202-736-5100
1010027	North American Communications Group	Not Available
1010028	American Long Distance Corporation	Not Available
1010029	Telecommunications Consultants, Inc.	1-817-261-3878
1010030	U.S. Long Distance, Inc.	1-210-525-6613
1010031	WorldCom Inc.	1-918-590-4581
1010032	United Communications Assn., Inc.	1-316-227-8645
1010033	Sprint	1-913-624-6881
1010034	Intellicall Operator Services	1-214-416-0022
1010035	LCI International	1-614-798-6884
1010036	Long Distance Savers	1-318-323-8600
1010037	BN1 Telecommunications, Inc.	1-330-762-4900
1010038	Citizens Communications	1-716-389-0380
1010040	LCI International	1-614-798-6884
1010041	VTA, Inc.	Not Available
1010042	TeleCommunication Systems	1-410-263-7616
1010043	Consolidated Comm. Public Services	1-217-235-4416
1010044	Frontier Communications Services, Inc.	1-716-777-8456
1010045	PSA, Inc.	1-904-257-4118
1010046	Cam-Net, Inc.	1-604-684-4111
1010047	Ranger Telecommunications	Not Available
1010048	ETSC	1-505-769-1823
1010049	Hedges & Associates	1-417-881-3425
1010050	WorldCom Inc.	1-918-590-4581
1010051	Fiberlink Communications Corp.	1-215-668-7950
1010052	West Coast Telecommunications, Inc.	1-805-963-2423

PIC Code	Company Name	Telephone Number
1010053	WorldCom Inc.	1-918-590-4581
1010054	Eastern Telephone Systems, Inc.	1-215-628-4111
1010055	WorldCom Inc.	1-918-590-4581
1010056	Qwest Communications	1-800-860-1020
1010057	Nationwide Long Distance	1-713-368-5300
1010058	Frontier Local Services, Inc.	1-716-777-8456
1010059	National Independent Carrier Exch., Inc.	1-908-490-3000
1010060	Economy Telephone, Inc.	1-619-279-5600
1010061	ACN Communications, Inc.	1-805-281-2100
1010062	Kentucky Telephone Corp.	1-502-562-0520
1010063	Coast International, Inc.	1-913-859-9000
1010064	Digital Network Services, Inc.	1-214-224-3000
1010066	Frontier Communications Services, Inc.	1-716-777-8456
1010068	Interstate Savings	1-215-830-0682
1010069	Hotel Connect, L.L.C.	1-209-339-4411
1010070	Qwest Communications	1-800-860-1020
1010071	Eclipse Telecommunications, Inc. (IXC-LD)	1-512-433-2456
1010073	Communications Options Inc.	1-614-345-2949
1010075	Allcomm Long Distance, Inc.	1-915-445-4556
1010076	International Telemedia Associates, Inc.	1-800-285-4263
1010077	General Communication Inc.	Not Available
1010078	Enhanced Services Billing, Inc. (ESBI)	Not Available
1010079	Red Rose Systems dba D&E Long Distance	1-717-738-7051
1010080	WorldCom Inc.	1-918-590-4581
1010081	Total-Tel USA, Inc.	1-800-864-4000
1010082	Discount Payphone	1-305-472-9969
1010084	WorldCom Inc.	1-918-590-4581
1010085	WesTel, Inc.	1-512-480-5500
1010086	Frontier Communications Int'l, Inc.	Not Available

continues

PIC Code	Company Name	Telephone Number
1010087	Telecom*USA [MCI]	1-972-729-5166
1010088	SBS/MCI	1-972-729-5166
1010090	WesTel, Inc.	1-512-480-5500
1010091	Call Technology Corp. of Philadelphia	1-215-595-1100
1010092	MCI	1-972-729-5166
1010093	Melbourne International Comm. Ltd.	1-407-952-9700
1010095	Apple Communications	1-512-338-0100
1010096	Citizens Communications	1-716-389-0380
1010097	TresCom Puerto Rico	1-954-627-6408
1010098	NETECH Comm. a US WEST Company	1-303-592-6422
1010099	Pac-West Telecomm, Inc. dba AmeriCall	1-209-469-3343
1010110	Tandem Access for Database Query	Not Available
1010111	Roseville Telephone Co.	1-916-786-1312
1010112	Business Discount Plan dba LD Discount Plan	1-714-798-7040
1010113	Ameritech Long Distance Services	1-708-248-2022
1010114	Telelink	1-416-925-9460
1010115	BKC Telecommunications, Inc.	1-512-288-4233
1010116	Telnet Global Communications	1-215-548-3630
1010117	Cellnet	Not Available
1010118	A & N Telecom	1-213-612-0336
1010120	TRT Telecommunications Corporation	1-202-879-2236
1010121	Future Telephone Communications	1-214-464-1537
1010122	MCI	1-972-729-5166
1010123	Americatel	1-305-716-8700
1010124	Horry Telephone Long Distance, Inc.	1-803-365-2151
1010125	Atlantic Telephone Company, Inc.	1-904-257-5588
1010126	Ameritech Communications, Inc.	1-847-928-4310
1010129	Baystar Satellite Paging	1-713-680-1313
1010130	Computer Telephone Corp.	1-617-466-1259
1010131	USP&C, Inc.	1-816-965-2600
1010132	MPC Bus. Comms. Systems, Inc./Easton Telecom Svcs.	1-954-968-1913

PIC Code	Company Name	Telephone Number
1010133	MCI	1-972-729-5166
1010134	Riktel Communications, Inc.	1-303-449-2459
1010135	Network One	1-404-980-0080
1010136	Eclipse Communications	1-757-873-1040
1010137	Access Network Services, Inc.	1-703-478-5772
1010138	Metcom Canada Limited	1-905-940-1616
1010139	Ascending Technologies	1-216-292-7005
1010140	Trans National Communications, Inc.	1-617-369-1129
1010141	IFC Communications	1-310-456-6660
1010142	WorldCom Inc.	1-918-590-4581
1010143	Digital Network, Inc.	1-972-756-2000
1010144	Association Communications	1-206-674-2000
1010145	American Communications Int'l, Ltd.	1-301-948-8777
1010146	Pioneer Long Distance	1-503-929-8223
1010147	Data & Electronic Services, Inc.	1-850-837-0077
1010149	Tel-Com Telecommunications, Inc.	1-903-935-2870
1010170	McLeod Network Services	1-319-398-7000
1010172	USP&C, Inc.	1-816-965-2600
1010176	WBC Communications, Inc.	1-510-568-6424
1010177	Sprint	1-913-624-6881
1010178	PDQ Communications Source	1-903-643-0064
1010179	Network Marketing Group	1-214-618-1611
1010180	Central Telephone Co.	1-214-424-2779
1010181	Digital Communications, Inc.	1-214-337-6426
1010182	Allgood Taylor Telephone	1-214-423-6020
1010183	MCI Metro	1-972-729-5166
1010184	Stone & Company	Not Available
1010185	GTC	1-214-238-7000
1010186	Standard Long Distance	1-214-232-5578
1010187	BellSouth Long Distance	1-770-352-3039

continues

PIC Code	Company Name	Telephone Number
1010188	MCI/1-800-COLLECT	1-972-729-5166
1010188	MCI/1-800-Collect	1-972-729-5166
1010189	State of Texas - GSC	1-512-475-2385
1010192	Amerinet Communications	1-404-460-1300
1010193	Landmark Communications Company, Inc.	1-913-749-1640
1010194	Easton Telecom Services, Inc.	1-216-659-6700
1010195	Starcom International Optics Corp.	1-604-688-4400
1010197	Comanche County Long Distance	1-817-893-7000
1010199	Crescent Communications	1-713-622-9000
1010200	US WATS	1-610-660-5022
1010201	North American Telephone	1-813-272-7000
1010202	Frontier Communications-North Central Region, Inc.	1-716-777-8456
1010203	Cypress Telecommunications Corp. (Cytel)	1-713-591-3000
1010204	United Telephone Long Distance	1-913-624-3667
1010205	Lone Star Telecom	Not Available
1010206	Global Com	Not Available
1010207	2JE Telecommunications	Not Available
1010210	NOS Communications, Inc.	1-702-547-8000
1010211	Frontier Communications Int'l, Inc.	1-716-777-8456
1010212	WorldCom Inc.	1-918-590-4581
1010213	Long Distance Telephone Savers	1-606-324-1726
1010214	LCC	1-409-633-6615
1010215	Pronto Long Distance Inc.	1-514-935-4733
1010216	MetroLink	1-312-551-3444
1010217	WorldCom Inc.	1-918-590-4581
1010218	Tel-Central of Jefferson City	1-314-634-5445
1010220	Telecom*USA [MCI]	1-972-729-5166
1010221	Capital Telecommunications, Inc.	1-717-848-8800
1010222	MCI	1-972-729-5166
1010223	Cable & Wireless Communications, Inc.	Not Available
1010224	Telecom*USA [MCI]	1-972-729-5166

PIC Code	Company Name	Telephone Number
1010225	Iowa Network Services, Inc.	1-515-830-0456
1010226	One Call Communications	1-317-843-1300
1010227	People's Telephone Company, Inc.	1-305-593-9667
1010228	USLink Long Distance	1-218-568-4000
1010229	U.S. ComNet	1-703-757-9900
1010231	Frontier Communications-North Central Region, Inc.	1-716-777-8456
1010232	Frontier Communications of the Great Lakes, Inc.	1-716-777-8456
1010233	ITC DeltaCom Communications, Inc.	1-706-645-8555
1010234	ACC Long Distance Corporation	1-716-987-3140
1010236	LCI International	1-614-798-6884
1010239	Brooks Fiber Communications [WorldCom]	1-918-590-4581
1010241	American Long Lines	1-215-442-9000
1010242	Sasktel	1-613-785-1120
1010243	Beehive Telephone	1-801-596-9512
1010244	Qwest Communications	1-303-260-4055
1010245	Frontier Communications Int'l, Inc.	1-716-777-8456
1010246	Shared Communications Services, Inc.	1-503-399-7000
1010248	Standard Communications Inc., dba SCI	1-813-938-4402
1010249	PSP Marketing Group, Inc.	1-601-932-5558
1010250	WorldCom Inc.	1-918-590-4581
1010251	Partners Telecom, Inc.	1-214-690-0692
1010252	Long Distance/USA [SPRINT]	1-913-624-6881
1010253	LCI International	1-614-798-6884
1010254	WorldCom Inc.	1-918-590-4581
1010255	Public, Phone	1-609-383-9444
1010256	Applied Signal Corporation	1-408-244-7844
1010257	ConQuest	1-614-791-3406
1010258	Metronet Long Distance Communications	1-517-694-1101
1010258	Metronet Long Distance Communications	1-517-694-1101
1010259	Call for Less Long Distance	1-817-483-7731

continues

PIC Code	Company Name	Telephone Number
1010260	Frontier Communications-North Central Region, Inc.	1-716-777-8456
1010261	Hertz Technologies, Inc.	1-405-720-5019
1010262	Carib Communications, L.P.	1-305-232-3635
1010263	WorldCom Inc.	1-918-590-4581
1010264	MEANS Telcom	1-612-230-4116
1010266	WorldCom Inc.	1-918-590-4581
1010267	WorldCom Inc.	1-918-590-4581
1010268	The CommuniGroup	1-601-353-9118
1010269	TEL AMERICA L.D.T.S.	Not Available
1010270	Cherry Communications	1-708-449-7000
1010272	Bell Atlantic Communications, Inc.	1-703-974-3547
1010273	EDS.	1-770-801-7215
1010274	WorldCom Inc.	1-918-590-4581
1010275	WorldXChange	1-619-625-5585
1010276	Bee Line Long Distance	1-801-262-9443
1010279	Associated Telenet Inc./ A CTI Company	1-717-848-8800
1010280	CEO Telecommunications, Inc. [Star Telecommunications, Inc.]	1-805-963-1619
1010281	Digital Technologies, Inc.	1-732-919-1400
1010282	GST Telecom	1-360-944-4521
1010283	Iowa Communications Network	1-515-323-4650
1010284	AmeriVision Communications, Inc.	1-405-879-0530
1010285	Federal TransTel, Inc. (FTT)	1-800-933-6600
1010286	Cincinnati Bell Long Distance	1-513-357-5120
1010287	LCI International	1-614-798-6884
1010288	AT&T Communications	1-908-580-8761
1010290	WorldCom Inc.	1-918-590-4581
1010291	Call Savers Inc.	1-209-292-1476
1010292	TCG	1-718-355-2762
1010293	Cincinnati Bell Long Distance	1-513-357-5120
1010295	Glens Falls Long Distance Service	1-518-793-8135

PIC Code	Company Name	Telephone Number
1010297	Long Distance Wholesale Club (Excel Communications)	1-214-863-8041
1010298	U.S. Net, Inc.	1-417-881-3425
1010299	LECNet, Inc.	1-601-352-2888
1010300	GST Telecom	1-360-944-4521
1010301	Western Telephone & Television	1-714-753-2814
1010302	Austin Bestline	1-512-328-9095
1010303	TCG	1-718-355-2762
1010304	Arch Telecom	1-713-751-1999
1010305	Motorola Inc.	1-708-576-5889
1010306	Colorado River Communications	1-702-641-5177
1010307	American Telnet, Inc.	1-305-932-2884
1010308	Network Operator Services, Inc.	1-903-758-9350
1010311	WorldCom Inc.	1-918-590-4581
1010312	WorldCom Inc.	1-918-590-4581
1010313	Star Tel, Inc.	1-409-821-2848
1010314	AT&T Wireless Services, Inc.	1-206-803-1232
1010315	WorldCom Inc.	1-918-590-4581
1010316	ABCO Communications, Inc.	1-707-584-1500
1010319	ConQuest	1-614-791-3406
1010321	Telecom*USA [MCI]	1-972-729-5166
1010322	Frontier Communications-North Central Region, Inc.	1-716-777-8456
1010323	BC Tel	1-613-781-7971
1010324	TELUS Communications (Edmonton) Inc. (TCE)	1-613-781-0815
1010325	Econo. Call Long Distance Services	1-505-524-1594
1010326	National Fibernet, Inc.	1-214-224-1335
1010327	ECI Communications	1-541-465-1375
1010328	Idaho State Government	1-208-334-2885
1010330	Tel-Share	Not Available
1010332	Northland Telephone Systems LTD.	1-315-797-6101
1010333	Sprint	1-913-624-6881

continues

PIC Code	Company Name	Telephone Number
1010335	Touch America, Inc.	1-406-523-3600
1010336	RCN Long Distance Company	1-609-734-3782
1010338	Midco Communications	1-605-334-1200
1010339	Communication Cable Laying Co., Inc.	1-417-881-3425
1010340	HUB Distributing Inc.	1-213-913-1000
1010341	National Tele-Sav Inc.	1-803-236-0963
1010342	Premier Long Distance Svcs. Inc.	1-313-981-5052
1010343	Chester Long Distance Services, Inc.	1-803-581-2111
1010344	GST Telecom	1-360-944-4521
1010345	ACC Long Distance Corporation	1-716-987-3140
1010346	GST Telecom	1-360-944-4521
1010347	Universal Communications Group, Inc.	1-212-889-7500
1010348	Sprint Canada, Inc.	1-416-496-4951
1010349	Communication Cable Laying Co., Inc.	1-417-881-3425
1010350	FiberNet Telemanagement, Inc.	1-800-401-4141
1010351	Call America of Riverside	1-714-369-8090
1010352	Standard TelCom, Inc.	Not Available
1010353	WorldCom Inc.	1-918-590-4581
1010354	Discount Long Distance of America	1-314-434-9009
1010355	U. S. Link	1-218-568-4000
1010356	Bluegrass Long Distance, Inc.	1-606-245-5739
1010358	LCI International	1-614-798-6884
1010359	Empire One Telecommunications, Inc.	1-212-929-2030
1010360	Touch America, Inc.	1-406-523-3600
1010361	Dakota Telecommunications Group, Inc.	1-605-263-3301
1010362	AmeriSystems, Inc.	Not Available
1010363	Bell Canada	1-613-785-1120
1010364	Equicom Communications Inc.	1-614-793-0200
1010365	EMI Communications Corp.	1-315-433-0022
1010366	American Telco, Inc.	1-713-880-7247
1010367	Wholesale Communications	1-214-519-1934

PIC Code	Company Name	Telephone Number
1010368	Budget Call Long Distance	1-716-777-8456
1010369	Loma International, Inc.	1-809-258-1052
1010370	American Network Exchange Inc., sub. of AMNEX, Inc.	1-407-246-6411
1010372	Pacific Bell Communications	1-415-278-1916
1010373	USC Telecom, Inc. (EqualNet)	1-281-529-4648
1010374	Connect Americom Corp.	1-210-492-8200
1010375	AT&T EasyLink Services	1-973-331-4723
1010376	Northern Telecom Inc.	1-615-734-4657
1010377	BellSouth Long Distance	1-770-352-3039
1010378	Tel Serv	1-605-225-1837
1010379	Professional Fusion Enterprises, Inc.	1-714-979-3532
1010380	TeleServ Corporation	1-703-205-0050
1010381	USN Communications	1-630-645-4300
1010382	Long Distance Management Inc.	1-405-236-2255
1010383	Caribbean Telephone & Telegraph Inc.	1-760-325-5618
1010384	TLD, Inc.	1-809-273-5629
1010385	The Switchboard	1-405-254-2255
1010386	MediaOne, Inc.	1-510-273-8686
1010387	AT&T Communications	1-908-580-8761
1010388	KDD America, Inc.	1-212-832-4078
1010389	EATELNET	1-504-621-4213
1010390	ONE-2-ONE Communications	1-334-433-6300
1010391	Omnicall Communications Corporation	1-810-737-2600
1010392	HSS Vending Distributors	1-412-264-9040
1010393	Intermedia Communications Inc.	1-813-829-0011
1010394	TresCom U.S.A., Inc./TresCom Caribbean	1-954-627-6408
1010395	USC Telecom, Inc. (EqualNet)	1-281-529-4648
1010397	DavelTel Inc.	1-813-623-3545
1010399	Telco Holdings, Inc.	1-703-631-5600
1010400	Frontier Communications-North Central Region, Inc.	1-716-777-8456

continues

PIC Code	Company Name	Telephone Number
1010401	NTI	1-507-452-8263
1010402	Integretel Inc.	1-408-362-4184
1010403	Nationwide Long Distance	1-713-368-5300
1010404	International Telcom, Ltd.	1-206-301-7001
1010405	Alternate Communications Technology Inc.	1-317-575-9556
1010406	WorldCom Inc.	1-918-590-4581
1010407	Nuestra Telefonica	1-212-541-9200
1010408	WorldCom Inc.	1-918-590-4581
1010409	US Buying Group, Inc.	1-708-489-9400
1010410	Call America/Palm Desert	1-619-340-2112
1010411	American Express Travel Related Services	1-602-766-2554
1010412	Penn Telecom, Inc.	1-412-443-9666
1010413	Alternative Long Distance Inc. dba Money $avers	1-512-404-2250
1010414	USC Telecom, Inc. (EqualNet)	1-281-529-4648
1010415	ESPI, Inc.	1-519-351-1957
1010416	Ameritel c/o Network Telephone Svcs, Inc	1-818-992-4300
1010417	Pioneer Telecom	1-608-723-2181
1010419	H.G. Telecom, Inc.	1-817-339-1700
1010420	Qwest Communications	1-303-260-4055
1010421	WorldCom Inc.	1-918-590-4581
1010422	Island Tel, PEI	1-613-785-1120
1010423	Nickel Fone	1-512-377-3216
1010424	Telus Communications Inc.	1-613-781-0815
1010425	Capital Network Systems Inc., sub. of AMNEX, Inc.	1-407-246-6411
1010426	Voyager Networks Inc.	1-212-571-2000
1010427	Western Telecom, Inc.	1-713-777-8227
1010428	WorldCom Inc.	1-918-590-4581
1010429	Extelcom dba Express Tel	1-801-521-0200
1010431	Star Tel of Abilene/Western Telenet Inc.	Not Available
1010432	Qwest Communications	1-800-860-1020
1010433	INFO-TEL, Inc.	Not Available

PIC Code	Company Name	Telephone Number
1010434	Maritime Tel & Tel	1-613-785-1120
1010435	Global TeleMedia International, Inc.	1-770-667-6088
1010438	Sam's Discount Long Distance, Inc.	1-817-483-5145
1010439	Star Tel, Inc.	1-409-821-2848
1010440	WorldCom Technologies, Inc.	1-918-590-4581
1010441	Escondido Telephone Company	1-708-449-7000
1010442	WorldCom Inc.	1-918-590-4581
1010443	Western Oklahoma Information Systems	1-405-323-0505
1010444	Frontier Communications Services, Inc.	1-716-777-8456
1010445	NewTel Communications	1-613-781-0815
1010446	WorldCom Inc.	1-918-590-4581
1010447	FaxNet Corporation	1-617-557-4300
1010448	NB Tel	1-613-660-3414
1010450	WorldCom Inc.	1-918-590-4581
1010451	LCI International	1-614-798-6884
1010452	LCI International	1-614-798-6884
1010453	WorldCom Inc.	1-918-590-4581
1010456	WorldCom Inc.	1-918-590-4581
1010457	Telco Communications Group dba Dial & Save (Excel Comms.)	1-214-863-8041
1010458	Telemanagement Consultants Corporation	1-414-885-2860
1010460	Independent Network Services, Inc.	1-208-387-0000
1010461	TTE OF CHARLESTON	1-803-744-0150
1010462	LCI International	1-614-798-6884
1010463	Redwood Long Distance	1-507-644-3844
1010464	WorldCom Inc.	1-918-590-4581
1010465	Intelco	1-719-592-1211
1010466	Virgin Islands Tele-Com	1-809-776-1716
1010467	Chickasaw Long Distance Co.	1-405-622-5223
1010468	ITC Networks	1-801-487-7495

continues

PIC Code	Company Name	Telephone Number
1010469	GMW Company	1-806-762-4565
1010470	American Tel Group, Inc.	1-505-294-4440
1010471	WorldCom Inc.	1-918-590-4581
1010472	USC Telecom, Inc. (EqualNet)	1-281-529-4648
1010475	Firstel	1-605-332-3232
1010476	TEK Communications, Inc.	1-202-789-7860
1010477	POPP Telcom	1-612-546-9707
1010478	ITC Networks	1-801-487-7495
1010479	Fibertech Telecom, Inc.	1-713-988-0928
1010480	Vista Group International	1-216-808-2201
1010481	TeleData International, Inc.	1-404-436-1000
1010482	Tele-Sys, Inc.	1-615-482-2140
1010483	Xpedite Systems, Inc.	1-732-389-3900
1010484	Community Long Distance	1-803-328-2534
1010485	Teltrust, Inc.	1-801-535-2000
1010486	Ironton Long Distance Co.	1-610-799-7283
1010488	WorldCom Inc.	1-918-590-4581
1010489	Tel-Optic, Inc. dba Universal Network Services (Uni-Net)	1-501-443-1355
1010491	Northern Arizona Communications Corp.	1-602-774-2686
1010492	Coastal Long Distance Services, Inc.	1-912-368-3300
1010493	Extelcom dba Express Tel	1-801-521-0200
1010494	TransAmerica Communications, Inc.	1-407-241-6515
1010495	Winstar	1-248-539-7877
1010497	Econ-A-Call Inc. of Hays	1-913-628-1750
1010498	Norlight Telecommunications, Inc.	1-218-723-8253
1010499	Norlight Telecommunications, Inc.	1-218-723-8253
1010500	Frontier Communications of the Great Lakes, Inc.	1-716-777-8456
1010501	Carrier Concepts International Corp.	1-214-233-6400
1010502	WorldXChange	1-619-625-5585
1010503	Fone America, Inc.	1-503-620-2400
1010505	Century Telecommunications, Inc.	1-512-754-5690

PIC Code	Company Name	Telephone Number
1010506	Friendship Long Distance	1-214-390-2897
1010507	Fonorola	1-914-631-3666
1010508	INTEX	1-404-395-1855
1010509	Olympic Telecommunications, Inc.	1-206-505-5518
1010510	Innovative Communications, Inc.	1-410-461-7966
1010511	Frontier Communications-North Central Region, Inc.	1-716-777-8456
1010512	TCG	1-718-355-2762
1010513	Intercontinental Communications Group, Inc. dba ICG	1-561-274-8044
1010514	Dominican Communications	1-212-491-3800
1010515	Frontier Communications Int'l, Inc.	1-802-660-0378
1010516	Frontier Communications Int'l, Inc.	1-810-433-4208
1010518	Telecon Communications Corporation	1-518-762-3456
1010519	RSL COM U.S.A.	1-818-888-7600
1010520	Tel-Span Communications, Inc.	1-615-320-0836
1010522	Transaction Network Services	1-703-453-8316
1010523	WorldCom Inc.	1-918-590-4581
1010524	Whitman College	1-509-527-5172
1010525	Lexington Telephone L.D. Co., Inc.	1-910-249-5729
1010526	Poka-Lambro Telecommuncations, Inc.	1-806-924-7234
1010527	Independence Telephone Co.	1-216-524-9292
1010529	Telecom West	1-503-245-3322
1010530	CoreComm	1-614-825-9722
1010531	Farmers Long Distance, Inc.	1-803-382-2350
1010532	Equal Access of Washington	1-202-588-8000
1010533	Long Distance Discount Inc.	1-314-651-3373
1010534	Touch 1 Communications	1-334-368-8600
1010535	WorldCom Inc.	1-918-590-4581
1010536	Long Distance Management	1-502-443-6302
1010537	LCI International	1-614-798-6884
1010538	WorldCom Inc.	1-918-590-4581

continues

PIC Code	Company Name	Telephone Number
1010539	Frontier Communications Services, Inc.	1-716-777-8456
1010540	American Long Distance Exchange, Inc.	Not Available
1010543	Digitran Corp.	Not Available
1010544	United Telephone Co. dba TELAMERICA L.D.	1-504-387-4438
1010545	Keystone Telecom, Inc.	1-717-344-7748
1010546	WorldCom Inc.	1-918-590-4581
1010547	Telefonica Larga Distancia	1-787-273-5479
1010548	Cleartel Communications	1-202-463-8500
1010549	National Brands, Inc. dba Sharenet Communications Company	1-602-269-3201
1010550	Century Long Distance	1-608-796-5834
1010551	Access-Plus, Inc.	1-414-226-2727
1010552	Lake States Communications, Inc.	1-608-233-5544
1010553	Parkway Communications, Inc.	1-214-326-1200
1010554	CellToll Corporation	1-213-245-0444
1010555	WorldCom Inc.	1-918-590-4581
1010556	U.S. Billing	1-210-949-7150
1010557	GST Telecom	1-360-944-4521
1010558	Midcom of Arizona, Inc.	Not Available
1010560	DTG Communications, Inc.	1-605-263-3301
1010561	LCC	1-409-633-6615
1010562	LCI	1-605-582-7527
1010563	LinkUSA Corporation	1-319-363-7570
1010565	Metro One Telecommunications, Inc.	1-503-643-9500
1010566	T-NET (Cable & Wireless)	1-703-760-3993
1010567	Americom Communications	1-513-224-9764
1010568	USC Telecom, Inc. (EqualNet)	1-281-529-4648
1010569	West Coast Telecommunications, Inc.	1-805-963-2423
1010571	Chautauqua & Erie Communications, Inc.	1-716-326-4911
1010572	AirTouch Cellular	1-925-279-6240
1010573	JC&N Satellite Telecommunications	1-619-296-9821

PIC Code	Company Name	Telephone Number
1010574	U.S. Connect Corp.	1-210-492-8200
1010576	U.S. Fiberline Communications, Inc.	1-619-268-0700
1010577	London Telecom Network Corp.	1-612-793-3000
1010578	TTI Telecommunications, Inc.	1-206-441-3100
1010579	Aliant Systems Inc.	1-402-486-7205
1010581	Ben Lomand Communications, Inc.	1-615-668-4132
1010582	International Telemedia Associates, Inc.	1-800-285-4263
1010583	GST Telecom	1-360-944-4521
1010584	Hereford Long Distance Services	1-806-364-3331
1010585	Custom Teleconnect, Inc.	1-702-368-3324
1010586	United Digital Network, Inc. (UDNI)	1-972-756-2089
1010587	Tel-Optic, Inc. dba Universal Network Services (Uni-Net)	1-501-443-1355
1010588	WorldCom Inc.	1-918-590-4581
1010589	WorldCom Inc.	1-918-590-4581
1010590	CoreComm	1-614-825-9722
1010591	Intel Communications	1-903-759-1957
1010593	Transaction Networks, Inc.	1-904-730-4304
1010594	EagleCom, Inc.	1-405-338-4222
1010595	U.S. Republic Communications, Inc.	1-214-230-7200
1010596	U.S. Advantage Long Distance	Not Available
1010597	Pacific Gateway Exchange	1-650-375-6700
1010598	American Discount Telecommunications Inc.	1-214-283-1111
1010599	IntelCom Group, Inc.	1-303-572-5994
1010601	North American Intelecom	1-512-227-1918
1010604	EconoPhone Inc.	1-206-923-2372
1010605	Intercontinental Telcom Inc.	1-817-460-7448
1010606	Biz Tel Long Distance Telephone Co.	1-407-697-5155
1010607	ONE-2-ONE Communications	1-334-433-6300
1010609	Teleglobe USA, Inc.	1-703-821-4835
1010610	Pioneer Long Distance	1-316-356-2374

continues

PIC Code	Company Name	Telephone Number
1010612	EqualNet Corporation	1-281-529-4648
1010613	Cybernet International, Inc.	1-503-224-2022
1010614	Cincinnati Bell Long Distance	1-513-357-5120
1010615	PRIMUS Telecommunications Canada	1-604-891-0829
1010617	AMVOX	1-408-957-4150
1010618	RSL COM U.S.A.	1-818-888-7600
1010619	Colorado River Communications	1-702-641-5177
1010620	Telehop Communications Inc.	1-905-836-9238
1010621	Winstar	1-248-539-7877
1010622	BMG	1-303-779-8735
1010623	NTI	1-507-452-8263
1010624	American Telesource International, Inc.	1-210-558-6090
1010625	EDS	1-818-786-4626
1010626	Tel-One	1-209-462-9828
1010627	Nationwide Emergency Telecomm. System (NETS)	Not Available
1010628	Star Telephone Long Distance	1-910-564-7827
1010629	WorldXChange	1-619-625-5585
1010630	Telegroup	1-515-472-5000
1010631	Long Distance of Michigan	1-313-873-5500
1010633	Frontier Communications-North Central Region, Inc.	1-716-777-8456
1010635	Metro Telephone Inc.	1-309-692-4926
1010636	VarTec Telecom dba Clear Choice Communications	1-214-230-7200
1010637	Fox Communications Corp.	1-206-562-2900
1010638	Northwest Telecom, Ltd.	1-719-592-1211
1010639	NEP Long Distance Co.	1-717-785-2201
1010640	Communications Brokers, Inc.	1-214-418-1885
1010641	Telecommunications Service Center, Inc.	1-813-933-6350
1010643	WinStar	1-248-539-7877
1010644	Arcada Communications	1-206-441-5022
1010645	American Communications Technology, Inc.	1-702-348-8841
1010646	Contact America, Inc.	1-816-646-2923

PIC Code	Company Name	Telephone Number
1010647	Pioneer Long Distance, Inc.	1-405-375-0139
1010648	Winstar	1-248-539-7877
1010649	Working Assets	1-415-788-0777
1010650	EDS	1-818-786-4626
1010651	O.L.C. Company	1-713-880-7255
1010652	Bell Atlantic Communications, Inc.	1-703-974-3547
1010653	Specialized Telecommunications	1-510-783-6300
1010654	Cincinnati Bell Long Distance	1-513-357-5120
1010655	T-NETIX, Inc.	1-303-705-5500
1010656	National Network Corp.	1-801-521-0200
1010657	National Telecom of Florida	1-305-491-9300
1010658	OCI	1-301-571-8694
1010659	CTA Comm. Inc. dba CTA Long Distance	1-503-266-8111
1010660	Connect America Communications, Inc.	1-210-492-8200
1010661	Coastal Telephone Co.	1-713-960-0500
1010662	Valuline Long Distance	1-505-271-9008
1010663	American Telco, Inc.	1-713-880-7247
1010664	Total Telephone, Inc. of Utah	1-801-299-7500
1010665	LCI International	1-614-798-6884
1010666	Systems 1000	1-714-758-2814
1010667	Communications Inc.dba ECI	1-918-254-5700
1010668	U.S. FiberCom Network, Inc.	1-212-302-3365
1010669	TCA Long Distance	1-806-374-6974
1010670	Cameron Long Distance	1-318-583-7000
1010671	Digital Telecommunications, Inc.	1-901-423-0655
1010672	Century Communications	1-214-823-4506
1010674	Venser, Inc.	1-809-273-5629
1010675	Convergent Communications Inc.	1-303-749-3000
1010677	WATS/800, Inc.	1-407-877-5454
1010678	Birch Telecom	1-316-343-7071

continues

PIC Code	Company Name	Telephone Number
1010679	Feist Long Distance	1-913-268-9547
1010680	StormTel, Inc.	1-941-945-2335
1010681	Huntleigh Telecomm. Group, Inc.	1-915-543-6570
1010682	Americall Communications	1-713-729-4617
1010683	WorldCom Inc.	1-918-590-4581
1010684	LCC	1-409-633-6615
1010685	Intl.800 Telecom dba Telecall Long Dist.	1-303-691-2115
1010686	AT&T Canada Long Distance Services Co.	1-416-345-2697
1010687	NTS Communications Inc.	1-806-762-4565
1010688	Mustang Tele-Communications, Inc.	1-713-871-9711
1010689	Telemanagement Consultants Corporation	1-414-885-2860
1010690	LCI International	1-614-798-6884
1010691	Hamilton Telecommunications	1-402-694-5101
1010693	Deluxe Data Systems	1-414-341-5123
1010694	Frontier Long Distance of America	1-716-777-8456
1010695	Opticall Communications Services	1-619-245-6784
1010696	Integrated Systems Corporation	1-405-528-7500
1010697	Matrix Telecom	1-817-581-9380
1010698	Bell Atlantic Communications	1-703-974-3547
1010699	U.S. TeleServices, Inc.	1-703-691-2220
1010700	Tel America	1-801-521-0200
1010701	Continental Long Distance	1-512-404-5751
1010703	Keystone Telecommunications Inc.	1-717-541-8140
1010704	Fibernet Telecommunications, Inc.	1-602-788-6100
1010705	Frontier Communications-North Central Region, Inc.	1-716-777-8456
1010706	ICON Communications Corporation [GST Telecom]	1-360-944-4521
1010707	TelVue Corporation	1-609-273-8888
1010708	Light Link Inc/dba Taylor Comm. Grp.	1-210-525-0028
1010709	Tel America	1-801-521-0200
1010711	Las Vegas Convention & Visitors Authority	1-702-892-7450
1010712	WCS/DIAL ONE	1-406-245-6102

PIC Code	Company Name	Telephone Number
1010713	Northern Wisconsin L.D.S.	1-715-356-2330
1010715	Latatel de America, Inc.	1-212-874-6286
1010716	Nationwide Communications, Inc.	1-800-968-0412
1010717	Network One, Inc.	1-904-730-0050
1010718	U.S. West Long Distance	1-303-672-1057
1010719	STARTEC, Inc.	1-301-365-8959
1010721	Voice Technical Corporation	1-208-389-1151
1010722	HI-PLAINS NTS COMMUNICATIONS	1-806-665-0706
1010723	Capital Telecommunications, Inc.	1-717-848-8800
1010724	WorldCom Inc.	1-918-590-4581
1010725	Consolidated Network Inc.	1-314-434-9889
1010726	ProCom, Inc.	1-304-379-2238
1010727	Switch 2000, Inc.	1-612-425-1521
1010728	Peoples Communication, Inc.	1-903-763-4941
1010729	Tel America	1-801-521-0200
1010730	ATNT of United Business & Comm. Svcs.	Not Available
1010731	Telescan Inc.	1-423-282-5043
1010732	AT&T Communications	1-908-580-8761
1010733	WorldCom Inc.	1-918-590-4581
1010734	Scherers Communications Group, Inc.	1-614-847-6161
1010735	I-Link Communications	1-602-264-8644
1010736	Xnet, Inc.	Not Available
1010737	WorldCom Inc.	1-918-590-4581
1010738	WorldCom Inc.	1-918-590-4581
1010741	WorldCom Inc.	1-918-590-4581
1010742	WorldCom Inc.	1-918-590-4581
1010743	Peninsula Long Distance Service Inc.	1-414-743-1060
1010744	GT Com Long Distance	1-850-227-7272
1010746	National Telephone Exchange (PA)	1-717-232-8201
1010748	CommNet Cellular, Inc.	1-303-694-8935

continues

PIC Code	Company Name	Telephone Number
1010750	Hi-Rim Communications, Inc.	1-702-734-3719
1010751	WorldCom Inc.	1-918-590-4581
1010752	Excel Telecommunications, Inc.	1-972-705-5500
1010754	IBM	1-847-240-3067
1010755	IBM	1-847-240-3067
1010756	ZeroPlus Dialing Inc.	Not Available
1010757	LCI International	1-614-798-6884
1010758	LCI International	1-614-798-6884
1010759	Telenet Comm. Corp. [Sprint]	1-913-624-6881
1010760	Alternative Long Distance, Inc.	1-303-623-2385
1010762	State of California - CALNET	1-916-657-9447
1010763	Southern New England Telephone (SNET)	1-860-947-7605
1010764	Network Plus	1-617-786-4000
1010765	Eclipse Communications	1-757-873-1040
1010766	Yavapai Telephone Exchange	1-602-678-0463
1010767	Payline Systems Inc.	1-503-692-6846
1010769	Omni Communications, Inc.	1-561-625-1900
1010770	Souris River Telecommunications Company	1-701-722-3711
1010771	Telecom*USA [MCI]	1-972-729-5166
1010772	IBM	1-847-240-3067
1010773	Sprint Canada, Inc.	1-416-496-4951
1010774	CityNet Communications Inc.	1-313-626-1710
1010775	Pencor Services dba Palmerton Long Distance	1-610-826-9140
1010776	Priority One Long Distance	1-909-483-1240
1010777	AlternaTel [Sprint]	1-913-624-6881
1010778	Show-Me Long Distance, Inc.	1-512-448-2831
1010779	Autumn Communications, Inc.	1-210-697-0766
1010780	Matrix Telecom	1-817-581-9380
1010781	WXL Communications, Ltd. (WorldxChange)	1-613-787-1041
1010782	WorldCom Inc.	1-918-590-4581
1010783	MTS Communications Inc.	1-613-785-1120

PIC Code	Company Name	Telephone Number
1010784	Sunshine Telephone Inc. dba SUNTEL	1-407-872-0470
1010786	WorldCom Inc.	1-918-590-4581
1010787	Star Tel of Abilene/Western Telenet Inc.	Not Available
1010788	C-COM	1-303-938-1417
1010789	WorldCom Inc.	1-918-590-4581
1010790	Affiliated Telecom Svcs. Inc.	1-214-283-1111
1010791	B.R. Communications	1-214-283-1111
1010792	SouthTel Corporation	1-210-826-8613
1010793	Southwest Texas Long Distance Co.	1-830-683-1924
1010794	Ameritel	1-707-257-3898
1010795	CapRock Telemanagement	1-972-239-9137
1010796	Indiantown Telephone Long Distance	1-561-597-3636
1010797	WorldCom Inc. dba Touch One Long Distance	1-918-590-4581
1010799	Long Distance International, Inc.	1-954-522-3300
1010800	WorldCom Inc.	1-918-590-4581
1010801	WorldCom Inc.	1-918-590-4581
1010802	Electric Lightwave, Inc.	1-360-896-3265
1010803	Low Country Carrier dba Hargray L.D. Co.	1-843-686-1111
1010805	OCI	1-301-571-8694
1010806	NACT	1-801-225-6248
1010807	South Carolina Network, Inc.	1-803-382-2350
1010808	Eastern Telecom dba InterQuest	1-706-645-8658
1010809	Asia International Services Corp. (AIC)	1-604-298-8810
1010810	Winstar	1-248-539-7877
1010811	VarTec Telecom, Inc.	1-214-230-7200
1010813	American Telecommunications Enterprises	1-315-453-2323
1010814	Discount America	1-512-392-6284
1010816	Consolidated Technologies, Inc. (CTI)	1-604-893-1555
1010817	Value-Added Communications	1-706-628-6606
1010818	VarTec Telecom, Inc.	1-214-230-7200

continues

PIC Code	Company Name	Telephone Number
1010819	Cablevision Lightpath Inc.	1-516-393-3456
1010820	G.E. Exchange	1-770-644-7680
1010822	Athena International L.L.C.	1-303-595-0800
1010824	WorldCom Inc.	1-918-590-4581
1010826	Telecom*USA [MCI]	1-972-729-5166
1010827	MVP Communications, Inc.	1-314-651-0505
1010828	Excel Telecommunications, Inc.	1-972-705-5500
1010829	Caribbean Telecommunications Consortium, Inc.	1-415-908-1250
1010830	Public Service Company of NM	1-505-848-2858
1010831	Frontier Communications-North Central Region, Inc.	1-716-777-8456
1010832	Telecom*USA [MCI]	1-972-729-5166
1010833	Business Telecom, Inc. (BTI)	1-919-510-7270
1010834	CTS Telcom of Florida	1-619-547-5700
1010835	Telecom*USA [MCI]	1-972-729-5166
1010836	Branson Telephone	1-417-335-5123
1010837	Norlight Telecommunications, Inc.	1-218-723-8253
1010838	PhoneTel Technologies Inc.	1-216-241-2555
1010839	Cable & Wireless Communications, Inc.	Not Available
1010840	World Pass Communications Corp.	1-305-935-5475
1010841	First Financial Management Corp.	Not Available
1010842	World Access Communications Corp. (WACC)	1-305-577-9700
1010843	Advanced Telecom Systems	1-408-988-3639
1010844	Preferred Telecom, Inc.	1-972-726-1939
1010845	TeleCable Corporation	Not Available
1010846	WorldCom Inc	1-918-590-4581
1010847	VIP Connections, Inc.	1-808-544-0900
1010848	Primus Telecommunications, Inc.	1-954-967-6226
1010849	Correctional Billing Services	1-334-875-3377
1010851	UTEL-CALL	1-608-328-6283
1010852	Telecom*USA [MCI]	1-972-729-5166
1010853	Digital Network, Inc.	1-972-756-2000

PIC Code	Company Name	Telephone Number
1010855	Union Telephone Company	1-307-782-6131
1010856	CFW NETWORK INC.	1-540-946-3596
1010857	Telecom*USA [MCI]	1-972-729-5166
1010858	AT&T Canada Long Distance Services Co.	1-416-345-2697
1010859	Valu-Line of Longview, Inc.	Not Available
1010860	Metro Telecomm Svcs., Inc. dba MetroComm	1-703-506-6650
1010861	Telco Holdings, Inc.	1-703-631-5600
1010862	WorldCom Inc.	1-918-590-4581
1010864	CEO Telecommunications [Star Telecommunications, Inc.]	1-805-963-1619
1010865	Express Communications, Inc.	1-605-334-7432
1010866	Alascom, Inc.	1-907-264-8473
1010867	Brooks Fiber Communications [WorldCom]	1-918-590-4581
1010868	WorldCom Inc.	1-918-590-4581
1010869	AT&T Canada Long Distance Services Co.	1-416-345-2697
1010870	Eclipse Communications	1-757-873-1040
1010871	Network Billing and Collections, Inc.	1-210-698-0931
1010872	Sprint	1-913-624-6881
1010873	One Star Long Distance	1-812-471-5870
1010874	WorldCom Inc.	1-918-590-4581
1010876	Telecom*USA [MCI]	1-972-729-5166
1010877	Willamette Valley Telecom	1-800-799-7000
1010879	EqualNet Corporation	1-281-529-4648
1010880	One Call Communications	1-317-843-1300
1010881	Coastal Telephone Co.	1-713-960-0500
1010882	Home Owners L.D. dba HOLD Billing Svcs.	1-210-690-2340
1010883	Tease Communications	Not Available
1010884	WorldCom Inc.	1-918-590-4581
1010885	The CommuniGroup Of KC	1-913-722-6005
1010886	Guide Network International	1-214-222-5058
1010887	Telemanagement Consultants Corporation	1-414-885-2860

continues

PIC Code	Company Name	Telephone Number
1010888	MCI	1-972-729-5166
1010889	Valu-Line of St. Joseph	1-816-232-2283
1010890	North County Communications Corporation	Not Available
1010892	Sound Communications West	1-206-881-1564
1010893	Concord Telephone Long Distance (CT Long Distance)	1-704-788-0274
1010895	WorldCom Inc.	1-918-590-4581
1010896	The Real Public Telephone Company, Inc.	1-407-843-8778
1010897	ITC Network of Utah	1-801-531-9230
1010898	MCI	1-972-729-5166
1010899	Telephone Express	1-719-592-1211
1010900	MCI	1-972-729-5166
1010902	Coast to Coast Telecommunications	1-810-623-6700
1010903	VRS Billing Systems, Inc.	1-408-362-4184
1010904	Interlink Telecommunications	1-404-787-1505
1010905	Pizza Hut, Inc.	1-316-687-8482
1010907	Uni-Tel of Farmington	1-505-326-4571
1010908	NTC, Inc.	1-800-881-9300
1010909	Chadwick Telephone	1-610-866-4444
1010910	WorldCom Inc.	1-918-590-4581
1010911	WorldCom Inc.	1-918-590-4581
1010912	Norlight Telecommunications, Inc.	1-414-792-7788
1010914	Century Telecommunications, Inc.	1-512-754-5690
1010915	Tele Tech Inc.	1-605-335-4142
1010917	Pay Tel Communications, Inc.	1-910-852-7419
1010918	WorldCom Inc.	1-918-590-4581
1010919	Tel Net, Inc.	1-409-297-3030
1010920	Hongkong Telecom (Canada)	1-604-668-9888
1010921	WorldCom Inc.	1-918-590-4581
1010922	FEB Corporation	1-206-646-9600
1010923	Thrifty Call, Inc.	1-512-392-6284
1010924	XTEL	1-609-596-4000

PIC Code	Company Name	Telephone Number
1010925	Kelhorn Communications, Inc.	1-315-449-0388
1010926	La Conexion Familiar, Inc.	Not Available
1010927	Advanced Radio Communications Systems	1-702-358-7000
1010928	Low Country Carrier dba Hargray L.D. Co.	1-843-686-1111
1010929	Stenocall	1-806-762-0811
1010930	Pilgrim Telephone, Inc.	1-617-225-7000
1010931	L.D. Network, Inc.	Not Available
1010932	Midtel Long Distance Minot	1-701-852-1228
1010934	ComCentral dba Southnet Services, Inc.	1-813-287-2880
1010935	USC Telecom, Inc. (EqualNet)	1-281-529-4648
1010936	Communications Network Exchange, Inc. (COMNEX)	1-561-243-3300
1010937	Access Long Distance	1-801-363-9600
1010938	WestCom Inc. (Western Telecom, Inc.)	1-713-777-8227
1010939	Vista-United Telecommunications	1-407-827-2112
1010941	U.S. Fibercom	1-214-283-1111
1010942	QCC, Inc.	1-913-492-1230
1010943	International Cellular, Inc. (ICI)	1-770-953-3300
1010945	New Times, Inc.	1-303-293-3582
1010946	Westinghouse Electric Corporation	1-412-244-6601
1010947	JSM Tele-Page	1-414-467-2281
1010948	IXC Communications Services, Inc. (IXC-CSI)	1-512-433-2456
1010949	Commonwealth of Pennsylvania	1-717-257-3003
1010950	Department of the Treasury, IRS	Not Available
1010951	WorldCom Inc.	1-918-590-4581
1010952	Econocom Long Distance	1-806-794-4652
1010953	WorldCom Inc.	1-918-590-4581
1010954	Prime Time Communications	1-414-633-6001
1010955	United Communications, Inc.	1-541-388-8711
1010956	City Telecom Inc. (CITI)	1-416-502-1836
1010957	Western Telecommunication, Inc. (WTCI)	1-303-267-5962

continues

PIC Code	Company Name	Telephone Number
1010958	Frontier Communications-North Central Region, Inc.	1-716-777-8456
1010959	Mid-Plains Telephone, Inc.	1-608-836-4213
1010960	London Telecom	1-905-570-8700
1010961	Telephone Systems of Georgia	1-904-224-3918
1010962	Gulf Long Distance, Inc.	1-334-952-7590
1010963	Capital Telecommunications, Inc.	1-717-848-8800
1010964	Interstate Telecom Svcs. Inc.	1-214-283-1111
1010965	LCI International	1-614-798-6884
1010966	AUC Communications	1-302-324-9980
1010967	Euronet Communications Corporation	1-732-972-7300
1010968	Dedicated Communications Corp.	1-602-532-9000
1010969	WorldCom Inc.	1-918-590-4581
1010972	Spectranet, Inc.	1-972-756-2000
1010973	Universal Telephone & Telegraph	1-201-492-0900
1010974	Caribsat Telecommunications, Inc.	1-809-793-8700
1010975	Ameritel Long Distance, Inc.	1-214-234-5422
1010976	Preferred Network	1-714-753-2814
1010977	Convergent Communications Inc.	1-303-749-3000
1010978	Westel Telecommunications, Ltd.	1-604-990-2000
1010979	Vortel Communications, Inc.	1-415-543-7810
1010981	Warwick Valley Long Distance Co., Inc.	1-914-986-2313
1010983	Star Tel of Victoria, Inc.	1-512-572-8000
1010984	Star Tel Transmission Co. Inc.	1-512-572-8120
1010986	MCI	1-972-729-5166
1010987	WorldCom Inc.	1-918-590-4581
1010988	AT&T EasyLink Services	1-973-331-4723
1010989	KRB Telecom	1-605-582-7527
1010991	Access Long Distance	1-801-363-9600
1010993	SouthWest United Communication, Inc.	1-214-228-8111
1010994	Touch America, Inc.	1-406-523-3600
1010995	WorldCom Inc.	1-918-590-4581

PIC Code	Company Name	Telephone Number
1010996	Midco Communications	1-605-334-1200
1010997	Gas Company of New Mexico	1-505-848-2700
1010998	The CommuniGroup Of KC	1-913-722-6005
1010999	WorldCom Inc.	1-918-590-4581

This appendix covers the following topics:

- RIP Routing Table
- RIP Routing Convergence
- RIP Concerns
- RIP Routing Protocol Summary

RIP (Routing Information Protocol)

RIP is a simple distance-vector routing protocol, and because RIP is an open standard, it is a safe presumption that any network routing device is capable of supporting RIP. RIP is an Interior Gateway Protocol (IGP) and is designed for use in small, simple networks. RIP was designed and engineered to support only Classful Routing and has no support for Classless Routing, such as CIDR (Classless Inter-Domain Routing).

NOTE Interior Gateway Protocols (IGPs) are designed to convey routing updates within their own routing domain or autonomous system. Exterior Gateway Protocols (EGPs) are designed to convey routing updates between routing domains or autonomous systems.

RIP configured routers build a routing table, calculated from the information shared by the exchanging of routing information with each router's immediate neighbors. This routing table consists of one entry for each known (and reachable) destination. This entry is the lowest-cost path to that destination.

NOTE The term *cost* when applied to routing tables and metrics is the total calculated value of that route. This cost is compared with the cost of other routes to determine the ideal path for traffic; the lower the cost value (closer to zero), the better the path.

RIP Routing Table

Each RIP routing table contains an entry for the Destination IP Address, a specific network host, and a subnet or a default route.

Technical Note: Default Routes

A default route is used when no other route is available to the specified destination. In most cases, the default route points to the Internet Service Provider (ISP) and is configured within the Cisco IOS as follows:

```
Router(config)# ip route 0.0.0.0 0.0.0.0 network_address network_mask
```

There are five fields in the RIP routing table. Table B-1 gives a brief explanation of each.

Table B-1 *RIP Routing Table Fields*

Field	Description
Destination IP Address	This is the destination of any data packet the RIP router receives. The RIP router looks up the destination address of the packet in its routing table to determine where to send the packet.
Metric	This is the total cost of carrying the packet from origination to destination. This field contains the sum of the costs associated with the network links comprising the end-to-end path across the network. RIP link costs are equal to 1 per link, with a total cost, or metric, of 16 being an unreachable destination.
Next Hop IP Address	This is the IP address of the next router interface in the network path to the ultimate destination. This field is populated in the router's table if the destination IP address is on a network not otherwise directly connected to the router.
Route Change	Specified in RFC 1058 this field is not always implemented by router vendors. This field is used to identify changes in routes to specific destination entries.
Route Timers	There are three timers associated with each route: • **Update timer**—Initiates routing updates. • **Route timeout**—Amount of time (default is 180 seconds) without a route update before the route is marked as invalid. • **Route-flush**—Amount of time (default is 90 seconds) after the route timeout timer has expired before the route is flushed, or purged, from the routing table.

The following network topology, illustrated in Figure B-1, is used to demonstrate the abbreviated contents of a RIP routing table, focusing on hop count (distance-vector metric):

NOTE	The default cost for each hop is 1; however, the network administrator can manually adjust the cost so that links with less bandwidth (such as 56Kbps) could have a cost of 10, giving a weight to those links with more bandwidth (for example, T1).

Figure B-1 *Five-node RIP Routed Network*

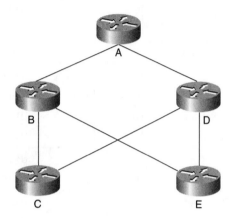

Table B-2 reflects the RIP routing table for the network illustrated in Figure B-1.

Table B-2 *RIP Routing Table for Five-Node Network (Figure B-1)*

Router Name	Destination Host	Next Hop	Number of Hops	Via Network Path
A	Any B Network	B	1	Directly Connected
	Any C Network	B	2	B-C
		D	2	D-C
		D	4	D-E-B-C
	Any D Network	D	1	Directly Connected
	Any E Network	B	2	B-E
		D	2	D-E
		B	4	B-C-D-E
B	Any A Network	A	1	Directly Connected
		C	3	C-D-A
		E	3	E-D-A

continues

Table B-2 *RIP Routing Table for Five-Node Network (Figure B-1) (Continued)*

Router Name	Destination Host	Next Hop	Number of Hops	Via Network Path
B	Any C Network	C	1	Directly Connected
		A	3	A-D-C
	Any D Network	A	2	A-D
		C	2	C-D
		E	2	E-D
	Any E Network	E	1	Directly Connected
		A	3	A-D-E
		C	3	C-D-E
C	Any A Network	B	2	B-A
		D	2	D-A
		B	4	B-E-D-A
		D	4	D-E-B-A
	Any B Network	B	1	Directly Connected
		D	3	D-A-B
	Any D Network	D	1	Directly Connected
		B	3	B-A-D
	Any E Network	B	2	B-E
		D	2	D-E
		B	4	B-A-D-E
		D	4	D-A-B-E
D	Any A Network	A	1	Directly Connected
		C	3	C-B-A
		E	3	E-B-A
	Any B Network	A	2	A-B
		C	2	C-B
		E	2	E-B
	Any C Network	C	1	Directly Connected
		A	3	A-B-C
		E	3	E-B-C

Table B-2   *RIP Routing Table for Five-Node Network (Figure B-1) (Continued)*

Router Name	Destination Host	Next Hop	Number of Hops	Via Network Path
D	Any E Network	E	1	Directly Connected
		A	3	A-B-E
		C	3	C-B-E
E	Any A Network	B	2	B-A
		D	2	D-A
		B	4	B-C-D-A
		D	4	D-C-B-A
	Any B Network	B	1	Directly Connected
		D	3	D-A-B
		D	3	D-C-B
	Any C Network	B	2	B-C
		D	2	D-C
		B	4	B-A-D-C
		D	4	D-A-B-C
	Any D Network	D	1	Directly Connected
		B	3	B-A-D
		B	3	B-C-D

RIP Routing Convergence

Any time there is a change in the network topology, each router must converge on the change—the most significant of which is a change to an immediate neighboring router. Simply stated, *convergence* is the mechanism by which each router agrees with the other on what the new network topology looks like.

In the previous figure, if the link between Router C and Router D fails, each interconnected router will converge and update its routing tables as a consequence. If Router B fails, the same process occurs whereby each Router A, C, D, and E will update its tables, marking any path involving Router B as being unavailable.

There are several mechanisms in place that affect the convergence of RIP routers:

- Count to Infinity (∞)
- Split Horizon
- Poison Reverse
- Triggered Updates
- Hold-Down Timers

Each of these is discussed in the following sections.

Count to Infinity (∞)

Counting to infinity is when each router adds 1 to the hop count before advertising the route. This hop count continues to increase by 1 until infinity is reached, rendering the destination network unreachable. In RIP implementations, infinity is 16 hops. Figure B-2 illustrates a three-node network that has experienced a link failure between Router A and Router C.

Figure B-2 *RIP Network with Failed Link*

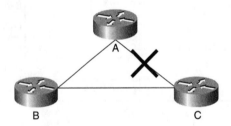

Table B-3 shows the routing table for each router prior to the network failure.

Table B-3 *Routing Table Prior to Failure*

Router Name	Destination Host	Next Hop	Number of Hops	Via Network Path
A	Any B Network	B	1	Directly Connected
		C	2	C-B
	Any C Network	C	1	Directly Connected
		B	2	B-C
B	Any A Network	A	1	Directly Connected
		C	2	C-A

Table B-3   *Routing Table Prior to Failure (Continued)*

Router Name	Destination Host	Next Hop	Number of Hops	Via Network Path
B	Any C Network	C	1	Directly Connected
		A	2	A-C
C	Any A Network	A	1	Directly Connected
		B	2	B-A
	Any B Network	B	1	Directly Connected
		A	2	A-B

Something unique starts to happen when Routers A and C detect the failed link, however. Router A is trying to connect to Router C, but it has no direct connection. Router A learns that Router B has a connection to Router C. However, Router B advertises that it also can get to Router C directly or through Router A; Router A in turn advertises that it can get to Router C through Router B. This will go back and forth between the two routes, adding 1 to the hop count, until the next routing update (180 seconds) takes place.

Table B-4 shows what the routing table will look like after each router has counted to infinity to determine the reachability of each node after the network link failure.

Table B-4   *Routing Table After Link Failure*

Router Name	Destination Host	Next Hop	Number of Hops	Via Network Path
A	Any B Network	B	1	Directly Connected
		C	2	C-B
	Any C Network	C	1	Directly Connected
		B	2	B-C
B	Any A Network	A	1	Directly Connected
		C	16	Unreachable
	Any C Network	C	1	Directly Connected
		A	16	Unreachable
C	Any A Network	A	16	Unreachable
		B	2	B-A
	Any B Network	B	1	Directly Connected
		A	2	A-B

The issue here is the amount of time taken for the 16 hop count (unreachable) to be achieved. During this time, datagram traffic is circling around between the two nodes, never reaching its ultimate destination until the next routing update is converged upon.

There are two methods used to avoid the count-to-infinity problem: split horizon and triggered updates. These are discussed in the next sections.

Split Horizon

Split horizon essentially divides the routed network (the horizon) into logical pieces. Split horizon is based on a simple premise: The router will not advertise a route over the same interface from which it was learned.

NOTE   In a Frame Relay network where the network manager/administrator has implemented multiple subinterfaces, the recommendation is to disable split horizon on the serial interface if you want remote sites to see each other across the network.

There is a drawback to simply implementing split horizon—each router must wait for the destination to be marked as unreachable. By the time a route has timed out and been flushed from the table (a process that takes six update messages, at 30 seconds each), more than three minutes have passed before each routing table is updated with the inactive link. During this time, there are five update intervals that can pass where each router can misinform another as to the reachability of certain destinations. Split horizon coupled with a poison reverse addresses and solves this problem.

RIP Split Horizon with Poison Reverse

Where split horizon is designed to prevent routing loops in an internetwork, split horizon with poison reverse makes this a bit more effective in that six update cycles do not have to pass to stop a routing loop (see the sections, "Count to Infinity" and "Split Horizon," earlier in this chapter). Split horizon with poison reverse takes a more proactive stance in managing and updating the routing tables in that upon detection of an inactive link, RIP with poison reverse sets the metric for that destination to infinity for the next routing update.

Although split horizon with poison reverse is the preference over (standalone) split horizon, there are still concerns with larger internetworks with multiple paths in that RIP is still subject to the counting to infinity problem of routing updates. Triggered updates were introduced to solve the problem of routing loops caused by the "counting to infinity" operations.

RIP Triggered Updates

Triggered updates are used to speed up convergence of a RIP routed network. Triggered updates are rules in the routing protocol that require routers to immediately broadcast an update message whenever there is a change to a route metric, without waiting for the next 30-second regular update interval to pass.

Triggered updates are designed to overcome the time issues that are still involved when dealing with split horizon or split horizon with poison reverse.

RIP Hold-Down Timers

Although triggered updates are a significant mechanism compared to split horizon and poison reverse, there is still the issue of time. Will each router in the internetwork receive and update its tables in a reasonable amount of time, an interval that passes before traffic is to be transmitted?

Hold-down timers solve this potential problem by working in conjunction with triggered updates. Essentially, when a triggered update has been sent, a clock starts counting down (to zero). Until this hold-down timer hits zero, the router will not accept any neighbor updates for the route in question.

The use of a hold-down timer prevents a RIP router from accepting and converging on updates for a route that has been invalidated over a period of time. Hold-down timers prevent a router from believing that another router may have a path to an invalid destination.

RIP Limitations

Although RIP has been a mainstay of internetwork routing for quite a long time, there are still some concerns and limitations that need to be addressed. These are as follows:

- Inability to support paths with more than 15 hops
- (Static) Fixed metrics for route calculation
- Network bandwidth consumption for routing table updates
- Slow convergence
- No dynamic load-balancing support

These issues are discussed in the following sections.

Hop Count Limitations

RIP was designed to support networks of relatively small diameter, enforcing a strict hop count of 15 hops maximum, with 16 hops being marked as unreachable.

NOTE The *network diameter* is categorized as the longest path, measured in hops, between two end-nodes.

As data packets are forwarded across a RIP router, their hop counters are incremented by the cost of the link over which they traversed; usually, 1 is the default. If the data packet's hop counter hits 15 and the packet is not at its intended destination, it is dropped and the destination is considered unreachable.

Fixed Metrics

RIP cannot update its cost metrics in a real-time environment to adapt to changes in the network topology. RIP metrics can be changed only manually and are static for the duration. It is because of these fixed, static metrics that RIP is not ideal in supporting real-time applications.

Network Bandwidth Consumption for Routing Table Updates

RIP routers broadcast their entire routing table out to every RIP-enabled interface every 30 seconds, rather than sending an update of the affected route. In large internetworks, this can consume a fair amount of network bandwidth that would otherwise be used to carry data traffic.

Slow Convergence

RIP routing updates are sent every 30 seconds, which is nearly an eternity in "network time." Several things could happen during this 30-second time, such as data traffic being transmitted, or another change occurring in the network topology. Additionally, a single RIP router takes up 180 seconds (three minutes) to invalidate a route. As the network topology grows, this convergence time also grows to a nearly unmanageable state.

This convergence time poorly supports real-time networked applications.

Dynamic Load Balancing

RIP does not have the capability to dynamically load balance across two or more links. If RIP learns of a 56 Kbps path to a destination first, and learns of a T1 Mbps path to the same destination in a later update, RIP will continue to use the 56 Kbps path because that was the first one learned. A RIP router will only use the T1 path if the 56 Kbps path is marked as unreachable (due to a link failure or the like).

Summary

RIP was designed for use with small networks with both static configurations and stable links. Because of issues with no dynamic load balancing, slow convergence, bandwidth consumption of routing updates, fixed cost metrics, and hop count limit, RIP is not well suited to large internetworks or to internetworks supporting real-time networked applications.

This appendix covers the following topics:

- RIPv2 Authentication
- RIPv2 Subnet Mask Support
- RIPv2 Next Hop Identification
- RIPv2 Multicasting
- RIPv2 Concerns

RIP Version 2 (RIPv2)

RIPv2 is an improvement over RIP in that RIPv2 is ideal for small internetworks. RIPv2 is ideal because it optimizes IP Address assignments, minimizing the wasted IP Address spaces. This optimization is accomplished through the use of Variable-Length Subnet Masks (VLSMs) for network addresses, enabling a Classless Interdomain Routing (CIDR) addressing scheme.

RIPv2 provides for more efficient use of IP address space with support for VLSM, CIDR, and subnets (small networks that are part of a larger network). RIPV2 also enables authentication methods, such as MD5 and plain text, and improved support over RIP for routing updates. RIPv2 multicasts (updates sent to RIPv2 routers) rather than broadcasting (updates sent to all routers, RIPv2 and non-RIPv2) are used for advertising routing updates.

RIPv2 was created in January 1993 and is backward compatible with RIPv1. RIPv2 added the following features not supported in RIP:

- RIPv2 authentication
- Subnet mask support (CIDR)
- Next hop IP addresses
- RIPv2 message multicasting

RIPv2 Authentication

RIPv2 authentication is used to authenticate routing messages that are propagated throughout the network. Authentication of these routing response messages prevents the routing tables from being corrupted by routes from fraudulent sources.

Authentication is achieved with a 16-octet maximum password with no encryption. Consequently, RIPv2 authentication messages are susceptible to attack by anyone with direct access to the network.

RIPv2 Subnet Mask Support

RIPv2 added a four-octet field behind the packet's IP address to carry the subnet mask of a destination IP address. The implementation of subnet mask support enables RIPv2 to route to a specific subnet, whether fixed or variable length.

Technical Note: Subnetting and Subnet Masks

Subnets are portions of a network sharing a common address component. On TCP/IP networks, subnets are defined as all devices whose IP addresses have the same prefix. For example, all devices with an IP address starting with 100.100.100 would be part of the same subnet. Dividing a network into subnets is useful for security and performance reasons. IP networks are divided using a subnet mask.

Subnet masks are used to determine the subnet to which an IP address belongs. An IP address has two components: the network address and the host address. For example, consider the IP address 150.215.017.009. Assuming that this is part of a Class B network, the first two numbers (150.215) represent the Class B network address, and the second two numbers (017.009) identify a particular host on the 150.215 network.

Subnetting enables network administrators to divide the host part of the address into two or more subnets. In this case, a part of the host address identifies the particular subnet.

Subnetting often is easier to see when the IP address is shown in binary format. This is the binary format for the 150.215.017.009 address:

    10010110.11010111.00010001.00001001

The Class B network part is as follows:

    10010110.11010111

The host address is shown here:

    00010001.00001001

If this network is divided into 14 subnets, the first 4 bits of the host address (0001) identify the subnet.

The subnet mask is the network address plus bits reserved for identifying the subnetwork. In this case, the subnet mask is 11111111.11111111.11110000.00000000. It's called a mask because it identifies the subnet to which an IP address belongs by performing a Boolean algebraic AND operation on the mask and the IP address. The result is the following subnetwork address:

Subnet Mask	255.255.240.000	11111111.11111111.11110000.00000000
IP Address	150.215.017.009	10010110.11010111.00010001.00001001
Subnet Address	150.215.016.000	10010110.11010111.00010000.00000000

Therefore, the subnet address for 150.215.017.009 is 150.215.016.000.

RIPv2 Next Hop Identification

The inclusion of a next hop identification field helps make RIPv2 more efficient than RIP. The next hop identification prevents unnecessary hops between end-points in a network. In a RIPv2-only network, the identification of the next hop does not add significant value; however, when RIPv2 is implemented with other (dissimilar) routing protocols, without the next hop identification, it is possible that some routes would never be discovered.

RIPv2 Multicasting

RIPv2 multicasting enables the simultaneous delivery of routing table updates to multiple neighbors rather than repeatedly unicasting the routing update to each neighbor on an individual basis. RIPv2 multicasting also can implement filters to prevent RIPv2 routing updates from being received by RIPv1 routers.

RIPv2 Concerns

Although RIPv2 provides significant improvements over its predecessor, RIPv1, some concerns regarding RIPv2's operation remain. These are as follows:

- Maximum hop count (15)
- Count to Infinity (∞)
- (Static) Fixed metrics for route calculation
- Lack of alternative routing support

RIPv2 Maximum Hop Count (15)

RIPv2 inherited the maximum hop count limit of 15 from RIPv1. This inheritance was preserved so that RIPv2 could maintain its backward compatibility with RIPv1.

RIPv2 Count to Infinity (∞)

RIPv2, like its predecessor RIPv1, relies on the "count to infinity" mechanism to resolve certain network error conditions. Counting to infinity becomes problematic because routing loops are permitted for potentially lengthy periods of time before the "loop" is detected by the hop count and the route is marked as unreachable.

RIPv2 (Static) Fixed Metrics for Route Calculation

RIPv2, like RIPv1, selects routes based on a fixed cost metric—hop count. This cost metric may be adjusted manually by the network administrator but remains static until manually changed again.

RIPv2 Lack of Alternative Routing Support

RIPv2, like RIPv1, maintains only a single route in its routing tables to a specific destination, providing no support for dynamic load balancing. If the "known" route fails, RIPv2 must wait for another routing update to determine the next optimal path to a destination.

It is this convergence time that makes RIPv2 unsuitable for large networks. Other routing protocols such as EIGRP or OSPF are more suitable for larger networks.

Summary

RIPv2 is a more modern, updated version of RIP. RIPv2 was designed as an update to RIP, allowing RIP legacy internetworking devices a smooth transition to RIPv2. Both RIP and RIPv2 are better suited for the SOHO (Small Office / Home Office) market than mid-size or larger enterprise networks.

Customers implementing RIPv2 can make more efficient use of their allocated address space by implementing Variable Length Subnet Masks (VLSM) within their networks. This route summarization, through the use of VLSM, is a key method to managing the growth and scaling of the Internet routing system as a whole.

This appendix covers the following topics:

- BGP Multihoming
- IBGP Versus EBGP
- Common BGP Implementation
- BGP Attributes
- BGP Route Selection
- BGP Peering
- BGP Route Reflectors
- BGP Confederations
- BGP Administrative Distances
- BGP Timers

Border Gateway Protocol, Version 4 (BGP4)

The Border Gateway Protocol (BGP) is used to exchange routing information between Internet Service Provider (ISP) networks, and between ISP networks and customer networks. BGP also can be used as a routing protocol for large-scale enterprise networks. BGP often is the routing protocol used to exchange information between two or more autonomous networks.

NOTE	Every network sharing a common network administration and common routing policies is referred to as an *autonomous network*.

An interior gateway routing protocol such as RIP or OSPF is often used within a customer's autonomous network. BGP is used when exchanging network routing information between ISPs or an ISP and its customers.

BGP is a robust and scalable routing protocol and the most widely used routing protocol for the Internet, with over 90,000 BGP routing table entries currently maintained in Internet Service Provider networks. BGP provides scalability by using well-defined route parameters, called *attributes*, providing for a stable routing environment and sophisticated routing behaviors.

BGP supports Classless Interdomain Routing (CIDR). CIDR reduces the size of the Internet routing tables. For example, suppose that an ISP owns the IP address block 195.10.x.x from the traditional Class C address space. This block consists of 256 Class C address blocks, 195.10.0.x – 195.10.255.x. Presume this ISP assigns a Class C block to each of its customers. Without CIDR, the ISP would advertise 256 (Class C) address blocks to its BGP peers. With CIDR, BGP can supernet (aggregate or summarize) the address space and advertise one block, 195.10.x.x.

BGP neighbors exchange full routing information when the TCP connection between neighbors is first established. When changes to the routing table are detected, the BGP routers send to their neighbors only those routes that have changed. Unlike some other routing protocols, such as OSPF or RIP, BGP routers do not send periodic routing updates, advertising only the optimal path to a destination network.

BGP was developed in June 1989 and was published as RFC 1105. BGP was born out of the requirement to move away from a backbone-centered tree-topology and into a more distributed-backbone, autonomous-system–based topology.

BGP is an exterior gateway protocol (EGP) and is used to pass routing information between autonomous systems (ASes). BGP is still a routing protocol and, like other routing protocols, BGP passes routing information and uses a metrics for route determination. BGP advertises which networks can be reached and can act in either an interior (IBGP) or exterior (EBGP) mode. IBGP or EBGP configurations mean that BGP can be configured to advertise networks within an AS (Autonomous System) or between different ASes. The key to BGP operation is in the configuration of which networks to advertise and whether they are directly connected.

NOTE   BGP uses TCP (port 179) to communicate with other routers. If a BGP router is in operation behind a network firewall, the firewall must be configured to allow TCP port 179 traffic to pass through; otherwise, BGP will not be able to operate.

The primary purpose of BGP4 is to exchange network reachability information with other BGP autonomous systems. Figure D-1 illustrates how the Internet is constructed with multiple BGP autonomous systems.

Figure D-1   *Connectivity Example with Random ASNs*

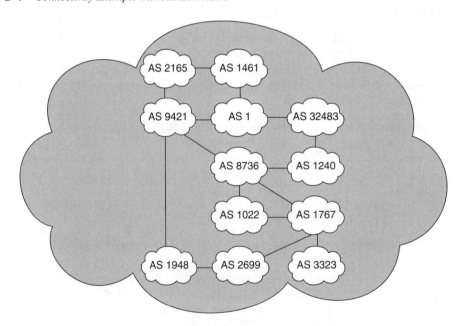

BGP is classified as a path-vector routing protocol. Path vector protocols are similar to distance vector routing protocols. The primary difference between path and distance vector routing protocols lies in that distance vector routing protocols use hop count to calculate the best path to a destination whereas path vector routing protocols advertise the reachable destinations to its neighbors. The border router (BR) advertises these destinations, as well as the attributes of the path to the destination. These path vector attributes include the number of hops and the administrative distance of each hop. Interior (IBGP-based) learned routes are given more "weight," or preference, than those learned from an Exterior BGP (EBGP) advertisement.

BGP Multihoming

BGP's popularity stems from its ability to add redundancy in support of critical networks and their connections for two-way traffic (inbound and outbound). BGP also can be used to load balance, or load share, traffic across multiple links. Load balancing of BGP traffic is possible when a BGP AS speaker (router) learns of two EBGP paths for an IP prefix from a neighboring autonomous system. By default, the BGP routing process will select the path with the lowest router ID to enter into its routing table. BGP multipath must be enabled for BGP to take advantage of multiple paths to a destination.

BGP can support up to eight paths to a destination, either load balancing or load sharing across each path.

NOTE   *Load balancing* is an equal distribution of the traffic load across all available links. *Load sharing* is the shared distribution of traffic load across all available links, but not necessarily equal. Load balanced traffic is load shared; load shared traffic is not always load balanced.

For example, a customer might have Internet connections with two (or more) ISPs for network connectivity redundancy. Rather than have one line carry all the traffic and the other(s) sit idle, active only when the primary connection has failed, load sharing enables the customer to spread his Internet traffic across all his ISP connections.

Interior (IBGP) Versus Exterior (EBGP)

Internal BGP neighbors are in the same autonomous system; external BGP neighbors are in different autonomous systems. In general, external neighbors are adjacent to each other and share a common subnet, whereas internal neighbors may be anywhere in the same autonomous system. Figures D-2, D-3, and D-4 illustrate both an External BGP peering session and an Internal BGP peering session between two peers.

Figure D-2 *External BGP Session Between Two BGP Peers*

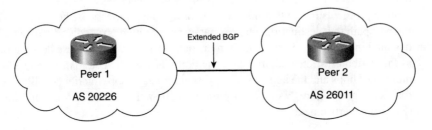

Figure D-3 *Internal BGP Session Between Two Peers*

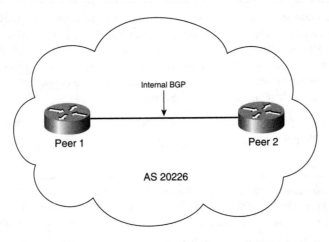

The following figure illustrates routers exchanging both Internal and External BGP sessions.

Figure D-4   *Internal (IBGP) and External (EBGP) Peering Sessions*

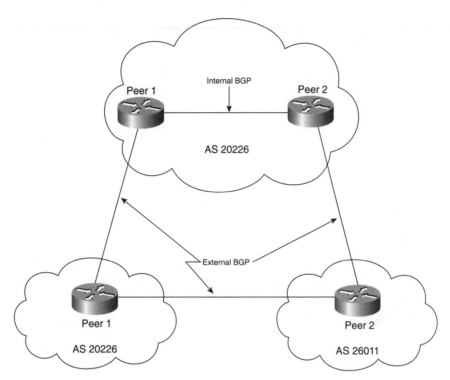

Common BGP Implementation

 for backup purposes. Figure D-5 illustrates a customer WAN with dual Internet connections—a T1 each to ISP#1 and ISP#2. This customer announces private Autonomous
System Number (ASN) of 65162 to both ISPs and will receive route updates from ISP
#1 (ASN 4276) and ISP #2 (ASN 174).

As with OSPF, a BGP-configured router first exchanges the entire routing table. After a
peering relationship has been established, only changes are sent. BGP routers send keep-
alives, ensuring that connections are still active and available. Like OSPF and EIGRP, BGP
uses AS numbers. BGP uses a single metric for path selections that may be manually configured to "fine-tune" the network to meet determined design needs.

Figure D-5 *Dual (Multi) Homed BGP Implementation*

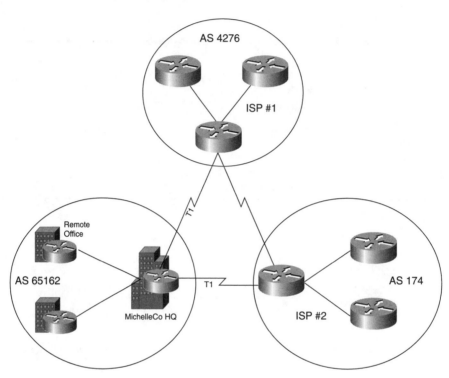

BGP4 uses Autonomous Systems Numbers (ASNs) to identify to which system a router belongs. These ARNs are allocated by the IANA (Internet Administration Numbering Authority) to the national registries and range from 1 to 64511. ASNs 64512 to 65535 are assigned by ARIN for private use and will be seen only by the upstream service provider; they are not propagated into other ASNs.

BGP Attributes

BGP's flexibility comes from configurable parameters called *attributes* that may be adjusted manually in the Cisco IOS. BGP attributes are classified into four categories:

- **Well-known**—Must be implemented in all BGP routers.
- **Mandatory**—Must be present in all BGP update messages; otherwise, the BGP connection is incompatible and will fail.

- **Discretionary**—May or may not be present in all BGP update messages; however, if they are present, discretionary attributes must be recognized by all BGP implementations.

- **Optional**—Do not have to be recognized by all BGP implementations because the type of optional attribute determines whether the information is passed on to other peers if the option is unrecognized. The two types of attributes are as follows:

  — Transitive optional attributes are passed on to other peers.

  — Non-transitive optional attributes, if unrecognized, are ignored and not passed on to other BGP peers.

BGP attributes are translated into a community value by the route map, which is in turn translated back into a BGP attribute by the receiving EBGP Peer. A community attribute provides BGP routers a way of grouping destinations, called *communities*, for which routing decisions (such as acceptance, preference, and redistribution) can be applied as a whole. Community Values identify these attributes.

The initial BGP specification (RFC 1771) defines seven attributes, as detailed in Table D-1.

Table D-1   *RFC 1771 BGP Attributes*

Attribute	Type	Flags	Value
ORIGIN	1	Well known	IGP (0)
			EGP (1)
			Incomplete (2)
AS_PATH	2	Well known	ASNs in the path
NEXT_HOP	3	Well known	Address of the next router
MULTI_EXIT_DESC (MED)	4	Optional, local	32 bit metric
LOCAL_PREF	5	Well known	32 bit metric
ATROMIC_AGGREGATE	6	Well known	Flags certain aggregations
AGGREGATOR	7	Operational, transitive	AS number and router ID

AS-Path Attribute

The AS-path attribute is a list of all the autonomous systems (ASes) a routing update has traversed. When an update passes through an AS, BGP prepends its AS number onto the existing AS path in the update.

Origin Attribute

The origin attribute indicates how reachability information through the path was obtained from the source, or origin, of the BGP update. This attribute has the following three values:

- **IGP (Internal)**—Indicates that the route originated within the AS of the advertising router.

- **EGP (External)**—Indicates that the route was learned via another router using an exterior gateway protocol, such as EBGP.

- **Incomplete**—Indicates that the origin of the route was learned by some means other than EGP or redistributed from an IGP.

Next Hop Attribute

Before a BGP peer can be told what the next hop is for reaching a particular AS, the router sending the updates adjusts the value of the next hop attributes. For EBGP, this attribute is usually the IP address. For IBGP, this attribute often is the address of the EBGP peer in the neighboring AS.

The next hop attribute is used to optimize BGP routing.

Weight Attribute

This is a Cisco proprietary BGP attribute that was added to assist in the BGP path selection process. Adjustments to the weight attribute can affect which route is preferred when multiple paths exist to the same destination. The weight attribute is present only on the local router and is not propagated to other BGP peers. Routes originated by the router are assigned a default weight of 32768; the range for this attribute is 0 to 65535; the larger the weight, the greater the preference of that path. Other paths learned by the router are assigned a value of zero.

Multi-Exit Discriminator (MED) Attribute

The MED is a non-transitive attribute and is defined as a metric that is used to convey the relative preference of entry points into an AS. The MED is assigned a value of zero by default when an update is generated. Lower MED values are the preferred values in an update. The MED is used to calculate the cost of using a particular router for reaching the next group in the AS.

Unlike the local preference attribute, the MED attribute is exchanged between ASes. However, because the MED attribute is non-transitive, the MED value for a destination is reset to zero when it leaves the neighboring Autonomous System, unless the AS is configured explicitly to propagate MED information into other ASes.

A set of path exchanges by BGP routers (internal to an AS) may include several nearly identical paths to destination, with the MED value and the next-hop attributes being the only differentiator. These paths should not be aggregated, or summed, by the router because they should use the MED value to select the preferred, or "best," exit point from the AS.

MED values received for the same destination from multiple ASes are usable only if the receiving router has the **bgp always-compare-med** configured. If the MED comparison is not configured, the MED value of the routing updates will not be used in the path selection process.

Local Preference Attribute

The local preference attribute is another way (aside from the weight attribute) used to affect the path selection process. Unlike the weight attribute, the local preference attribute is propagated via routing updates to other routers in the AS. The values for this attribute range from 0 to 255, with a local preference value of 100 being the default. The path with a highest preference is the preferred.

The various AS border routers may learn several paths that lead to the same routing prefixes. These paths will be propagated inside the AS; however, each of the BGP border gateways will select the path with the lowest local preference value.

Atomic Aggregate Attribute

The atomic aggregate attribute does not have content; its length is always zero. This attribute indicates that the router chose to pass an aggregated prefix. The aggregated prefix is a prefix that aggregates, or summarizes, several short prefixes. There may be more specific routes for longer network prefixes, but the BGP router chose to hide them to reduce the size of the AS path parameters.

Aggregator Attribute

The aggregator attribute is inserted by the AS that made the decision to aggregate the network prefix. This value is six octets in length, consisting of the 16-bit ASN and the 32-bit IP address of the router performing the aggregation.

Additional Attributes

There are additional attributes supported by BGP, developed in later RFCs, that are beyond the scope of this book. Following is a complete list of these attributes and their respective RFC specification.

Table D-2 *BGP Full Attribute Values (as of April 30, 2001)*

Attribute Value	Description	Reference
1	ORIGIN	RFC 1771
2	AS_PATH	RFC 1771
3	NEXT_HOP	RFC 1771
4	MULTI_EXIT_DISC	RFC 1771
5	LOCAL_PREF	RFC 1771
6	ATOMIC_AGGREGATE	RFC 1771
7	AGGREGATOR	RFC 1771
8	COMMUNITY	RFC 1997
9	ORIGINATOR ID	RFC 1998
10	CLUSTER_LIST	RFC 1998
11	DPA	Chen
12	ADVERTISER	RFC 1863
13	RCID_PATH / CLUSTER_ID	RFC 1863
14	MP_REACH_NLRI	RFC 2283
15	MP_UNREACH_NLRI	RFC 2283
16	EXTENDED COMMUNITIES	Rosen
17–255	Reserved for future development	-----

BGP Route Selection

The following steps are taken by a BGP router when determining the preferred path to a destination. After a BGP path criterion has been selected, the path selection process ends for that session.

The following list identifies the steps BGP follows when selecting routes to a network destination:

1 Verify the next hop is accessible.

2 (Internal Paths Only] If synchronization is enabled, the route must exist in the IGP order to be selected.

3 (Cisco Proprietary) Use the path with the largest weight because the weight gives the path preference.

4 If routes have identical weights, use the route with the higher local preference.

5 If routes have identical local preference, use the route that the local router originated.

6 If no route was originated, use the shorter AS path.

7 If AS paths are identical lengths, choose the external path over an internal path.

8 If all routes are external, use the route with the lowest origin code.

9 If the origin codes are the same and the paths came from the same AS, use the path with the lowest MULTI_EXIT_DISC (MED) attribute.

10 The EBGP path holds preference over the IBGP path.

11 Select the shortest path within the AS (the lowest IGP metric).

12 If multipath (Cisco IOS "**maximum-path**") is enabled at this point, multiple paths may be inserted into the routing table, if both (or all) paths are external routes and originated from the same autonomous system.

13 Use the route with the lowest IP address value for the BGP Router ID (RID).

14 If IGP is disabled and only internal paths are left, use the path through the closest neighbor.

BGP Peering

BGP mandates that each external router establishes an internal BGP connection with each of the other external routers in the same AS. These external peered routers will be linked by a "fully meshed graph" of route paths. The internal interconnections are used to propagate external routing information, independent of whatever Interior Gateway Protocol (IGP) might be running, such as OSPF or EIGRP.

These internal interconnections also are used among BGP routers to reach an agreement on the best route to an external destination network. This ensures that only the router managing the best path inserts information into the AS internal routing tables through the IGP in use.

There are two types of BGP peers:

- **Internal**—BGP peers that are connected within the same Autonomous System (with Intra AS Links).

- **External**—BGP peers that are interconnected between two Autonomous Systems (with Inter AS Links).

Figure D-6 illustrates Internal and External BGP Peers, with respective Inter- and Intra-AS Links.

Figure D-6 *Internal and External BGP Peers*

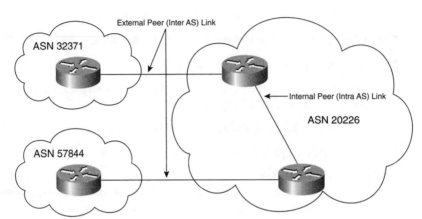

BGP Route Reflectors

To help reduce the amount of peers a router will have in an Autonomous System, BGP employs the use of route reflectors. The routers peer with another router, or concentration router. These peers are then known as clients. They receive updates from and send updates to the route reflector.

The use of route reflectors is one way to reduce the size of the IBGP routing mesh. The issue with meshed IBGP routes is scalability. Routing meshes are subject to the *N-squared* algorithm, $N^2-N/2$, also represented as $N(N-1)/2$, where N is the number of nodes in the network. As internetworks and autonomous systems grow, so will the size of each BGP router's routing table at the rate of $N(N-1)/2$ for each additional node (N), as illustrated in Figure D-7.

In a BGP Autonomous System, there can be several routers exchanging route information. To reduce the amount of peers a router has to establish, a concentration router or route reflector router can be configured. Reflect clients are configured to exchange information with a central concentration router (route reflector). Reflect clients (client peers) peer only with the central concentration router instead of every router in the Autonomous System. The central router (route reflector) is responsible for sending updates to the reflector clients. The reflector clients are responsible for sending updates to the central concentration router instead of every router in the AS. Routers not configured as route reflector clients are known as *non-client peers*. The route reflector "reflects" routes between client peers and non-client peers and is illustrated in Figure D-8.

Figure D-7 *BGP Route Reflector Topology*

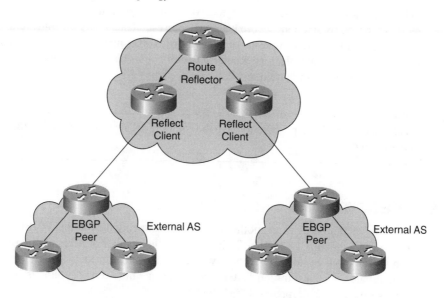

Figure D-8 *BGP With and Without Route Reflectors*

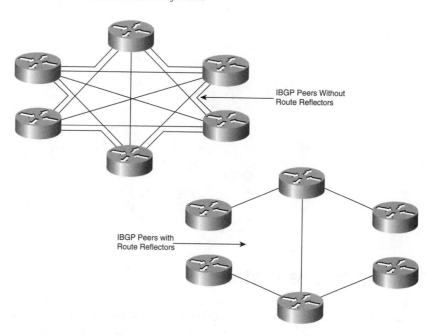

As the previous figure shows, the benefit of route reflectors is that IBGP peers do not have to be fully meshed with each other to receive full-mesh routing updates. The sole requirement is for each IBGP client peer to have a session established with the route reflector. Non-client peers will require full-mesh connectivity with other non-client peers, and those must be configured as route reflectors. Router reflector clients can communicate only with the route reflector, not with non-client peers.

NOTE   It is a good networking practice to have the router reflector topology mirror the physical network topology.

BGP Confederations

BGP Confederations provide another method of managing the number of IBGP mesh routes in an Autonomous System. To help reduce the number of peers a router will have in an Autonomous System, BGP employs the use of route reflectors. The routers peer with another router, or concentration router. These peers are then known as clients. They receive updates from and send updates to the route reflector.

The other networks see the confederation as a single AS. The sub-ASes, or mini-ASes, are transparent to the outside world. Similar to using route reflectors, this method reduces the number of IBGP mesh paths (see Figure D-9).

Figure D-9   *BGP Confederation*

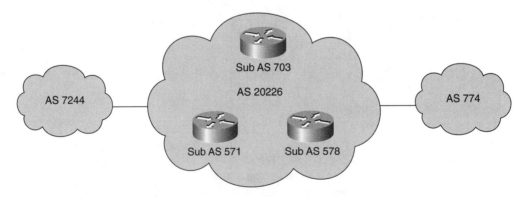

BGP Administrative Distances

Administrative distance is a way to set the preference of different routing protocols. Routers use administrative distances as a tiebreaker, with the lower administrative distance being the winner and subsequently entered into the router's routing table. BGP does not use administrative distances during the route selection process. BGP uses administrative distances to select which routes are placed in the routing table.

Three administrative distances are associated with BGP:

- **Internal (IBGP)**—Routes are learned from IBGP peers. Default administrative distance is 200.

- **External (EBGP)**—Routes are learned from EBGP peers. Default administrative distance is 20.

- **Local**—Routes are generated locally. Default administrative distance is 20.

BGP Timers

BGP uses two timers to manage protocol functions:

- **Keepalive**—Default is 60 seconds. The keepalive timer is the maximum amount of time a BGP router will let pass between routing updates.

- **Hold-down**—Default is 180 seconds. The hold-down timer is the maximum amount of time a BGP route will hold the route in its table after the keepalive timer has passed with no update.

The amount of time for routing updates, keepalive, and hold-down is negotiated between BGP peers upon session initialization. In the absence of a timer, the defaults are used. These timers may be manually configured; however, the BGP router will use the lower value discovered during session negotiation.

Summary

BGP was born out of the requirement to move away from a backbone-centered tree-topology and into a more distributed-backbone, autonomous-system–based topology. BGP version 4 (BGP4) makes it possible to ensure reliable routing that enables route aggregation, multihoming, and policy-based routing.

BGP provides support for multihoming across up to eight paths to a destination. BGP's flexibility and complexity lie in its use of attributes (carried by community values) in route maps to "customize" a network topology. The attributes as defined by RFC 1771 are listed here:

- ORIGIN
- AS_PATH
- NEXT_HOP
- MULTI_EXIT_DESC (MED)

- LOCAL_PREF
- ATROMIC_AGGREGATE
- AGGREGATOR

BGP develops a network topology map of connectivity, exchanging network reachability information with other BGP systems, using this information to prevent routing loops. BGP uses route, path, and community filtering to control the flow of BGP updates between BGP autonomous systems (ASes). BGP provides a scalable and flexible Internet routing protocol to provide for loop-free routing information and connectivity between Internet Service Providers and customers and for large enterprise networks.

Network reachability information between BGP systems is accomplished with the use of route aggregation, BGP confederations, and route reflectors.

BGP does not use administrative distances during the route selection process. Instead, BGP uses administrative distances to select the routes that are placed in the routing table.

Three administrative distances are associated with BGP:

- **Internal (IBGP)**—Routes are learned from IBGP peers. Default administrative distance is 200.
- **External (EBGP)**—Routes are learned from EBGP peers. Default administrative distance is 20.
- **Local**—Routes are generated locally. Default administrative distance is 20.

BGP is a very complex routing protocol, about which volumes of books have been published. Here is some recommended reading if you want to learn more about BGP:

- *Internet Routing Architectures*, Second Edition. Sam Halabi (published by Cisco Press, 2000).
- *Cisco BGP-4 Command and Configuration Handbook*. William R. Parkhurst, PhD (published by Cisco Press, 2001).
- *Routing in the Internet*, Second Edition. Christian Huitema (published by Prentice Hall, 2000).
- *RFC 1771 A Border Gateway Protocol 4 (BGP-4)*. Y. Rekhter, T. Li. March 1995.

The following topics are covered in this appendix:

- IGRP Metrics
- Metric Calculation
- IGRP Timers
- IGRP Convergence Mechanisms
- IGRP Load Balancing

Interior Gateway Routing Protocol (IGRP)

Cisco Systems developed the Interior Gateway Routing Protocol (IGRP) in the early 1980s as an answer to the limitations of RIPv1 (Routing Information Protocol, version 1), while preserving its ease of implementation.

The principal goal in creating IGRP was to provide a robust protocol for routing within an autonomous system (AS). Such protocols are known as *Interior Gateway Routing Protocols*. Although RIP was quite useful for routing within small- to moderate-sized, relatively homogeneous internetworks, its limits were being pushed by network growth. In particular, RIP's small hop-count limit (16) restricted the size of internetworks; single metric (hop count) did not allow for routing flexibility in complex environments.

The popularity of Cisco routers and the robustness of IGRP encouraged many organizations with large internetworks to replace RIP with IGRP. Cisco's initial IGRP implementation worked in Internet Protocol (IP) networks.

IGRP Metrics

IGRP is a distance-vector routing protocol designed for use within autonomous systems. IGRP, like other distance-vector routing protocols (such as RIP and RIPv2), forwards its entire routing table on a regular basis. IGRP, unlike other distance-vector protocols (RIP and RIPv2), uses a series of metrics rather than a single hop-count metric. These metrics are as follows:

- Hop count
- Packet size — MTU (Maximum Transmission Unit)
- Link bandwidth
- Delay
- Load
- Reliability

IGRP supports multipath routing, load balancing across two, three, or four links, with automatic link recovery from a failed link.

Like RIP, IGRP is a classful routing protocol, with no support for VLSM (Variable Length Subnet Masking) or CIDR (Classless Inter-Domain Routing).

IGRP Hop Count

IGRP supports incrementing hop count as one method of determining the distance to a specific destination. Unlike RIP, which has a maximum hop count of 16, IGRP has a maximum hop count of 100, which may be further increased to 255.

IGRP does not use the hop counter as a metric to determine optimal paths to a destination, but rather as a means to detect routing loops in the network. Any route with a hop count in excess of the stated, or configured, maximum is automatically invalidated.

IGRP Packet Size (MTU)

The MTU (Maximum Transmission Unit) identifies the largest datagram that an IGRP router will accept for transmission. IGRP does not use the MTU to calculate a route or use it as a factor in its metrics. IGRP routers exchange MTU information with each other, identifying the maximum datagram size they can support. Datagrams larger than the MTU size will be broken down into manageable "pieces" by the router.

NOTE Large MTU sizes may result in what is called a *performance penalty*. Routers will buffer these incoming datagrams for transmission until it can be determined where they are to be forwarded. The performance penalty lies in the delay to determine the next hop and the amount of router buffer (memory) space consumed waiting for the entire datagram to be received for transmission.

IGRP Link Bandwidth

IGRP uses the link bandwidth as one of the metrics to calculate the total cost of a network path. The default bandwidth statement is 1.544 Mbps (T1), but it can range from 1200 bps to 10 Gbps.

IGRP looks at the defined bandwidth on each outbound interface router port for a given route and will select the smallest bandwidth statement, which is the bandwidth limit for that route. This bandwidth number is then divided by 10^7 (10,000,000) to determine the bandwidth measurable in kilobits per second (kbps).

IGRP Delay

The IGRP delay metric measures the approximate amount of time needed to traverse a network link, based on no other link usage at the time. The aggregated delay metric of a route is the sum of all delays attributed to each outbound router interface in the path. This delay sum is divided by 10 to express the delay result in microseconds (μs). The metric value for delay ranges from 1 to 16,777,215 ($2^{24} - 1$).

IGRP Load

The IGRP load metric measures the amount of bandwidth currently available across a given link. The heavier the link utilization, the more time is required for data traffic to traverse that link. This metric enables IGRP to factor current link utilization levels into the network's optimal route calculation.

This metric can be configured manually to any value between 1 and 255, although it is not recommended you do this, as there could be adverse impacts on network convergence and route distribution throughout the network.

IGRP Reliability

The reliability metric keeps track of the current error rate per transmission facility. The error rate is a ratio of packets received by a destination without error.

This metric is between the range of 1 and 255; the higher the metric value, the more unreliable the link.

Metric Calculation

IGRP calculates and uses a composite metric of the previous values to calculate the route optimization. The metric value ranges from 1 to 16,277,215 ($2^{24} - 1$), and for purposes of route calculation, the lower the number (closer to zero), the better the route.

This composite metric reflects the various weights of each of the previously listed metrics. The general formula for this composite metric is as follows:

```
Metric = (K1 × Bandwidth) + (K2 × Bandwidth)/(256 - Load) + (K3 × Delay)
```

K1, K2, and K3 are constants used to weigh the effect of these routing metrics; the default values for K1 and K3 is 1, and the default for K2 is 0.

There are two other constant values, K4 and K5, both of which default to 0 and are not used if they are left at the default value. The network administrator can change these values because they are not changed dynamically by IGRP operation.

The mathematical simplification of the composite metric, provided that all values remain at their defaults, is as follows:

```
Metric = Bandwidth + Delay
```

The reliability metric, K5, is a constant and is used only if the reliability metric is greater than the default of 0. The composite operation used to determine the metric for K5 (Reliability) > 0 is shown here:

```
Metric = Metric × [K5/(Reliability + K4)]
```

Delay is in units of 10 microseconds. This gives a range of 10 microseconds to 168 seconds.

Bandwidth is the inverse minimum bandwidth of the path in bits per second scaled by a factor of 10e10. The range is from a 1200bps line to 10Gbps.

Table E-1 lists the default delay values used by IGRP.

Table E-1   *IGRP Default Delay Values*

Media	Delay	Bandwidth
Satellite	200,000 (2 sec)	20 (500 Mbit)
Ethernet	100 (1 ms)	1,000
1.544 Mbit	2000 (20 ms)	6,476
64 Kbit	2000 (20 ms)	156,250
56 Kbit	2000 (20 ms)	178,571
10 Kbit	2000 (20 ms)	1,000,000
1 Kbit	2000 (20 ms)	10,000,000

IGRP Timers

The default IGRP timer intervals are as follows:

- **Update Timer** (90 seconds)—How often the router is to initiate routing table updates.
- **Hold Timer** (280 seconds: 3 × Update Timer + 10 seconds)—The amount of time the IGRP routing table will hold down routing updates.
- **Route Invalid Timer** (270 seconds: 3 × Update Timer)—The amount of time a router will wait, in the absence of routing update messages about a specific route, before declaring the route invalid.
- **Route-Flush Timer** (630 seconds: 7 × Update Timer)—The amount of time before a route is flushed from the routing table.

IGRP Convergence Mechanisms

IGRP uses similar convergence mechanisms to that of RIP. The convergence mechanisms used by IGRP are as follows:

- Flash Update
- Hold-Downs
- Split Horizon
- Poison Reverse Update

Each of these is discussed in more detail in the following sections.

IGRP Flash Update

Rather than wait for the update timer to elapse before sending a routing update, IGRP uses flash updates to send a routing change immediately to its routing neighbors. This results in significantly reduced convergence time compared to other distance-vector routing protocols, such as RIP or RIPv2.

IGRP Hold-Downs

Although IGRP flash updates are a significant improvement over "traditional" routing table updates (timer-based versus event-based updates), the issue of time still remains. The question is whether each router in the internetwork will receive and update its tables in a reasonable amount of time, an interval that passes before traffic is to be transmitted.

Hold-down timers solve this potential problem by working with triggered updates. Essentially when a triggered update has been sent, a clock starts counting down (to zero). Until this hold-down timer hits zero, the router will not accept neighbor updates for the route in question.

The use of a hold-down timer prevents an IGRP router from accepting and converging on updates for a route that has been invalidated over a period of time. Hold-down timers prevent a router from believing that another router may have a path to an invalid destination.

IGRP Split Horizon

Like RIP, IGRP's split horizon is based on a simple premise: The router will not advertise a route over the same interface from which it was learned.

NOTE   If you are operating a Frame Relay internetwork with multiple subinterfaces, be sure to disable split horizon on the interface if you want the remote sites to see each other across the network.

However, there is a drawback to simply implementing split horizon. Each router must wait for the destination to be marked as unreachable; after a route has timed out and been flushed from the table, a process that takes six update messages (90 seconds each), totaling upward of nine minutes before each routing table is updated with the inactive link. During this time, there are five update intervals that can pass where each router can misinform another as to the reachability of certain destinations. IGRP uses hold-down timers with split horizon to prevent routing instability caused by the misinformation traded between neighboring routers.

IGRP Poison Reverse

IGRP uses poison reverse updates to invalidate a route learned from a neighbor if that router believes the route to be looping. When an IGRP node receives a routing table update from a neighbor, it compares the learned information with the routing table information currently in memory. If the learned, or updated, information includes a routing metric whose value has increased 10 percent or more since the last routing update, that route is assumed to be invalid, based on the generalization that increases in routing metrics are caused by routing loops.

IGRP Load Balancing

IGRP has the capability to perform multipath routing, up to four different routes to a given destination. This multipath routing enables IGRP to perform load balancing of both an equal-cost and unequal-cost nature.

IGRP Equal-Cost Load Balancing

Equal-cost load balancing is the balancing of traffic across redundant, or multiple, links of equal cost. Equal-cost load balancing may be achieved on a per-packet or a per-destination basis.

Per-packet load balancing means that sequential packets in a data stream, bound for the same destination, may be transmitted out different interfaces. The drawback to this type of operation is that data packets may be received late or out of sequence, causing possible application performance issues.

Per-destination load balancing means that packets in a data stream bound for the same destination will be forwarded via the same route, alleviating the potential for issues caused by per-packet load balancing. Per-destination load balancing can result in a less-than-ideal equal-cost traffic distribution, however.

IGRP determines which of these approaches to use based on its ability to perform route caching, a technique used to keep a route cached in memory. Route caching is per-destination-based load balancing and can be memory intensive. If route caching is disabled, per-packet load balancing will automatically be performed.

IGRP Unequal-Cost Load Balancing

Unequal-cost load balancing sends traffic across up to four paths of unequal cost, with the lowest-cost link being the primary path. Paths with higher cost are used as alternatives, providing redundant link connectivity to a single, or multiple, destination(s).

IGRP Feasibility and Feasible Successors

IGRP feasibility means that each network path conforms to three basic principles:

- Alternative path metrics must be within the specified variance range of the local best metric.

- The best local metric must be greater than the metric for the same destination that is learned from the next router; simply stated, the next hop must be closer to the destination than the current router.

- The variance value, multiplied against the best local metric for a destination, must be greater than or equal to the cost metric for that destination on the next router.

IGRP can be used to establish a hierarchy of feasible successors in a multipath routing environment. *Feasible successors* are routes whose costs are greater than the specified variance from the optimal route to a given destination. As such, they are not feasible for unequal-cost load balancing, but are feasible routes in the event the primary route becomes unavailable.

Summary

IGRP is a proprietary routing protocol that was developed by Cisco Systems, Inc. in the early 1990s and was built with functional similarity to RIP, but with the additional features of weighted metrics.

To enable networks to achieve greater efficiency, size, stability, and control over resources, IGRP uses a composite metric calculated by factoring weighted mathematical values for network delay, bandwidth, reliability, and load.

These metric ranges are complemented by user-definable constants, as noted previously and in the list that follows (k1– k5), enabling a network administrator to influence route selection. These constants are used in an algorithm yielding a single, composite metric. This composite metric enables the network administrator to influence route selection by giving higher or lower weighting to specific metrics. This flexibility enables administrators to fine-tune IGRP's automatic route selection.

IGRP permits multipath routing, enabling dual equal-bandwidth lines to run a single stream of traffic in round-robin fashion, with automatic switchover to the second line if one line goes down. Multiple paths can have unequal metrics and still be valid multipath routes. For example, if one path is three times better than another path (its metric is three times lower), the better path will be used three times as often.

Cisco Systems developed an enhancement to IGRP, aptly named the Enhanced Interior Gateway Routing Protocol (EIGRP) in the early 1990s.

The composite IGRP metric is computed according to the following formula:

```
Metric = (K1 × Bandwidth) + (K2 × Bandwidth)/(256 - Load) + (K3 × Delay) × [K5/
(Reliability + K4)]
```

The default *K* values are as follows:

- K1 = 1
- K2 = 0
- K3 = 1
- K4 = 0
- K5 = 0
- If K5 = 0, there is no reliability term.

IGRP has proven to be one of the most successful routing protocols. No small part of its success has been due to its functional similarity to RIP, a simple yet highly successful and widely deployed routing protocol. Cisco took great pains to carefully preserve many of the effective features of RIP, while greatly expanding its capabilities. Today, IGRP is showing its age; it lacks support for variable-length subnet masks (VLSM). Rather than develop an IGRP version 2 to incorporate that capability, Cisco has built upon IGRP's legacy of success with Enhanced IGRP.

The following topics are covered in this appendix:

- OSPF Areas
- OSPF Convergence
- OSPF Route Summarization
- OSPF Authentication

OSPF (Open Shortest Path First)

Open Shortest Path First (OSPF) is a routing protocol developed for Internet Protocol (IP) networks by the Interior Gateway Protocol (IGP) working group of the Internet Engineering Task Force (IETF). OSPF was created in the mid-1980s because RIP (Routing Information Protocol) was (and is) incapable of serving large, heterogeneous internetworks.

OSPF has two primary characteristics:

- The protocol is open, which means that its specification is in the public domain. The OSPF specification is based on Request For Comments (RFC) 1247.

- OSPF is based on the SPF algorithm. The SPF algorithm in turn is based on the Dijkstra Algorithm. The Dijkstra Algorithm enables route selection based on link state versus distance vectors.

OSPF is a link-state routing protocol that sends link-state advertisements (LSAs) to all routers within the same hierarchical area. Information on attached interfaces, metrics used, and other variables are included in these LSAs. As OSPF routers accumulate link-state information, they use the SPF algorithm to calculate the shortest path to each node.

OSPF features include least-cost routing, multipath routing, and load balancing. OSPF was derived from an early version of the IS-IS protocol.

NOTE   OSPF is based on the mathematical concept known as *Graph Theory*. Graph Theory is a branch of mathematics, called *discrete math*, focusing on the properties of a variety of graphs. A good start to learning about graph theory can be found at this web site: `http://campus.northpark.edu/wicksBook/GraphTheory/Intro/`

OSPF, and later OSPFv2, calculates routes based on the destination IP address found in IP datagram headers, with no provisions made for route calculation to non-IP destinations. OSPF was designed to detect quickly and adapt to changes in the network topology (autonomous system). OSPF routing decisions are based on the state of the router interconnecting links within the autonomous system. Each OSPF router maintains a database of network link states, including information regarding its usable interfaces, known-reachable neighbors, and link-state information.

Routing table updates, known as *link-state advertisements (LSAs)* are transmitted, or flooded, to all other neighbors within a router's area.

OSPF was introduced to overcome some of the limitations found with RIP and RIPv2, such as these:

- RIP and RIPv2 both have a limit of 15 hops. A RIP network that spans more than 15 hops (15 routers) is considered unreachable.

- RIP cannot handle Variable Length Subnet Masks (VLSM); however, RIPv2 can. Given the shortage of IP addresses and the flexibility VLSM gives in the efficient assignment of IP addresses, this is considered a major flaw.

- Periodic broadcasts of the full routing table consume a large amount of bandwidth. This is a major issue with large networks, especially on slow links and WAN clouds.

- RIP and RIPv2 both converge slower than OSPF. In large networks, convergence gets to be in the order of minutes. RIP routers will go through a period of a hold-down and garbage collection and will slowly time-out information that has not been received recently. This is inappropriate in large environments and could cause routing inconsistencies.

- RIP and RIPv2 have no concept of network delays and link costs. Routing decisions are based on hop counts. The path with the lowest hop count to the destination is always preferred even if the longer path has a better aggregate link bandwidth and slower delays.

- RIP and RIPv2 networks are flat networks. There is no concept of areas or boundaries. With the introduction of classless routing and the use of network aggregation and summarization, RIP networks struggle to provide a coherent networking infrastructure.

NOTE   Although RIPv2 supports address summarization with the use of VLSM, the concept of areas is not supported.

Link-state protocols, such as OSPF, provide for several networking features that enable a more robust and flexible internetworking environment. These OSPF-enabled features are as follows:

- There is no hop count limitation.

- VLSM support is very useful in IP address allocation.

- OSPF uses IP multicast to send link-state updates. This ensures less processing on routers that are not listening to OSPF packets.

- OSPF updates are "event triggered," sent only in the case of routing changes occurring within the network instead of periodically.

- OSPF allows for better load balancing.

- OSPF allows for a logical definition of networks in a hierarchical network structure where routers can be divided into areas. This will limit the explosion of link-state updates over the whole network. This also provides a mechanism for aggregating routes and cutting down on the unnecessary propagation of subnet information.

- OSPF allows for the transfer and tagging of external routes injected into an Autonomous System. This keeps track of external routes injected by exterior protocols such as BGP.

OSPF Areas

OSPF's rapid convergence is due to its use of areas. Areas are the compartmentalization of an internetwork (autonomous systems) into smaller pieces; a collection of networked end systems, routers, and transmission facilities.

OSPF area numbers are 32 bits in length. Area IDs range from 1 to 4,294,967,295 (the theoretical maximum number of OSPF supported areas).

OSPF Area Router Types

Based on area membership, there are three types of routers within an OSPF network, as illustrated in Figure F-1:

- **Internal routers**—All router interfaces are defined in the same area, but not Area 0 (Backbone Area).

- **Area border routers**—These interconnect the backbone and its area members.

- **Backbone routers**—At least one defined interface belongs to Area 0 (Backbone Area).

Figure F-1 *OSPF Areas*

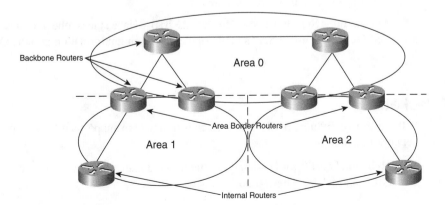

OSPF Routing Types

OSPF supports four different types of routing:

- **Default**—If an explicit route cannot be found for a given IP network or subnetwork, the router will forward the packet to the destination specified in the default route.

- **Inter-area**—This exchanges data between different areas. All inter-area routing must traverse through Area 0. Nonzero OSPF areas are not permitted to communicate directly with each other.

- **Intra-area**—Routing is self-contained and is limited to the routers that are internal to a single area.

- **External routes**—When different ASes exchange routing information, the routes they exchange are referred to as external routes.

OSPF Area Types

The area types, listed here, determine which LSAs the area will receive:

- **Stub Area**—Does not accept external LSAs. LSA Type 5s are rejected. Can accept route summaries. Stub areas carry a default route, intra-area routes, and inter-area routes, but they do not carry external routes. Stub areas are recommended for areas that have only one area border router, and they are often useful in areas with multiple area border routers.

- **Totally Stubby Areas**—Will not accept LSAs with external routes or summaries.

- **Internal Routers**—Exchange LSAs 1 and LSAs 2. They share the same routing databases, and all interfaces are within the same area.

- **Backbone Routers (BBR)**—Exchange LSAs 1 and LSAs 2. Share at least one interface in Area 0.

- **Area Border Router (ABR)**—Share an interface with another OSPF area. This router keeps a database for each area.

- **Autonomous System Border Router (ASBR)**—Have at least one interface in a non-OSPF network; uses LSA 5s to distribute this routing information into the OSPF network.

OSPF Packets

OSPF uses five different packet types. Each is designed to support a different specific network function:

- **Hello packets (Type 1)**—Used to establish and maintain relationships, or adjacencies, between neighboring nodes.

- **Database description packets (Type 2)**—Exchanged between two OSPF routers as they initialize an adjacency. This is used to describe the contents of an OSPF router's link-state database.

- **Link-state request packets (Type 3)**—Used to request specific pieces of a neighboring router's link-state database.

- **Link-state update packets (Type 4)**—Used to transport LSAs to neighboring nodes. There are 11 types of LSAs:

  — **LSA1: Router Links LSA**—Sends information about the router's links.

  — **LSA2: Network Link LSA**—Sent by the DR to all routers in the AS, containing a list of routers in the segment.

  — **LSA3: Summary Link LSA**—Sent by ASBRs, containing a list of networks available outside the area.

  — **LSA4: Summary Link LSA**—Sent by ASBRs, containing a list of networks available outside the area.

  — **LSA5: External Link LSA**—Sent by ASBRs, containing a list of external network routes.

  — **LSA6: Group Membership LSA**—Part of MOSPF (Multicast OSPF), which routes multicast packets. As of this writing, Cisco does not support MOSPF.

  — **LSA7: NSSA External LSA**—Originated by ASBRs in not-so-stubby areas (NSSAs). LSA7s operate in the same fashion as LSA5s, except that LSA7s are limited to NSSAs.

  — **LSA8: External Attributes LSA**

  — **LSA9: Opaque LSA (link-local scope)**

  — **LSA10: Opaque LSA (area-local scope)**

  — **LSA11: Opaque LSA (AS scope)**

- LSA types 8, 9, 10, and 11 have been proposed but have not been implemented.

- **Link-state acknowledgement packets (Type 5)**—OSPF features a reliable distribution of LSA packets. This reliable distribution means that packet receipt must be acknowledged; otherwise, source nodes would have no mechanism to determine actual receipt of the LSA.

OSPF Convergence

Regardless of which fashion OSPF uses, the cost of any given route path is the sum of the costs of all interfaces encountered along the path. OSPF calculates route costs in one of two fashions:

- A non-bandwidth-sensitive default value can be used for each OSPF interface.

- OSPF can calculate automatically the cost of using individual router interfaces.

At a minimum, OSPF uses bandwidth to calculate the cost of a route, using the formula $(10^8/\text{Bandwidth})$. Table F-1 demonstrates some of these calculated costs.

Table F-1 *OSPF Link Costs*

Interface	OSPF Cost
100 Mbps FDDI/Ethernet	1
45 Mbps T3	2
10 Mbps Ethernet	10
1.544 Mbps T1	~64 (64.7)
56 Kbps	1,768

OSPF convergence is based on the adjacency mechanism, discussed in the next section.

OSPF Adjacencies

Adjacency is the next step after the OSPF neighboring process. Adjacent routers are routers that go beyond the simple Hello protocol exchange and proceed into the database exchange process. To minimize the amount of information exchange on a particular segment, OSPF elects one router to be a designated router (DR) and one router to be a backup designated router (BDR) on each multi-access segment. The BDR is elected as a backup mechanism in case the DR goes down. The idea behind this is that routers have a central point of contact for information exchange. Instead of each router exchanging updates with every other router on the segment, every router exchanges information with the DR and BDR. The DR and BDR relay the information to everybody else.

OSPF routers become adjacent when each router has the same link-state database. Following is a brief summary of the states an interface passes through before becoming adjacent to another router:

- **Down**—No information has been received from anybody on the segment.

- **Attempt**—On non-broadcast multi-access clouds, such as Frame Relay, this state indicates that no recent information has been received from the neighbor. An effort should be made to contact the neighbor by sending Hello packets at the reduced rate poll interval.

- **Init**—The interface has detected a Hello packet coming from a neighbor, but bi-directional communication has not yet been established.
- **Two-way**—There is bi-directional communication with a neighbor. The router has seen itself in the Hello packets coming from a neighbor. At the end of this stage, the DR and BDR election would have been done. At the end of the two-way stage, routers will decide whether to proceed in building an adjacency. The decision is based on whether one of the routers is a DR or BDR or the link is a point-to-point or a virtual link.

NOTE   Area 0 is the backbone area and is connected to each OSPF area in the internetwork. In some rare instances, it is impossible to have an area physically connected to the backbone. In this case, a virtual link is used. The virtual link will provide the disconnected area with logical path to the backbone.

- **Exstart**—Routers are trying to establish the initial sequence number that is going to be used in the information exchange packets. The sequence number ensures that routers always get the most recent information. One router will become the primary router and the other will become secondary. The primary router will poll the secondary for information.
- **Exchange**—Routers will describe their entire link-state database by sending database description packets. At this state, packets could be flooded to other interfaces on the router.
- **Loading**—At this state, routers are finalizing the information exchange. Routers have built a link-state request list and a link-state retransmission list. Any information that looks incomplete or outdated will be put on the request list. Any update that is sent will be put on the retransmission list until it is acknowledged.
- **Full**—At this state, the adjacency is complete. The neighboring routers are fully adjacent. Adjacent routers will have a similar link-state database.

OSPF Route Summarization

Route summarization is the consolidation of multiple routes in a single route advertisement. Route summarization is normally performed at the area boundaries by the ABRs (Area Border Routers). It is recommended that you summarize directly into the backbone (Area 0), although summarization may be configured between any two areas. By summarizing routes directly into the backbone, the backbone will then turn around and inject these routes into other areas as part of the normal link-state advertisement.

There are two types of summarization:

- **Inter-area route summarization**—Inter-area route summarization is done on ABRs and it applies to routes from within the AS. It does not apply to external routes injected into OSPF via redistribution.

- **External route summarization**—External route summarization is specific to external routes that are injected into OSPF via redistribution. It is imperative to ensure that external address ranges being summarized are contiguous. The summarization of overlapping ranges from two different routers could cause packets to be sent to the wrong destination. It is also imperative to ensure that all subnets being summarized are in use within the network; otherwise, routing "black holes" could be created, leading to dropped traffic.

OSPF Authentication

OSPF provides for link security in the form of routing update authentication. OSPF packets can be authenticated so that routers can participate in routing domains based on predefined passwords. By default, a router uses a Null authentication, which means that routing exchanges over a network are not authenticated. Two other authentication methods exist:

- **Simple password authentication**—Simple password authentication allows a password (key) to be configured per area. Routers in the same area that want to participate in the routing domain will have to be configured with the same key. The drawback of this method is that it is vulnerable to passive attacks. Anybody with a link analyzer could easily get the password off the wire.

- **Message Digest authentication (MD-5)**—Message Digest authentication is a cryptographic authentication. A key (password) and key-id are configured on each router. The router uses an algorithm based on the OSPF packet, the key, and the key-id to generate a "message digest" that is appended to the packet. Unlike the simple authentication, the key is not exchanged over the wire. A non-decreasing sequence number also is included in each OSPF packet to protect against replay attacks.

- **Replay attack protection**—*Replay attacks* are attacks in which a valid data transmission is maliciously or fraudulently repeated, either by the originator or by an adversary intercepting the data and retransmitting it, often as part of a masquerade attack against the enterprise network.

Summary

OSPF is a powerful and feature-rich routing protocol due to its flexibility. OSPF provides a high functionality open protocol standard, enabling inter-vendor networking with the TCP/IP protocol suite. Here are some of the benefits of OSPF:

- Faster convergence than standard distance-vector routing protocols (such as RIP and RIPv2)
- VLSM support
- Authentication
- Hierarchical segmentation
- Route summarization and aggregation, which is needed to handle large and complicated networks

The following topics are covered in this appendix:

- Neighbor Discovery and Recovery
- Reliable Transport Protocol
- DUAL Finite-State Machine
- Protocol-Specific Modules
- EIGRP Tables
- EIGRP Packet Types
- EIGRP Convergence

EIGRP (Enhanced Interior Gateway Routing Protocol)

The Enhanced Interior Gateway Routing Protocol (EIGRP) is an evolution from its predecessor IGRP, resulting from the demands of diverse and large-scale internetworks. EIGRP integrates the capabilities of link-state and distance vector protocols.

EIGRP provides backward compatibility and seamless interoperation with IGRP routers. An automatic-redistribution mechanism allows IGRP routes to be imported into Enhanced IGRP and vice versa, making it possible to migrate EIGRP into an existing IGRP network. Because the metrics for both protocols are directly translatable, they are as easy to compare as though they were routes that originated in their own autonomous systems (ASes).

Key capabilities distinguishing Enhanced IGRP from other routing protocols include fast convergence, VLSM (variable-length subnet mask) support, partial route update support, and support for multiple network layer protocols, such as Novell's IPX or AppleTalk. Enhanced IGRP does not make periodic updates. Instead, it sends partial updates only when the metric for a route changes. Propagation of partial updates is automatically bounded so that only those routers that need the information are updated. As a result of these two capabilities, Enhanced IGRP consumes significantly less bandwidth than IGRP.

Enhanced IGRP includes support for AppleTalk, IP, and Novell NetWare. The AppleTalk implementation redistributes routes learned from Apple's Routing Table Maintenance Protocol (RTMP). The IP implementation redistributes routes learned from OSPF (Open Shortest Path First), RIP (Routing Information Protocol), IS-IS (Intermediate System-to-Intermediate System), or BGP (Border Gateway Protocol).

Cisco Systems, Inc. developed EIGRP, and like its predecessor IGRP (Interior Gateway Routing Protocol), EIGRP is Cisco proprietary. EIGRP is considered a hybrid routing protocol in that although it shares the distance-vector mechanisms found in IGRP, it differs greatly in the mechanics of operation. EIGRP introduces several features:

- Neighbor Discovery and Recovery
- Reliable Transport Protocol
- DUAL Finite-State Machine
- Protocol-Specific Modules

EIGRP also introduces a new route determination and update algorithm, the Diffusing Update Algorithm (DUAL). DUAL enables EIGRP routers to determine whether a path advertised by a neighbor is looped or loop free. DUAL also allows an EIGRP router to find alternative routes to destinations without waiting for routing updates from neighboring routers.

EIGRP, unlike IGRP, supports both VLSM (Variable Length Subnet Masking) and CIDR (Classless Inter-Domain Routing).

EIGRP was designed to be completely compatible with IGRP. EIGRP uses the same composite metrics as IGRP, as well as the same distance vectors and their respective mathematical weights. EIGRP and IGRP's metrics are directly comparable and can be used interchangeably after translation.

NOTE   The only difference between the IGRP and EIGRP algorithms is the calculation of the composite metric; IGRP is 20 bits long and EIGRP is 32 bits long, resulting in the EIGRP metric being 256 times larger than a comparable IGRP metric. The larger EIGRP metric enables a better and finer mathematical comparison of potential routes.

Neighbor Discovery and Recovery

The *neighbor discovery/recovery* mechanism enables routers to dynamically learn the status of other routers on directly attached networks, such as up, down, or unreachable (router is up, but connection cannot be established). This neighbor discovery process is achieved by periodically sending small Hello packets. As long as an EIGRP router receives Hello packets from a neighboring router, the router presumes that the neighbor is functioning, and the two can exchange routing information. EIGRP does not rely solely on the use of timers for routing table maintenance; instead, EIGRP uses periodic communication to perform the following tasks:

- Dynamically learn of new routers that may join the network
- Identify routers that become either unreachable or inoperable
- Rediscover routers that had previously been unreachable

The initial exchange of routing tables is accomplished with the EIGRP Hello packet between neighbors. Hello packets are discussed later in this appendix in the section "EIGRP Packet Types."

Reliable Transport Protocol

EIGRP can provide guaranteed and reliable delivery of its various packets, whereas other routing protocols rely on other mechanisms, such as time, to determine whether a packet needs to be retransmitted. EIGRP uses the Reliable Transport Protocol (RTP) to provide reliable delivery of its own packets.

RTP is a transport layer (OSI Layer-4) protocol that correlates to the functions found in TCP (Transmission Control Protocol) and UDP (User Datagram Protocol); however, RTP is not an open protocol standard.

RTP is responsible for guaranteed ordered delivery of EIGRP packets and is used to transport all EIGRP messages through an internetwork. RTP supports unicasting and multicasting, even simultaneously for different peers.

DUAL Finite-State Machine

The DUAL Finite-State Machine Engine contains all the logic used to calculate and compare EIGRP routes in an internetwork. DUAL tracks all routes advertised by neighbors and uses the composite metric of each route to compare them. Selected route paths must be both loop-free and have the lowest cost. These route paths then are inserted into the routing table by the DUAL engine.

Routes selected for routing table insertion also are evaluated by the feasible successor process, as described for use by IGRP. *Feasible successors* are routes to a destination where the neighbor router is the next hop in a least-cost path.

The *DUAL finite-state machine* embodies the decision process for all route computations by tracking all routes advertised by all neighbors. DUAL uses distance information to select efficient, loop-free paths and selects routes for insertion in a routing table based on feasible successors.

As noted previously, a feasible successor is a neighboring router used for packet forwarding that is a least-cost path to a destination that is guaranteed not to be part of a routing loop. When a routing neighbor changes a metric or a topology change occurs, DUAL tests for feasible successors. If a successor is found, DUAL uses feasible successors to avoid unnecessarily recomputing the route. When no feasible successors exist but neighbors still advertise the destination, the router performs a recomputation (also known as a *diffusing computation*) to determine a new successor.

Protocol-Specific Modules

EIGRP was developed to be completely independent from routed protocols—IP, Novell's IPX, and AppleTalk, for example— and as such implemented a modular approach to supporting these routed protocols.

EIGRP's modular support provides for the following protocols:

- **AppleTalk (AT-EIGRP)**—EIGRP can redistribute routes learned from RTMP (Routing Table Maintenance Protocol).

- **Novell IPX (IPX-EIGRP)**—EIGRP can redistribute routes learned from Novell's proprietary RIP as well as SAP (Service Advertisement Protocol) and NLSP (Novell Link State Protocol).

- **IP (IP-EIGRP)**—EIGRP can redistribute routes learned from OSPF (Open Shortest Path First), RIP (Routing Information Protocol), IS-IS (Intermediate System-to-Intermediate System), EGP (Exterior Gateway Protocol), and BGP (Border Gateway Protocol).

EIGRP Tables

EIGRP stores routing-related information in three tables, each dedicated to the organization and storage of network data. These tables are as follows:

- **Neighbor Table**—Neighbor relationships are tracked in this table and provide the basis for all of EIGRP's routing update and convergence activities.

- **Routing Table**—This contains least-cost routes that DUAL calculated for all known destinations. EIGRP tracks up to six routes to each destination.

- **Topology Table**—This stores all information needed to calculate a set of distances and vectors to all known and reachable destinations. This information includes the following:

  - **Bandwidth**—The bandwidth of the slowest interface in the path to a destination.

  - **Total Delay**—The total of delay expected in that route.

  - **Reliability**—Path reliability identical to the IGRP Reliability metric.

  - **Load**—Load of the path.

  - **MTU (Maximum Transmission Unit)**—The size of the smallest MTU supported by the router interfaces in the path. EIGRP will notify all routers in advance of the maximum MTU on each path to a given destination.

  - **Reported Distance**—The distance reported by an adjacent neighbor to a specific destination. This metric does not include the distance between this originating (advertising) router and the adjacent neighbor.

  - **Feasible Distance**—The lowest calculated metric to each destination.

  - **Route Source**—The identification number of the router that originally advertised a route. This field is populated only for routes learned from outside the EIGRP network.

Topology table entries are in one of two states:

- **Active**—A route currently being recomputed; the process of recalculating routes in search of new successors. This process is time- and resource-intensive. DUAL is designed to use any and all available feasible successors before recomputing routes. Recomputing will occur only when there are no successors, feasible or otherwise, to a route.

- **Passive**—A route currently stable and available for use.

Technical Note: Cisco IOS Command

If upon executing the **show ip eigrp topology all** command several routes continue to appear to be in ACTIVE states, this in an indication of an unstable network and should be investigated immediately.

EIGRP Packet Types

EIGRP uses five specialized packets for routing table maintenance. These are as follows:

- **Hello**—Used to (re)discover and track other network EIGRP routers. Hello packets are multicast for neighbor discovery/recovery and do not require acknowledgment. Neighbor rediscovery sometimes occurs during the convergence process.

  — The fixed hello interval is 60 seconds for serial interfaces less than T1 or configured for multipoint (for example, Frame Relay, ATM or X.25).

  — Serial interfaces with links T1 or greater have a Hello interval of five seconds.

  — Hold-timer is defaulted to three times the Hello interval, either 15- or 180-seconds, depending on the interface.

- **Acknowledgement**—Used to acknowledge receipt of any EIGRP packet that requires reliable delivery. An acknowledgment packet is a Hello packet that has no data.

- **Update**—Used to convey routing information to known destinations. Update packets are used to either provide a complete topological data dump to a new EIGRP router or to provide an update to a topological change in the network, such as a downed link or change in link cost.

- **Query**—Used whenever a router needs specific information from one or all of its neighbors. Queries are sent only when a destination becomes active. When the network is stable, all routes in the topology table are marked as PASSIVE, making it unnecessary (and a waste of bandwidth) to send EIGRP query packets.

- **Reply**—Sent in reply to EIGRP query packets. These packets instruct the originator not to recompute the route because feasible successors exist. Both query and reply packets are transmitted reliably.

EIGRP Convergence

EIGRP convergence occurs rapidly in an internetwork, due in no small part to EIGRP supporting up to six parallel paths to all destinations in the network.

EIGRP convergence time is very low, based on both the RTP (Reliable Transport Protocol) and EIGRP update packets. Rapid convergence is based upon the feasible successors, which are determined by the DUAL engine.

The DUAL finite-state machine uses distance information to select efficient, loop-free paths, and it selects routes for insertion in a routing table based on feasible successors. The *feasible successor* is a neighboring router used for packet forwarding that is a least-cost path to a destination guaranteed not to be part of a routing loop. When a neighbor changes a metric, or when a topology change occurs, DUAL tests for feasible successors. If one is found, DUAL uses it to avoid recomputing the route unnecessarily. When no feasible successors exist but neighbors still advertise the destination, a recomputation (also known as a *diffusing computation*) must occur to determine a new successor. Although recomputation is not processor-intensive, it does affect convergence time, so it is best to avoid unnecessary recomputations.

Because of the combination of the DUAL finite-state machine and the EIGRP topology table packets, EIGRP convergence can occur within a few seconds, making it the premier choice for Cisco internetworks.

Summary

EIGRP is Cisco Systems, Inc. proprietary and is one of the most feature-rich and vigorous routing protocols developed and used today. EIGRP's combination of features blends the best attributes of distance vector protocols with the best attributes of link-state protocols. The result is a hybrid routing protocol that defies easy categorization with conventional protocols, such as BGP or OSPF.

EIGRP is easy to configure, enabling efficient operation in the support of IP(v4), AppleTalk, and IPX routed protocol traffic.

E

O

P

S

T

X-Y-Z

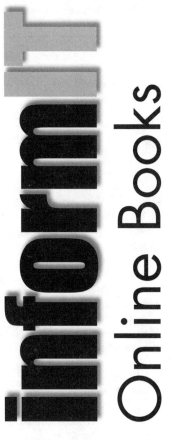

Train with authorized Cisco Learning Partners.

Discover all that's possible on the Internet.

One of the biggest challenges facing networking professionals is how to stay current with today's ever-changing technologies in the global Internet economy. Nobody understands this better than Cisco Learning Partners, the only companies that deliver training developed by Cisco Systems.

Just go to **www.cisco.com/go/training_ad**. You'll find more than 120 Cisco Learning Partners in over 90 countries worldwide.* Only Cisco Learning Partners have instructors that are certified by Cisco to provide recommended training on Cisco networks and to prepare you for certifications.

To get ahead in this world, you first have to be able to keep up. Insist on training that is developed and authorized by Cisco, as indicated by the Cisco Learning Partner or Cisco Learning Solutions Partner logo.

Visit **www.cisco.com/go/training_ad** today.

CISCO SYSTEMS

EMPOWERING THE
INTERNET GENERATION™

Cisco Press Solutions

High Availability Network Fundamentals

Chris Oggerino

1-58713-017-3 • **Available Now**

High Availability Network Fundamentals discusses the need for and the mathematics of availability, then moves on to cover the issues affecting availability, including hardware, software, design strategies, human error, and environmental considerations. After setting up the range of common problems, it then delves into the details of how to design networks for fault tolerance and provides sample calculations for specific systems. Also included is a complete, end-to-end example showing availability calculations for a sample network.

Performance and Fault Management

Paul Della Maggiora, Kent Phelps, Christopher Elliott, James Thompson, Robert Pavone

1-57870-180-5 • **Available Now**

Performance and Fault Management is a comprehensive guide to designing and implementing effective strategies for monitoring performance levels and correctng problems in Cisco networks. It provides an overview of router and LAN switch operations to help you understand how to manage such devices, as well as guidance on the essential MIBs, traps, syslog messages, and show commands for managing Cisco routers and switches.

Cisco Press Solutions

Managing Cisco Network Security

Mike Wenstrom
1-57870-103-1 • **Available Now**

Managing Cisco Network Security focuses on implementing IP network security and contains a wealth of case study material, configuration examples, command summaries, helpful tables and diagrams, and chapter-ending review questions, making this book an effective preparation tool for the MCNSportion of the Cisco Security Specialist certification, part of the new Cisco Qualified Specialist certification track.

Cisco Secure PIX Firewalls

David W. Chapman Jr. and Andy Fox
1-58705-035-8 • **Available Now**

Whether you are preparing for the Cisco Security Specialist 1 certification or simply want to understand and make the most efficient use of PIX Firewalls, *Cisco Secure PIX Firewalls* provides you with a complete solution for planning, deploying, and managing PIX Firewall protected networks.

Cisco Press Solutions

Cisco Secure Virtual Private Networks

Andrew Mason
1-58705-033-1 • **Available Now**

Cisco Secure Virtual Private Networks provides you with the knowledge to plan, administer, and maintain a virtual private network (VPN). Learn how to reduce network cost, enable network scalability, and increase remote access efficiency by deploying Cisco-based VPNs. You will also learn how to configure and test IPSec in Cisco IOS Software and PIX Firewalls; secure remote access connections to corporate networks with IPSec; create a secure tunnel to a Cisco VPN Concentrator and PIX Firewall; and configure the Cisco VPN Concentrator, Cisco router, and PIX Firewall for interoperability.

Cisco Secure Intrustion Detection System

Earl Carter
1-58705-034-X • **Available Now**

Cisco Secure Intrusion Detection Systems provides a clear explanation of why network security is crucial in today's converged networking environment, how the Cisco Secure Intrusion Detection System (CSIDS) improves the security on a network, and how to install and configure CSIDS. The CSIDS is a real-time, network-based IDS designed to detect, report, and terminate unauthorized activity throughout a network. The industry's first and now the market-leading IDS, CSIDS is the dynamic security component of Cisco's end-to-end security product line.

IF YOU'RE USING CISCO PRODUCTS, YOU'RE QUALIFIED TO RECEIVE A FREE SUBSCRIPTION TO CISCO'S PREMIER PUBLICATION, *PACKET*™ MAGAZINE.

Packet delivers complete coverage of cutting-edge networking trends and innovations, as well as current product updates. A magazine for technical, hands-on Cisco users, it delivers valuable information for enterprises, service providers, and small and midsized businesses.

Packet is a quarterly publication. To start your free subscription, click on the URL and follow the prompts: www.cisco.com/go/packet/subscribe

CISCO SYSTEMS

☐ YES! I'm requesting a **free** subscription to *Packet*™ magazine.

☐ No. I'm not interested at this time.

☐ Mr.
☐ Ms.

First Name (Please Print)   Last Name

Title/Position (Required)

Company (Required)

Address

City   State/Province

Zip/Postal Code   Country

Telephone (Include country and area codes)   Fax

E-mail

Signature (Required)   Date

☐ I would like to receive additional information on Cisco's services and products by e-mail.

1. Do you or your company:
- A ☐ Use Cisco products
- B ☐ Resell Cisco products
- C ☐ Both
- D ☐ Neither

2. Your organization's relationship to Cisco Systems:
- A ☐ Customer/End User
- B ☐ Prospective Customer
- C ☐ Cisco Reseller
- D ☐ Cisco Distributor
- E ☐ Integrator
- F ☐ Non-Authorized Reseller
- G ☐ Cisco Training Partner
- I ☐ Cisco OEM
- J ☐ Consultant
- K ☐ Other (specify):

3. How many people does your entire company employ?
- A ☐ More than 10,000
- B ☐ 5,000 to 9,999
- C ☐ 1,000 to 4,999
- D ☐ 500 to 999
- E ☐ 250 to 499
- F ☐ 100 to 249
- G ☐ Fewer than 100

4. Is your company a Service Provider?
- A ☐ Yes
- B ☐ No

5. Your involvement in network equipment purchases:
- A ☐ Recommend
- B ☐ Approve
- C ☐ Neither

6. Your personal involvement in networking:
- A ☐ Entire enterprise at all sites
- B ☐ Departments or network segments at more than one site
- C ☐ Single department or network segment
- F ☐ Public network
- D ☐ No involvement
- E ☐ Other (specify):

7. Your Industry:
- A ☐ Aerospace
- B ☐ Agriculture/Mining/Construction
- C ☐ Banking/Finance
- D ☐ Chemical/Pharmaceutical
- E ☐ Consultant
- F ☐ Computer/Systems/Electronics
- G ☐ Education (K–12)
- U ☐ Education (College/Univ.)
- H ☐ Government—Federal
- I ☐ Government—State
- J ☐ Government—Local
- K ☐ Health Care
- L ☐ Telecommunications
- M ☐ Utilities/Transportation
- N ☐ Other (specify):

CPRESS

PACKET™

Packet magazine serves as the premier publication linking customers to Cisco Systems, Inc. Delivering complete coverage of cutting-edge networking trends and innovations, *Packet* is a magazine for technical, hands-on users. It delivers industry-specific information for enterprise, service provider, and small and midsized business market segments. A toolchest for planners and decision makers, *Packet* contains a vast array of practical information, boasting sample configurations, real-life customer examples, and tips on getting the most from your Cisco Systems' investments. Simply put, *Packet* magazine is straight talk straight from the worldwide leader in networking for the Internet, Cisco Systems, Inc.

We hope you'll take advantage of this useful resource. I look forward to hearing from you!

Cecelia Glover
Packet Circulation Manager
packet@external.cisco.com
www.cisco.com/go/packet

PACKET™